JAVA
EXAMPLES
IN A NUTSHELL

*A Tutorial Companion
to Java in a Nutshell*

THE JAVA™ SERIES

Exploring Java™

Java™ Threads

Java™ Network Programming

Java™ Virtual Machine

Java™ AWT Reference

Java™ Language Reference

Java™ Fundamental Classes Reference

Database Programming with
  JDBC™ and Java™

Java™ Distributed Computing

Developing Java Beans™

Java™ Security

Java™ Cryptography

Java™ Swing

Java™ Servlet Programming

Java™ I/O

Java™ 2D Graphics

Enterprise JavaBeans™

Also from O'Reilly

Java™ in a Nutshell

Java™ in a Nutshell, Deluxe Edition

Java™ Examples in a Nutshell

Java™ Enterprise in a Nutshell

Java™ Foundation Classes in
a Nutshell

Java™ Power Reference: A
Complete Searchable
Resource on CD-ROM

JAVA™
EXAMPLES
IN A NUTSHELL

*A Tutorial Companion
to Java in a Nutshell*

David Flanagan

O'REILLY™

Beijing · Cambridge · Farnham · Köln · Paris · Sebastopol · Taipei · Tokyo

Java Examples in a Nutshell
by David Flanagan

Copyright © 1997 O'Reilly & Associates, Inc. All rights reserved.
Printed in the United States of America.

Published by O'Reilly & Associates, Inc., 101 Morris Street, Sebastopol, CA 95472.

Editor: Paula Ferguson

Production Editor: Nicole Gipson Arigo

Printing History:

> September 1997:   First Edition.

ISBN: 1-56592-371-5
[M]

[4/00]

Table of Contents

Preface

This book is a companion volume to *Java in a Nutshell*. While that book is a quick-reference at heart, it also includes an accelerated introduction to Java programming and a small set of example programs. I wrote *Java Examples in a Nutshell* to pick up where *Java in a Nutshell* leaves off, providing a suite of example programs for novice Java programmers and experts alike.

This book was a lot of fun to write. It came about when Java 1.1 was released at more than double the size of Java 1.0. While I was busy writing additional examples for the second edition of *Java in a Nutshell*, the engineers at Sun were busy turning Java into something that could no longer quite fit in a nutshell. With its quick-reference section expanding so much, *Java in a Nutshell* could no longer hold many examples. We were able to include some examples of new Java 1.1 features, but we had to cut many more than we could include. This was a hard decision to make—the examples in *Java in a Nutshell* were one of its most popular features.

This book is the result of those cuts, and I am glad that we made the decision we did. Given the freedom to devote an entire book to examples, I was able to write the examples I really wanted to write. I was able to go into more depth than I ever would have before, and I found myself really enjoying the exploration and experimentation that went into developing the examples. As you study these examples, I hope that you can use them as a starting point for your own explorations, and that you get a taste of the same excitement I felt while writing them.

As its name implies, this book teaches by example, which is how many people learn best. There is not a lot of hand-holding, nor will you find detailed documentation of the exact syntax and behavior of Java statements. This book is designed to work in tandem with *Java in a Nutshell*, so you will probably find that volume quite useful while studying the examples here. You may also be interested in a number of the other books in the O'Reilly Java series. Those books are listed below.

You can read the chapters of this book in more-or-less whatever order suits you. The first ten chapters cover core Java topics. The remaining seven chapters cover more advanced, specialized Java programming topics, such as the JavaBeans API, internationalization, and the Java Enterprise APIs. Chapters 1 and 2, *Java Basics* and *Objects, Classes, and Interfaces*, are aimed at programmers who are just starting out with Java. Seasoned Java programmers can skip them. Chapters 4, 5, and 6, *Graphics, Events*, and *Graphical User Interfaces*, build on each other and should probably be read in order. Similarly, Chapters 8 and 9, *Input/Output* and *Networking*, work best when read one after the other.

Related Books

O'Reilly & Associates is developing an entire series of books on Java. This series consists of introductory books, reference manuals, and advanced programming guides.

The following books on Java are currently available from O'Reilly & Associates:

Exploring Java, by Patrick Niemeyer and Joshua Peck
> A comprehensive tutorial that provides a practical, hands-on approach to learning Java.

Java Language Reference, by Mark Grand
> A complete reference for the Java programming language itself.

Java AWT Reference, by John Zukowski
> A complete reference manual for the AWT-related packages in the core Java API.

Java Fundamental Classes Reference, by Mark Grand and Jonathan Knudsen
> A complete reference manual for the `java.lang`, `java.io`, `java.net`, and `java.util` packages, among others, in the core Java API.

Java Virtual Machine, by Jon Meyer and Troy Downing
> A programming guide and reference manual for the Java virtual machine.

Java Threads, by Scott Oaks and Henry Wong
> An advanced programming guide to working with threads in Java.

Java Network Programming, by Elliotte Rusty Harold
> A complete guide to writing sophisticated network applications.

Database Programming with JDBC and Java, by George Reese
> An advanced tutorial on JDBC that presents a robust model for developing Java database programs.

Developing Java Beans, by Robert Englander
> A complete guide to writing components that work with the JavaBeans API.

Look for additional advanced programming guides on such topics as distributed computing and electronic commerce from O'Reilly in the near future.

Java Examples Online

The web site for this book is *http://www.oreilly.com/catalog/jenut/*. You will find the examples from this book at that location, available for download.

Licensing Information

You may study, use, modify, and distribute these examples for any non-commercial purpose, as long as the copyright notice at the top of each example is retained. If you would like to use the code in a commercial product, you may purchase a commercial use license from the author for a nominal fee. Visit *http://www.davidflanagan.com/javaexamples/* for information on obtaining such a license.

Please note that the examples are provided as-is, with no warranty of any kind.

Conventions Used in This Book

Italic is used for:

- Pathnames, filenames, and program names
- New terms where they are defined
- Internet addresses, such as domain names and URLs

Boldface is used for:

- Particular keys on a computer keyboard
- Names of user interface buttons and menus

Letter Gothic is used for:

- Anything that might appear in a Java program, including keywords, data types, constants, method names, variables, class names, and interface names
- Command lines and options that should be typed verbatim on the screen
- All Java code listings
- Tags that might appear in an HTML document

Letter Gothic Oblique is used for:

- Method parameters, and general placeholders that indicate that an item is replaced by some actual value in your own program
- Variable expressions in command-line options

Request for Comments

Please help us to improve future editions of this book by reporting any errors, inaccuracies, bugs, misleading or confusing statements, and plain old typos that you find anywhere in the book. Email your bug reports and comments to us at: *bookquestions@oreilly.com*. (Before sending a bug report, however, you may want to check for an errata list at *http://www.oreilly.com/catalog/jenut/* to see if the bug has already been submitted.)

Please also let us know what we can do to make this book more useful to you. We take your comments seriously and will try to incorporate reasonable suggestions into future editions.

Acknowledgments

My thanks go, once again, to my editor Paula Ferguson for pulling my seventeen separate chapters together into one coherent book. I left her in the lurch through that process this time, but she good-naturedly took care of all the finishing touches I'd left town without doing. Thanks also to Frank Willison and Tim O'Reilly for being willing and enthusiastic to try this all-example book format.

George Reese, author of O'Reilly's *Database Programming with JDBC and Java*, was kind enough to look over the JDBC examples in Chapter 16 and make suggestions. Jim Farley, author of the forthcoming *Java Distributed Computing*, reviewed the RMI examples in Chapter 15 and offered some useful suggestions. And finally, Jonathan Knudsen, O'Reilly's Java staff writer who has contributed to a number of Java books, looked over the security material in Chapter 17. I appreciate the help of all these reviewers.

The production team at O'Reilly & Associates has again done a great job of turning the manuscript I submitted into a honest-to-goodness book. As usual, I am grateful to them, and awestruck by them. Nicole Gipson Arigo was the production editor and project manager. Jane Ellin and Sheryl Avruch performed quality control checks. Seth Maislin and Marilyn Rowland wrote the index. Robert Romano created the figures. Edie Freedman designed the cover, and Nancy Priest designed the interior format of the book. Lenny Muellner carefully implemented the format in *troff*.

Finally, I want to thank Christie, for reasons too numerous to list here.

David Flanagan
July 1997

CHAPTER 1

Java Basics

This chapter contains examples that demonstrate the basic syntax of Java; it is meant to be used in conjunction with Chapter 2 of *Java in a Nutshell*. If you have substantial programming experience with C or C++, you should find the material in this chapter straightforward. If you are coming to Java from another language, however, you may need to study the examples here more carefully.

The most important step in learning a new programming language is mastering the basic control statements of the language. With Java, this means learning the if/else branching statement and the while and for looping statements. Learning to program well is like learning to do word problems in high-school algebra class: you have to translate the problem from an abstract description into the concrete language of algebra (or, in this case, the language of Java). Once you learn to think in if, while, and for statements, other Java statements, such as break, continue, switch, and try/catch/finally, should be easy to pick up.

The examples in this chapter are standalone Java programs, not Java applets. That means that you run them by invoking the Java interpreter, rather than by loading them into a Java-enabled Web browser. Although Java is an object-oriented language, we won't discuss objects until Chapter 2, *Objects, Classes and Interfaces*.

So, with that as preface, and with mastery of basic syntax as our goal, let's jump right in and start writing Java programs.

Hello World

As long ago as 1978, Brian Kernighan and Dennis Ritchie wrote, in their classic book *The C Programming Language*, that "the first program to write is the same for all languages." They were referring, of course, to the "Hello World" program. The Java implementation of "Hello World" is shown in Example 1-1.

Example 1-1: Hello.java

```
public class Hello {                          // Everything in Java is a class
  public static void main(String[] args) {    // All programs must have main()
    System.out.println("Hello World!");       // Say hello!
  }                                           // This marks the end of main()
}                                             // Marks the end of the Hello class
```

The value of "Hello World" is that it is a template that you can expand on in your later experiments with Java. The first two lines of Example 1-1 are a required part of the template. Every program and every applet—every piece of Java code—you write is part of a class. The first line of the example says that we're writing a class named Hello that is a public class, which means that it can be used by anyone.

Every standalone Java program requires a main() method. This is where the Java interpreter begins running a Java program. As we'll see later, the rules are different for Java applets; they don't have main() methods. The second line of the example declares this main() method. It says that the method is public, that it has no return value (i.e., its return value is void), and that it is passed an array of strings as its argument. The name of the array is args. The line also says that main() is a static method. In this chapter, we'll work exclusively with static methods. In Chapter 2, when we start working with objects, you'll see that non-static methods are actually the norm.

In any case, you might as well go ahead and memorize this line:

```
public static void main(String[] args)
```

Every standalone Java program you ever write will contain a line that looks exactly like this one. (Actually, you can name the array of strings anything you want, but it is usually called args.)

The fourth and fifth lines of Example 1-1 simply mark the end of the main() method and of the Hello class. Like most modern programming languages, Java is a block-structured language. This means that things like classes and methods have bodies that comprise a "block" of code. In Java, the beginning of a block is marked by a { and the end is marked by a matching }. Method blocks are always defined within class blocks, and as we'll see in later examples, methods blocks can contain things like if statements and for loops that form sub-blocks within the method. Furthermore, these sorts of statement blocks can be nested arbitrarily deep within each other.

The first two lines and the last two lines of Example 1-1 are part of the basic framework of a Java application. It is the third line of the example that is of primary interest to us. This is the line that prints the words "Hello World!" The System.out.println() method sends a line of output to "standard output," which is usually the screen. We'll see this method used throughout this chapter and in many other chapters in this book. It isn't until we reach Chapter 8, *Input/Output*, however, that we'll really understand what it is doing. If you are curious before then, look up the java.lang.System and java.io.PrintStream classes in *Java in a Nutshell* (or some other Java reference manual).

One final point to note about this program is the use of comments. Example 1-1 uses C++-style comments that begin with // and continue until the end of the line.

Thus, anything between the // characters and the end of a line is ignored by the Java compiler. You'll find that the examples in this book are thoroughly commented. The code and the comments are worth studying because the comments often explain things, or draw your attention to points that are not mentioned in the main text of the book.

Compiling and Running "Hello World"

Before you can run the "Hello World" program, you must compile it. If you are using the Java Development Kit (JDK) from Sun, you do this with the *javac* command.* Save the program in a file named *Hello.java* and run this command:

```
% javac Hello.java
```

Assuming that the JDK has been properly installed and that your CLASSPATH is set up correctly, *javac* runs for a short while and then produces a file named *Hello.class*. This file contains the compiled version of the program. As I said earlier, everything you write in Java is a class, as the *.class* extension on this file indicates. One important rule about compiling Java programs is that the name of the file minus the *.java* extension must match the name of the class defined in the file. Thus, if you typed in Example 1-1 and saved it in a file named *HelloWorld.java*, you would not be able to compile it.

To run the program (again using the JDK) type:

```
% java Hello
```

This command should produce the output:

```
Hello World!
```

The *java* command is the Java interpreter program; it runs the Java Virtual Machine. You pass *java* the name of the class that you want to run. Note that you are specifying the class name, Hello, not the name of the file, *Hello.class*, that contains the compiled class.

All standalone Java programs are compiled and run in this way, so we won't go through these steps again.

FizzBuzz

FizzBuzz is a game I learned long ago in elementary school French class, as a way to practice counting in that language. The players take turns counting, starting with one and going up. The rules are simple: when your turn arrives, you say the next number. However, if that number is a multiple of five, you should say the word "fizz" (preferably with a French accent) instead. If the number is a multiple of seven, you should say "buzz." And if it is a multiple of both, you should say "fizzbuzz." If you mess up, you're out, and the game continues without you.

---

*If you are using some other Java programming environment, read and follow the vendor's instructions for compiling and running programs.

Example 1-2 is a Java program named FizzBuzz that plays a version of the game. Actually, it isn't a very interesting version of the game because the computer plays by itself and it doesn't count in French! What is interesting to us is the Java code that goes into this example. It demonstrates the use of a for loop to count from 1 to 100 and the use of if/else statements to decide whether to output the number or one of the words "fizz", "buzz", or "fizzbuzz". (In this case, the if/else statement is used as a if/elseif/elseif/else statement, as we'll discuss shortly.)

This program introduces System.out.print(). This method is just like System.out.println(), except that it does not terminate the line of output. Whatever is output next appears on the same line.

The example also shows another style for comments. Anything, on any number of lines, between the characters /* and the characters */ is a comment in Java, and is ignored by the compiler. When one of these comments begins with /**, as the one in this example does, then it is additionally a "doc comment", which means its contents are used by the *javadoc* program that automatically generates API documentation from Java source code.

Example 1-2: FizzBuzz.java

```
/**
 * This program plays the game "Fizzbuzz".  It counts to 100, replacing each
 * multiple of 5 with the word "fizz", each multiple of 7 with the word "buzz",
 * and each multiple of both with the word "fizzbuzz".  It uses the modulo
 * operator (%) to determine if a number is divisible by another.
 **/
public class FizzBuzz {                         // Everything in Java is a class
  public static void main(String[] args) {      // Every program must have main()
    for(int i = 1; i <= 100; i++) {             // count from 1 to 100
      if (((i % 5) == 0) && ((i % 7) == 0))     // A multiple of both?
        System.out.print("fizzbuzz");
      else if ((i % 5) == 0) System.out.print("fizz"); // else a multiple of 5?
      else if ((i % 7) == 0) System.out.print("buzz"); // else a multiple of 7?
      else System.out.print(i);                 // else just print it
      System.out.print(" ");
    }
    System.out.println();
  }
}
```

The for and if/else statements may require a bit of explanation for programmers who have not encountered them before. A for statement sets up a loop, so that some code can be executed multiple times. The for keyword is followed by three Java expressions that specify the parameters of the loop. The syntax is:

```
for(initialize ; test ; update)
    body
```

The *initialize* expression does any necessary initialization. It is run once, before the loop starts. Usually, it sets an initial value for a "loop counter" variable. Often, as in this example, the loop counter is used only within the loop, so the *initialize* expression also declares the variable.

The *test* expression checks whether the loop should continue. It is evaluated before each execution of the loop body. If it evaluates to true, the loop is executed. When it evaluates to false, however, the loop body is not executed and the loop terminates.

The *update* expression is evaluated at the end of each iteration of the loop; it does anything necessary to set the loop up for the next iteration. Usually, it simply increments or decrements the "loop counter" variable.

Finally, the *body* is the Java code that is run each time through the loop. It can either be a single Java statement or a whole block of Java code, enclosed by curly braces.

This explanation should make it clear that the for loop in Example 1-2 counts from 1 to 100.

The if/else statement is simpler than the for statement. Its syntax is:

```
if (expression)
    statement1
else
    statement2
```

When Java encounters an if statement, it evaluates the specified *expression*. If the expression evaluates to true, *statement1* is executed. Otherwise, *statement2* is evaluated. That is all if/else does; there is no looping involved, so the program continues with the next statement following if/else. The else clause and *statement2* that follows it are entirely optional. If they are omitted, and the *expression* evaluates to false, the if statement does nothing. The statements following the if and else clauses can either be single Java statements or entire blocks of Java code, contained within curly braces.

The thing to note about the if/else statement (and the for statement, for that matter) is that it can contain other statements, including other if/else statements. This is how the statement was used in Example 1-2, where we saw what looked like an if/elseif/elseif/else statement. In fact, this is simply an if/else statement within an if/else statement within an if/else statement. This structure becomes clearer if the code is rewritten to use curly braces:

```
if (((i % 5) == 0) && ((i % 7) == 0))
  System.out.print("fizzbuzz");
else {
  if ((i % 5) == 0)
    System.out.print("fizz");
  else {
    if ((i % 7) == 0)
      System.out.print("buzz");
    else
      System.out.print(i);
  }
}
```

Note, however, that this sort of nested if/else logic is not typically written out with a full set of curly braces in this way. The elseif programming construct is a commonly used idiom that you will quickly become accustomed to. You may have also noticed that I use a compact coding style that keeps everything on a single line wherever possible.

Thus, you'll often see:

```
if (expression) statement
```

I do this so that the code remains compact and manageable, and therefore easier to study in the printed form in which it appears here. You may prefer to use a more highly structured, less compact style in your own code.

The Fibonacci Series

The Fibonacci numbers are a sequence of numbers in which each successive number is the sum of the two preceding numbers. The sequence begins 1, 1, 2, 3, 5, 8, 13, and goes on from there. Example 1-3 shows a program that computes and displays the first 20 numbers in this sequence. There are several things to note about the program. First, it again uses a `for` statement as its main loop. It also declares and uses variables to hold the last two numbers in the sequence, so that these numbers can be added together to produce the next number in the sequence.

Example 1-3: Fibonacci.java

```
/**
 * This program prints out the first 20 numbers in the Fibonacci sequence.
 * Each number is formed by adding together the previous two numbers in the
 * sequence, starting with the numbers 0 and 1.
 **/
public class Fibonacci {
  public static void main(String[] args) {
    int current, prev = 1, prevprev = 1;// Initialize some variables
    System.out.print("1 1 ");            // Output the initial two values
    for(int i = 2; i < 20; i++) {        // Loop, outputting remaining values
      current = prev + prevprev;         // Next number is sum of previous two
      System.out.print(current + " ");   // Print it out
      prevprev = prev;                   // First previous becomes 2nd previous
      prev = current;                    // And current number becomes previous
    }
    System.out.println();                // Terminate the line, and flush output
  }
}
```

Using Command-Line Arguments

As we've seen, every standalone Java program must declare a method with exactly the following signature:

```
public static void main(String[] args)
```

This signature says that an array of strings is passed to the `main()` method. What are these strings, and where do they come from? The `args` array contains any arguments passed to the Java interpreter on the command line, following the name of the class to be run. Example 1-4 shows a program, `Echo`, that reads these arguments and prints them back out. For example, you can invoke the program this way:

```
% java Echo this is a test
```

The program responds:

```
this is a test
```

In this case, the args array has a length of four. The first element in the array, args[0], is the string "this" and the last element of the array, args[3], is "test". As you can see, Java arrays begin with element 0. If you are coming from a language that uses arrays that are one-based, this can take quite a bit of getting used to. In particular, you must remember that if the length of an array a is n, the last element in the array is a[n-1]. You can determine the length of an array by appending .length to its name, as shown in Example 1-4.

This example also demonstrates the use of a while loop. A while loop is a simpler form of the for loop; it requires you to do your own initialization and update of the loop counter variable. Any for loop can be written as a while loop, but the compact syntax of the for loop makes it the more commonly used statement. A for loop would have been perfectly acceptable, and even preferable, in this example.

Example 1-4: Echo.java

```
/**
 * This program prints out all its command-line arguments.
 **/
public class Echo {
  public static void main(String[] args) {
    int i = 0;                           // Initialize the loop variable
    while(i < args.length) {             // Loop until we reach end of array
      System.out.print(args[i] + " ");   // Print each argument out
      i++;                               // Increment the loop variable
    }
    System.out.println();                // Terminate the line
  }
}
```

Echo in Reverse

Example 1-5 is a lot like the Echo program of Example 1-4, except that it prints out the command line arguments in reverse order, and it prints out the characters of each argument backwards. Thus, the Reverse program can be invoked as follows, with the following output:

```
% java Reverse this is a test
tset a si siht
```

This program is interesting because its nested for loops count backward instead of forward. It is also interesting because it manipulates String objects by invoking methods of those objects and the syntax starts to get a little complicated. For example, consider the expression at the heart of this example:

```
args[i].charAt(j)
```

This expression first extracts the ith element of the args[] array. We know from the declaration of the array in the signature of the main() method that it is a String array—that is, it contains String objects. (Strings are not a primitive type, like integers and boolean values in Java—they are full-fledged objects.) Once we have extracted the ith String from the array, we invoke the charAt() method of that object, passing the argument j. (The . character in the expression is used to refer to a method or a field of an object.) As you can surmise from the name (and verify, if you want, in a reference manual), this method extracts the specified character from the String object. Thus, this expression extracts the jth character from the ith command-line argument. Armed with this understanding, you should be able to make sense of the rest of Example 1-5.

Example 1–5: Reverse.java

```
/**
 * This program echos the command-line arguments backwards.
 **/
public class Reverse {
  public static void main(String[] args) {
    // Loop backwards through the array of arguments
    for(int i = args.length-1; i >= 0; i--) {
      // Loop backwards through the characters in each argument
      for(int j=args[i].length()-1; j>=0; j--) {
        // Print out character j of argument i.
        System.out.print(args[i].charAt(j));
      }
      System.out.print(" ");  // add a space at the end of each argument
    }
    System.out.println();     // and terminate the line when we're done.
  }
}
```

FizzBuzz Switched

Example 1-6 is another version of the FizzBuzz game. This version uses a switch statement instead of nested if/else statements to determine what its output should be for each number. Take a look at the example first, then read the explanation of switch below.

Example 1–6: FizzBuzz2.java

```
/**
 * This class is much like the FizzBuzz class, but uses a switch statement
 * instead of repeated if/else statements
 **/
public class FizzBuzz2 {
  public static void main(String[] args) {
    for(int i = 1; i <= 100; i++) { // count from 1 to 100
      switch(i % 35) {                    // What's the remainder when divided by 35?
      case 0:                             // For multiples of 35...
        System.out.print("fizzbuzz ");    // print "fizzbuzz"
        break;                            // Don't forget this statement!
      case 5: case 10: case 15:           // If the remainder is any of these
      case 20: case 25: case 30:          // then the number is a multiple of 5
        System.out.print("fizz ");        // so print "fizz"
        break;
      case 7: case 14: case 21: case 28:  // For any multiple of 7...
        System.out.print("buzz ");        // print "buzz"
        break;
```

Example 1–6: FizzBuzz2.java (continued)

```
        default:                      // For any other number...
          System.out.print(i + " ");  // print the number
          break;
      }
    }
    System.out.println();
  }
}
```

The `switch` statement acts like a switch operator at a busy railyard, switching a train (or the execution of a program) to the appropriate track (or piece of code) out of many potential tracks. A `switch` statement is often an alternative to repeated `if/else` statements, but it only works when the value being tested is a primitive integral type (e.g., not a `double` or a `String`) and when the value is being tested against constant values. The basic syntax of the `switch` statement is:

```
switch(expression) {
    statements
}
```

The `switch` statement is followed by an *expression* in parentheses and a block of code in curly braces. After evaluating the *expression*, the `switch` statement executes certain code within the block, depending on the integral value of the expression. How does the `switch` statement know where to start executing code for which values? This information is indicated by `case:` labels and with the special `default:` label. Each `case:` label is followed by an integral value. If the *expression* evaluates to that value, the `switch` statement begins executing code immediately following that `case:` label. If there is no `case:` label that matches the value of the expression, the `switch` statement starts executing code following the `default:` label, if there is one. If there is no `default:` label, `switch` does nothing.

The `switch` statement is an unusual one because each case does not have its own unique block of code. Instead, `case:` and `default:` labels simply mark various entry points into a single large block of code. Typically, each label is followed by several statements and then a `break` statement, which causes the flow of control to exit out of the block of the `switch` statement. If you don't use a `break` statement at the end of the code for a label, the execution of that case "drops through" to the next case. If you want to see this in action, remove the `break` statements from Example 1-6 and see what happens when you run the program. Forgetting `break` statements within a `switch` statement is a common source of bugs.

Computing Factorials

The factorial of an integer is the product of that number and all of the positive integers smaller than it. Thus the factorial of 5, written 5!, is the product 5*4*3*2*1, or 120. Example 1-7 shows a class, `Factorial`, that contains a method, `factorial()` that computes factorials. This class is not a program in its own right, but the method it defines can be used by other programs. The method itself is quite simple; we'll see several variations of it in the following sections. As a exercise, you might think about how you could rewrite this example using a `while` loop instead of a `for` loop.

Example 1-7: Factorial.java

```
/**
 * This class doesn't define a main() method, so it isn't a program by itself.
 * It does define a useful method that we can use in other programs, though.
 **/
public class Factorial {
  /** Compute and return x!, the factorial of x */
  public static int factorial(int x) {
    int fact = 1;
    for(int i = 2; i <= x; i++)     // loop
      fact *= i;                    // shorthand for: fact = fact * i;
    return fact;
  }
}
```

Recursive Factorials

Example 1-8 shows another way to compute factorials. This example uses a programming technique called "recursion." Recursion happens when a method calls itself, or in other words, invokes itself "recursively." The recursive algorithm for computing factorials relies on the fact that n! is equal to n*(n-1)!. Computing factorials in this fashion is a classic example of recursion. It is not a particularly efficient technique in this case, but there are many important uses for recursion, and this example demonstrates that it is perfectly legal in Java. This example also switches from the int data type, which is a 32-bit integer, to the long data type, which is a 64-bit integer. Factorials become very large, very quickly, so the extra capacity of a long makes the factorial() method more useful.

Example 1-8: Factorial2.java

```
/**
 * This class shows a recursive method to compute factorials.  This method
 * calls itself repeatedly based on the formula: n! = n * (n-1)!
 **/
public class Factorial2 {
  public static long factorial(long x) {
    if (x <= 1) return 1;
    else return x * factorial(x-1);
  }
}
```

Caching Factorials

Example 1-9 shows a refinement to our previous factorial examples. Factorials are an ideal candidate for caching because they are slightly time consuming to compute, and more importantly, there are only a few factorials that we can actually compute, due to the limitations of the long data type. So, in this examples, once a factorial is computed, its value is stored for future use.

Besides introducing the technique of caching, this example demonstrates several new things. First, it declares "static fields" within the Factorial3 class:

```
static long[] table = new long[21];
static int last = 0;
```

A field that is declared static still acts as a variable. The difference between a static field and a "regular" field is that a static field retains its value between invocations of the factorial() method, while a non-static field does not. This means that static fields can be used to cache values computed in one invocation for use by the next invocation.

Second, this example shows how to create an array:

```
static long[] table = new long[21];
```

The first half of this line (before the = sign) declares the static field table to be an array of long values. The second half of the line actually creates an array of 21 long values using the new operator.

Finally, this example demonstrates how to "throw an exception":

```
throw new IllegalArgumentException("Overflow; x is too large.");
```

An exception is a kind of Java object; it is created with the new keyword, just as the array was. When a program throws an exception object with the throw statement, it indicates that some sort of unexpected circumstance or error has arisen. When an exception is thrown, program control transfers to the nearest containing catch clause of a try/catch statement. This clause should contain code to handle the exceptional condition. If an exception is never "caught," the program terminates with an error.

Example 1-9 throws an exception to notify the calling procedure that the argument it passed is too big or too small. The argument is too big if it is greater than 20, since we cannot compute factorials beyond 20!. The argument is too small if it is less than 0, as factorial is only defined for non-negative integers. Examples later in the chapter demonstrate how to catch and handle exceptions.

Example 1–9: Factorial3.java

```
/**
 * This class computes factorials and caches the results in a table for reuse.
 * 20! is as high as we can go using the long data type, so check the argument
 * passed and "throw an exception" if it is too big or too small.
 **/
public class Factorial3 {
  // Create an array to cache values 0! through 20!.
  static long[] table = new long[21];
  // A "static initializer": initialize the first value in the array
  static { table[0] = 1; }  // factorial of 0 is 1.
  // Remember the highest initialized value in the array
  static int last = 0;

  public static long factorial(int x) throws IllegalArgumentException {
    // Check if x is too big or too small.  Throw an exception if so.
    if (x >= table.length)   // ".length" returns length of any array
      throw new IllegalArgumentException("Overflow; x is too large.");
    if (x < 0) throw new IllegalArgumentException("x must be non-negative.");

    // Compute and cache any values that are not yet cached.
    while(last < x) {
```

Example 1-9: Factorial3.java (continued)

```
    table[last + 1] = table[last] * (last + 1);
    last++;
  }
  // Now return the cached factorial of x.
  return table[x];
}
}
```

Computing Big Factorials

In the previous section, we learned that 20! is the largest factorial that can fit in a 64-bit integer. But what if we want to compute 50! or 100!? Java 1.1 includes a class, java.math.BigInteger, that represents arbitrarily-large integer values and provides methods to perform arithmetic operations on these very large numbers. Example 1-10 uses the BigInteger class to compute factorials of any size. It also includes a simple main() method that defines a standalone test program for our factorial() method. This test program tells us, for example, that 50! is the following 65-digit number:

30414093201713378043612608166064768844377641568960512000000000000

Example 1-10 introduces the import statement. This statement must appear at the top of a Java file, before any class is defined. It provides a way to tell the compiler what classes we are using in a program. Once a class like java.math.BigInteger has been imported, we no longer have to type its full name; instead we can refer to it simply as BigInteger. You can also import an entire "package" of classes, as we do with the line:

```
import java.util.*
```

Example 1-10 uses the same caching technique that Example 1-9 did. However, because there is no upper bound on the number of factorials that can be computed with this class, we cannot use a fixed-sized array for the cache. Instead, we use the java.util.Vector class, which is a utility class that implements an array-like data structure that can grow to be as large as we need it to be. Because a Vector is an object, rather than an array, we use methods like size(), addElement(), and elementAt() to work with it. By the same token, a BigInteger is an object rather than a primitive value, so we cannot simply use the * operator to multiply BigInteger objects. We must use the multiply() method instead.

Example 1-10: Factorial4.java

```
// Import some other classes we'll use in this example.
// Once we import a class, we don't have to type its full name.
import java.math.BigInteger;  // Import BigInteger from java.math package
import java.util.*;  // Import all classes (including Vector) from java.util

/**
 * This version of the program uses arbitrary precision integers, so it does
 * not have an upper-bound on the values it can compute.  It uses a Vector
 * object to cache computed values instead of a fixed-size array.  A Vector
 * is like an array, but can grow to any size.  The factorial() method is
 * declared "synchronized" so that it can be safely used in multi-threaded
```

Example 1-10: Factorial4.java (continued)

```
 * programs.  Look up java.math.BigInteger and java.util.Vector while
 * studying this class.
 **/
public class Factorial4 {
  protected static Vector table = new Vector();        // create cache
  static { table.addElement(BigInteger.valueOf(1)); } // initialize 1st element

  /** The factorial() method, using BigIntegers cached in a Vector */
  public static synchronized BigInteger factorial(int x) {
    if (x < 0) throw new IllegalArgumentException("x must be non-negative.");
    for(int size = table.size(); size <= x; size++) {
      BigInteger lastfact = (BigInteger)table.elementAt(size-1);
      BigInteger nextfact = lastfact.multiply(BigInteger.valueOf(size));
      table.addElement(nextfact);
    }
    return (BigInteger) table.elementAt(x);
  }

  /**
   * A simple main() method that we can use as a standalone test program
   * for our factorial() method.
   **/
  public static void main(String[] args) {
    for(int i = 1; i <= 50; i++) System.out.println(i + "! = " + factorial(i));
  }
}
```

Handling Exceptions

Example 1-11 shows a program that uses the `Integer.parseInt()` method to convert a string specified on the command line to a number. The program then computes and prints the factorial of that number, using the `Factorial4.factorial()` method defined in Example 1-10. That much is simple; it takes only two lines of code. The rest of the example is concerned with "exception handling," or with taking care of all of the things that can go wrong. You use the `try/catch` statement in Java for exception handling. The `try` clause encloses a block of code from which exceptions may be thrown. It is followed by any number of `catch` clauses; the code in each `catch` clause takes care of a particular type of exception.

In Example 1-11, there are three possible user input errors that can prevent the program from executing normally. Therefore, the two main lines of program code are wrapped in a `try` clause that is followed by three `catch` clauses. Each clause notifies the user about a particular error by printing an appropriate message. This example is fairly straightforward. You may want to read the section titled "Exceptions and Exception Handling" in Chapter 2 of *Java in a Nutshell*. It explains exceptions in more detail.

Example 1-11: FactComputer.java

```
/**
 * This program computes and displays the factorial of a number specified
 * on the command line.  It handles possible user input errors with try/catch.
 **/
public class FactComputer {
```

Example 1-11: FactComputer.java (continued)

```java
public static void main(String[] args) {
    // Try to compute a factorial.  If something goes wrong, handle it below.
    try {
        int x = Integer.parseInt(args[0]);
        System.out.println(x + "! = " + Factorial4.factorial(x));
    }
    // The user forgot to specify an argument.  Thrown if args[0] is undefined.
    catch (ArrayIndexOutOfBoundsException e) {
        System.out.println("You must specify an argument");
        System.out.println("Usage: java FactComputer <number>");
    }
    // The argument is not a number.  Thrown by Integer.parseInt().
    catch (NumberFormatException e) {
        System.out.println("The argument you specify must be an integer");
    }
    // The argument is < 0.  Thrown by Factorial4.factorial()
    catch (IllegalArgumentException e) {
        // Display the message sent by the factorial() method:
        System.out.println("Bad argument: " + e.getMessage());
    }
}
}
```

Interactive Input

Example 1-12 shows yet another program for computing factorials. Unlike Example 1-11, however, it does not just compute one factorial and quit. Instead, it prompts the user to enter a number, reads that number, prints its factorial, and then loops and asks the user to enter another number. The most interesting thing about this example is the technique it uses to read user input from the keyboard. It uses the readLine() method of a BufferedReader object to do this. The line that creates the BufferedReader may look confusing. For now, take it on faith that it works; you do not really need to understand how it works until we reach Chapter 8. Another feature of note in Example 1-12 is the use of the equals() method of the String object line to check whether the user has typed "quit".

The code for parsing the user's input and computing and printing the factorial is the same as in Example 1-11, and again, it is enclosed within a try clause. In Example 1-12, however, there is only a single catch clause to handle the possible exceptions. This one handles any exception object of type Exception. Exception is the "superclass" of all exception types, so this one catch clause is invoked no matter what type of exception is thrown.

Example 1-12: FactQuoter.java

```java
import java.io.*; // Import all classes in java.io package.  Saves typing.

/**
 * This program displays factorials as the user enters values interactively
 **/
public class FactQuoter {
    public static void main(String[] args) throws IOException {
        // This is how we set things up to read lines of text from the user.
        BufferedReader in = new BufferedReader(new InputStreamReader(System.in));
```

Example 1–12: FactQuoter.java (continued)

```
    // Loop forever
    for(;;) {
      // Display a prompt to the user
      System.out.print("FactQuoter> ");
      // Read a line from the user
      String line = in.readLine();
      // If we reach the end-of-file, or if the user types "quit", then quit
      if ((line == null) || line.equals("quit")) break;
      // Try to parse the user's input, and compute and print the factorial
      try {
        int x = Integer.parseInt(line);
        System.out.println(x + "! = " + Factorial4.factorial(x));
      }
      // If anything goes wrong, display a generic error message
      catch(Exception e) { System.out.println("Invalid Input"); }
    }
  }
}
```

Using a StringBuffer

One of the things you may have noticed about the String class that is used to represent strings in Java is that it is "immutable." In other words, there are no methods that allow you to change the contents of a string. Methods that operate on a string return a new string, not a modified copy of the old one. When you want to operate on a string in place, you must use a StringBuffer object instead.

Example 1-13 demonstrates the use of a StringBuffer. It interactively reads a line of user input, as Example 1-12 did, and creates a StringBuffer to contain the line. The program then encodes each character of the line using the *rot13* substitution cipher, which simply "rotates" each letter 13 places through the alphabet, wrapping around from Z back to A when necessary. Because we are using a String-Buffer object, we can replace each character in the line one-by-one. A session with this Rot13Input program might look like this:

```
% java Rot13Input
> Hello there.  Testing, testing!
Uryyb gurer.  Grfgvat, grfgvat!
> quit
%
```

The main() method of Example 1-13 calls another method, rot13(), to perform the actual encoding of a character. This method demonstrates the use of the primitive Java char type and character literals (i.e., characters that are used literally in a program within single quotes).

Example 1–13: Rot13Input.java

```
import java.io.*;  // We're doing input, so import I/O classes

/**
 * This program reads lines of text from the user, encodes them using the
 * trivial "Rot13" substitution cipher, and then prints out the encoded lines.
 **/
```

Example 1–13: Rot13Input.java (continued)

```
public class Rot13Input {
  public static void main(String[] args) throws IOException {
    // Get set up to read lines of text from the user
    BufferedReader in = new BufferedReader(new InputStreamReader(System.in));
    for(;;) {                                   // Loop forever
      System.out.print("> ");                   // Print a prompt
      String line = in.readLine();              // Read a line
      if ((line == null) || line.equals("quit")) // If EOF or "quit" then...
        break;                                  // ... break out of the loop
      StringBuffer buf = new StringBuffer(line); // Convert to a StringBuffer
      for(int i = 0; i < buf.length(); i++)     // For each character...
        buf.setCharAt(i, rot13(buf.charAt(i))); //   read, encode, put it back
      System.out.println(buf);                  // Print encoded line
    }
  }

  /**
   * This method performs the Rot13 substitution cipher.  It "rotates"
   * each letter 13 places through the alphabet.  Since the Latin alphabet
   * has 26 letters, this method both encodes and decodes.
   **/
  public static char rot13(char c) {
    if ((c >= 'A') && (c <= 'Z')) {  // For uppercase letters
      c += 13;                       // Rotate forward 13
      if (c > 'Z') c -= 26;          // And subtract 26 if necessary
    }
    if ((c >= 'a') && (c <= 'z')) {  // Do the same for lowercase letters
      c += 13;
      if (c > 'z') c -= 26;
    }
    return c;                        // Return the modified letter
  }
}
```

Sorting Numbers

Example 1-14 implements a simple (but inefficient) algorithm for sorting an array of numbers. This example does not introduce any new elements of Java syntax, but it is interesting because it reaches a real-world level of complexity. The sorting algorithm manipulates array entries using an if statement within a for loop that is itself within another for loop. You should take the time to study this short program carefully. Make sure that you understand exactly how it goes about sorting its array of numbers.

Example 1–14: SortNumbers.java

```
/**
 * This class demonstrates how to sort numbers using a simple algorithm
 **/
public class SortNumbers {
  /**
   * This is a very simple sorting algorithm that is not very efficient
   * when sorting large numbers of things
   **/
  public static void sort(double[] nums) {
    // Loop through each element of the array, sorting as we go.
```

Example 1-14: SortNumbers.java (continued)

```
      // Each time through, find the smallest remaining element, and move it
      // to the first unsorted position in the array.
      for(int i = 0; i < nums.length; i++) {
        int min = i;  // holds the index of the smallest element
        // find the smallest one between i and the end of the array
        for(int j = i; j < nums.length; j++) {
          if (nums[j] < nums[min]) min = j;
        }
        // Now swap the smallest one with element i.
        // This leaves all elements between 0 and i sorted.
        double tmp;
        tmp = nums[i];
        nums[i] = nums[min];
        nums[min] = tmp;
      }
    }

    /** This is a simple test program for the algorithm above */
    public static void main(String[] args) {
      double[] nums = new double[10];      // Create an array to hold numbers
      for(int i = 0; i < nums.length; i++) // Generate random numbers
        nums[i] = Math.random() * 100;
      sort(nums);                          // Sort them
      for(int i = 0; i < nums.length; i++) // Print them out
        System.out.println(nums[i]);
    }
  }
```

Computing Primes

Example 1-15 computes the largest prime number less than a specified value,
using the "Sieve of Eratosthenes" algorithm. The algorithm finds primes by elimi-
nating multiples of all lower prime numbers. Like Example 1-14, this example
introduces no new Java syntax, but is a nice, non-trivial program with which to
end this introductory chapter. The program may seem deceptively simple, but
there's actually a fair bit going on, so be sure you understand how it is ruling out
prime numbers

Example 1-15: Sieve.java

```
/**
 * This program computes prime numbers using the Sieve of Eratosthenes
 * algorithm: rule out multiples of all lower prime numbers, and anything
 * remaining is a prime.  It prints out the largest prime number less than
 * or equal to the supplied command-line argument
 **/
public class Sieve {
  public static void main(String[] args) {
    // We will compute all primes less than the supplied command line argument
    // Or, if no argument, all primes less than 100
    int max = 100;                            // Assign a default value
    try { max = Integer.parseInt(args[0]); } // Try to parse user-supplied arg
    catch (Exception e) {}                    // Silently ignore exceptions.

    // Create an array that specifies whether each number is prime or not.
    boolean[] isprime = new boolean[max+1];
```

Example 1-15: Sieve.java (continued)

```
    // Assume that all numbers are primes, until proven otherwise.
    for(int i = 0; i <= max; i++) isprime[i] = true;

    // However, we know that 0 and 1 are not primes.  Make a note of it.
    isprime[0] = isprime[1] = false;

    // To compute all primes less than max, we need to rule out
    // multiples of all integers less than the square root of max.
    int n = (int) Math.ceil(Math.sqrt(max));  // See java.lang.Math class

    // Now, for each integer i from 0 to n:
    //   If i is a prime, then none of its multiples are primes, so
    //   indicate this in the array.
    //   If i is not a prime, then its multiples have already been
    //   ruled out by one of the prime factors of i, so we can skip this case.
    for(int i = 0; i <= n; i++) {
      if (isprime[i])                          // If i is a prime,
        for(int j = 2*i; j <= max; j = j + i)  // loop through its multiples
          isprime[j] = false;                  // noting they are not prime.
    }

    // Now go look for the largest prime:
    int largest;
    for(largest = max; !isprime[largest]; largest--) ;  // empty loop body

    // Output the result
    System.out.println("The largest prime less than or equal to " + max +
                       " is " + largest);
  }
}
```

Exercises

1-1. Write a program that counts from 1 to 15, printing out each number, and then counts backwards by twos back to 1, again printing out each number.

1-2. Each term of the Fibonacci series is formed by adding the previous two terms. What sort of series do you get if you add the previous three terms? Write a program to print the first 20 terms of this series.

1-3. Write a program that takes two numbers and a string as command-line arguments, and prints out the substring of the string specified by the two numbers. For example:

```
    % java Substring hello 1 3
```

Should print out:

```
    ell
```

Handle all possible exceptions that might arise because of bad input.

1-4. Write a program that interactively reads lines of input from the user and prints them back out, reversed. The program should exit if the user types tiuq.

1-5. The SortNumbers class shows how you can sort an array of doubles. Write a program that uses this class to sort an array of 100 floating-point numbers. Then, interatively prompt the user for numeric input and display the next larger and next smaller number from the array. You should use an efficient binary search algorithm to find the desired position in the sorted array.

CHAPTER 2

Objects, Classes, and Interfaces

This chapter provides examples that highlight the object-oriented nature of Java. It is designed to be read in conjunction with Chapter 3 of *Java in a Nutshell*. That chapter offers a complete introduction to the object-oriented concepts and syntax you must understand to program in Java. A number of the examples here also use nested and/or inner classes. These Java constructs are new in Java 1.1; they are completely documented in Chapter 5 of the Second Edition of *Java in a Nutshell*. The following paragraphs give a quick summary of Java's object-oriented terminology.

An *object* is a collection of data values, or *fields*, plus *methods* that operate on that data. The data type of an object is called a *class*; an object is often referred to as an *instance* of its class. The class defines the type of each field in the object, and it provides the methods that operate on data contained in an instance of the class. An object is created using the new operator, which invokes a *constructor* method of the class to initialize the new object. The fields and methods of an object are accessed and invoked using the . operator.

Methods that operate on the fields of an object are known as "instance methods." They are different from the "static methods," or "class methods," that we saw in Chapter 1, *Java Basics*. Class methods are declared static; they operate on the class itself, rather than on an individual instance of the class. Fields of a class may also be declared static, which makes them "class fields" instead of "instance fields." While each object has its own copy of each instance field, there is only one copy of a class field and it is shared by all instances of the class.

The fields and methods of a class may have different "visibility levels," including public, private, and protected. These different levels of visibility allow fields and methods to be used in different contexts. Every class has a *superclass*, from which it *inherits* fields and methods. When a class inherits from another class, it is called a *subclass* of that class. Classes in Java form a *class hierarchy*. The java.lang.Object class is root of this hierarchy; Object is the ultimate superclass of all other classes in Java.

An *interface* is a Java construct that defines methods, like a class, but does not provide any implementations for those methods. A class can *implement* an interface by defining an appropriate implementation for each of the methods in the interface.

A Rectangle Class

Example 2-1 shows a class that represents a rectangle. Each instance of this Rect class has four fields, x1, y1, x2, and y2, that define the coordinates of the corners of the rectangle. The Rect class also defines a number of methods that operate on those coordinates.

Note the toString() method. This method overrides the toString() method of java.lang.Object, which is the implicit superclass of the Rect class. toString() produces a String that represents a Rect object. As we'll see, this method is quite useful for printing out Rect values.

Example 2-1: Rect.java

```
/**
 * This class represents a rectangle.  Its fields represent the coordinates
 * of the corners of the rectangle.  Its methods define operations that can
 * be performed on Rect objects.
 **/
public class Rect {
  // These are the data fields of the class
  public int x1, y1, x2, y2;

  /**
   * The is the main constructor for the class.  It simply uses its arguments
   * to initialize each of the fields of the new object.  Note that it has
   * the same name as the class, and that it has no return value declared in
   * its signature.
   **/
  public Rect(int x1, int y1, int x2, int y2) {
    this.x1 = x1;
    this.y1 = y1;
    this.x2 = x2;
    this.y2 = y2;
  }

  /**
   * This is another constructor.  It defines itself in terms of the one above
   **/
  public Rect(int width, int height) { this(0, 0, width, height); }

  /** This is yet another constructor. */
  public Rect() { this(0, 0, 0, 0); }

  /** Move the rectangle by the specified amounts */
  public void move(int deltax, int deltay) {
    x1 += deltax; x2 += deltax;
    y1 += deltay; y2 += deltay;
  }

  /** Test whether the specified point is inside the rectangle */
  public boolean isInside(int x, int y) {
```

Example 2-1: Rect.java (continued)

```
    return ((x >= x1) && (x <= x2) && (y >= y1) && (y <= y2));
  }

  /**
   * Return the union of this rectangle with another.  I.e. return the
   * smallest rectangle that includes them both.
   **/
  public Rect union(Rect r) {
    return new Rect((this.x1 < r.x1) ? this.x1 : r.x1,
                    (this.y1 < r.y1) ? this.y1 : r.y1,
                    (this.x2 > r.x2) ? this.x2 : r.x2,
                    (this.y2 > r.y2) ? this.y2 : r.y2);
  }

  /**
   * Return the intersection of this rectangle with another.
   * I.e. return their overlap.
   **/
  public Rect intersection(Rect r) {
    Rect result =  new Rect((this.x1 > r.x1) ? this.x1 : r.x1,
                            (this.y1 > r.y1) ? this.y1 : r.y1,
                            (this.x2 < r.x2) ? this.x2 : r.x2,
                            (this.y2 < r.y2) ? this.y2 : r.y2);
    if (result.x1 > result.x2) { result.x1 = result.x2 = 0; }
    if (result.y1 > result.y2) { result.y1 = result.y2 = 0; }
    return result;
  }

  /**
   * This is a method of our superclass, Object.  We override it so that
   * Rect objects can be meaningfully converted to strings, can be
   * concatenated to strings with the + operator, and can be passed to
   * methods like System.out.println()
   **/
  public String toString() {
    return "[" + x1 + "," + y1 + "; " + x2 + "," + y2 + "]";
  }
}
```

Testing the Rect Class

Example 2-2 is a standalone program named RectTest that puts the Rect class of Example 2-1 through its paces. Note the use of the new keyword and the Rect() constructor to create new Rect objects. The program uses the . operator to invoke methods of the Rect objects and to access their fields. The test program also relies implicitly on the toString() method of Rect when it uses the string concatenation operator (+) to create strings to be displayed to the user.

Example 2-2: RectTest.java

```
/** This class demonstrates how you might use the Rect class */
public class RectTest {
  public static void main(String[] args) {
    Rect r1 = new Rect(1, 1, 4, 4);    // Create Rect objects
    Rect r2 = new Rect(2, 3, 5, 6);
```

Example 2-2: RectTest.java (continued)

```
    Rect u = r1.union(r2);           // Invoke Rect methods
    Rect i = r2.intersection(r1);

    if (u.isInside(r2.x1, r2.y1))    // Use Rect fields and invoke a method
      System.out.println("(" + r2.x1 + "," + r2.y1 + ") is inside the union");

    // These string concatenations implicitly call the Rect.toString() method
    System.out.println(r1 + " union " + r2 + " = " + u);
    System.out.println(r1 + " intersect " + r2 + " = " + i);
  }
}
```

A Rect Subclass

Example 2-3 is a simple subclass of the Rect class of Example 2-1. This DrawableRect class inherits the fields and methods of Rect and adds its own method, draw(), that draws a rectangle using a specified java.awt.Graphics object. (We'll see more of the Graphics object in Chapter 3, *Applets*, and study it in detail in Chapter 4, *Graphics*.) DrawableRect also defines a constructor that does nothing more than pass its arguments on to the corresponding Rect constructor. Note the use of the extends keyword to indicate that Rect is the superclass of DrawableRect.

Example 2-3: DrawableRect.java

```
/**
 * This is a subclass of Rect that allows itself to be drawn on a screen.
 * It inherits all the fields and methods of Rect
 * It relies on the java.awt.Graphics object to perform the drawing.
 **/
public class DrawableRect extends Rect {
  /** The DrawableRect constructor just invokes the Rect() constructor */
  public DrawableRect(int x1, int y1, int x2, int y2) { super(x1,y1,x2,y2); }

  /** This is the new method defined by DrawableRect */
  public void draw(java.awt.Graphics g) {
    g.drawRect(x1, y1, (x2 - x1), (y2-y1));
  }
}
```

Another Subclass

Example 2-4 shows another subclass. ColoredRect is a subclass of DrawableRect (see Example 2-3), which makes it a sub-subclass of Rect (see Example 2-1). This class inherits the fields and methods of DrawableRect and of Rect (and of Object, which is the implicit superclass of Rect). ColoredRect adds two new fields that specify the border color and fill color of the rectangle when it is drawn. (These fields are of type java.awt.Color, which we'll learn about in Chapter 4.) The class also defines a new constructor that allows these fields to be initialized. Finally, ColoredRect overrides the draw() method of the DrawableRect class. The draw() method defined by ColoredRect draws a rectangle using the specified colors, rather than simply using the default colors as the method in DrawableRect did.

Example 2-4: ColoredRect.java

```java
import java.awt.*;

/**
 * This class subclasses DrawableRect and adds colors to the rectangle it draws
 **/
public class ColoredRect extends DrawableRect {
  // These are new fields defined by this class.
  // x1, y1, x2, and y2 are inherited from our super-superclass, Rect.
  protected Color border, fill;

  /**
   * This constructor uses super() to invoke the superclass constructor, and
   * also does some initialization of its own.
   **/
  public ColoredRect(int x1, int y1, int x2, int y2, Color border, Color fill){
    super(x1, y1, x2, y2);
    this.border = border;
    this.fill = fill;
  }

  /**
   * This method overrides the draw() method of our superclass so that it
   * can make use of the colors that have been specified.
   **/
  public void draw(Graphics g) {
    g.setColor(fill);
    g.fillRect(x1, y1, (x2 - x1), (y2 - y1));
    g.setColor(border);
    g.drawRect(x1, y1, (x2 - x1), (y2 - y1));
  }
}
```

Complex Numbers

Example 2-5 shows the definition of a class that represents complex numbers. You may recall from algebra class that a complex number is the sum of a real number and an imaginary number. The imaginary number i is the square root of -1. This ComplexNumber class defines two double fields, which represent the real and imaginary parts of the number. These fields are declared private, which means that they can only be used within the body of the class; they are inaccessible outside of the class. Because the fields are inaccessible, the class defines two "accessor" methods, real() and imaginary(), that simply return their values. This technique of making fields private and defining accessor methods is called *encapsulation*. Encapsulation hides the implementation of a class from its users, which means that you can change the implementation without it affecting the users.

Notice that the ComplexNumber class does not define any methods, other than the constructor, that set the values of its fields. Once a ComplexNumber object is created, the number it represents can never be changed. This property is known as *immutability*; it is sometimes useful to design objects that are immutable like this.

ComplexNumber defines two add() methods and two multiply() methods that perform addition and multiplication of complex numbers. The difference between the two versions of each method is that one is an instance method and one is a class, or static, method. Consider the add() methods, for example. The instance method adds the value of the current instance of ComplexNumber to another specified ComplexNumber object. The class method does not have a current instance; it simply adds the values of two specified ComplexNumber objects. The instance method is invoked through an instance of the class, like this:

```
ComplexNumber sum = a.add(b);
```

The class method, however, is invoked through the class itself, rather than through an instance:

```
ComplexNumber sum = ComplexNumber.add(a, b);
```

Example 2–5: ComplexNumber.java

```java
/**
 * This class represents complex numbers, and defines methods for performing
 * arithmetic on complex numbers.
 **/
public class ComplexNumber {
  // These are the instance variables.  Each ComplexNumber object holds
  // two double values, known as x and y.  They are private, so they are
  // not accessible from outside this class.  Instead, they are available
  // through the real() and imaginary() methods below.
  private double x, y;

  /** This is the constructor.  It initializes the x and y variables */
  public ComplexNumber(double real, double imaginary) {
    this.x = real;
    this.y = imaginary;
  }

  /**
   * An accessor method.  Returns the real part of the complex number.
   * Note that there is no setReal() method to set the real part.  This means
   * that the ComplexNumber class is "immutable".
   **/
  public double real() { return x; }

  /** An accessor method.  Returns the imaginary part of the complex number */
  public double imaginary() { return y; }

  /** Compute the magnitude of a complex number */
  public double magnitude() { return Math.sqrt(x*x + y*y); }

  /**
   * This method converts a ComplexNumber to a string.  This is a method of
   * Object that we override so that complex numbers can be meaningfully
   * converted to strings, and so they can conveniently be printed out with
   * System.out.println() and related methods
   **/
  public String toString() { return "{" + x + "," + y + "}"; }

  /**
   * This is a static class method.  It takes two complex numbers, adds them,
   * and returns the result as a third number.  Because it is static, there is
   * no "current instance" or "this" object.  Use it like this:
   * ComplexNumber c = ComplexNumber.add(a, b);
   **/
  public static ComplexNumber add(ComplexNumber a, ComplexNumber b) {
```

Example 2-5: ComplexNumber.java (continued)

```
    return new ComplexNumber(a.x + b.x, a.y + b.y);
}

/**
 * This is a non-static instance method by the same name.  It adds the
 * specified complex number to the current complex number.  Use it like this:
 * ComplexNumber c = a.add(b);
 **/
public ComplexNumber add(ComplexNumber a) {
  return new ComplexNumber(this.x + a.x, this.y+a.y);
}

/** A static class method to multiply complex numbers */
public static ComplexNumber multiply(ComplexNumber a, ComplexNumber b) {
  return new ComplexNumber(a.x*b.x - a.y*b.y, a.x*b.y + a.y*b.x);
}

/** An instance method to multiply complex numbers */
public ComplexNumber multiply(ComplexNumber a) {
  return new ComplexNumber(x*a.x - y*a.y, x*a.y + y*a.x);
}
}
```

Computing Pseudo-Random Numbers

So far, all of the classes we've defined have represented real-world objects. (A complex number is an abstract mathematical concept, but it's not too hard to think of it as a real-world object.) In some cases, however, you need to create a class that does not represent some kind of object, or even an abstract concept. Example 2-6, which defines a class that can be used to compute pseudo-random numbers, is just this kind of class.

The Randomizer class obviously does not implement some kind of object. In turns out, however, that the simple algorithm we use for generating pseudo-random numbers requires a state variable, seed, that stores the random-number seed. Because we need to keep track of some state, we cannot simply define a static random() method as we did for methods like Factorial.factorial() in Chapter 1. When a method requires state to be saved between one invocation and the next, the method typically needs to be an instance method of an object that contains the necessary state, even if the object itself has no obvious real-world or abstract counterpart.

Thus, our Randomizer class defines a single instance variable, seed, that saves the necessary state for generating pseudo-random numbers. The other fields in Randomizer are declared static and final, which makes them constants in Java. In other words, for each static final field, there is a field associated with the class itself whose value never changes.

Example 2-6: Randomizer.java

```
/**
 * This class defines methods for computing pseudo-random numbers, and it defines
 * the state variable that needs to be maintained for use by those methods.
 **/
```

Example 2-6: Randomizer.java (continued)

```java
public class Randomizer {
  // Carefully chosen constants from the book "Numerical Recipes in C".
  // All "static final" fields are constants.
  static final int m = 233280;
  static final int a = 9301;
  static final int c = 49297;

  // The state variable maintained by each Randomizer instance
  int seed = 1;

  /**
   * The constructor for the Randomizer() class.  It must be passed some
   * arbitrary initial value or "seed" for its pseudo-randomness.
   **/
  public Randomizer(int seed) { this.seed = seed; }

  /**
   * This method computes a pseudo-random number between 0 and 1 using a very
   * simple algorithm.  Math.random() and java.util.Random are actually a lot
   * better at computing randomness.
   **/
  public float randomFloat() {
    seed = (seed * a + c) % m;
    return (float)seed/(float)m;
  }

  /**
   * This method computes a pseudo-random integer between 0 and the specified
   * maximum.  It uses randomFloat() above.
   **/
  public int randomInt(int max) {
    return Math.round(max * randomFloat());
  }

  /**
   * This nested class is a simple test program: it prints 10 random integers.
   * Note how the Randomizer object is seeded using the current time.
   **/
  public static class Test {
    public static void main(String[] args) {
      Randomizer r = new Randomizer((int)new java.util.Date().getTime());
      for(int i = 0; i < 10; i++) System.out.println(r.randomInt(100));
    }
  }
}
```

Example 2-6 introduces an important new feature. The Randomizer class defines a nested top-level (i.e., static) class named Test. This class, Randomizer.Test, contains a main() method and is thus a standalone program suitable for testing the Randomizer class. When you compile the *Randomizer.java* file, you get two class files, *Randomizer.class* and *Randomizer$Test.class*. Running this nested Randomizer.Test class is a little tricky. You *ought* to be able to do so like this:

```
% java Randomizer.Test
```

Objects, Classes, and Interfaces

However, current versions of the JDK do not correctly map from the class name Randomizer.Test to the class file *Randomizer$Test.class.** So to run the test program, you must invoke the Java interpreter using a $ character instead of a . character in the class name:

```
% java Randomizer$Test
```

On a UNIX system, however, you should be aware that the $ character has special significance and must be escaped. Therefore, on such a system, you have to type:

```
% java Randomizer\$Test
```

Or:

```
% java 'Randomizer$Test'
```

Computing Statistics

Example 2-7 shows a class that computes some simple statistics for a set of numbers. As numbers are passed to the addDatum() method, the Averager class updates its internal state so that its other methods can easily return the average and standard deviation of the numbers that have been passed to it so far. Like Randomizer, the Averager class does not represent any kind of real-world object or abstract concept. Nevertheless, Averager does maintains some state (this time as private fields) and it has methods that operate on that state, so it is implemented as an object.

Like Example 2-6, Example 2-7 defines a nested Test class that contains a main() method that implements a test program for Averager.

Example 2-7: Averager.java

```
/**
 * A class to compute the running average of numbers passed to it
 **/
public class Averager {
  // Private fields to hold the current state.
  private int n = 0;
  private double sum = 0.0, sumOfSquares = 0.0;

  /**
   * This method adds a new datum into the average.
   **/
  public void addDatum(double x) {
    n++;
    sum += x;
    sumOfSquares += x * x;
  }

  /** This method returns the average of all numbers passed to addDatum() */
  public double getAverage() { return sum / n; }

  /** This method returns the standard deviation of the data */
  public double getStandardDeviation() {
```

---

*Hopefully, this situation will be fixed in a future release.

Example 2–7: Averager.java (continued)

```
    return Math.sqrt(((sumOfSquares - sum*sum/n)/n));
  }

  /** This method returns the number of numbers passed to addDatum() */
  public double getNum() { return n; }

  /** This method returns the sum of all numbers passed to addDatum() */
  public double getSum() { return sum; }

  /** This method returns the sum of the squares of all numbers. */
  public double getSumOfSquares() { return sumOfSquares; }

  /** This method resets the Averager object to begin from scratch */
  public void reset() { n = 0; sum = 0.0; sumOfSquares = 0.0; }

  /**
   * This nested class is a simple test program we can use to check that
   * our code works okay.
   **/
  public static class Test {
    public static void main(String args[]) {
      Averager a = new Averager();
      for(int i = 1; i <= 100; i++) a.addDatum(i);
      System.out.println("Average: " + a.getAverage());
      System.out.println("Standard Deviation: " + a.getStandardDeviation());
      System.out.println("N: " + a.getNum());
      System.out.println("Sum: " + a.getSum());
      System.out.println("Sum of squares: " + a.getSumOfSquares());
    }
  }
}
```

Objects, Classes, and Interfaces

A Linked List Class

Example 2-8 displays a class, LinkedList, that implements a linked list data structure. The example also defines a Linkable interface. If an object is to be "linked" into a LinkedList, the class of that object must implement the Linkable interface. Recall that an interface defines methods, but does not provide any bodies for those methods. A class "implements" an interface by providing an implementation for each of the methods in the interface and by using the implements keyword in its declaration. Any instance of a class that implements Linkable can be treated as an instance of Linkable. A LinkedList object treats all of the objects in its list as instances of Linkable, and therefore does not need to know anything about their true types.

LinkedList defines a single state field, head, that refers to the first Linkable item in the list. The class also defines a number of methods for adding items to and removing items from the list. Note that the Linkable interface is nested within the LinkedList class. While this is a convenient and useful way to define the interface, it is by no means necessary to nest things in this way. Linkable could just as easily be defined as an ordinary, top-level interface.

The LinkedList class also defines a nested top-level Test class, which, once again, is a standalone program for testing the class. In this example, however, the nested

Test class itself contains a nested class, LinkableInteger. This class implements Linkable; instances of it are linked into a list by the test program.

Example 2–8: LinkedList.java

```java
/**
 * This class implements a linked list that can contain any type of object
 * that implements the nested Linkable interface.  Note that the methods are
 * all synchronized, so that it can safely be used by multiple threads at
 * the same time.
**/
public class LinkedList {
  /**
   * This interface defines the methods required by any object that can be
   * linked into a linked list.
  **/
  public interface Linkable {
    public Linkable getNext();         // Returns the next element in the list
    public void setNext(Linkable node); // Sets the next element in the list
  }

  // This class has a default constructor: public LinkedList() {}

  /** This is the only field of the class.  It holds the head of the list */
  Linkable head;

  /** Return the first node in the list */
  public synchronized Linkable getHead() { return head; }

  /** Insert a node at the beginning of the list */
  public synchronized void insertAtHead(Linkable node) {
    node.setNext(head);
    head = node;
  }

  /** Insert a node at the end of the list */
  public synchronized void insertAtTail(Linkable node) {
    if (head == null) head = node;
    else {
      Linkable p, q;
      for(p = head; (q = p.getNext()) != null; p = q);
      p.setNext(node);
    }
  }

  /** Remove and return the node at the head of the list */
  public synchronized Linkable removeFromHead() {
    Linkable node = head;
    if (node != null) {
      head = node.getNext();
      node.setNext(null);
    }
    return node;
  }

  /** Remove and return the node at the end of the list */
  public synchronized Linkable removeFromTail() {
    if (head == null) return null;
    Linkable p = head, q = null, next = head.getNext();
    if (next == null) {
```

Example 2-8: LinkedList.java (continued)

```
      head = null;
      return p;
    }
   while((next = p.getNext()) != null) {
     q = p;
     p = next;
   }
   q.setNext(null);
   return p;
 }


/**
 * Remove a node matching the specified node from the list.
 * Use equals() instead of == to test for a matched node.
 **/
public synchronized void remove(Linkable node) {
  if (head == null) return;
  if (node.equals(head)) {
    head = head.getNext();
    return;
  }
  Linkable p = head, q = null;
  while((q = p.getNext()) != null) {
    if (node.equals(q)) {
      p.setNext(q.getNext());
      return;
    }
    p = q;
  }
}


/**
 * This nested class defines a main() method that tests the LinkedList class
 **/
public static class Test {
  /**
   * This is a test class that implements the Linkable interface
   **/
  static class LinkableInteger implements Linkable {
    int i;          // The data contained in the node
    Linkable next;  // A reference to the next node in the list
    public LinkableInteger(int i) { this.i = i; }    // Constructor method
    public Linkable getNext() { return next; }        // Part of Linkable
    public void setNext(Linkable node) { next = node; } // Part of Linkable
    public String toString() { return i + ""; }       // For easy printing
    public boolean equals(Object o) {                 // For comparison
      if (this == o) return true;
      if (!(o instanceof LinkableInteger)) return false;
      if (((LinkableInteger)o).i == this.i) return true;
      return false;
    }
  }

  /**
   * The test program.  Insert some nodes, remove some nodes, then
   * print out all elements in the list.  It should print out the
   * numbers 4, 6, 3, 1, and 5
   **/
```

Example 2-8: LinkedList.java (continued)

```java
public static void main(String[] args) {
    LinkedList ll = new LinkedList();           // Create a list
    ll.insertAtHead(new LinkableInteger(1));    // Insert some stuff
    ll.insertAtHead(new LinkableInteger(2));
    ll.insertAtHead(new LinkableInteger(3));
    ll.insertAtHead(new LinkableInteger(4));
    ll.insertAtTail(new LinkableInteger(5));    // Insert some more stuff
    ll.insertAtTail(new LinkableInteger(6));
    System.out.println(ll.removeFromHead());    // Remove and print a node
    System.out.println(ll.removeFromTail());    // Remove and print another
    ll.remove(new LinkableInteger(2));          // Remove another one

    // Now print out the contents of the list.
    for(Linkable l = ll.getHead(); l != null; l = l.getNext())
      System.out.println(l);
  }
 }
}
```

Advanced Sorting

In Chapter 1, we saw an example of a simple, unsophisticated algorithm for sorting an array of numbers. Example 2-9 defines a class, Sorter, that supports more efficient and general-purpose sorting. Sorter defines a multitude of static sort() methods that each take slightly different arguments. A number of these methods sort strings in various ways, while others sort other types of objects. The last of these sort() methods implements the quicksort algorithm to efficiently sort an array of objects. All of the other methods are variants; each one ultimately invokes the general sorting method.

The sort() methods that sort strings take advantage of some of the new internationalization features of Java 1.1. In particular, they use the java.util.Locale, java.text.Collator, and java.text.CollationKey classes. We examine these classes in more detail in Chapter 14, *Internationalization*.

In order to sort an array of objects, Sorter needs some way to compare two objects to determine which one should come before the other in the sorted array. Sorter defines two nested interfaces, Comparer and Comparable, that provide two different ways of implementing this comparison. You can sort arbitrary objects by passing a Comparer object to one of the sort() methods. A Comparer object defines a compare() method that compares arbitrary objects. Alternatively, the object classes that you need to sort can implement the Comparable interface. In this case, the objects themselves have compareTo() methods, so they can be compared directly.

Example 2-9 rounds out this chapter. If you've skimmed ahead and looked at the program, you probably noticed that it is a rather complex example. As such, it is worth studying carefully. In particular, the program makes heavy use of inner classes, so you should be sure you understand how inner classes work before you examine this code in detail. (You may want to read Chapter 5 of the Second Edition of *Java in a Nutshell* to brush up on inner classes.) As usual, there is a nested

Test class at the end of the example, but nested classes and interfaces, as well as anonymous classes, are used throughout the program.

Example 2-9: Sorter.java

```
// These are some classes we need for internationalized string sorting
import java.text.Collator;
import java.text.CollationKey;
import java.util.Locale;

/**
 * This class defines a bunch of static methods for efficiently sorting
 * arrays of Strings or other objects.  It also defines two interfaces that
 * provide two different ways of comparing objects to be sorted.
 **/
public class Sorter {
  /**
   * This interface defines the compare() method used to compare two objects.
   * To sort objects of a given type, you must provide an appropriate Comparer
   * object with a compare() method that orders those objects as desired
   **/
  public static interface Comparer {
    /**
     * Compare objects and return a value that indicates their relative order:
     * if (a > b) return > 0;
     * if (a == b) return 0;
     * if (a < b) return < 0.
     **/
    public int compare(Object a, Object b);
  }

  /**
   * This is an alternative interface that can be used to order objects.  If a
   * class implements this Comparable interface, then any two instances of that
   * class can be directly compared by invoking the compareTo() method.
   **/
  public static interface Comparable {
    /**
     * Compare objects and return a value that indicates their relative order:
     * if (this > other) return > 0
     * if (this == other) return 0
     * if (this < other) return < 0
     **/
    public int compareTo(Object other);
  }

  /**
   * This is an internal Comparer object (created with an anonymous class)
   * that compares two ASCII strings.
   * It is used in the sortAscii methods below.
   **/
  private static Comparer ascii_comparer = new Comparer() {
    public int compare(Object a, Object b) {
      return ((String)a).compareTo((String)b);
    }
  };

  /**
   * This is another internal Comparer object.  It is used to compare two
   * Comparable objects.  It is used by the sort() methods below that take
```

Example 2-9: Sorter.java (continued)

```
 * Comparable objects as arguments instead of arbitrary objects
 */
private static Comparer comparable_comparer = new Comparer() {
  public int compare(Object a, Object b) {
    return ((Comparable)a).compareTo(b);
  }
};

/** Sort an array of ASCII strings into ascending order */
public static void sortAscii(String[] a) {
  // Note use of the ascii_comparer object
  sort(a, null, 0, a.length-1, true, ascii_comparer);
}

/**
 * Sort a portion of an array of ASCII strings into ascending or descending
 * order, depending on the argument up
 **/
public static void sortAscii(String[] a, int from, int to, boolean up) {
  // Note use of the ascii_comparer object
  sort(a, null, from, to, up, ascii_comparer);
}

/** Sort an array of ASCII strings into ascending order, ignoring case */
public static void sortAsciiIgnoreCase(String[] a) {
  sortAsciiIgnoreCase(a, 0, a.length-1, true);
}

/**
 * Sort an portion of an array of ASCII strings, ignoring case.  Sort into
 * ascending order if up is true, otherwise sort into descending order.
 **/
public static void sortAsciiIgnoreCase(String[] a, int from, int to,
                                       boolean up) {
  if ((a == null) || (a.length < 2)) return;
  // Create a secondary array of strings that contains lowercase versions
  // of all the specified strings.
  String b[] = new String[a.length];
  for(int i = 0; i < a.length; i++) b[i] = a[i].toLowerCase();
  // Sort that secondary array, and rearrange the original array
  // in exactly the same way, resulting in a case-insensitive sort.
  // Note the use of the ascii_comparer object
  sort(b, a, from, to, up, ascii_comparer);
}

/**
 * Sort an array of strings into ascending order, using the correct
 * collation order for the default locale
 **/
public static void sort(String[] a) {
  sort(a, 0, a.length-1, true, false, null);
}

/**
 * Sort a portion of an array of strings, using the collation order of
 * the default locale.  If up is true, sort ascending, otherwise, sort
 * descending.  If ignorecase is true, ignore the capitalization of letters
 **/
```

Example 2-9: Sorter.java (continued)

```java
public static void sort(String[] a, int from, int to,
                        boolean up, boolean ignorecase) {
  sort(a, from, to, up, ignorecase, null);
}

/**
 * Sort a portion of an array of strings, using the collation order of
 * the specified locale.  If up is true, sort ascending, otherwise, sort
 * descending.  If ignorecase is true, ignore the capitalization of letters
 **/
public static void sort(String[] a, int from, int to,
                        boolean up, boolean ignorecase,
                        Locale locale) {
  // Don't sort if we don't have to
  if ((a == null) || (a.length < 2)) return;

  // The java.text.Collator object does internationalized string compares
  // Create one for the specified, or the default locale.
  Collator c;
  if (locale == null) c = Collator.getInstance();
  else c = Collator.getInstance(locale);

  // Specify whether or not case should be taken into account in the sort.
  // Note: this option does not seem to work correctly in JDK 1.1.1
  // using the default American English locale.
  if (ignorecase) c.setStrength(Collator.SECONDARY);

  // Use the Collator object to create an array of CollationKey objects that
  // correspond to each of the strings.
  // Comparing CollationKeys is much quicker than comparing Strings
  CollationKey[] b = new CollationKey[a.length];
  for(int i = 0; i < a.length; i++) b[i] = c.getCollationKey(a[i]);

  // Now define a Comparer object to compare collation keys, using an
  // anonymous class.
  Comparer comp =  new Comparer() {
    public int compare(Object a, Object b) {
      return ((CollationKey)a).compareTo((CollationKey)b);
    }
  };

  // Finally, sort the array of CollationKey objects, rearranging the
  // original array of strings in exactly the same way.
  sort(b, a, from, to, up, comp);
}

/** Sort an array of Comparable objects into ascending order */
public static void sort(Comparable[] a) {
  sort(a, null, 0, a.length-1, true);
}

/**
 * Sort a portion of an array of Comparable objects.  If up is true,
 * sort into ascending order, otherwise sort into descending order.
 **/
public static void sort(Comparable[] a, int from, int to, boolean up) {
  sort(a, null, from, to, up, comparable_comparer);
}
```

Example 2-9: Sorter.java (continued)

```
/**
 * Sort a portion of array a of Comparable objects.  If up is true,
 * sort into ascending order, otherwise sort into descending order.
 * Re-arrange the array b in exactly the same way as a.
 **/
public static void sort(Comparable[] a, Object[] b,
                        int from, int to, boolean up) {
  sort(a, b, from, to, up, comparable_comparer);
}


/**
 * Sort an array of arbitrary objects into ascending order, using the
 * comparison defined by the Comparer object c
 **/
public static void sort(Object[] a, Comparer c) {
  sort(a, null, 0, a.length-1, true, c);
}


/**
 * Sort a portion of an array of objects, using the comparison defined by
 * the Comparer object c.  If up is true, sort into ascending order,
 * otherwise sort into descending order.
 **/
public static void sort(Object[] a, int from,int to, boolean up, Comparer c){
  sort(a, null, from, to, up, c);
}


/**
 * This is the main sort() routine.  It performs a quicksort on the elements
 * of array a between the element from and the element to.  The up argument
 * specifies whether the elements should be sorted into ascending (true) or
 * descending (false) order.  The Comparer argument c is used to perform
 * comparisons between elements of the array.  The elements of the array b
 * are reordered in exactly the same way as the elements of array a are.
 **/
public static void sort(Object[] a, Object[] b,
                        int from, int to,
                        boolean up, Comparer c)
{
  // If there is nothing to sort, return
  if ((a == null) || (a.length < 2)) return;

  // This is the basic quicksort algorithm, stripped of frills that can make
  // it faster but even more confusing than it already is.  You should
  // understand what the code does, but don't have to understand just
  // why it is guaranteed to sort the array...
  // Note the use of the compare() method of the Comparer object.
  int i = from, j = to;
  Object center = a[(from + to) / 2];
  do {
    if (up) {  // an ascending sort
      while((i < to) && (c.compare(center, a[i]) > 0)) i++;
      while((j > from) && (c.compare(center, a[j]) < 0)) j--;
    } else {   // a descending sort
      while((i < to) && (c.compare(center, a[i]) < 0)) i++;
      while((j > from) && (c.compare(center, a[j]) > 0)) j--;
    }
    if (i < j) {
```

Example 2-9: Sorter.java (continued)

```
        Object tmp = a[i]; a[i] = a[j]; a[j] = tmp;           // swap elements
        if (b != null) { tmp = b[i]; b[i] = b[j]; b[j] = tmp; }// swap b, too
      }
      if (i <= j) { i++; j--; }
    } while(i <= j);
    if (from < j) sort(a, b, from, j, up, c); // recursively sort the rest
    if (i < to) sort(a, b, i, to, up, c);
  }

  /**
   * This nested class defines a test program that demonstrates several
   * ways to use the Sorter class to sort ComplexNumber objects
   **/
  public static class Test {
    /**
     * This subclass of ComplexNumber implements the Comparable interface
     * and defines a compareTo() method for comparing complex numbers.
     * It compares numbers based on their magnitude. I.e. on their distance
     * from the origin.
     **/
    static class SortableComplexNumber extends ComplexNumber
                               implements Sorter.Comparable {
      public SortableComplexNumber(double x, double y) { super(x, y); }
      public int compareTo(Object other) {
        return sign(this.magnitude()-((ComplexNumber)other).magnitude());
      }
    }

    /** This is the test program.  It sorts complex numbers in various ways. */
    public static void main(String[] args) {
      // Define an array of SortableComplexNumber objects.  Initialize it
      // to contain random complex numbers.
      SortableComplexNumber[] a = new SortableComplexNumber[5];
      for(int i = 0; i < a.length; i++)
        a[i] = new SortableComplexNumber(Math.random()*10, Math.random()*10);

      // Now sort it using the SortableComplexNumber compareTo() method, which
      // sorts by magnitude, and print the results out.
      System.out.println("Sorted by magnitude:");
      Sorter.sort(a);
      for(int i = 0; i < a.length; i++) System.out.println(a[i]);

      // Sort the complex numbers again, using a Comparer object that
      // compares them based on the sum of their real and imaginary parts
      System.out.println("Sorted by sum of real and imaginary parts:");
      Sorter.sort(a, new Sorter.Comparer() {
        public int compare(Object a, Object b) {
          ComplexNumber i = (ComplexNumber)a, j = (ComplexNumber)b;
          return sign((i.real() + i.imaginary()) -
                      (j.real() + j.imaginary()));
        }
      });
      for(int i = 0; i < a.length; i++) System.out.println(a[i]);

      // Sort them again using a Comparer object that compares their real
      // parts, and then their imaginary parts
      System.out.println("Sorted descending by real part, then imaginary:");
      Sorter.sort(a, 0, a.length-1, false, new Sorter.Comparer() {
```

Example 2-9: Sorter.java (continued)

```
    public int compare(Object a, Object b) {
      ComplexNumber i = (ComplexNumber) a, j = (ComplexNumber) b;
      double result = i.real() - j.real();
      if (result == 0) result = i.imaginary() - j.imaginary();
      return sign(result);
    }
  });
  for(int i = 0; i < a.length; i++) System.out.println(a[i]);
}

/** This is a convenience routine used by comparison routines */
public static int sign(double x) {
  if (x > 0) return 1;
  else if (x < 0) return -1;
  else return 0;
}
}
}
```

Exercises

2-1. Write a Circle class that is similar to the Rect class. Define a move() method and an isInside() method. (Recall that a circle is defined as all points within a given radius from the center. Test for insideness by using the Pythagorean theorem to compute the distance between a point and the center of the circle.) Also, define a boundingBox() method that returns the smallest Rect that encloses the complete Circle. Write a simple program to test the methods you've implemented.

2-2. Write a class that represents a person's mailing address. It should have separate fields for the name, street address, city, state, and ZIP code. Define a toString() method that produces nicely formatted output.

2-3. Using the Sort.Comparer and/or the Sort.Comparable interfaces, write a static search() method for a class named Search that peforms an efficient binary search for a specified object within a sorted array of objects. If the object is found in the array, search() should return the array index at which it was found. Otherwise, it should return −1.

CHAPTER 3

Applets

This chapter demonstrates the techniques of applet writing. It proceeds from a trivial "Hello World" applet to more sophisticated applets. Along the way, it explains how to:

- Draw graphics in your applet.

- Handle and respond to simple user input.

- Read and use values of applet parameters, allowing customization of an applet.

- Load and display images and load and play sounds.

- Package an applet and related files into a JAR file.

- Attach a digital signature to an applet.

Note that this chapter merely introduces the framework for writing applets. Applets, like other Java programs, use features from throughout the Java API. See Chapter 5, *Events*, in particular, for details on event processing in Java applets and applications. You may find it useful to refer to reference material for the java.applet package while studying these examples.

Introduction to Applets

An applet, as the name implies, is a kind of mini-application, designed to be run by a Web browser, or in the context of some other "applet viewer." Applets differ from regular applications in a number of ways. One of the most important is that there are a number of security restrictions on what applets are allowed to do. An applet often consists of untrusted code, so it cannot be allowed access to the local file system, for example.

From a programmer's standpoint, one of the biggest differences between an applet and an application is that an applet does not have a main() method, or other single entry point from which the program starts running. Instead, to write an applet, you subclass the Applet class and override a number of standard methods. At appropriate times, under well-defined circumstances, the Web browser or applet viewer invokes the methods you have defined. The applet is not in control of the thread of execution; it simply responds when the browser or viewer tells it to. For this reason, the methods you write must take the necessary action and return promptly—they are not allowed to enter time-consuming (or infinite) loops. In order to perform a time-consuming or repetitive task, such as animation, an applet must create its own thread, over which it does have complete control.

The task of writing an applet, then, comes down to defining the appropriate methods. A number of these methods are defined by the Applet class:

init()
> Called when the applet is first loaded into the browser or viewer. It is typically used to perform applet initialization, in preference to a constructor method. (The Web browser doesn't pass any arguments to an applet's constructor method, so defining one isn't too useful.)

destroy()
> Called when the applet is about to be unloaded from the browser or viewer. It should free any resources, other than memory, that the applet has allocated.

start()
> Called when the applet becomes visible and should start doing whatever it is that it does. Often used with animation and with threads.

stop()
> Called when the applet becomes temporarily invisible, for example, when the user has scrolled it off the screen. Tells the applet to stop performing an animation or other task.

getAppletInfo()
> Called to get information about the applet. Should return a string suitable for display in a dialog box.

getParameterInfo()
> Called to obtain information about the parameters the applet responds to. Should return strings describing those parameters.

In addition to these Applet methods, there are a number of other methods, inherited from superclasses of Applet, that the browser invokes at appropriate times, and that an applet should override. The most obvious of these methods is paint(), which the browser or viewer invokes to ask the applet to draw itself on the screen. In Java 1.1, a related method is print(), which an applet should override if it wants to display itself on paper differently than it does on the screen. There are quite a few other methods that applets should override to respond to events. For example, if an applet wants to respond to mouse clicks, it should override mouseDown(). (As we'll see in Chapter 5, however, there are other, preferred, ways to receive mouse events in Java 1.1.)

The `Applet` class also defines some methods that are commonly used by applets:

getImage()
> Loads an image file from the network and returns a `java.awt.Image` object.

getAudioClip()
> Loads a sound clip from the network and returns a `java.applet.AudioClip` object.

getParameter()
> Looks up and returns the value of a named parameter, specified in the HTML file that refers to the applet with the `<PARAM>` tag.

getCodeBase()
> Returns the base URL from which the applet class file was loaded.

getDocumentBase()
> Returns the base URL of the HTML file that refers to the applet.

showStatus()
> Displays a message in the status line of the browser or applet viewer.

getAppletContext()
> Returns the `java.applet.AppletContext` object for the applet. `AppletContext` defines the useful `showDocument()` method that asks the browser to load and display a new Web page.

A First Applet

Figure 3-1 shows what is probably the simplest possible applet you can write in Java. Example 3-1 lists its code. This example introduces the `paint()` method, which is invoked by the applet viewer (or Web browser) when the applet needs to be drawn. This method should perform graphical output—such as drawing text or lines or displaying images—for your applet. The argument to `paint()` is a `java.awt.Graphics` object that you use to do the drawing.

Example 3–1: FirstApplet.java

```
import java.applet.*;   // Don't forget this import statement!
import java.awt.*;      // Or this one for the graphics!

/** This applet just says "Hello World!" */
public class FirstApplet extends Applet {
  // This method displays the applet.
  // The Graphics class is how you do all drawing in Java.
  public void paint(Graphics g) {
    g.drawString("Hello World", 25, 50);
  }
}
```

To display an applet, you need an HTML file that references it. Here is an HTML fragment that can be used with our first applet:

```
<APPLET code="FirstApplet.class" width=150 height=100>
</APPLET>
```

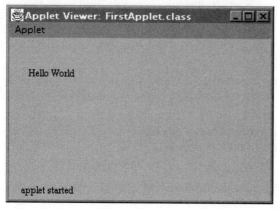

Figure 3-1: A simple applet

With an HTML file that references the applet, you can now view the applet with an applet viewer or Web browser. Note that the WIDTH and HEIGHT attributes of this HTML tag are required. For most applet examples in this book, we show only the Java code and not the corresponding HTML file that goes with it. Typically, that HTML file contains a tag as simple as the one shown here.

Drawing Graphics

Example 3-2 shows a fancier version of our simple applet. As you can see from Figure 3-2, we've made the graphical display more interesting. This applet also does all of its drawing in the paint() method. It demonstrates the use of java.awt.Font and java.awt.Color objects.

This example also introduces the init() method, which is typically used in place of a constructor to perform any initialization that is necessary when the applet is first created. The paint() method may be invoked many times in the life of an applet, so this example uses init() to create the Font object that paint() uses.

Example 3-2: SecondApplet.java

```
import java.applet.*;
import java.awt.*;

/**
 * This applet spices up "Hello World" with graphics, colors, and a font.
 **/
public class SecondApplet extends Applet {
  static final String message = "Hello World";
  private Font font;

  // One-time initialization for the applet
  // Note: no constructor defined.
  public void init() {
    font = new Font("sansserif", Font.BOLD, 48);
  }
```

Example 3-2: SecondApplet.java (continued)

```
// Draw the applet whenever necessary.  Do some fancy graphics.
public void paint(Graphics g) {
  // The pink oval
  g.setColor(Color.pink);
  g.fillOval(10, 10, 330, 100);

  // The red outline. Java doesn't support wide lines, so we
  // try to simulate a 4-pixel wide line by drawing four ovals.
  g.setColor(Color.red);
  g.drawOval(10,10, 330, 100);
  g.drawOval(9, 9, 332, 102);
  g.drawOval(8, 8, 334, 104);
  g.drawOval(7, 7, 336, 106);

  // The text
  g.setColor(Color.black);
  g.setFont(font);
  g.drawString(message, 40, 75);
}
}
```

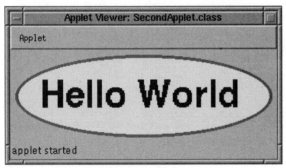

Figure 3-2: A fancier applet

Handling Events

The previous two applets have only displayed output. If an applet is to be interactive in any way, it has to receive and respond to user input. Example 3-3 shows a simple applet that lets the user do a freehand sketch (or scribble) with the mouse. Figure 3-3 shows such a scribble.

The mouseDown() and mouseDrag() methods are called by the system when the user presses a mouse button and moves the mouse with the button down, respectively. This very simple applet draws lines directly in response to these events. It does not have a paint() method, which means that the user's scribble is lost any time that the applet is redrawn (for example, if the user scrolls down a page and then scrolls back up again).

Note that both mouseDown() and mouseDrag() return true. This is to tell the system that they've handled the Event object that was passed to them, and that the event should not be processed any further.

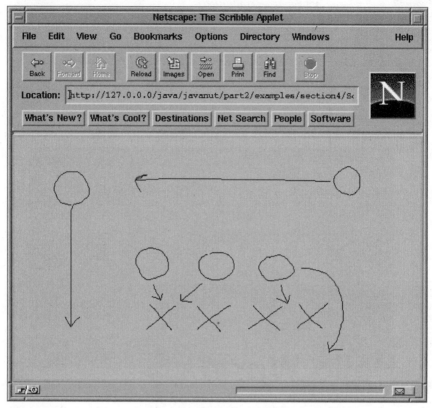

Figure 3-3: Scribbling with the scribble applet

The `mouseDown()` and `mouseDrag()` methods shown here work in both Java 1.0 and Java 1.1, but they (and related methods) have been deprecated in Java 1.1 and replaced with a new, more flexible, event handling model. Event processing is often the central task of applets and of GUI-based applications, and is a big topic in its own right. Chapter 5 explains and demonstrates the Java 1.1 and 1.0 event processing models in more detail.

Example 3-3: Scribble.java

```java
import java.applet.*;
import java.awt.*;

/**
 * This applet lets the user scribble with the mouse.  It demonstrates
 * the Java 1.0 event model.
 **/
public class Scribble extends Applet {
    private int last_x = 0, last_y = 0;  // Fields to store a point in.

    // Called when the user clicks.
    public boolean mouseDown(Event e, int x, int y) {
        last_x = x; last_y = y;              // Remember the location of the click.
```

Example 3-3: Scribble.java (continued)

```
    return true;
  }

  // Called when the mouse moves with the button down
  public boolean mouseDrag(Event e, int x, int y)  {
    Graphics g = getGraphics();         // Get a Graphics to draw with.
    g.drawLine(last_x, last_y, x, y);   // Draw a line from last point to this.
    last_x = x; last_y = y;             // And update the saved location.
    return true;
  }
}
```

Reading Applet Parameters

Example 3-4 shows an extension to our Scribble applet. The ColorScribble class is a subclass of Scribble that adds the ability to scribble in a configurable foreground color over a configurable background color. (The ColorScribble applet looks a lot like the Scribble applet of Figure 3-3 and is not pictured here.)

ColorScribble has an init() method that reads the value of two "applet parameters" that can be optionally specified with the <PARAM> tag in the applet's HTML file. The String values returned by getParameters() are converted to colors and specified as the default foreground and background colors for the applet. Note that the init() method invokes its superclass' init() method, just in case a future version of Scribble defines that method to perform initialization.

This example also introduces the getAppletInfo() and getParameterInfo() methods. These methods provide textual information about the applet (its author, its version, its copyright, etc.) and the parameters that it can accept (the parameter names, their types, and their meanings). An applet should generally define these methods, although the current generation of Web browsers do not actually ever make use of them. (The *appletviewer* application in the JDK does call these methods, however.)

Example 3-4: ColorScribble.java

```
import java.applet.*;
import java.awt.*;

/**
 * A version of the Scribble applet that reads two applet parameters
 * to set the foreground and background colors.  It also returns
 * information about itself when queried.
 **/
public class ColorScribble extends Scribble {
  // Read in two color parameters and set the colors.
  public void init() {
    super.init();
    Color foreground = getColorParameter("foreground");
    Color background = getColorParameter("background");
    if (foreground != null) this.setForeground(foreground);
    if (background != null) this.setBackground(background);
  }
```

Example 3–4: ColorScribble.java (continued)

```
// Read the specified parameter.  Interpret it as a hexadecimal
// number of the form RRGGBB and convert it to a color.
protected Color getColorParameter(String name) {
  String value = this.getParameter(name);
  try { return new Color(Integer.parseInt(value, 16)); }
  catch (Exception e) { return null; }
}


// Return information suitable for display in an About dialog box.
public String getAppletInfo() {
  return "ColorScribble v. 0.02.  Written by David Flanagan.";
}


// Return info about the supported parameters.  Web browsers and applet
// viewers should display this information, and may also allow users to
// set the parameter values.
public String[][] getParameterInfo() { return info; }


// Here's the information that getParameterInfo() returns.
// It is an array of arrays of strings describing each parameter.
// Format: parameter name, parameter type, parameter description
private String[][] info = {
  {"foreground", "hexadecimal color value", "foreground color"},
  {"background", "hexadecimal color value", "background color"}
};
}
```

The following HTML fragment references the applet, and demonstrates how parameter values can be set with the <PARAM> tag:

```
<APPLET code="ColorScribble.class" width=300 height=300>
<PARAM name="foreground" value="0000FF">
<PARAM name="background" value="FFCCCC">
</APPLET>
```

Images and Sounds

Example 3-5 shows a Java applet that implements a simple client-side imagemap that has the ability to highlight the "hot spots" in the image and play a sound clip when the user clicks on the image. Figure 3-4 shows what this applet might look like, when configured with an appropriate image.

This applet demonstrates quite a few important applet techniques:

- getParameter() looks up the name of the image to display and the audio clip to play when the user clicks, and it also reads a list of rectangles and URLs that define the hot spots and hyperlinks of the imagemap.

- The getImage() and getDocumentBase() methods load the image (an Image object) in the init() method, and Graphics.drawImage() displays the image in the paint() method.

- getAudioClip() loads a sound file (an AudioClip object) in the init() method, and AudioClip.play() plays the sound in the mousePressed() method.

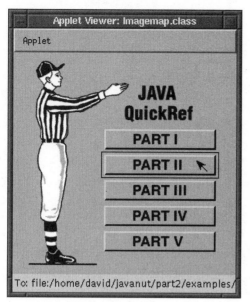

Figure 3-4: An imagemap applet

- Events are handled by an "event listener" object that is defined by an inner class. This is an example of the Java 1.1 event handling model (see Chapter 5). Therefore, this applet only runs in Web browsers that support Java 1.1.

- The showStatus() method displays the destination URL when the user presses the mouse button over a hot spot, while the AppletContext.showDocument() method makes the browser display that URL when the user releases the mouse button.

- The applet uses the "XOR mode" of the Graphics class to highlight an area of the image in a way that can be easily "un-highlighted" by redrawing.

- The individual hot spots are represented by instances of ImagemapRectangle, a nested top-level class. The java.util.Vector class stores the list of hot spot objects, and java.util.StringTokenizer parses the descriptions of those hot spots.

The following HTML fragment shows an example of the properties read by this applet:

```
<APPLET code="Soundmap.class" width=288 height=288>
<PARAM name="image" value="image.gif">
<PARAM name="sound" value="sound.au">
<PARAM name="rect0" value="114,95,151,33,#part1">
<PARAM name="rect1" value="114,128,151,33,#part2">
<PARAM name="rect2" value="114,161,151,33,#part3">
<PARAM name="rect3" value="114,194,151,33,#part4">
<PARAM name="rect4" value="114,227,151,33,#part5">
</APPLET>
```

Example 3-5: Soundmap.java

```java
import java.applet.*;
import java.awt.*;
import java.awt.event.*;
import java.net.*;
import java.util.*;

/**
 * A Java applet that simulates a client-side imagemap.
 * Plays a sound whenever the user clicks on one of the hyperlinks.
 */
public class Soundmap extends Applet {
  protected Image image;        // The image to display.
  protected Vector rects;       // A list of rectangles in it.
  protected AudioClip sound;    // A sound to play on user clicks in a rectangle.

  /** Initialize the applet */
  public void init() {
    // Look up the name of the image, relative to a base URL, and load it.
    // Note the use of three Applet methods in this one line.
    image = this.getImage(this.getDocumentBase(), this.getParameter("image"));

    // Lookup and parse a list of rectangular areas and the URLs they map to.
    // The convenience routine getRectangleParameter() is defined below.
    rects = new Vector();
    ImagemapRectangle r;
    for(int i = 0; (r = getRectangleParameter("rect" + i)) != null; i++)
      rects.addElement(r);

    // Look up a sound to play when the user clicks one of those areas.
    sound = this.getAudioClip(this.getDocumentBase(),
                              this.getParameter("sound"));

    // Specify an "event listener" object to respond to mouse button
    // presses and releases.  Note that this is the Java 1.1 event model.
    // Note that it also uses a Java 1.1 inner class, defined below.
    this.addMouseListener(new Listener());
  }

  /** Called when the applet is being unloaded from the system.
   * We use it here to "flush" the image we no longer need. This may
   * result in memory and other resources being freed more quickly. */
  public void destroy() { image.flush(); }

  /** To display the applet, we simply draw the image. */
  public void paint(Graphics g) { g.drawImage(image, 0, 0, this); }

  /** We override this method so that it doesn't clear the background
   * before calling paint().  No clear is necessary, since paint() overwrites
   * everything with an image.  Causes less flickering this way. */
  public void update(Graphics g) { paint(g); }

  /** Parse a comma-separated list of rectangle coordinates and a URL.
   * Used to read the imagemap rectangle definitions from applet parameters */
  protected ImagemapRectangle getRectangleParameter(String name) {
    int x, y, w, h;
    URL url;
    String value = this.getParameter(name);
    if (value == null) return null;
```

Example 3–5: Soundmap.java (continued)

```
  try {
    StringTokenizer st = new StringTokenizer(value, ",");
    x = Integer.parseInt(st.nextToken());
    y = Integer.parseInt(st.nextToken());
    w = Integer.parseInt(st.nextToken());
    h = Integer.parseInt(st.nextToken());
    url = new URL(this.getDocumentBase(), st.nextToken());
  }
  catch (NoSuchElementException e) { return null; }
  catch (NumberFormatException e) { return null; }
  catch (MalformedURLException e) { return null; }

  return new ImagemapRectangle(x, y, w, h, url);
}
/**
 * An instance of this inner class is used to respond to mouse events
 */
class Listener extends MouseAdapter {
  /** The rectangle that the mouse was pressed in. */
  private ImagemapRectangle lastrect;

  /** Called when a mouse button is pressed. */
  public void mousePressed(MouseEvent e) {
    // On button down, check if we're inside one of the specified rectangles.
    // If so, highlight the rectangle, display a message, and play a sound.
    // The utility routine findrect() is defined below.
    ImagemapRectangle r = findrect(e);
    if (r == null) return;
    Graphics g = Applet.this.getGraphics();
    g.setXORMode(Color.red);
    g.drawRect(r.x, r.y, r.width, r.height);    // highlight rectangle
    Applet.this.showStatus("To: " + r.url);     // display URL
    sound.play();                               // play the sound
    lastrect = r;     // Remember the rectangle so it can be un-highlighted.
  }

  /** Called when a mouse button is released. */
  public void mouseReleased(MouseEvent e) {
    // When the button is released, unhighlight the rectangle.  If the
    // mouse is still inside it, ask the browser to go to the URL.
    if (lastrect != null) {
      Graphics g = Applet.this.getGraphics();
      g.setXORMode(Color.red);
      g.drawRect(lastrect.x, lastrect.y, lastrect.width, lastrect.height);
      Applet.this.showStatus("");    // Clear the message.
      ImagemapRectangle r = findrect(e);
      if ((r != null) && (r == lastrect))  // If still in the same rectangle
        Applet.this.getAppletContext().showDocument(r.url); // Go to the URL
      lastrect = null;
    }
  }

  /** Find the rectangle we're inside. */
  protected ImagemapRectangle findrect(MouseEvent e) {
    int i, x = e.getX(), y = e.getY();
    for(i = 0; i < rects.size(); i++)  {
      ImagemapRectangle r = (ImagemapRectangle) rects.elementAt(i);
      if (r.contains(x, y)) return r;
```

Example 3-5: Soundmap.java (continued)

```
        }
        return null;
    }
}

/**
 * A helper class.  Just like java.awt.Rectangle, but with a URL field.
 * Note the use of a nested toplevel class for neatness.
 */

static class ImagemapRectangle extends Rectangle {
    URL url;
    public ImagemapRectangle(int x, int y, int w, int h, URL url) {
        super(x, y, w, h);
        this.url = url;
    }
}
}
```

JAR Files

The Soundmap applet defined in the previous section requires five files to operate: the class file for the applet itself, the class files for the two nested classes it contains, the image file, and the sound clip file. It can be loaded using an <APPLET> tag like this:

```
<APPLET code="Soundmap.class" width=288 height=288>
    ...
</APPLET>
```

When the applet is loaded in this manner, however, each of the five files is transferred in uncompressed form using a separate HTML request. As you might imagine, this is quite inefficient.

In Java 1.1, you can instead combine the five files into a single JAR (Java ARchive) file. This single, compressed file (it is a ZIP file) can be transferred from Web server to browser much more efficiently. To create a JAR file, use the *jar* tool, which has a syntax reminiscent of the UNIX *tar* command:

```
% jar cf soundmap.jar *.class image.gif sound.au
```

This command creates a new file, *soundmap.jar*, that contains all of the *.class* files in the current directory, as well as the files *image.gif* and *sound.au*.

To use a JAR file, you specify it as the value of the ARCHIVE attribute of the <APPLET> tag:

```
<APPLET archive="soundmap.jar" code="Soundmap.class" width=288 height=288>
    ...
</APPLET>
```

Note that the ARCHIVE attribute does not replace the CODE attribute. ARCHIVE specifies where to look for files, but CODE is still required to tell the browser which of the files in the archive is the applet class file to be executed. The ARCHIVE attribute may actually specify a comma-separated list of JAR files. The Web browser or applet viewer searches these archives for any files the applet requires. If a file is not found in an archive, however, the browser falls back upon its old behavior and attempts to load the file from the Web server using a new HTTP request.

Signed Applets

In Java 1.1, it is possible to circumvent the security restrictions placed on an applet by attaching a digital signature to a JAR file. When a Web browser or applet viewer loads a JAR file that has been signed by a trusted entity (the user specifies whom she trusts), the browser may grant the applet contained in the JAR file special privileges, such as the ability to read and write local files, that are not available to untrusted applets.

Signing an applet with the *javakey* tool provided by the JDK is a somewhat cumbersome task. First, of course, you must have a security database set up. The database must contain the certificate and the public and private keys that you want to use to sign the applet. Once you have a properly configured security database, you must create a simple "directive file" that gives *javakey* the information it needs to sign your JAR file. A directive file might look like this:

```
# The entity doing the signing
signer=david
# The certificate number to use
cert=1
# Currently unused
chain=0
# The base name of the signature files to be added to the JAR manifest
signature.file=DAVIDSIG
```

Having created a directive file named *mysig*, for example, you could then sign a JAR file like this:

```
% javakey -gs mysig soundmap.jar
```

This command creates a new JAR file named *soundmap.jar.sig* that you can use in an HTML archive attribute just as you would use an unsigned JAR file.

The *javakey* tool is used for all aspects of administering the Java system security database. One of the other things you can do with it is to declare which entities are trusted. You do this with the -t option.

For example, you might declare your trust for the author as follows:

```
% javakey -t DavidFlanagan true
```

Or you could revoke your trust like this:

```
% javakey -t DavidFlanagan false
```

The *appletviewer* program makes use of any trust values declared in this way. Note that *javakey* and *appletviewer* support only untrusted entities and fully-trusted entities, without any gradations in between. We may see additional levels of trust in the future.

Bear in mind that the *javakey* techniques described here apply only to the JDK. Other vendors may provide other mechanisms for signing applets, and Web browsers may provide other ways of declaring trusted entities.

Exercises

3-1. Look up the java.awt.Graphics class in a Java reference manual. Modify the SecondApplet applet to try out various drawing methods of Graphics. Be creative!

3-2. Modify the Scribble applet so that it draws the word "Erase" in the upper-left hand corner of the window. Then, modify the applet so that if the user clicks the mouse anywhere approximatly over the word "Erase", it erases any scribbles in the applet.

3-3. Write an applet that reads applet parameters named "line1", "line2", "line3", and so on until it finds a parameter that does not exist. The value for each parameter should contain four integers separated by spaces. Parse these integers, interpret them as (x1, y1), (x2, y2) coordinates, and draw a line between those coordinates. Consider the possibility of writing a general-purpose drawing-displayer applet that displays lines, rectangles, and ellipses specified with applet parameters.

CHAPTER 4

Graphics

This chapter demonstrates many of the techniques used to display graphics in Java programs. It shows you how to:

- Draw lines, rectangles, ovals, and other graphical primitives using the Graphics object.

- Display text and work with fonts.

- Work with colors.

- Display and manipulate images.

- Create animations.

- Provide flicker-free animations using double-buffering and clipping.

- Print applets and generate custom hardcopy output.

Drawing with the Graphics Object

The java.awt.Graphics class encapsulates most of the graphics functionality of the Java API. An instance of this class represents a "graphics context" in which you perform graphical operations. The context it defines includes the color in which drawing is done, the font with which text is displayed, the drawing origin relative to which all drawing coordinates are interpreted, and a clipping region outside of which no drawing is done.

A Graphics object has methods to query and set its state values, and, more importantly, it also has methods to draw lines, draw rectangles, fill rectangles, and perform a number of other primitive graphical operations. Example 4-1 defines a GraphicsSampler applet that shows how you can use these methods; Figure 4-1 shows what the resulting graphics primitives look like. The paint() method of the applet is where most of the action takes place, of course. Other points of interest in this example are the tile() method that shows how you can tile an image across the background of an applet, and the `centerText()` method that shows how you can use the `java.awt.FontMetrics` class to measure the size of lines of text and display those lines centered within a specified rectangle.

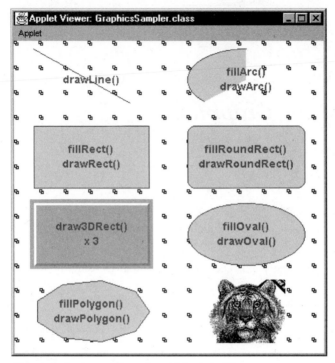

Figure 4-1: A sampling of graphics primitives

Example 4-1: GraphicsSampler.java

```
import java.applet.*;
import java.awt.*;

/**
 * An applet that demonstrates most of the graphics primitives in java.awt.Graphics.
 **/
public class GraphicsSampler extends Applet
{
  Image image;
  Image background;

  // Initialize the applet
  public void init()
  {
    this.setBackground(Color.lightGray);
    image = this.getImage(this.getDocumentBase(), "tiger.gif");
    background = this.getImage(this.getDocumentBase(), "background.gif");
  }

  // Draw the applet whenever necessary
  public void paint(Graphics g)
  {
```

Example 4-1: GraphicsSampler.java (continued)

```
Color fill = new Color(200, 200, 200);
Color outline = Color.blue;
Color textcolor = Color.red;
Font font = new Font("sansserif", Font.BOLD, 14);
g.setFont(font);

// get a background image and tile it
tile(g, this, background);

// Draw a line
g.setColor(outline);
g.drawLine(25, 10, 150, 80);
centerText("drawLine()", null, g, textcolor, 25, 10, 150, 80);

// Draw an arc
g.setColor(fill);
g.fillArc(225, 10, 150, 80, 90, 135);
g.setColor(outline);
g.drawArc(225, 10, 150, 80, 90, 135);
centerText("fillArc()", "drawArc()", g, textcolor, 225, 10, 150, 80);

// Draw a rectangle
g.setColor(fill);
g.fillRect(25, 110, 150, 80);
g.setColor(outline);
g.drawRect(25, 110, 150, 80);
centerText("fillRect()", "drawRect()", g, textcolor, 25, 110, 150, 80);

// Draw a rounded rectangle
g.setColor(fill);
g.fillRoundRect(225, 110, 150, 80, 20, 20);
g.setColor(outline);
g.drawRoundRect(225, 110, 150, 80, 20, 20);
centerText("fillRoundRect()", "drawRoundRect()", g, textcolor,
           225, 110, 150, 80);

// Draw a 3D rectangle (clear an area for it first)
g.setColor(fill);
g.clearRect(20, 205, 160, 90);
g.draw3DRect(25, 210, 150, 80, true);
g.draw3DRect(26, 211, 148, 78, true);
g.draw3DRect(27, 212, 146, 76, true);
centerText("draw3DRect()", "x 3", g, textcolor, 25, 210, 150, 80);

// Draw an oval
g.setColor(fill);
g.fillOval(225, 210, 150, 80);
g.setColor(outline);
g.drawOval(225, 210, 150, 80);
centerText("fillOval()", "drawOval()", g, textcolor, 225, 210, 150, 80);

// Draw a polygon
int numpoints = 9;
int[] xpoints = new int[numpoints+1];
int[] ypoints = new int[numpoints+1];
for(int i=0; i < numpoints; i++) {
  double angle = 2*Math.PI * i / numpoints;
  xpoints[i] = (int)(100 + 75*Math.cos(angle));
```

Graphics

Example 4–1: GraphicsSampler.java (continued)

```
      ypoints[i] = (int)(350 - 40*Math.sin(angle));
    }
    g.setColor(fill);
    g.fillPolygon(xpoints, ypoints, numpoints);
    g.setColor(outline);
    xpoints[numpoints] = xpoints[0];  ypoints[numpoints] = ypoints[0];
    g.drawPolygon(xpoints, ypoints, numpoints+1);
    centerText("fillPolygon()", "drawPolygon()", g, textcolor,
               25, 310, 150, 80);

    // Center and draw an image
    int w = image.getWidth(this);
    int h = image.getHeight(this);
    g.drawImage(image, 225 + (150-w)/2, 310 + (80-h)/2, this);
    centerText("drawImage()", null, g, textcolor,  225, 310, 150, 80);
  }

  // Utility method to tile an image on the background
  protected void tile(Graphics g, Component c, Image i)
  {
    Rectangle r = c.getBounds();  // use c.bounds() in Java 1.0.x
    int iw = i.getWidth(c);
    int ih = i.getHeight(c);
    if ((iw <= 0) || (ih <= 0)) return;
    for(int x=0; x < r.width; x += iw)
      for(int y=0; y < r.height; y += ih)
        g.drawImage(i, x, y, c);
  }

  // Utility method to center text in a rectangle
  protected void centerText(String s1, String s2, Graphics g, Color c,
                            int x, int y, int w, int h)
  {
    Font f = g.getFont();
    FontMetrics fm = Toolkit.getDefaultToolkit().getFontMetrics(f);
    int ascent = fm.getAscent();
    int height = fm.getHeight();
    int width1=0, width2 = 0, x0=0, x1=0, y0=0, y1=0;
    width1 = fm.stringWidth(s1);
    if (s2 != null) width2 = fm.stringWidth(s2);
    x0 = x + (w - width1)/2;
    x1 = x + (w - width2)/2;
    if (s2 == null)
      y0 = y + (h - height)/2 + ascent;
    else {
      y0 = y + (h - (int)(height * 2.2))/2 + ascent;
      y1 = y0 + (int)(height * 1.2);
    }
    g.setColor(c);
    g.drawString(s1, x0, y0);
    if (s2 != null) g.drawString(s2, x1, y1);
  }
}
```

Fonts

Fonts are represented in Java with the `java.awt.Font` class. You create a `Font` object by specifying a font family name, a font style, and a point size. In order to use a `Font`, you pass it to the `setFont()` method of the `Graphics` object before calling `drawString()` or one of the other text-drawing methods of `Graphics`.

To promote platform independence, Java defines only a small number of font family names and a similarly small number of styles. Example 4-2 is a simple applet that shows each of the standard fonts in each of the available styles. Its output is shown in Figure 4-2.

Figure 4-2: The standard fonts and styles

Example 4-2: FontList.java

```
import java.applet.*;
import java.awt.*;

/**
 * An applet that displays the standard fonts and styles.
 **/
public class FontList extends Applet
{
  // The available font families
  String[] families = {"Serif",        // "TimesRoman" in Java 1.0
                       "SansSerif",     // "Helvetica" in Java 1.0
```

Example 4-2: FontList.java (continued)

```
                        "Monospaced",    // "Courier" in Java 1.0
                        "Dialog",        // unchanged
                        "DialogInput" }; // unchanged

  // The available font styles
  int[] styles = {Font.PLAIN, Font.ITALIC, Font.BOLD, Font.ITALIC+Font.BOLD};
  String[] stylenames = {"Plain", "Italic", "Bold", "Bold Italic"};

  public void paint(Graphics g) {
    for(int family=0; family < families.length; family++) { // for each family
      for(int style = 0; style < styles.length; style++) {    // for each style
        Font f = new Font(families[family], styles[style], 16); // create font
        String s = families[family] + " " + stylenames[style];  // create name
        g.setFont(f);                                          // set font
        g.drawString(s, 10, (family*4 + style + 1) * 20);       // display name
      }
    }
  }
}
```

Colors

A color in Java is represented by the java.awt.Color class. The Color class defines a number of constants that refer to pre-defined Color objects for commonly used colors, such as Color.black and Color.white. You can also create your own custom Color objects by specifying the red, green, and blue components of the color. Both of these methods of obtaining Color objects were demonstrated in Example 4-1. Additionally, the static getHSBColor() method allows you to create a Color object based on hue, saturation, and brightness values.

Java 1.1 also defines a java.awt.SystemColor subclass of Color. This class defines a number of constant SystemColor objects that represent standard colors in the system desktop palette. If you do any custom drawing in your Java application or applet, you can use these colors to have your application match the desktop color scheme.

Example 4-3 presents an applet that displays each of the predefined SystemColor colors. It demonstrates the use of the SystemColor class, and also shows you how to use the getRed(), getGreen(), and getBlue() methods of the Color class to manipulate the individual color components of a Color. Figure 4-3 shows the output of this applet.

Example 4-3: SystemColorList.java

```
import java.applet.*;
import java.awt.*;

/**
 * An applet that displays all of the predefined system colors.
 **/
public class SystemColorList extends Applet {
  String[] color_names = {
    "desktop", "activeCaption", "activeCaptionText", "activeCaptionBorder",
    "inactiveCaption", "inactiveCaptionText", "inactiveCaptionBorder",
```

Example 4–3: SystemColorList.java (continued)

```
    "window", "windowBorder", "windowText", "menu", "menuText", "text",
    "textText", "textHighlight", "textHighlightText", "textInactiveText",
    "control", "controlText", "controlHighlight", "controlLtHighlight",
    "controlShadow", "controlDkShadow", "scrollbar", "info", "infoText"
  };
  SystemColor[] colors = {
    SystemColor.desktop, SystemColor.activeCaption,
    SystemColor.activeCaptionText, SystemColor.activeCaptionBorder,
    SystemColor.inactiveCaption, SystemColor.inactiveCaptionText,
    SystemColor.inactiveCaptionBorder, SystemColor.window,
    SystemColor.windowBorder, SystemColor.windowText,
    SystemColor.menu, SystemColor.menuText, SystemColor.text,
    SystemColor.textText, SystemColor.textHighlight,
    SystemColor.textHighlightText, SystemColor.textInactiveText,
    SystemColor.control, SystemColor.controlText, SystemColor.controlHighlight,
    SystemColor.controlLtHighlight, SystemColor.controlShadow,
    SystemColor.controlDkShadow, SystemColor.scrollbar, SystemColor.info,
    SystemColor.infoText
  };

  public void init() {
    // Use a bunch of Label objects arranged in a grid to display the colors.
    this.setLayout(new GridLayout(0, 3, 5, 5));
    for(int i = 0; i < colors.length; i++) {
      // Create a label object to display a system color and its name
      Label l = new Label(color_names[i], Label.CENTER);
      this.add(l);
      // compute a foreground color to contrast with the background
      Color bg  = colors[i], fg;
      int r = bg.getRed(), g = bg.getGreen(), b = bg.getBlue();
      int avg = (r + g + b) / 3;
      if (avg > 128) fg = Color.black;
      else fg = Color.white;
      // And assign the colors.
      l.setBackground(bg);
      l.setForeground(fg);
    }
  }
}
```

Graphics

Cursors

Java defines 14 different platform-independent mouse cursors. In Java 1.0, these cursors were represented by constants in the java.awt.Frame class, and could only be specified for an entire Frame. In Java 1.1, cursors are represented by the java.awt.Cursor class and can be specified on individual components. Note that the Cursor class does not allow custom cursors to be defined: only the 14 standard cursors may be used.

Example 4-4 is a simple applet that displays 14 buttons, each one using a different cursor. The applet is not pictured here, but Figure 4-4 shows what the cursors look like on a UNIX system running the X Window System. In addition, Table 4-1 lists the names of the cursors and describes their typical uses.

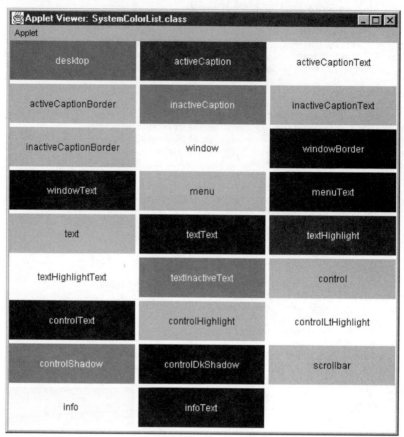

Figure 4-3: The standard system colors

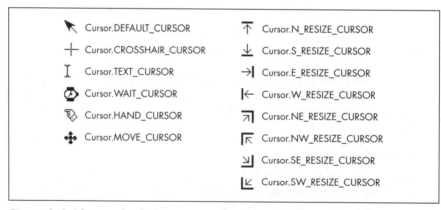

Figure 4-4: The standard Java cursors, on a UNIX platform

Table 4-1: Standard Java Cursors

Cursor Constant	Description
Cursor.CROSSHAIR_CURSOR	A simple crosshair
Cursor.DEFAULT_CURSOR	The platform-dependent default cursor; usually an arrow
Cursor.E_RESIZE_CURSOR	A right-pointing arrow; used to indicate that the right edge of something is to be dragged
Cursor.HAND_CURSOR	A hand; used to indicate that a selection is to be made
Cursor.MOVE_CURSOR	A four-directional arrow; used to indicate that something is to be moved
Cursor.NE_RESIZE_CURSOR	An upper-right-pointing arrow; used to indicate that the upper-right corner of something is to be dragged
Cursor.NW_RESIZE_CURSOR	An upper-left-pointing arrow; used to indicate that the upper-left corner of something is to be dragged
Cursor.N_RESIZE_CURSOR	An upward-pointing arrow; used to indicate that the top edge of something is to be dragged
Cursor.SE_RESIZE_CURSOR	A lower-right-pointing arrow; used to indicate that the lower-right corner of something is to be dragged
Cursor.SW_RESIZE_CURSOR	A lower-left-pointing arrow; used to indicate that the lower-left corner of something is to be dragged
Cursor.S_RESIZE_CURSOR	A downward-pointing arrow; used to indicate that the bottom edge of something is to be dragged
Cursor.TEXT_CURSOR	Often an I-bar; used to indicate editable text
Cursor.WAIT_CURSOR	Often a wristwatch or an hourglass; used to indicate that the program is busy and that the user should wait
Cursor.W_RESIZE_CURSOR	A left-pointing arrow; used to indicate that the left edge of something is to be dragged

Example 4-4: Cursors.java

```
import java.applet.*;
import java.awt.*;

/**
 * An applet that uses each of the predefined cursor types in a bunch
 * of buttons.
 **/
public class Cursors extends Applet {
    int[] cursor_types = {      // Constants for the 14 predefined types
        Cursor.DEFAULT_CURSOR, Cursor.CROSSHAIR_CURSOR, Cursor.TEXT_CURSOR,
        Cursor.WAIT_CURSOR, Cursor.HAND_CURSOR, Cursor.MOVE_CURSOR,
        Cursor.N_RESIZE_CURSOR, Cursor.S_RESIZE_CURSOR, Cursor.E_RESIZE_CURSOR,
        Cursor.W_RESIZE_CURSOR, Cursor.NE_RESIZE_CURSOR, Cursor.NW_RESIZE_CURSOR,
        Cursor.SE_RESIZE_CURSOR, Cursor.SW_RESIZE_CURSOR
    };
    String[] cursor_names = { // The cursor names as strings
```

Graphics

Example 4-4: Cursors.java (continued)

```
    "DEFAULT_CURSOR", "CROSSHAIR_CURSOR", "TEXT_CURSOR", "WAIT_CURSOR",
    "HAND_CURSOR", "MOVE_CURSOR", "N_RESIZE_CURSOR", "S_RESIZE_CURSOR",
    "E_RESIZE_CURSOR", "W_RESIZE_CURSOR", "NE_RESIZE_CURSOR",
    "NW_RESIZE_CURSOR", "SE_RESIZE_CURSOR", "SW_RESIZE_CURSOR"
  };

  /** Create a grid of buttons each using a different cursor */
  public void init() {
    this.setLayout(new GridLayout(0, 2, 5, 5));
    for(int i = 0; i < cursor_types.length; i++) {
      Button b = new Button(cursor_names[i]);
      // This is how we obtain a Cursor object and set it on a Component
      b.setCursor(Cursor.getPredefinedCursor(cursor_types[i]));
      this.add(b);
    }
  }
}
```

Simple Animation

All of the applets we've seen so far in this chapter have static displays—they draw exactly the same graphics each time paint() is called. Creating an animation is simply a matter of drawing something different each time paint() is called and making sure that paint() is called frequently enough that the individual "frames" of the animation blur into what appears to be continuous motion.

This sounds simple enough, but there is one catch. In the applet programming model, the applet is not in control of the thread of execution—it must passively respond when the Web browser or applet viewer invokes its methods. In order to display an animation, the applet must be able to repeatedly redraw itself. The only way to accomplish this is by creating a new thread of execution, one that the applet *is* in control of.

Example 4-5 presents an applet that animates a red circle in the applet window, bouncing it off the edges. (The applet is not pictured here because any single frame of the applet is pretty uninteresting.) Notice the following points about the program:

- It consists of two classes and an interface. BouncingCircle is the applet itself. AnimationTimer is a subclass of java.lang.Thread—it creates the extra thread required to perform animation. The Animation interface is used to connect the applet to the timer thread in a modular, reusable way.

- The main feature of the AnimationTimer class, as with all threads, is the run() method. This method constitutes the body of the thread. When you create a Thread object and invoke its start() method, a new thread of execution begins running at the run() method. When the run() method exits, the thread terminates. In this case, the run() method is an infinite loop. It calls the animate() method of the Animation object it is passed (our applet, in this case), and then uses the Thread.sleep() method to pause (for 100 milliseconds) before calling the animate() method all over again.

- In the BouncingCircle class, the paint() method simply draws a red circle at the current position, specified by the x and y fields. The animate() method, from the Animation interface we defined, is the more interesting method. It updates the current position of the circle, implementing a "bounce" algorithm if the circle hits any of the edges of the applet, and then calls repaint(). repaint() tells the system that the applet needs to be redrawn. The browser responds by invoking the paint() method of the applet the next time it has a moment, which is usually right away.

This applet overrides the start() and stop() methods of the Applet class. Recall that these methods are used to tell an applet to start doing whatever it does and to temporarily stop doing whatever it does, respectively. In this case, those methods invoke AnimationTimer methods that suspend and resume the timer thread, causing the animation to pause and resume.

Example 4-5: BouncingCircle.java

```
import java.applet.*;
import java.awt.*;

/** An applet that displays a simple animation */
public class BouncingCircle extends Applet implements Animation {
  int x = 150, y = 50, r=50;    // position and radius of the circle
  int dx = 11, dy = 7;          // trajectory of circle

  /** A timer for animation: call our animate() method ever 100
   *  milliseconds.  Creates a new thread. */
  AnimationTimer timer = new AnimationTimer(this, 100);

  /** Draw the circle at its current position */
  public void paint(Graphics g) {
    g.setColor(Color.red);
    g.fillOval(x-r, y-r, r*2, r*2);
  }

  /** Move and bounce the circle and request a redraw.
   *  The timer calls this method periodically. */
  public void animate() {
    // Bounce if we've hit an edge.
    if ((x - r + dx < 0) || (x + r + dx > bounds().width)) dx = -dx;
    if ((y - r + dy < 0) || (y + r + dy > bounds().height)) dy = -dy;
    // Move the circle.
    x += dx;  y += dy;
    // Ask the browser to call our paint() method to draw the circle
    // at its new position.
    repaint();
  }

  /** Start the timer when the browser starts the applet */
  public void start() { timer.start_animation(); }

  /** Pause the timer when browser pauses the applet */
  public void stop() { timer.pause_animation(); }
}

/** This interface for objects that can be animated by an AnimationTimer */
interface Animation { public void animate(); }
```

Graphics

Example 4–5: BouncingCircle.java (continued)

```
/** The thread class that periodically calls the animate() method */
class AnimationTimer extends Thread {
  Animation animation;  // The animation object we're serving as timer for
  int delay;            // How many milliseconds between "animation frames"

  public AnimationTimer(Animation animation, int delay) {
    this.animation = animation;
    this.delay = delay;
  }

  public void start_animation() {
    if (isAlive()) super.resume();
    else start();
  }
  public void pause_animation() { suspend(); }

  /** Loop forever, calling animate(), and then pausing the specified time. */
  public void run() {
    for(;;) {
      animation.animate();
      try { Thread.sleep(delay); } catch (InterruptedException e) { ; }
    }
  }
}
```

Animation with Double-Buffering

Our next example animates a red circle, just as Example 4-5 does, but this new example demonstrates two important techniques for smooth animation: double-buffering and clipping. It also demonstrates another way to use threads.

Before we describe double-buffering and clipping, you must understand how this example uses threads. Unlike the previous example, this example does not use a separate AnimationTimer thread object. Instead, the applet itself implements the java.lang.Runnable interface, so it contains a run() method. This run() method becomes the body of the new thread that is created.

To use a thread in this way, you use the Thread() constructor to create the thread. You must pass a Runnable object to the Thread() constructor. The constructor returns a Thread object that, when started with the start() method, begins running the run() method of the specified Runnable object as a separate thread of execution. The start() method of the applet calls the Thread() constructor to create a thread, and then it calls the thread's start() method to begin the animation. The stop() method of the applet sets a flag that causes the run() method to exit, terminating the animation.

Note also that the user can start and stop the animation by clicking a mouse button. The Java 1.0 event model is used so that this applet works correctly in either a Java 1.0 or a Java 1.1 Web browser.

With this threading technique explained, we can return to the discussion of producing smooth animations with double-buffering and clipping. Double-buffering is the practice of doing all your drawing into an off-screen "buffer," and then copying the contents of the buffer to the screen all at once. This prevents the flicker that would otherwise result from erasing and redrawing the figure. In Java, our "buffer" is an off-screen `java.awt.Image` object, created with one of the `Component.createImage()` methods. To draw into an off-screen image, we simply use the `Graphics` object obtained with the `Image.getGraphics()` method. Once the drawing is complete in the off-screen image, we copy the off-screen image onto the screen all at once.

The reason this technique works is because the on-screen display is being updated completely for each frame. When we copy the image from the off-screen buffer we are updating both the foreground and the background of the display. Thus, there is no need to clear the on-screen display before drawing the image. It is this repeated clearing of the screen that causes flickering in the first place.

In order to make this all work, however, we must override the `update()` method of our applet. When an applet calls `repaint()` to request that it be redrawn, the `paint()` method is not invoked directly. Instead, the applet's `update()` method is invoked. The default implementation of `update()` clears the screen and then calls `paint()`, which allows the `paint()` method to rely on the fact that it starts off with a blank screen. Because we are using double-buffering in this applet, however, we do not need or want the screen to be cleared. So we override `update()` and have it invoke `paint()` without clearing the screen. You should always remember to override the `update()` method when using double-buffering.

Clipping is another important technique for making animations smooth and speedy. Animation often involves erasing and redrawing only a small region of a larger area. Unfortunately, the `paint()` method must be written to redraw the entire applet, not small regions of it. What we can do, though, is to set a rectangular "clipping region" in the `Graphics` objects we use. Such a clipping region tells the system that it only needs to draw within the specified rectangle and that it can ignore any drawing requests outside of that rectangle. When we know the portion of an applet that needs to be redrawn, we can specify a clipping rectangle that surrounds that area and do a full redraw, knowing that the applet will only be redrawn inside the specified rectangle. This is usually much faster than doing the full redraw without clipping.

While it is possible to explicitly set a clipping region for a `Graphics` object, there is an easier technique, which we use in this example. When you call `repaint()` with no arguments, it requests a complete redraw of the applet. But if you pass the position and size of a rectangle to the four-argument version of `repaint()`, it automatically sets that rectangle as the clipping region in the `Graphics` object that is passed to `update()` (and that `update()` passes to `paint()`). Therefore, by telling `repaint()` the exact region you want redrawn, you can improve the efficiency of the redrawing in your application.

In our example, there are two rectangular regions that need to be redrawn: the old position of the circle and the new position of the circle. We could combine these two rectangles into one slightly larger rectangle that contains them both and pass this larger rectangle to `repaint()`. What we do instead is simply call `repaint()` twice, once for each of the rectangles. `repaint()` does not call `update()` immediately; it merely places a repaint event on the event queue, where it is handled in an asynchronous manner. When multiple repaint requests for the same on-screen area are on the event queue, they are combined into a single request, merging the regions that need to be redrawn. Thus, our two calls to repaint() result in only a single call to update(), and thus to paint().

Note that our use of clipping in this example is not as efficient as it could be. For simplicity, we do not use a clipping region when drawing into the off-screen buffer, only when copying that buffer back to the screen. The drawing would be even faster if we copied the clipping region from the on-screen Graphics object into the off-screen Graphics object.

Now, without any further ado, Example 4-6 shows our fast, flicker-free animation applet.

Example 4-6: SmoothCircle.java

```
import java.applet.*;
import java.awt.*;

/**
 * An applet that displays a simple animation using double-buffering
 * and clipping
 **/
public class SmoothCircle extends Applet implements Runnable {
  int x = 150, y = 100, r=50;      // Position and radius of the circle
  int dx = 8, dy = 5;              // Trajectory of circle
  Dimension size;                  // The size of the applet
  Image buffer;                    // The off-screen image for double-buffering
  Graphics bufferGraphics;         // A Graphics object for the buffer
  Thread animator;                 // Thread that performs the animation
  boolean please_stop;             // A flag asking animation thread to stop

  /** Set up an off-screen Image for double-buffering */
  public void init() {
    size = this.size();
    buffer = this.createImage(size.width, size.height);
    bufferGraphics = buffer.getGraphics();
  }

  /** Draw the circle at its current position, using double-buffering */
  public void paint(Graphics g)`{
    // Draw into the off-screen buffer.
    // Note, we could do even better clipping by setting the clip rectangle
    // of bufferGraphics to be the same as that of g.
    // In Java 1.1:  bufferGraphics.setClip(g.getClip());
    bufferGraphics.setColor(this.getBackground());
    bufferGraphics.fillRect(0, 0, size.width, size.height); // clear the buffer
    bufferGraphics.setColor(Color.red);
    bufferGraphics.fillOval(x-r, y-r, r*2, r*2);            // draw the circle

    // Then copy the off-screen buffer onto the screen
    g.drawImage(buffer, 0, 0, this);
  }

  /** Don't clear the screen; just call paint() immediately
   *    It is important to override this method like this for double-buffering */
  public void update(Graphics g) { paint(g); }

  /** The body of the animation thread */
  public void run() {
```

Example 4-6: SmoothCircle.java (continued)

```
while(!please_stop) {
  // Bounce the circle if we've hit an edge.
  if ((x - r + dx < 0) || (x + r + dx > size.width)) dx = -dx;
  if ((y - r + dy < 0) || (y + r + dy > size.height)) dy = -dy;

  // Move the circle.
  x += dx;  y += dy;

  // Ask the browser to call our paint() method to redraw the circle
  // at its new position.  Tell repaint what portion of the applet needs
  // be redrawn: the rectangle containing the old circle and the
  // the rectangle containing the new circle.  These two redraw requests
  // will be merged into a single call to paint()
  repaint(x-r-dx, y-r-dy, 2*r, 2*r);   // repaint old position of circle
  repaint(x-r, y-r, 2*r, 2*r);         // repaint new position of circle

  // Now pause 1/10th of a second before drawing the circle again.
  try { Thread.sleep(100); } catch (InterruptedException e) { ; }
}
animator = null;
}

/** Start the animation thread */
public void start() {
  if (animator == null) {
    please_stop = false;
    animator = new Thread(this);
    animator.start();
  }
}

/** Stop the animation thread */
public void stop() { please_stop = true; }

/** Allow the user to start and stop the animation by clicking */
public boolean mouseDown(Event e, int x, int y) {
  if (animator != null) please_stop = true;  // if running request a stop
  else start();                               // otherwise start it.
  return true;
}
}
```

Graphics

Animation with Images

A common kind of animation uses images. Each frame of the animation is a separate Image object, so producing the animation is simply a matter of displaying one image after the other. Example 4-7 shows how to implement this kind of animation.

As with all animations, this example uses a thread. It implements the Runnable interface and defines the body of the thread in the run() method, just as we saw in Example 4-6.

An interesting feature of an animation performed with images is that each frame completely overwrites the previous one. In effect, a kind of double-buffering is taking place, and to make this as efficient as possible, we need to prevent each frame from being explicitly erased before the next frame is drawn. For this reason, we override the update() method just as we did in the previous example.

There is only one tricky element to animation with images: images are loaded asynchronously. When you call the getImage() method of the Applet class, an Image object is returned immediately, but the actual image data for that Image may need to be downloaded from the network (or read in from a cache), so it is not available until some time in the future. Obviously, we'd like to have some way to wait until all of the images used by our animation have finished loading. We can do this using the java.awt.MediaTracker class. In Example 4-7, we create our Image objects in the init() method, and register each one with a MediaTracker object. (Notice also the use of getParameter() to look up the number of images and a base name for the images.) Then in the run() method, we use the Media-Tracker.waitForID() method to ensure that all the images are loaded before we begin the animation.

Example 4-7: ImageAnimator.java

```
import java.applet.*;
import java.awt.*;
import java.net.*;
import java.util.*;

/**
 * This applet displays an image animation.  It uses the MediaTracker class
 * to load the images and verify that there are no errors.
 */
public class ImageAnimator extends Applet implements Runnable {
  protected int num_frames;              // Number of frames in animation
  protected Image[] frames;              // The frames themselves
  protected int framenum;                // Current frame number
  protected MediaTracker tracker;        // Tracker class to wait for images
  protected Thread animator_thread = null; // The thread for animation

  /** Read the basename and num_frames parameters.
   *  Then read in the images, using the specified base name.
   *  For example, if basename is images/anim, read images/anim0,
   *  images/anim1, etc.  These are relative to the current document URL.
   */
  public void init() {
    String basename = this.getParameter("basename");
    try { num_frames = Integer.parseInt(this.getParameter("num_frames")); }
    catch (NumberFormatException e) { num_frames = 0; }

    // getImage() creates an Image object from a URL specification,
    // but it doesn't actually load the images; that is done  asynchronously.
    // Store all the images in a MediaTracker so we can block until
    // they have all loaded.  This method must return promptly, so we don't
    // wait for them to load here.
    tracker = new MediaTracker(this);
    frames = new Image[num_frames];
    for(int i = 0; i < num_frames; i++) {
      frames[i] = this.getImage(this.getDocumentBase(), basename+i);
      tracker.addImage(frames[i], i);  // Add image to tracker, assigning an ID
    }
  }
}
```

Example 4-7: ImageAnimator.java (continued)

```
/** Draw the current frame of the animation */
public void paint(Graphics g) { g.drawImage(frames[framenum], 0, 0, this); }

/** Don't clear the screen before calling paint() */
public void update(Graphics g) { paint(g); }

/** Create the animation thread and start it running */
public void start() {
  if (animator_thread == null) {
    animator_thread = new Thread(this);
    animator_thread.start();
  }
}
/** Stop the animation thread */
public void stop() {
  if ((animator_thread != null) && animator_thread.isAlive())
    animator_thread.stop();
  animator_thread = null;
}

/** This is the body of the thread--the method that does the animation. */
public void run() {
  // First, wait until all images have loaded completely.
  for (int i = 0; i < num_frames; i++) {
    this.showStatus("Loading frame: " + i);
    // Block until the specified image is loaded.  The ID argument is the
    // one we passed to addImage().
    try { tracker.waitForID(i); } catch (InterruptedException e) {;}
    // Check for errors loading it.  Display an error message if necessary
    if (tracker.isErrorID(i)) {
      this.showStatus("Error loading frame " + i + "; quitting.");
      return;
    }
  }
  this.showStatus("Loading frames: done.");  // Done loading all frames

  // Now do the animation: increment the framenumber, redraw, pause
  while(true) {
    if (++framenum >= frames.length) framenum = 0;
    repaint();
    try { Thread.sleep(200); } catch (InterruptedException e) { ; }
  }
}
}
```

Graphics

Image Scaling, Cropping, and Flipping

In Java 1.1, the Graphics object supports a new version of the drawImage() method. This new version is passed integers that specify source and destination rectangles. By providing appropriate values for these eight integers, you can display, scale, crop, and flip images, or perform any combination of these operations.

Example 4-8 shows how to use drawImage() to perform these operations; Figure 4-5 shows the output of the applet.

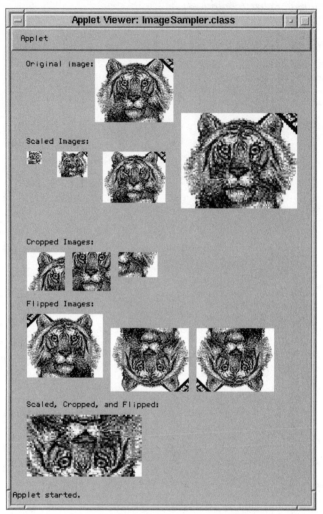

Figure 4–5: Scaled, cropped, and flipped images

Example 4–8: ImageSampler.java

```
import java.applet.*;
import java.awt.*;

/** An applet that demonstrates image scaling, cropping, and flipping */
public class ImageSampler extends Applet {
  Image i;

  /** Load the image */
  public void init() {  i = getImage(this.getDocumentBase(), "tiger.gif"); }

  /** Display the image in a variety of ways */
  public void paint(Graphics g) {
```

Example 4-8: ImageSampler.java (continued)

```
        g.drawString("Original image:", 20, 20);     // Display original image
        g.drawImage(i, 110, 10, this);               // Old version of drawImage()

        g.drawString("Scaled Images:", 20, 120);     // Display scaled images
        g.drawImage(i, 20, 130, 40, 150, 0, 0, 100, 100, this);  // New version
        g.drawImage(i, 60, 130, 100, 170, 0, 0, 100, 100, this);
        g.drawImage(i, 120, 130, 200, 210, 0, 0, 100, 100, this);
        g.drawImage(i, 220, 80, 370, 230, 0, 0, 100, 100, this);

        g.drawString("Cropped Images:", 20, 250);     // Display cropped images
        g.drawImage(i, 20, 260, 70, 310, 0, 0, 50, 50, this);
        g.drawImage(i, 80, 260, 130, 310, 25, 25, 75, 75, this);
        g.drawImage(i, 140, 260, 190, 310, 50, 50, 100, 100, this);

        g.drawString("Flipped Images:", 20, 330);     // Display flipped images
        g.drawImage(i, 20, 340, 120, 440, 100, 0, 0, 100, this);
        g.drawImage(i, 130, 340, 230, 440, 0, 100, 100, 0, this);
        g.drawImage(i, 240, 340, 340, 440, 100, 100, 0, 0, this);

        g.drawString("Scaled, Cropped, and Flipped:", 20, 460);  // Do all three
        g.drawImage(i, 20, 470, 170, 550, 90, 70, 10, 20, this);
    }
}
```

Filtering Images

The classes in the java.awt.image package can be quite confusing. Java uses a stream-based model for its image processing API, involving "image producers," "image consumer," and "image filters." Although you do not often have to work with these abstractions directly, it is sometimes useful to implement an Image-Filter to modify an image on-the-fly.

Example 4-9 shows how you can use an image filter to alter the colors of an image. A common way to specify that a portion of a graphical user interface is currently inactive is to "gray it out." When a GUI displays images, we need a way to create "grayed out" versions of those images. Our example is an applet that demonstrates a simple way to create these grayed-out images. Figure 4-6 shows an image and the grayed-out version created by this applet.

The init() method of this example demonstrates how you can use a source image, a FilteredImageSource object, and an ImageFilter object to produce a new, filtered image. The contents of this new image depends, of course, on the image filter. In this example, we define a GrayFilter as a subclass of RGBImage-Filter. The body of this filter is the filterRGB() method, which takes an RGB color value as input, averages it with gray, and returns the result. This makes all the colors in the image more gray. Note that we are careful in this example not to modify the alpha transparency value stored in the top eight bits of the color value.

Note that the filterRGB() method does not use its x and y arguments. The filtering it performs is position independent, which means that the filter can be used more efficiently on the entries of a colormap instead of on each pixel of the image. To indicate that our GrayFilter is position independent, we set the can-FilterIndexColorModel variable to true in the constructor. On the other hand, if

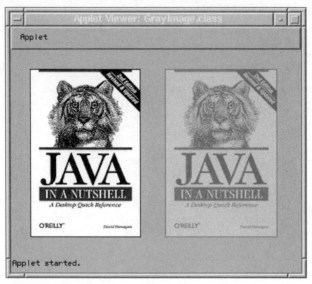

Figure 4-6: Filtered image colors

we were implementing an RGBImageFilter that produced a blurring effect, for example, the filter would be position dependent, and we would have to set can-FilterIndexColorModel to false.

Example 4-9: GrayImage.java

```
import java.applet.*;
import java.awt.*;
import java.awt.image.*;

/** An applet that display an image, and a filtered version of the image */
public class GrayImage extends Applet {
  Image orig, gray;  // the original and grayed-out versions of the image

  /**
   * Load the image.  Create a new image that is a grayer version of it, using
   * a FilteredImageSource, ImageProducer and a the GrayFilter class, below.
   */
  public void init() {
    orig = this.getImage(this.getDocumentBase(), "cover.gif");
    ImageFilter filter = new GrayFilter();
    ImageProducer producer = new FilteredImageSource(orig.getSource(), filter);
    gray = this.createImage(producer);
  }

  /** Display the original image and gray version side-by-side */
  public void paint(Graphics g) {
    g.drawImage(orig, 25, 25, this);
    g.drawImage(gray, 200, 25, this);
  }
}
```

Example 4-9: GrayImage.java (continued)

```
/** Filter an image by computing a weighted average of its colors with gray */
class GrayFilter extends RGBImageFilter {
  public GrayFilter() { canFilterIndexColorModel = true; }
  public int filterRGB(int x, int y, int rgb) {
    int a = rgb & 0xff000000;
    int r = (((rgb & 0xff0000) + 0x1800000)/3) & 0xff0000;
    int g = (((rgb & 0x00ff00) + 0x018000)/3) & 0x00ff00;
    int b = (((rgb & 0x0000ff) + 0x000180)/3) & 0x0000ff;
    return a | r | g | b;
  }
}
```

Printing an Applet

An exciting new feature of Java 1.1 is the ability for programs to generate hard-copy. You draw on a page in Java just as you draw on the screen: by invoking methods of a Graphics object. The difference, of course, is in the Graphics object. When drawing to the screen, you are given an instance of one subclass of Graphics, and when printing, you are given an instance of some other subclass. The two subclasses implement the necessary functionality for on-screen drawing and printing, respectively.

To print in Java, follow these steps:

- First, you must begin the "print job." You do this by calling the getPrintJob() method of the java.awt.Toolkit object. This method displays a dialog box to the user to request information about the print job, such as the name of the printer it should be sent to. getPrintJob() returns a java.awt.PrintJob object.

- To begin printing a page, you call the getGraphics() method of the PrintJob object. This returns a Graphics object that implements the java.awt.PrintGraphics interface, to distinguish it from an on-screen Graphics object.

- Now you can use the various methods of the Graphics object to draw your desired output on the page.

- When you are done drawing the page, you call the dispose() method of the Graphics object to send that page description to the printer. If you need to print another page, you can call the getGraphics() method of the PrintJob again to obtain a new Graphics object for the next page, and repeat the process of drawing and calling dispose().

- When you have printed all of your pages, you end the print job itself by calling the end() method of the PrintJob object.

Printing AWT components and hierarchies of components is particularly easy. You simply pass a PrintGraphics object to the print() method of the component you want to print. By default, print() simply passes this Graphics object to the paint() method. If a component wants to display itself differently on paper than it does on screen, however, it might implement a custom print() method. To print a complete hierarchy of components, you simply call the `printAll()` method of the root component of the hierarchy.

An important restriction on printing is that applets cannot initiate print jobs. This does not mean that they cannot print themselves, merely that the Web browser or applet viewer must initiate the print job and invoke the `printAll()` method of the applet.

Example 4-10 shows a modified version of the `Scribble` applet from Chapter 3, *Applets*. This version has a new **Print** button, and it has been converted to be a standalone application, since applets cannot initiate print jobs. When the **Print** button is pressed, the application creates a `PrintJob`, obtains a `Graphics` object from it, and passes that `Graphics` object to the `printAll()` method of the `Frame`. The result of this printing process (the printed results, not a screen-dump of the on-screen version) is shown in Figure 4-7.

Bear in mind that an application may well want to print something other than a hard-copy version of its on-screen appearance. We'll see a character output stream example in Chapter 8, *Input/Output*, that allows a program to print out multiple pages of arbitrary text.

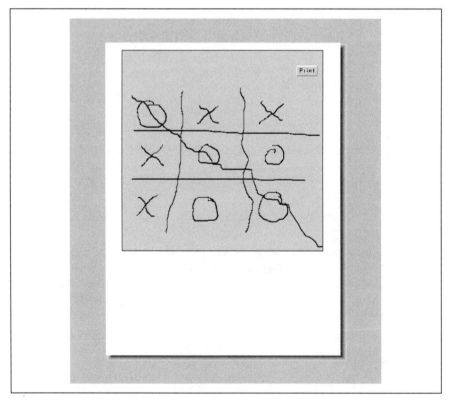

Figure 4-7: Printed output of a Java application

Example 4-10: PrintScribble.java

```java
import java.awt.*;
import java.awt.event.*;
import java.util.*;

/** An application that can print the user's scribbles */
public class PrintScribble extends Frame {
  private short last_x = 0, last_y = 0;            // last click posistion
  private Vector lines = new Vector(256,256);      // store the scribble
  private Properties printprefs = new Properties(); // store user preferences

  public PrintScribble() {
    super("PrintScribble");

    // Add a print button.
    this.setLayout(new FlowLayout(FlowLayout.RIGHT, 5, 5));
    Button b = new Button("Print");
    this.add(b);

    // Call the print() method when the button is clicked.
    // Note anonymous class.
    b.addActionListener(new ActionListener() {
      public void actionPerformed(ActionEvent e) { print(); }
    });

    // Exit when the user closes the window.
    this.addWindowListener(new WindowAdapter() {
      public void windowClosing(WindowEvent e) { System.exit(0); }
    });

    // Register other event types we're interested in -- for scribbling
    enableEvents(AWTEvent.MOUSE_EVENT_MASK |
                 AWTEvent.MOUSE_MOTION_EVENT_MASK);

    // Set our initial size and pop the window up.
    this.setSize(400, 400);
    this.show();
  }

  /** Redraw (or print) the scribble based on stored lines */
  public void paint(Graphics g)
  {
    for(int i = 0; i < lines.size(); i++) {
      Line l = (Line)lines.elementAt(i);
      g.drawLine(l.x1, l.y1, l.x2, l.y2);
    }
  }

  /** Print out the scribble */
  void print() {
    // Obtain a PrintJob and a Graphics object to use with it
    Toolkit toolkit = this.getToolkit();
    PrintJob job = toolkit.getPrintJob(this, "PrintScribble", printprefs);
    if (job == null) return; // If the user clicked Cancel in the print dialog
    Graphics g = job.getGraphics();

    // Give the output a larger top and left margin.  Otherwise it will
    // be scrunched up in the upper-left corner of the page.
    g.translate(100, 100);
```

Example 4-10: PrintScribble.java (continued)

```java
  // Draw a border around the output area.
  Dimension size = this.getSize();
  g.drawRect(-1, -1, size.width+1, size.height+1);

  // Set a clipping region so our scribbles don't go outside the border
  // On-screen this happens automatically, but not on paper.
  g.setClip(0, 0, size.width, size.height);

  // Print this component and all components it contains
  this.printAll(g); // Use print() if you don't want the button to show

  // Finish up.
  g.dispose();      // End the page
  job.end();        // End the job
}

/** Called when the user clicks */
public void processMouseEvent(MouseEvent e)
{
  if (e.getID() == MouseEvent.MOUSE_PRESSED) {
    last_x = (short)e.getX();                    // remember click position
    last_y = (short)e.getY();
  }
  else super.processMouseEvent(e);
}

/** Called when the the user drags the mouse: does the scribbling */
public void processMouseMotionEvent(MouseEvent e)
{
  if (e.getID() == MouseEvent.MOUSE_DRAGGED) {
    Graphics g = getGraphics();
    g.drawLine(last_x, last_y, e.getX(), e.getY());  // draw the line
    lines.addElement(new Line(last_x, last_y,         // and save the line
                              (short) e.getX(), (short)e.getY()));
    last_x = (short) e.getX();   last_y = (short) e.getY();
  }
  else super.processMouseMotionEvent(e);
}

/** The main method.  Create a PrintScribble() object and away we go! */
public static void main(String[] args)
{
  PrintScribble s = new PrintScribble();
}

/** This nested toplevel helper class stores the coordinates
 *  of one line of the scribble. */
class Line {
  public short x1, y1, x2, y2;
  public Line(short x1, short y1, short x2, short y2) {
    this.x1 = x1; this.y1 = y1; this.x2 = x2; this.y2 = y2;
  }
}
}
```

Exercises

4-1. You can obtain a FontMetrics object for a Font by passing the font to the getFontMetrics() method of an applet or any other AWT component. Use the FontMetrics class to write a method that draws a single-line string vertically centered and horizontally right-justified with a given rectangle.

4-2. Use the animation techniques demonstrated in this chapter to write an applet that scrolls a textual message across the screen. The text to scroll should be read from an applet parameter specified with a <PARAM> tag in an HTML file.

4-3. Experiment with the graphics capabilities of the Graphics object and write an applet that displays some kind of interesting and dynamic graphics. You may want to take your inspiration from any of the many screensaver programs on the market. For example, you might draw filled rectangles on the screen, using random sizes, positions, and colors. You may also want to make use of the random() method of the java.lang.Math class. Be creative!

Graphics

CHAPTER 5

Events

The heart of any applet or graphical user interface is the event processing code. Graphical applications are event-driven: they do nothing until the user moves the mouse or clicks a button or types a key. An event-driven program is structured around its event-processing model, so a solid understanding of event handling mechanisms is crucial for good programming.

Unfortunately, the Java event handling model has changed between Java 1.0 and Java 1.1. The Java 1.0 model is a simple one, well suited to writing basic applets. It has a number of shortcomings, however, and does not scale well to complicated interfaces. Although the 1.0 event model is deprecated in Java 1.1, you'll still need to use it for any applets that you want to run on Web browsers based on Java 1.0. The Java 1.1 event model solves many of the shortcomings of the 1.0 model it replaces, but would be quite cumbersome to use if it were not for the new inner classes features also introduced in Java 1.1. This chapter covers both event models and provides examples of each.

The Java 1.0 Event Model

In Java 1.0, all events are represented by the java.awt.Event class. This class has a number of instance variables that describe the event. One of these variables, id, specifies the type of the event. Event defines a number of constants that are the possible values for the id field. The target field specifies the object (typically a java.awt.Component) that generated the event, or on which the event occurred (i.e., the source of the event). The other fields may or may not be used, depending on the type of the event. For example, the x and y fields are defined when id is BUTTON_EVENT, but not when it is ACTION_EVENT. The arg field can provide additional type-dependent data.

Java 1.0 events are dispatched first to the handleEvent() method of the Component on which they occurred. The default implementation of this method checks the id field of the Event object and dispatches the most commonly used types of events to various type-specific methods, listed in Table 5-1.

Table 5-1: Java 1.0 Event Processing Methods of Component

action()	lostFocus()	mouseExit()
gotFocus()	mouseDown()	mouseMove()
keyDown()	mouseDrag()	mouseUp()
keyUp()	mouseEnter()	

The methods listed in Table 5-1 are defined by the Component class. One of the primary characteristics of the Java 1.0 event model is that you must override these methods in order to process events. This means that you must create a subclass to define custom event-handling behavior, which is exactly what we do when we write an applet, for example. Notice, however, that not all of the event types are dispatched by handleEvent() to more specific methods. So, if you are interested in LIST_SELECT or WINDOW_ICONIFY events, for example, you have to override handleEvent() itself, rather than one of the more specific methods. If you do this, you should usually invoke super.handleEvent() to continue dispatching events of other types in the default way.

The handleEvent() method, and all of the type-specific methods, return boolean values. If an event-handling method returns false, as they all do by default, it means that the event was not handled, so it should be passed to the container of the current component to see if that container is interested in processing it. If a method returns true, on the other hand, it is a signal that the event *has* been handled and no further processing is needed.

The fact that unhandled events are passed up the containment hierarchy is important. It means that we can override the action() method (for example) in an applet in order to handle the ACTION_EVENT events that are generated by the buttons within the applet. If events were not propagated up as they are, we would have to create a custom subclass of Button for every button we wanted to add to an interface!

In programs that use the Java 1.0 event model, it is typical to handle events at the top-level component. In an applet, for example, you override the handleEvent() method, or some of the other type-specific methods, of the Applet subclass you create. Or, in a standalone program that creates its own window, you subclass Frame to provide definitions of the event-handling methods. When a program displays a dialog box, it subclasses Dialog to define the methods. With complex interfaces, the event-handling methods of the containers at the top of the hierarchy can become long and somewhat convoluted, so you need to be careful when writing them.

Components and Their Events

In the Java 1.0 model, there is no de-facto way to know what types of events are generated by what GUI components. You simply have to look this information up in the documentation. Additionally, different components use different fields of the Event object, and pass different values in the arg field of that object. Table 5-2 lists each of the AWT components, and for each one, lists the type of events it generates. The first column of the table specifies both the type of the component and the type of the event. The event type is the constant stored in the id field of the Event.

The second through sixth columns indicate whether the when (timestamp), x (mouse x coordinate), y (mouse y coordinate), key (the key that was pressed), and modifiers (modifier keys that were down) fields are set for a given event. If a dot appears in this column, the event sets a value for the corresponding field. The seventh column explains what occurred to trigger the event, and what the value of the arg field of the Event object is.

Events listed for Component apply to all java.awt.Component subclasses. The events listed for Window also apply to the Window subclasses, Dialog and Frame.

Table 5-2: AWT Components and the Java 1.0 Events They Generate

Component Event Type (id)	w h e n	x	y	k e y	m o d s	Event Meaning arg (Type: value)
Button ACTION_EVENT						User clicked on the button String: the button label
Checkbox ACTION_EVENT						User clicked on checkbox Boolean: new checkbox state
Choice ACTION_EVENT						User selected an item String: label of selected item
Component GOT_FOCUS						Got input focus *unused*
Component KEY_ACTION	•	•	•	•	•	User pressed a function key *unused*—key contains key constant
Component KEY_ACTION_RELEASE	•	•	•	•	•	User released a function key *unused*—key contains key constant
Component KEY_PRESS	•	•	•	•	•	User pressed a key *unused*—key contains ASCII key value
Component KEY_RELEASE	•	•	•	•	•	User released a key *unused*—key contains ASCII key value
Component LOST_FOCUS						Lost input focus *unused*

Component Event Type (id)	w h e n	x	y	k e y	m o d s	Event Meaning arg (Type: value)
Component MOUSE_ENTER	•	•	•			Mouse entered the Component *unused*
Component MOUSE_EXIT	•	•	•			Mouse left the Component *unused*
Component MOUSE_DOWN	•	•	•		•	User pressed mouse button *unused*
Component MOUSE_UP	•	•	•		•	User released mouse button *unused*
Component MOUSE_MOVE	•	•	•		•	User moved mouse *unused*
Component MOUSE_DRAG	•	•	•		•	User dragged mouse *unused*
List ACTION_EVENT						User double-clicked on an item String: label of activated item
List LIST_SELECT						User selected an item Integer: index of selected item
List LIST_DESELECT						User deselected an item Integer: index of deselected item
MenuItem ACTION_EVENT						User selected an item String: label of selected item
Scrollbar SCROLL_LINE_UP						User requested scroll Integer: position to scroll to
Scrollbar SCROLL_LINE_DOWN						User requested scroll Integer: position to scroll to
Scrollbar SCROLL_PAGE_UP						User requested scroll Integer: position to scroll to
Scrollbar SCROLL_PAGE_DOWN						User requested scroll Integer: position to scroll to
Scrollbar SCROLL_ABSOLUTE						User requested scroll Integer: position to scroll to
TextField ACTION_EVENT						User struck <Return> String: user's input text
Window WINDOW_DESTROY						Window was destroyed *unused*
Window WINDOW_ICONIFY						Window was iconified *unused*

Events

Table 5–2: AWT Components and the Java 1.0 Events They Generate (continued)

Component Event Type (id)	w h e n	x	y	k e y	m o d s	Event Meaning arg (Type: value)
Window WINDOW_DEICONIFY						Window was deiconified *unused*
Window WINDOW_MOVED		•	•			Window was moved *unused*

Key and Modifier Constants

The Event class contains the field key, which is filled in when a keyboard event has occurred, and the field modifiers, which lists the keyboard modifier keys currently in effect for key and mouse events.

Four modifier constants are defined by the Event class; they are listed in Table 5-3. They are mask values that are OR'ed into the modifiers field. You can test for them using AND. You can also check a given event for the first three of the modifiers with the Event methods shiftDown(), controlDown(), and metaDown().

Table 5–3: Java Keyboard Modifiers

Modifier Constant	Meaning
Event.SHIFT_MASK	**Shift** key is held down (or **Caps Lock** on)
Event.CTRL_MASK	**Control** key is held down
Event.META_MASK	**Meta** key is held down
Event.ALT_MASK	**Alt** key is held down

When a KEY_PRESS or KEY_RELEASE event occurs, it means that the user pressed a key that is a normal printing character, a control character, or a non-printing character with a standard ASCII value—one of **Return** (ASCII 10 or '\n'), **Tab** (ASCII 9 or '\t'), **Escape** (ASCII 27), **Backspace** (ASCII 8), or **Delete** (ASCII 127). In this case, the value of the key field in the event is simply the ASCII value of the key that was pressed or released.

When a KEY_ACTION or KEY_ACTION_RELEASE event occurs, it means that the user pressed some sort of function key, one which does not have an ASCII representation. Event defines constants for each of these function keys, which are listed in Table 5-4.

Table 5-4: Java Function Key Constants

Key Constant	Meaning
Event.HOME	**Home** key
Event.END	**End** key
Event.PGUP	**Page Up** key
Event.PGDN	**Page Down** key
Event.UP	**Up** arrow key
Event.DOWN	**Down** arrow key
Event.LEFT	**Left** arrow key
Event.RIGHT	**Right** arrow key
Event.F1 *to* Event.F12	Function keys 1 through 12

Mouse Buttons

In order to maintain platform independence, Java only recognizes a single mouse button—the Event class does not have any kind of mouseButton field to indicate which button has been pressed on a multi-button mouse. On platforms that support two- or three-button mouses, the right and center buttons generate mouse down, mouse drag, and mouse up events as if the user was holding down modifier keys, as shown in Table 5-5.

Table 5-5: Mouse Button Modifiers

Mouse Button	Flag Set in Event.modifiers Field
Left button	*none*
Right button	Event.META_MASK
Middle button	Event.ALT_MASK

Using keyboard modifiers to indicate the mouse button that has been pressed maintains compatibility with platforms that only have one-button mouses, but still allows programs to use the right and middle buttons on platforms that support them. Suppose, for example, you want to write a program that allows the user to draw lines with the mouse using two different colors. You might draw in the primary color if there are no modifier flags set, and draw in the secondary color when the META_MASK modifier is set. In this way, users with a two- or three-button mouse can simply use the left and right mouse buttons to draw in the two colors; and users with a one-button mouse can use the **Meta** key, in conjunction with the mouse, to draw in the secondary color.

Scribbling in Java 1.0

Example 5-1 shows a simple applet that uses the Java 1.0 event model. It overrides the mouseDown() and mouseDrag() methods to allow the user to scribble with the mouse. It overrides the keyDown() method and clears the screen when it detects the **C** key. And it overrides the action() method to clear the screen when the user clicks on a **Clear** button. We've seen applets much like this elsewhere in the book; this one is not pictured here.

Example 5–1: Scribble1.java

```java
import java.applet.*;
import java.awt.*;

/** A simple applet that uses the Java 1.0 event handling model */
public class Scribble1 extends Applet {
  private int lastx, lasty;    // remember last mouse coordinates
  Button clear_button;         // the Clear button
  Graphics g;                  // A Graphics object for drawing

  /** Initialize the button and the Graphics object */
  public void init() {
    clear_button = new Button("Clear");
    this.add(clear_button);
    g = this.getGraphics();
  }
  /** Respond to mouse clicks */
  public boolean mouseDown(Event e, int x, int y) {
    lastx = x; lasty = y;
    return true;
  }
  /** Respond to mouse drags */
  public boolean mouseDrag(Event e, int x, int y) {
    g.setColor(Color.black);
    g.drawLine(lastx, lasty, x, y);
    lastx = x; lasty = y;
    return true;
  }
  /** Respond to key presses */
  public boolean keyDown(Event e, int key) {
    if ((e.id == Event.KEY_PRESS) && (key == 'c')) {
      clear();
      return true;
    }
    else return false;
  }
  /** Respond to Button clicks */
  public boolean action(Event e, Object arg) {
    if (e.target == clear_button) {
      clear();
      return true;
    }
    else return false;
  }
  /** convenience method to erase the scribble */
  public void clear() {
    g.setColor(this.getBackground());
    g.fillRect(0, 0, bounds().width, bounds().height);
  }
}
```

Java 1.0 Event Details

Example 5-2 is an applet that handles all of the user input events that can occur in an applet and displays the event details. These are mouse and keyboard events primarily; the program does not define any GUI components, so it does not handle the higher-level "semantic" events that those components generate.

This example is interesting because it shows how to interpret modifiers and how to make sense of the various types of key events. If you find yourself writing complex event handling code, you may want to model pieces of it after this example.

Example 5–2: EventTester1.java

```
import java.applet.*;
import java.awt.*;
import java.util.*;

/** An applet that gives details about Java 1.0 events */
public class EventTester1 extends Applet {
  // Handle mouse events
  public boolean mouseDown(Event e, int x, int y)  {
    showLine(mods(e.modifiers) +  "Mouse Down: [" + x + "," + y + "]");
    return true;
  }
  public boolean mouseUp(Event e, int x, int y)  {
    showLine(mods(e.modifiers) + "Mouse Up: [" + x + "," + y + "]");
    return true;
  }
  public boolean mouseDrag(Event e, int x, int y)  {
    showLine(mods(e.modifiers) + "Mouse Drag: [" + x + "," + y + "]");
    return true;
  }
  public boolean mouseMove(Event e, int x, int y)  {
    showLine(mods(e.modifiers) + "Mouse Move: [" + x + "," + y + "]");
    return true;
  }
  public boolean mouseEnter(Event e, int x, int y)  {
    showLine("Mouse Enter: [" + x + "," + y + "]"); return true;
  }
  public boolean mouseExit(Event e, int x, int y)  {
    showLine("Mouse Exit: [" + x + "," + y + "]"); return true;
  }

  // Handle focus events
  public boolean gotFocus(Event e, Object what)  {
    showLine("Got Focus"); return true;
  }
  public boolean lostFocus(Event e, Object what)  {
    showLine("Lost Focus"); return true;
  }

  // Handle key down and key up events
  // This gets more confusing because there are two types of key events
  public boolean keyDown(Event e, int key)  {
    int flags = e.modifiers;
    if (e.id == Event.KEY_PRESS)                   // a regular key
      showLine("Key Down: " + mods(flags) + key_name(e));
    else if (e.id == Event.KEY_ACTION)             // a function key
      showLine("Function Key Down: " + mods(flags) + function_key_name(key));
```

Example 5-2: EventTester1.java (continued)

```
    return true;
  }
  public boolean keyUp(Event e, int key)  {
    int flags = e.modifiers;
    if (e.id == Event.KEY_RELEASE)                 // a regular key
      showLine("Key Up: " + mods(flags) + key_name(e));
    else if (e.id == Event.KEY_ACTION_RELEASE)   // a function key
      showLine("Function Key Up: " + mods(flags) + function_key_name(key));
    return true;
  }


  // The remaining methods help us sort out the various modifiers and keys

  // Return the current list of modifier keys
  private String mods(int flags) {
    String s = "[ ";
    if (flags == 0) return "";
    if ((flags & Event.SHIFT_MASK) != 0) s += "Shift ";
    if ((flags & Event.CTRL_MASK) != 0) s += "Control ";
    if ((flags & Event.META_MASK) != 0) s += "Meta ";
    if ((flags & Event.ALT_MASK) != 0) s += "Alt ";
    s += "] ";
    return s;
  }


  // Return the name of a regular (non-function) key.
  private String key_name(Event e) {
    char c = (char) e.key;
    if (e.controlDown()) {    // If CTRL flag is set, handle control chars.
      if (c < ' ') {
        c += '@';
        return "^" + c;
      }
    }
    else {                     // If CTRL flag is not set, then certain ASCII
      switch (c) {             // control characters have special meaning.
        case '\n': return "Return";
        case '\t': return "Tab";
        case '\033': return "Escape";
        case '\010': return "Backspace";
      }
    }
    // Handle the remaining possibilities.
    if (c == '\177') return "Delete";
    else if (c == ' ') return "Space";
    else return String.valueOf(c);
  }

  // Return the name of a function key.  Just compare the key to the
  // constants defined in the Event class.
  private String function_key_name(int key) {
    switch(key) {
      case Event.HOME: return "Home";      case Event.END: return "End";
      case Event.PGUP: return "Page Up";   case Event.PGDN: return "Page Down";
      case Event.UP: return "Up";          case Event.DOWN: return "Down";
      case Event.LEFT: return "Left";      case Event.RIGHT: return "Right";
      case Event.F1: return "F1";          case Event.F2: return "F2";
      case Event.F3: return "F3";          case Event.F4: return "F4";
```

Example 5-2: EventTester1.java (continued)

```
        case Event.F5: return "F5";      case Event.F6: return "F6";
        case Event.F7: return "F7";      case Event.F8: return "F8";
        case Event.F9: return "F9";      case Event.F10: return "F10";
        case Event.F11: return "F11";    case Event.F12: return "F12";
    }
    return "Unknown Function Key";
}

/** A list of lines to display in the window */
protected Vector lines = new Vector();
/** Add a new line to the list of lines, and redisplay */
protected void showLine(String s) {
    if (lines.size() == 20) lines.removeElementAt(0);
    lines.addElement(s);
    repaint();
}
/** This method repaints the text in the window */
public void paint(Graphics g) {
    for(int i = 0; i < lines.size(); i++)
        g.drawString((String)lines.elementAt(i), 20, i*16 + 50);
}
}
```

The Java 1.1 Event Model

The Java 1.1 event model is used by both the AWT and the JavaBeans API. In this model, different classes of events are represented by different Java classes. Every event is a subclass of java.util.EventObject. AWT events, which is what we are concerned with here, are subclasses of java.awt.AWTEvent. For convenience, the various types of AWT events, such as MouseEvent and ActionEvent, are placed in the new java.awt.event package.

Every event has a source object, which can be obtained with getSource(), and every AWT event has a type value, which can be obtained with getID(). This value is used to distinguish the various types of events that are represented by the same event class. For example, the FocusEvent has two possible types: Focus-Event.FOCUS_GAINED and FocusEvent.FOCUS_LOST. Event subclasses contain whatever data values are pertinent to the particular event type. For example, MouseEvent has getX(), getY(), and getClickCount() methods; it also inherits the getModifiers() and getWhen() methods, among others.

The 1.1 event handling model is based on the concept of an "event listener." An object interested in receiving events is an *event listener*. An object that generates events (an *event source*) maintains a list of listeners that are interested in being notified when events occur, and provides methods that allow listeners to add themselves and remove themselves from this list of interested objects. When the event source object generates an event (or when a user input event occurs on the event source object), the event source notifies all of the listener objects that the event has occurred.

An event source notifies an event listener object by invoking a method on it and passing it an event object (an instance of a subclass of EventObject). In order for a source to invoke a method on a listener, all listeners must implement the required method. This is ensured by requiring that all event listeners for a particular type of event implement a corresponding interface. For example, event listener objects for ActionEvent events must implement the ActionListener interface. The java.awt.event package defines an event listener interface for each of the event types it defines. (Actually for MouseEvent events, it defines two listener interfaces: MouseListener and MouseMotionListener.) All event listener interfaces themselves extend java.util.EventListener. This interface does not define any methods, but instead acts as a marker interface, clearly identifying all event listeners as such.

An event listener interface may define more than one method. For example, an event class like MouseEvent represents several different types of mouse events, such as button press events and button release events, and these different event types cause different methods in the corresponding event listener to be invoked. By convention, the methods of an event listener are passed a single argument, which is an event object of the type that corresponds to the listener. This event object should contain all the information a program needs to respond to the event. Table 5-6 lists the event types defined in java.awt.event, the corresponding listener (or listeners), and the methods defined by each listener interface.

Table 5-6: Java 1.1 Event Types, Listeners, and Listener Methods

Event Class	Listener Interface	Listener Methods
ActionEvent	ActionListener	actionPerformed()
AdjustmentEvent	AdjustmentListener	adjustmentValueChanged()
ComponentEvent	ComponentListener	componentHidden() componentMoved() componentResized() componentShown()
ContainerEvent	ContainerListener	componentAdded() componentRemoved()
FocusEvent	FocusListener	focusGained() focusLost()
ItemEvent	ItemListener	itemStateChanged()
KeyEvent	KeyListener	keyPressed() keyReleased() keyTyped()
MouseEvent	MouseListener	mouseClicked() mouseEntered() mouseExited() mousePressed() mouseReleased()
	MouseMotionListener	mouseDragged() mouseMoved()
TextEvent	TextListener	textValueChanged()

Event Class	Listener Interface	Listener Methods
WindowEvent	WindowListener	windowActivated() windowClosed() windowClosing() windowDeactivated() windowDeiconified() windowIconified() windowOpened()

For each of the event listener interfaces that contains more than one method, java.awt.event defines a simple "adapter" class that provides an empty body for each of the methods in the interface. When you are only interested in one or two of the defined methods, it is sometimes easier to subclass the adapter class than to implement the interface. If you subclass the adapter, you only have to override the methods of interest, but if you implement the interface directly you have to define all of the methods, which means you must provide empty bodies for all of the methods that are not of interest. These pre-defined no-op adapter classes bear the same name as the interfaces they implement, with "Listener" changed to "Adapter": MouseAdapter, WindowAdapter, etc.

Once you have implemented a listener interface, or subclassed an adapter class, you must instantiate your new class to define an individual event listener object. You then register that listener with the appropriate event source. In AWT programs, an event source is always some sort of AWT component. Event listener registration methods follow a standard naming convention: if an event source generates events of type *X*, it has a method named add*X*Listener() to add an event listener, and a method remove*X*Listener() to remove a listener. One of the nice features of the 1.1 event model is that it is easy to determine the types of events a component can generate—just look for the event listener registration methods. For example, by inspecting the API of the Button object, you can determine that it generates ActionEvent events. Table 5-7 lists the AWT components and the events they generate.

Table 5-7: AWT Components and the Java 1.1 Events They Generate

Component	Events Generated	Meaning
Button	ActionEvent	User clicked on the button
Checkbox	ItemEvent	User selected or deselected an item
CheckboxMenuItem	ItemEvent	User selected or deselected an item
Choice	ItemEvent	User selected or deselected an item
Component	ComponentEvent	Component moved, resized, hidden, or shown
	FocusEvent	Component gained or lost focus
	KeyEvent	User pressed or released a key

Component	Events Generated	Meaning
	MouseEvent	User pressed or released mouse button, mouse entered or exited component, or user moved or dragged mouse. Note: MouseEvent has two corresponding listeners, which are MouseListener and MouseMotionListener.
Container	ContainerEvent	Component added to or removed from container
List	ActionEvent	User double-clicked on list item
	ItemEvent	User selected or deselected an item
MenuItem	ActionEvent	User selected a menu item
Scrollbar	AdjustmentEvent	User moved the scrollbar
TextComponent	TextEvent	User changed text
TextField	ActionEvent	User finished editing text
Window	WindowEvent	Window opened, closed, iconified, deiconified, or close requested

Scribbling in Java 1.1

The Java 1.1 event model is quite flexible, and, as we'll see, there are quite a few different ways you can use it to structure your event-handling code. Example 5-3 shows the first technique. Once again, this is our basic Scribble applet, this time using the Java 1.1 event model. This version of the applet implements the MouseListener and MouseMotionListener interfaces itself, and registers itself with its own addMouseListener() and addMouseMotionListener() methods.

Example 5–3: Scribble2.java

```
import java.applet.*;
import java.awt.*;
import java.awt.event.*;

/** A simple applet that uses the Java 1.1 event handling model */
public class Scribble2 extends Applet
                    implements MouseListener, MouseMotionListener {
  private int last_x, last_y;

  public void init() {
    // Tell this applet what MouseListener and MouseMotionListener
    // objects to notify when mouse and mouse motion events occur.
    // Since we implement the interfaces ourself, our own methods are called.
    this.addMouseListener(this);
    this.addMouseMotionListener(this);
  }

  // A method from the MouseListener interface.  Invoked when the
  // user presses a mouse button.
```

Example 5–3: Scribble2.java (continued)

```
  public void mousePressed(MouseEvent e) {
    last_x = e.getX();
    last_y = e.getY();
  }

  // A method from the MouseMotionListener interface.  Invoked when the
  // user drags the mouse with a button pressed.
  public void mouseDragged(MouseEvent e) {
    Graphics g = this.getGraphics();
    int x = e.getX(), y = e.getY();
    g.drawLine(last_x, last_y, x, y);
    last_x = x; last_y = y;
  }

  // The other, unused methods of the MouseListener interface.
  public void mouseReleased(MouseEvent e) {;}
  public void mouseClicked(MouseEvent e) {;}
  public void mouseEntered(MouseEvent e) {;}
  public void mouseExited(MouseEvent e) {;}

  // The other method of the MouseMotionListener interface.
  public void mouseMoved(MouseEvent e) {;}
}
```

Scribbling with External Classes

Example 5-4 shows another version of the Scribble applet. This one defines two separate classes to serve as the MouseListener and MouseMotionListener objects. It is these classes that define the event-handling logic, and the body of the applet itself shrinks to contain only the init() method, which is what creates and registers the listeners. Note the use of the MouseAdapter and MouseMotionAdapter classes. It is easier to subclass them than it is to implement the MouseListener and MouseMotionListener interfaces.

Example 5–4: Scribble3.java

```
import java.applet.*;
import java.awt.*;
import java.awt.event.*;

/**
 * A simple applet that uses external classes to implement
 * the Java 1.1 event handling model
 **/
public class Scribble3 extends Applet {
  int last_x;
  int last_y;

  public void init() {
    MouseListener ml = new MyMouseListener(this);
    MouseMotionListener mml = new MyMouseMotionListener(this);

    // Tell this component what MouseListener and MouseMotionListener
    // objects to notify when mouse and mouse motion events occur.
    this.addMouseListener(ml);
    this.addMouseMotionListener(mml);
```

Example 5-4: Scribble3.java (continued)

```
  }
}

class MyMouseListener extends MouseAdapter {
  private Scribble3 scribble;
  public MyMouseListener(Scribble3 s) { scribble = s; }
  public void mousePressed(MouseEvent e)  {
    scribble.last_x = e.getX();
    scribble.last_y = e.getY();
  }
}

class MyMouseMotionListener extends MouseMotionAdapter {
  private Scribble3 scribble;
  public MyMouseMotionListener(Scribble3 s) { scribble = s; }
  public void mouseDragged(MouseEvent e) {
    Graphics g = scribble.getGraphics();
    int x = e.getX(), y = e.getY();
    g.drawLine(scribble.last_x, scribble.last_y, x, y);
    scribble.last_x = x; scribble.last_y = y;
  }
}
```

Scribbling with Inner Classes

Example 5-4 is not an entirely satisfactory solution to the problem of event handling in our applet. It places the event-handling logic in separate classes, external
to the applet. These classes have to be passed a reference to the applet so that
they can draw into it. Since we are using the Java 1.1 event model, this is an ideal
situation to use another new Java 1.1 feature: inner classes. Example 5-5 shows
what the applet looks like when the event listeners are implemented as anonymous inner classes. Note how succinct this representation is. This is perhaps the
most common way to use the Java 1.1 event model, so you'll probably see a lot of
code that looks like this. In this case, our simple applet is nothing but event-
handling code, so almost the entire applet becomes part of the two inner classes.

Note that we've added a feature to the applet. It now includes a **Clear** button. An
ActionListener object is registered with the button; it clears the scribble when the
appropriate event occurs.

Example 5-5: Scribble4.java

```
import java.applet.*;
import java.awt.*;
import java.awt.event.*;

/**
 * A simple applet that uses anonymous inner classes to implement
 * the Java 1.1 event handling model
 **/
public class Scribble4 extends Applet {
  int last_x, last_y;

  public void init() {
    // Define, instantiate and register a MouseListener object
```

Example 5-5: Scribble4.java (continued)

```
this.addMouseListener(new MouseAdapter() {
  public void mousePressed(MouseEvent e) {
    last_x = e.getX();
    last_y = e.getY();
  }
});

// Define, instantiate and register a MouseMotionListener object
this.addMouseMotionListener(new MouseMotionAdapter() {
  public void mouseDragged(MouseEvent e) {
    Graphics g = getGraphics();
    int x = e.getX(), y = e.getY();
    g.setColor(Color.black);
    g.drawLine(last_x, last_y, x, y);
    last_x = x; last_y = y;
  }
});

// Create a clear button
Button b = new Button("Clear");
// Define, instantiate, and register a listener to handle button presses
b.addActionListener(new ActionListener() {
  public void actionPerformed(ActionEvent e) {  // clear the scribble
    Graphics g = getGraphics();
    g.setColor(getBackground());
    g.fillRect(0, 0, getSize().width, getSize().height);
  }
});
// And add the button to the applet
this.add(b);
  }
}
```

Scribbling with Adapter Classes

Example 5-6 shows yet another variation on the Scribble theme. In this case, some of the event listener objects do not handle events themselves, but merely serve as "adapters" that pass events along to other objects. The word "adapter" is used in a couple of ways in the Java 1.1 event model. One usage describes convenience classes such as MouseAdapter and FocusAdapter, defined in java.awt.event. In this case, however, we're using "adapter" in a more general sense, to refer to any small, simple class that receives events and passes them on, serving simply to connect a GUI to the rest of the application. An adapter works just as a physical adapter might work to join two cables that use different types of connectors.

The adapter class, ScribbleActionListener, handles the ActionEvent objects for the buttons in this version of Scribble. ScribbleActionListener is implemented as a local class.

In Example 5-6, we've transformed our Scribble applet into a standalone application. The application provides high-level functionality; it implements its GUI as a separate class. This technique of enforcing a clear distinction between application and interface can be a very useful one, particularly with large applications.

Events

Example 5-6: Scribble5.java

```java
import java.applet.*;
import java.awt.*;
import java.awt.event.*;

/** The application class.  Processes high-level commands sent by GUI */
public class Scribble5 {
  /** main entry point.  Just create an instance of this application class */
  public static void main(String[] args) { new Scribble5(); }

  /** Application constructor:  create an instance of our GUI class */
  public Scribble5() { window = new ScribbleGUI(this); }
  protected Frame window;

  /** This is the application method that processes commands sent by the GUI */
  public void doCommand(String command) {
    if (command.equals("clear")) {          // clear the GUI window
      // It would be more modular to include this functionality in the GUI
      // class itself.  But for demonstration purposes, we do it here.
      Graphics g = window.getGraphics();
      g.setColor(window.getBackground());
      g.fillRect(0, 0, window.getSize().width, window.getSize().height);
    }
    else if (command.equals("print")) {}   // not yet implemented
    else if (command.equals("quit")) {     // quit the application
      window.dispose();                       // close the GUI
      System.exit(0);                         // and exit.
    }
  }
}

/** This class implements the GUI for our application */
class ScribbleGUI extends Frame {
  int lastx, lasty;   // remember last mouse click
  Scribble5 app;      // A reference to the application, to send commands to.

  /**
   * The GUI constructor does all the work of creating the GUI and setting
   * up event listeners.  Note the use of local and anonymous classes.
   */
  public ScribbleGUI(Scribble5 application) {
    super("Scribble");        // Create the window
    app = application;        // Remember the application reference

    // Create three buttons
    Button clear = new Button("Clear");
    Button print = new Button("Print");
    Button quit = new Button("Quit");

    // Set a LayoutManager, and add the buttons to the window.
    this.setLayout(new FlowLayout(FlowLayout.RIGHT, 10, 5));
    this.add(clear); this.add(print);  this.add(quit);

    // Here's a local class used for action listeners for the buttons
    class ScribbleActionListener implements ActionListener {
      private String command;
      public ScribbleActionListener(String cmd) { command = cmd; }
      public void actionPerformed(ActionEvent e) { app.doCommand(command); }
    }
```

Example 5–6: Scribble5.java (continued)

```
    // Define action listener adapters that connect the  buttons to the app
    clear.addActionListener(new ScribbleActionListener("clear"));
    print.addActionListener(new ScribbleActionListener("print"));
    quit.addActionListener(new ScribbleActionListener("quit"));

    // Handle the window close request similarly
    this.addWindowListener(new WindowAdapter() {
      public void windowClosing(WindowEvent e) { app.doCommand("quit"); }
    });

    // High-level action events are passed to the application, but we
    // still handle scribbling right here.  Register a MouseListener object.
    this.addMouseListener(new MouseAdapter() {
      public void mousePressed(MouseEvent e) {
        lastx = e.getX(); lasty = e.getY();
      }
    });

    // Define, instantiate and register a MouseMotionListener object
    this.addMouseMotionListener(new MouseMotionAdapter() {
      public void mouseDragged(MouseEvent e) {
        Graphics g = getGraphics();
        int x = e.getX(), y = e.getY();
        g.setColor(Color.black);
        g.drawLine(lastx, lasty, x, y);
        lastx = x; lasty = y;
      }
    });

    // Finally, set the size of the window, and pop it up
    this.setSize(400, 400);
    this.show();
  }
}
```

Inside the Java 1.1 Event Model

The listener-based event model we've seen in the sections above is ideal for creating a GUI out of pre-defined AWT components or out of Java beans. It becomes a little cumbersome, however, when developing custom AWT components. AWT components (but not beans) provide a lower-level interface to this event model that is sometimes more convenient to use.

When an AWTEvent is delivered to a component, there is some default processing that goes on before the event is dispatched to the appropriate event listeners. When you define a custom component (by subclassing), you have the opportunity to override methods and intercept the event before it is sent to listener objects. When an AWTEvent is delivered to a component, it is passed to the process-Event() method.

By default, processEvent() simply checks the class of the event object and dispatches the event to a class-specific method. For example, if the event object is an instance of FocusEvent, processEvent() dispatches it to a method named pro-cessFocusEvent(). Or, if the event is of type ActionEvent, it is dispatched to

Events

processActionEvent(). In other words, any event type *X*Event is dispatched to a corresponding process*X*Event() method. The exception is for MouseEvent events, which are dispatched either to processMouseEvent() or processMouseMotion-Event(), depending on the type of the mouse event that occurred.

For any given component, it is the individual process*X*Event() methods that are responsible for invoking the appropriate methods of all registered event listener objects. The processMouseEvent() method, for example, invokes the appropriate method for each registered MouseListener object. There is a one-to-one mapping between these methods and the event listener interfaces defined in java.awt.event. Each process*X*Event() method corresponds to an *X*Listener interface.

As you can see, there is a clear analogy between the Java 1.0 event model and this Java 1.1 low-level event model. processEvent() is analogous to the Java 1.0 handleEvent() method, and methods like processKeyEvent() are analogous to the Java 1.0 keyDown() and keyUp() methods. As with the Java 1.0 model, there are two levels at which you can intercept events: you can override processEvent() itself or you can rely on the default version of processEvent() to dispatch the events based on their class and instead override the individual event methods, such as processFocusEvent() and processActionEvent().

There is one additional requirement to make this low-level Java 1.1 event model work. In order to receive events of a particular type for a component, you must tell the component that you are interested in receiving that type of event. If you do not do this, for efficiency, the component does not bother to deliver that type of event. When using event listeners, the act of registering a listener is enough to notify the component that you are interested in receiving events of that type. But when you use the low-level model, you must register your interest explicitly. You do this by calling the enableEvents() method of the component and passing a bit mask that specifies each of the event types you are interested in. The bit mask is formed by ORing together various EVENT_MASK constants defined by the AWTEvent class.

Scribbling with Low-Level Event Handling

Example 5-7 is another variation on the Scribble applet. This one uses the Java 1.1 low-level event-handling model. It overrides the event-specific methods processMouseEvent(), processMouseMotionEvent() and processKeyEvent(). Note how it calls enableEvents() in its init() method to register interest in events of that type. Furthermore, it calls requestFocus() to ask that it be given the keyboard focus, so that it can receive key events. Notice also that it passes events it is not interested in to the superclass event-processing method. In this case, the superclass is not going to use those events, but this is still a good practice.

Example 5-7: Scribble6.java

```
import java.applet.*;
import java.awt.*;
import java.awt.event.*;

/** A simple applet that uses low-level event handling under Java 1.1 */
```

Example 5-7: Scribble6.java (continued)

```java
public class Scribble6 extends Applet {
  private int lastx, lasty;

  /** Tell the system we're interested in mouse events, mouse motion events,
   *  and keyboard events.  This is a required or events won't be sent.
   */
  public void init() {
    this.enableEvents(AWTEvent.MOUSE_EVENT_MASK |
                      AWTEvent.MOUSE_MOTION_EVENT_MASK |
                      AWTEvent.KEY_EVENT_MASK);
    this.requestFocus();  // Ask for keyboard focus so we get key events
  }

  /** Invoked when a mouse event of some type occurs */
  public void processMouseEvent(MouseEvent e) {
    if (e.getID() == MouseEvent.MOUSE_PRESSED) {  // check the event type
      lastx = e.getX(); lasty = e.getY();
    }
    else super.processMouseEvent(e); // pass unhandled events to our superclass
  }

  /** Invoked when a mouse motion event occurs */
  public void processMouseMotionEvent(MouseEvent e) {
    if (e.getID() == MouseEvent.MOUSE_DRAGGED) {  // check type
      int x = e.getX(), y = e.getY();
      Graphics g = this.getGraphics();
      g.drawLine(lastx, lasty, x, y);
      lastx = x; lasty = y;
    }
    else super.processMouseMotionEvent(e);
  }

  /** Called on key events:  clear the screen when 'c' is typed */
  public void processKeyEvent(KeyEvent e) {
    if ((e.getID() == KeyEvent.KEY_TYPED) && (e.getKeyChar() == 'c')) {
      Graphics g = this.getGraphics();
      g.setColor(this.getBackground());
      g.fillRect(0, 0, this.getSize().width, this.getSize().height);
    }
    else super.processKeyEvent(e);  // pass unhandled events to our superclass
  }
}
```

Scribbling with processEvent()

Example 5-8 is the last variation on the Scribble applet that we'll see in this chapter. It is much like Example 5-7, but it overrides processEvent(), rather than overriding the event-specific methods. One important thing to notice is that it passes all unhandled events to the processEvent() method of the superclass so they can be dispatched normally by that method. This version of the applet calls enableEvents(), just as the previous version did.

Example 5-8: Scribble7.java

```java
import java.applet.*;
import java.awt.*;
```

Example 5–8: Scribble7.java (continued)

```
import java.awt.event.*;

/** A simple applet that uses low-level event handling under Java 1.1 */
public class Scribble7 extends Applet {
  private int lastx, lasty;

  /** Specify the event types we care about, and ask for keyboard focus */
  public void init() {
    this.enableEvents(AWTEvent.MOUSE_EVENT_MASK |
                      AWTEvent.MOUSE_MOTION_EVENT_MASK |
                      AWTEvent.KEY_EVENT_MASK);
    this.requestFocus();  // Ask for keyboard focus so we get key events
  }

  /**
   * Called when an event arrives.  Do the right thing based on the event
   * type.  Pass unhandled events to the superclass for possible processing
   */
  public void processEvent(AWTEvent e) {
    MouseEvent me;
    Graphics g;
    switch(e.getID()) {
    case MouseEvent.MOUSE_PRESSED:
      me = (MouseEvent)e;
      lastx = me.getX(); lasty = me.getY();
      break;
    case MouseEvent.MOUSE_DRAGGED:
      me = (MouseEvent)e;
      int x = me.getX(), y = me.getY();
      g = this.getGraphics();
      g.drawLine(lastx, lasty, x, y);
      lastx = x; lasty = y;
      break;
    case KeyEvent.KEY_TYPED:
      if (((KeyEvent)e).getKeyChar() == 'c') {
        g = this.getGraphics();
        g.setColor(this.getBackground());
        g.fillRect(0, 0, this.getSize().width, this.getSize().height);
      }
      else super.processEvent(e);
      break;
    default: super.processEvent(e); break;
    }
  }
}
```

Java 1.1 Event Details

We end this chapter with a program that displays details about all the events that occur within it. Example 5-9 is much like the applet shown in Example 5-2, except that it uses the low-level Java 1.1 event model instead of the Java 1.0 model, and it is a standalone application instead of an applet. Figure 5-1 shows the output of the program.

Because this application does not create any GUI components, it only receives input events such as MouseEvent, KeyEvent, and WindowEvent. It does not receive

---

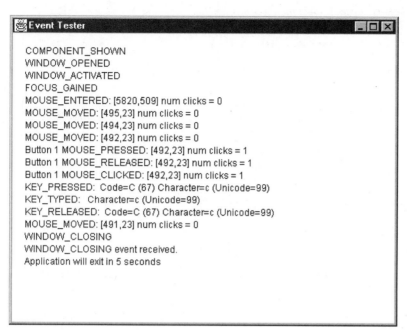

COMPONENT_SHOWN
WINDOW_OPENED
WINDOW_ACTIVATED
FOCUS_GAINED
MOUSE_ENTERED: [5820,509] num clicks = 0
MOUSE_MOVED: [495,23] num clicks = 0
MOUSE_MOVED: [494,23] num clicks = 0
MOUSE_MOVED: [492,23] num clicks = 0
Button 1 MOUSE_PRESSED: [492,23] num clicks = 1
Button 1 MOUSE_RELEASED: [492,23] num clicks = 1
Button 1 MOUSE_CLICKED: [492,23] num clicks = 1
KEY_PRESSED: Code=C (67) Character=c (Unicode=99)
KEY_TYPED: Character=c (Unicode=99)
KEY_RELEASED: Code=C (67) Character=c (Unicode=99)
MOUSE_MOVED: [491,23] num clicks = 0
WINDOW_CLOSING
WINDOW_CLOSING event received.
Application will exit in 5 seconds

Figure 5–1: Java 1.1 event details

the higher-level "semantic" events such as ActionEvent, ItemEvent, and TextEvent that are generated by AWT components. This is a useful example, however, because it demonstrates how to make use of the various pieces of information provided in MouseEvent, KeyEvent, and other event classes.

Example 5–9: EventTester2.java

```
import java.applet.*;
import java.awt.*;
import java.awt.event.*;
import java.util.*;

/** A program that displays all the events that occur in its window */
public class EventTester2 extends Frame
{
  /** The main method: create an EventTester frame, and pop it up */
  public static void main(String[] args) {
    EventTester2 et = new EventTester2();
    et.setSize(500, 400);
    et.show();
  }

  /** The constructor: register the event types we are interested in */
  public EventTester2() {
    super("Event Tester");
    this.enableEvents(AWTEvent.MOUSE_EVENT_MASK |
                      AWTEvent.MOUSE_MOTION_EVENT_MASK |
                      AWTEvent.KEY_EVENT_MASK |
                      AWTEvent.FOCUS_EVENT_MASK |
```

Example 5–9: EventTester2.java (continued)

```
                        AWTEvent.COMPONENT_EVENT_MASK |
                        AWTEvent.WINDOW_EVENT_MASK);
}

/**
 * Display mouse events that don't involve mouse motion.
 * The mousemods() method prints modifiers, and is defined below.
 * The other methods return additional information about the mouse event.
 * showLine() displays a line of text in the window.  It is defined
 * at the end of this class, along with the paint() method.
 */
public void processMouseEvent(MouseEvent e) {
  String type = null;
  switch(e.getID()) {
  case MouseEvent.MOUSE_PRESSED:   type = "MOUSE_PRESSED"; break;
  case MouseEvent.MOUSE_RELEASED:  type = "MOUSE_RELEASED"; break;
  case MouseEvent.MOUSE_CLICKED:   type = "MOUSE_CLICKED"; break;
  case MouseEvent.MOUSE_ENTERED:   type = "MOUSE_ENTERED"; break;
  case MouseEvent.MOUSE_EXITED:    type = "MOUSE_EXITED"; break;
  }
  showLine(mousemods(e) + type + ": [" + e.getX() + "," + e.getY() + "] " +
          "num clicks = " + e.getClickCount() +
          (e.isPopupTrigger()?"; is popup trigger":""));
}


/**
 * Display mouse moved and dragged mouse event.  Note that MouseEvent
 * is the only event type that has two methods, two EventListener interfaces
 * and two adapter classes to handle two distinct categories of events.
 * Also, as seen in init(), mouse motion events must be requested
 * separately from other mouse event types.
 */
public void processMouseMotionEvent(MouseEvent e) {
  String type = null;
  switch(e.getID()) {
  case MouseEvent.MOUSE_MOVED:   type = "MOUSE_MOVED"; break;
  case MouseEvent.MOUSE_DRAGGED: type = "MOUSE_DRAGGED"; break;
  }
  showLine(mousemods(e) + type + ": [" + e.getX() + "," + e.getY() + "] " +
          "num clicks = " + e.getClickCount() +
          (e.isPopupTrigger()?"; is popup trigger":""));
}

/** Return a string representation of the modifiers for a MouseEvent.
 *  Note that the methods called here are inherited from InputEvent.
 */
protected String mousemods(MouseEvent e) {
  int mods = e.getModifiers();
  String s = "";
  if (e.isShiftDown()) s += "Shift ";
  if (e.isControlDown()) s += "Ctrl ";
  if ((mods & InputEvent.BUTTON1_MASK) != 0) s += "Button 1 ";
  if ((mods & InputEvent.BUTTON2_MASK) != 0) s += "Button 2 ";
  if ((mods & InputEvent.BUTTON3_MASK) != 0) s += "Button 3 ";
  return s;
}
```

Example 5-9: EventTester2.java (continued)

```java
/**
 * Display keyboard events.
 * Note that there are three distinct types of key events, and that
 * key events are reported by key code and/or Unicode character.
 * KEY_PRESSED and KEY_RELEASED events are generated for all key strokes.
 * KEY_TYPED events are only generated when a key stroke produces a
 * Unicode character; these events do not report a key code.
 * If isActionKey() returns true, then the key event reports only
 * a key code, because the key that was pressed or released (such as a
 * function key) has no corresponding Unicode character.
 * Key codes can be interpreted by using the many VK_ constants defined
 * by the KeyEvent class, or they can be converted to strings using
 * the static getKeyText() method as we do here.
 */
public void processKeyEvent(KeyEvent e) {
  String eventtype, modifiers, code, character;
  switch(e.getID()) {
  case KeyEvent.KEY_PRESSED:  eventtype = "KEY_PRESSED"; break;
  case KeyEvent.KEY_RELEASED: eventtype = "KEY_RELEASED"; break;
  case KeyEvent.KEY_TYPED:    eventtype = "KEY_TYPED"; break;
  default: eventtype = "UNKNOWN";
  }

  // Convert the list of modifier keys to a string
  modifiers = KeyEvent.getKeyModifiersText(e.getModifiers());

  // Get string and numeric versions of the key code, if any.
  if (e.getID() == KeyEvent.KEY_TYPED) code = "";
  else code = "Code=" + KeyEvent.getKeyText(e.getKeyCode()) +
         " (" + e.getKeyCode() + ")";

  // Get string and numeric versions of the Unicode character, if any.
  if (e.isActionKey()) character = "";
  else character = "Character=" + e.getKeyChar() +
         " (Unicode=" + ((int)e.getKeyChar()) + ")";

  // Display it all.
  showLine(eventtype + ": " + modifiers + " " + code + " " + character);
}

/** Display keyboard focus events.  Focus can be permanently
 * gained or lost, or temporarily transferred to or from a component. */
public void processFocusEvent(FocusEvent e) {
  if (e.getID() == FocusEvent.FOCUS_GAINED)
    showLine("FOCUS_GAINED" + (e.isTemporary()?" (temporary)":""));
  else
    showLine("FOCUS_LOST" + (e.isTemporary()?" (temporary)":""));
}

/** Display Component events.  */
public void processComponentEvent(ComponentEvent e) {
  switch(e.getID()) {
  case ComponentEvent.COMPONENT_MOVED: showLine("COMPONENT_MOVED"); break;
  case ComponentEvent.COMPONENT_RESIZED: showLine("COMPONENT_RESIZED");break;
  case ComponentEvent.COMPONENT_HIDDEN: showLine("COMPONENT_HIDDEN"); break;
  case ComponentEvent.COMPONENT_SHOWN: showLine("COMPONENT_SHOWN"); break;
  }
}
```

Events

Example 5-9: EventTester2.java (continued)

```
/** Display Window events.  Note the special handling of WINDOW_CLOSING */
public void processWindowEvent(WindowEvent e) {
  switch(e.getID()) {
  case WindowEvent.WINDOW_OPENED: showLine("WINDOW_OPENED"); break;
  case WindowEvent.WINDOW_CLOSED: showLine("WINDOW_CLOSED"); break;
  case WindowEvent.WINDOW_CLOSING: showLine("WINDOW_CLOSING"); break;
  case WindowEvent.WINDOW_ICONIFIED: showLine("WINDOW_ICONIFIED"); break;
  case WindowEvent.WINDOW_DEICONIFIED: showLine("WINDOW_DEICONIFIED"); break;
  case WindowEvent.WINDOW_ACTIVATED: showLine("WINDOW_ACTIVATED"); break;
  case WindowEvent.WINDOW_DEACTIVATED: showLine("WINDOW_DEACTIVATED"); break;
  }

  // If the user requested a window close, quit the program.
  // But first display a message, force it to be visible, and make
  // sure the user has time to read it.
  if (e.getID() == WindowEvent.WINDOW_CLOSING) {
    showLine("WINDOW_CLOSING event received.");
    showLine("Application will exit in 5 seconds");
    update(this.getGraphics());
    try {Thread.sleep(5000);} catch (InterruptedException ie) { ; }
    System.exit(0);
  }
}

/** The list of lines to display in the window */
protected Vector lines = new Vector();

/** Add a new line to the list of lines, and redisplay */
protected void showLine(String s) {
  if (lines.size() == 20) lines.removeElementAt(0);
  lines.addElement(s);
  repaint();
}

/** This method repaints the text in the window */
public void paint(Graphics g) {
  for(int i = 0; i < lines.size(); i++)
    g.drawString((String)lines.elementAt(i), 20, i*16 + 50);
}
}
```

Exercises

5-1. Write an applet that responds to user keyboard events. When the user types a key, it should display the key in the Web browser's status line.

5-2. Write an applet that displays a red circle in the center of its display. When the user types any of the keyboard arrow keys, move the circle a few pixels in the appropriate direction. If the user clicks and drags the mouse over the circle, move the circle to follow the mouse. Optionally, change the color of the circle when the user types a function key, **F1** through **F10**.

5-3. Write an applet that can display multiple circles on the screen. When the user clicks the left mouse button over the background of the applet, it should display a new circle under the mouse. When the user clicks the left mouse button over an existing circle and drags it, move the circle to follow the mouse. When the user clicks the right mouse button (or holds down the appropriate modifier key while clicking the left button) over a circle, remove that circle from the display. In order to make this work, you will have to maintain a list of all circles that are currently displayed, along with their positions. Use the java.util.Vector object to maintain this list. Consider defining a nested top-level (i.e., static) Circle class to represent the position of each circle, and, perhaps, to draw each circle.

CHAPTER 6

Graphical
User Interfaces

We've seen that Java programs can draw themselves on the screen using the paint() method and can handle user input events using methods like mouse-Down() or processMouseEvent(). In theory, these drawing and event-handling methods are sufficient for us to design arbitrarily complex graphical user interfaces (GUIs). In practice, however, it is far too cumbersome to do all the drawing and event-handling for even a simple user interface. So instead, we build our GUIs out of pre-defined building blocks. Each building block knows how to display itself and how to handle events that occur on it. Many of these building blocks process low-level user input events, like mouse clicks, and then generate corresponding higher-level semantic events that notify us when a menu item has been selected or the user has pressed the **Return** key, for example.

To Motif programmers on UNIX systems, these GUI building blocks are known as "widgets." To Windows programmers, they are commonly called "controls." In Java, they are known as "components," and they are all subclasses of java.awt.Component.* The Abstract Windowing Toolkit (AWT) defines all of the GUI components in Java; these components comprise the java.awt package.

There are four basic steps to creating a GUI:

- *Create the components.* A GUI component is created just like any other object in Java—simply call the constructor. Consult the documentation for the individual components to determine what arguments the constructor expects. For example, to create a Button component that displays the label "Quit", you simply say:

    ```
    Button quit = new Button("Quit");
    ```

---

* Except menu-related components, which are all subclasses of java.awt.MenuComponent.

104

Components are typically created in the init() method of an applet or in the constructor of a standalone application (or in a private method invoked by one of those methods).

- *Add the components to a container.* All components must be placed within a container. Containers in Java are all subclasses of java.awt.Container. The Applet class is a container. So are the Frame and Dialog classes, which represent top-level windows and dialog boxes, respectively. A container is a type of component, so containers can be, and commonly are, nested within other containers. Panel is a container that is often used in this manner. In developing a GUI, you are really creating a containment hierarchy: the top-level window or applet contains containers that may contain other containers, which in turn contain components. To add a component to a container, you simply pass the component to the add() method of the container. For example, you might add a quit button to an applet with code like the following:

```
this.add(quit);
```

As you'll see later, there is also a two-argument version of add() that is sometimes used. Components are typically added to containers from the init() method of an applet or the constructor of an application.

- *Arrange, or lay out, the components within their containers.* In other words, you need to set the position and size of every component so that the GUI has a pleasing appearance. While it is possible to hardcode the position and size of each component, it is more common to use a LayoutManager object to automatically lay out the components of a container according to certain layout rules defined by the particular LayoutManager you have chosen. We'll learn more about layout management later in this chapter.

- *Handle the events generated by the components.* As we saw in Chapter 5, *Events*, there are different event-handling models in Java 1.1 and Java 1.0. Chapter 5 focused primarily on handling low-level user input events, such as keyboard and mouse events generated by the operating system. When working with GUIs, it is more common to handle the higher-level semantic events that are generated by the components themselves, in response to the lower-level input events. For example, an appropriate series of MouseEvent user input events over a Button object causes the button to generate a single ActionEvent semantic event. It is usually much easier for a program to respond to the single ActionEvent than to attempt to interpret the whole series of MouseEvent events. You can use either the Java 1.1 or Java 1.0 event model with your GUIs, although the Java 1.1 model is preferred for new applications where backwards compatibility is not an issue, of course. The event processing code for semantic events is very similar to the code we saw in Chapter 5 for handling input events.

The rest of this chapter discusses:

- The standard AWT components

- Nesting components with the Panel container

- Layout management using various LayoutManager classes

- Hardcoding component layout and writing custom layout managers

- Working with top-level windows through the Frame class

- Using pulldown and popup menus

- Creating dialog boxes with the Dialog class

- Creating custom components

Components

The AWT contains a number of pre-defined GUI components. Figure 6-1 and Figure 6-2 show UNIX and Windows versions of a Java application that uses each of these pre-defined components. Table 6-1 lists and describes all of the standard components, as well as the pre-defined containers in the AWT. Note that the menu components described in the table are actually subclasses of MenuComponent, rather than Component. Also note that while FileDialog is technically a subclass of Container, it is more useful to think of it as a Component. You may find it useful to refer to a class hierarchy diagram for the java.awt package in conjunction with this table (see Chapter 22 of the Second Edition of *Java in a Nutshell*, for example).

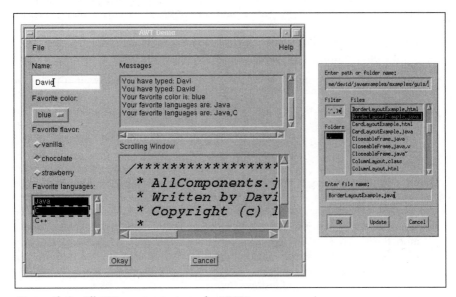

Figure 6-1: All GUI components under UNIX

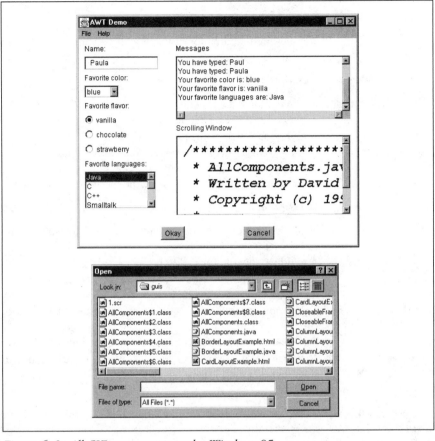

Figure 6–2: All GUI components under Windows 95

Table 6–1: Components, Menu Components, and Containers in the AWT

Component	Description
Button	A graphical push button that the user can click
Canvas	A blank component suitable for custom drawing or subclassing
Checkbox	A toggle button that can be selected and deselected
Choice	A "drop-down list" or "option menu"
Component	The root of the component hierarchy; suitable for subclassing in Java 1.1
FileDialog	A dialog box for browsing and selecting files
Label	A single-line text display
List	A list of selectable items
Scrollbar	A slider for scrolling

Component	Description
TextArea	A multi-line text area for displaying and editing text
TextField	A single-line text input area

Menu Component	**Description**
CheckboxMenuItem	A toggle button in a menu
Menu	A pulldown (or tear-off) menu pane
MenuBar	A component that holds pulldown menus
MenuComponent	The root of the menu component hierarchy
MenuItem	A menu button
PopupMenu	A menu pane that pops up under the mouse (Java 1.1 only)

Container	**Description**
Container	The root of the container hierarchy; suitable for subclassing in Java 1.1
Dialog	A window suitable for dialog boxes
Frame	A top-level window with a decorated border; can contain a menubar
Panel	An empty container, suitable for nested layouts or subclassing
ScrollPane	A container that scrolls its contents (Java 1.1 only)
Window	A top-level window with no border and no menubar; suitable for popup menus

Creating AWT components, menu components, and containers is simple—create them the same way you create any Java object. You'll need to consult Java reference material to determine the appropriate arguments to pass to a component's constructor and to discover any special-purpose methods defined by a component.

Containers

Table 6-1 lists the pre-defined containers provided by the AWT. The Frame and Dialog containers represent separate windows. The ScrollPane container, which was added in Java 1.1, has a special purpose—to scroll a single, large component within a smaller visible area. We'll see these containers later in this chapter. The Panel container is a generic container with no behavior of its own; it is suitable for nesting within other containers. Example 6-1 shows an example of such a hierarchy and Figure 6-3 shows the resulting GUI. Note the use of background color to indicate nesting depth (darker is deeper). In the code, note the use of the add() method to add a component (which may be another container) to a container.

Example 6–1: Containers.java

```
import java.applet.*;
import java.awt.*;
```

Figure 6-3: Nested components and containers

Example 6-1: Containers.java (continued)

```
/**
 * An applet that demonstrates nested container and components
 * It creates the hierarchy shown below, and uses different colors to
 * distinguish the different nesting levels of the containers
 *
 *    applet---panel1----button1
 *       |          |---panel2----button2
 *       |          |       |----panel3----button3
 *       |          |------panel4----button4
 *       |                        |----button5
 *       |---button6
 */
public class Containers extends Applet {
  public void init() {
    this.setBackground(Color.white);              // The applet is white
    this.setFont(new Font("Dialog", Font.BOLD, 24));

    Panel p1 = new Panel();
    p1.setBackground(new Color(200, 200, 200)); // Panel1 is darker than applet
    this.add(p1);                    // Panel 1 is contained in applet
    p1.add(new Button("#1"));        // Button 1 is contained in Panel 1

    Panel p2 = new Panel();
    p2.setBackground(new Color(150, 150, 150)); // Panel2 is darker than Panel1
    p1.add(p2);                      // Panel 2 is contained in Panel 1
    p2.add(new Button("#2"));        // Button 2 is contained in Panel 2

    Panel p3 = new Panel();
    p3.setBackground(new Color(100, 100, 100)); // Panel3 is darker than Panel2
    p2.add(p3);                      // Panel 3 is contained in Panel 2
    p3.add(new Button("#3"));        // Button 3 is contained in Panel 3

    Panel p4 = new Panel();
    p4.setBackground(new Color(150, 150, 150)); // Panel4 is darker than Panel1
    p1.add(p4);                      // Panel4 is contained in Panel 1
    p4.add(new Button("#4"));        // Button4 is contained in Panel4
    p4.add(new Button("#5"));        // Button5 is contained in Panel4

    this.add(new Button("#6"));      // Button6 is contained in applet
  }
}
```

Layout Management

As discussed at the beginning of this chapter, one of the important steps in creating a GUI is laying out your components within their containers. This is usually done by specifying an appropriate LayoutManager object for the container. A particular layout manager enforces a specific layout policy and automatically arranges the components within a container according to that policy. Table 6-2 lists the AWT layout manager classes and summarizes their layout policies. The sections that follow demonstrate the use of each of these layout managers.

Table 6-2: The AWT Layout Managers

Layout Manager	Description
BorderLayout	Lays out a maximum of five components: one along each of the four borders and one in the center of the container. Used with the two-argument version of add(); the additional argument specifies the position of the component.
CardLayout	Makes each component as large as the container, and displays only one at a time. Various methods change the displayed component.
FlowLayout	Arranges components like words on a page: from left to right in rows, and top to bottom as each row fills up. Rows may be left-justified, centered, or right-justified.
GridBagLayout	A flexible layout manager that arranges components in a grid with variable-sized cells. Allows explicit control over resize behavior of the components.
GridLayout	Makes all components the same size and arranges them in a grid of specified dimensions.

Layout managers all implement the LayoutManager interface, or in Java 1.1, they may implement the LayoutManager2 interface. A layout manager is created like any other object. Different layout manager classes take different constructor arguments to specify the parameters of their layout policy. You do not usually invoke the methods of a LayoutManager. Instead, you pass the layout manager object to the setLayout() method of the container that is to be managed—it is the container that invokes the various LayoutManager methods when necessary. Once you have set the layout manager, you can usually forget about it.

As you'll see in the following sections, most of the pre-defined AWT layout managers have fairly simple layout policies that are not much use on their own. They become much more useful, however, when used with nested panels. For example, to center a button at the bottom of a window, you might place it in a Panel that uses a FlowLayout manager, and then place that panel in a container that uses a BorderLayout manager and specify that it should be laid out along the bottom border of the container.

FlowLayout

The FlowLayout layout manager arranges its children like words on a page: from left to right in a row, and top to bottom. When there is not enough space remaining in the current row for the next component, the FlowLayout "wraps" and places the new component in a new row. When you create a FlowLayout, you can specify whether the rows should be left-justified, centered, or right-justified. You can also specify the amount of horizontal and vertical space that the layout manager leaves between components. FlowLayout makes no attempt to fit its components into the container; it leaves each component at its preferred size. If there is extra space, FlowLayout leaves it blank. If there is not enough room in the container, some of the components simply do not appear. Note that FlowLayout is the default layout manager for Panel containers. If you do not specify a different layout manager, a panel uses a FlowLayout that centers its rows and leaves five-pixels between components, both horizontally and vertically.

Example 6-2 shows a short applet that arranges buttons using a FlowLayout layout manager and Figure 6-4 shows the resulting output.

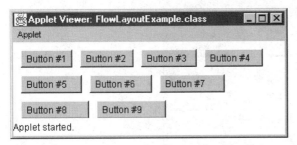

Figure 6–4: Components laid out with a FlowLayout

Example 6–2: FlowLayoutExample.java

```java
import java.applet.*;
import java.awt.*;

public class FlowLayoutExample extends Applet {
  public void init() {
    // Create and specify the layout manager for the applet container.
    // Leave 10 pixels of horizontal and vertical space between components.
    // Left justify rows.
    this.setLayout(new FlowLayout(FlowLayout.LEFT, 10, 10));
    String spaces = "";  // Used to make the buttons different sizes
    for(int i = 1; i <= 9; i++) {
      this.add(new Button("Button #" + i + spaces));
      spaces += " ";
    }
  }
}
```

GridLayout

GridLayout is a heavy-handed layout manager that arranges components left-to-right and top-to-bottom in an evenly-spaced grid of specified dimensions. When you create a GridLayout, you can specify the number of rows and columns in the grid, and you can also specify the horizontal and vertical space the GridLayout should leave between the components. Typically, you only specify the desired number of rows or the desired number of columns, and leave the other dimension set to 0. This allows the GridLayout to pick the appropriate number of rows or columns based on the number of components. GridLayout does not honor the preferred sizes of its components. Instead, it divides the size of the container into the specified number of equally-sized rows and columns and makes all of the components the same size.

Example 6-3 is a simple applet that arranges buttons in a grid using GridLayout. Figure 6-5 shows the output of the applet.

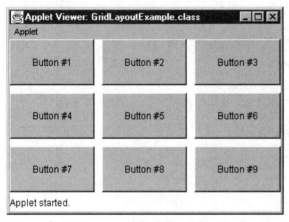

Figure 6-5: Components laid out with a GridLayout

Example 6-3: GridLayoutExample.java

```
import java.applet.*;
import java.awt.*;

public class GridLayoutExample extends Applet {
  public void init() {
    // Create and specify a layout manager for this applet.
    // Layout components into a grid three columns wide, with the number
    // of rows to depend on the number of components.  Leave 10 pixels
    // of horizontal and vertical space between components
    this.setLayout(new GridLayout(0, 3, 10, 10));
    for(int i = 1; i <= 9; i++)
      this.add(new Button("Button #" + i));
  }
}
```

BorderLayout

The BorderLayout layout manager arranges up to five components within a container. Four of the components are laid out against each of the edges of the container and one is placed in the center. When you add a component to a container that is managed by a BorderLayout layout manager, you must specify where you want the container laid out. You do this by using the two-argument version of add() and passing one of the strings "North", "East", "South", "West", or "Center". Remember that BorderLayout can only lay out one component in each of these positions. In Java 1.0, your code might look like this:

```
this.add("South", b);
```

In Java 1.1, there is another two-argument form of add() that is preferred. This form takes an arbitrary layout "constraint" object as the second argument. If you are using Java 1.1, therefore, the code should look like this:

```
this.add(b, "South");
```

BorderLayout does not honor the preferred sizes of the components it manages. Components specified laid out "North" or "South" are made as wide as the container, and retain their preferred height. "East" and "West" components are made as high as the container (minus the heights of the top and bottom components) and retain their preferred width. The "Center" component is made as large as whatever space remains in the center of the container after the specified number of pixels of horizontal and vertical space are allocated.

BorderLayout is the default layout manager for the Frame, Dialog, and Window containers. If you do not explicitly specify a layout manager for these containers, they use a BorderLayout configured to leave no horizontal or vertical space between components.

Example 6-4 shows a simple applet that arranges five buttons within a BorderLayout. Figure 6-6 shows the output of this program.

Example 6-4: BorderLayoutExample.java

```
import java.applet.*;
import java.awt.*;

public class BorderLayoutExample extends Applet {
  String[] borders = {"North", "East", "South", "West", "Center"};
  public void init() {
    // Create and specify a BorderLayout layout manager that leaves
    // 10 pixels of horizontal and vertical space between components
    this.setLayout(new BorderLayout(10, 10));
    for(int i = 0; i < 5; i++) {
      // Swap the order of these arguments in Java 1.1
      this.add(borders[i], new Button(borders[i]));
    }
  }
}
```

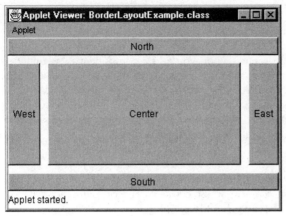

Figure 6–6: Components laid out with a BorderLayout

CardLayout

The CardLayout layout manager can manage any number of components, but it only displays one at a time. Each component is made as large as the container. CardLayout is one of the few layout managers that has methods that you invoke directly. The next( ), previous( ), first( ), last( ), and show( ) methods change the visible component. show( ) is passed the "name" of the component to be shown; this name should be specified when the component is added to the container, using the two-argument form of add( ).

Example 6-5 shows an example using CardLayout. Note the use of an anonymous inner class, ActionListener, to invoke the next( ) method of the CardLayout whenever one of the contained buttons is clicked. Because this program only displays a single, large button, it is not pictured here.

Example 6–5: CardLayoutExample.java

```
import java.applet.*;
import java.awt.*;
import java.awt.event.*;

public class CardLayoutExample extends Applet {
  public void init() {
    // Create a layout manager, and save a reference to it for future use.
    // This CardLayout leaves 10 pixels margins around the component.
    final CardLayout cardlayout = new CardLayout(10, 10);
    // Specify the layout manager for the applet
    this.setLayout(cardlayout);
    // Create a listener to invoke the next() method of card layout.
    ActionListener listener = new ActionListener() {
      public void actionPerformed(ActionEvent e) {  // When button is clicked
        cardlayout.next(CardLayoutExample.this);    // display the next one.
      }
    };
    for(int i = 1; i <= 9; i++) {
      Button b = new Button("Button #" + i);
      b.addActionListener(listener);
```

Example 6–5: CardLayoutExample.java (continued)

```
        this.add("Button" + i, b);   // Specify a name for each component
    }
  }
}
```

GridBagLayout

GridBagLayout is the most flexible and powerful of the AWT layout managers, but is also the most complicated, and sometimes the most frustrating. It arranges components according to a number of constraints, which are stored in a GridBag-Constraints object. In Java 1.1, you pass a GridBagConstraints object to the add() method, along with the component to be added. In Java 1.0, however, you must specify the constraints object for a component by calling the setConstraints() method of the GridBagLayout itself.

The basic GridBagLayout layout policy is to arrange components at specified positions in a grid. The grid may be of arbitrary size, and the rows and columns of the grid may be of arbitrary heights and widths. A component laid out in this grid may occupy more than one row or column. The gridx and gridy fields of GridBag-Constraints specify the position of the component in the grid, and the gridwidth and gridheight fields specify the number of columns and rows, respectively, that the component occupies in the grid. The insets field specifies the margins that should be left around each individual component, while fill specifies whether and how a component should grow when there is more space available for it than it needs for its default size. The anchor field specifies how a component should be positioned when there is more space available than it uses. GridBagConstraints defines a number of constants that are legal values for these last two fields. Finally, weightx and weighty specify how extra horizontal and vertical space should be distributed among the components when the container is resized. Consult reference material on GridBagConstraints for more details.

Example 6-6 shows a program that uses the GridBagLayout to produce the layout pictured in Figure 6-7. Note that the program reuses a single GridBagConstraints object, which is perfectly legal. To convert this program to run in a Java 1.0 browser, you have to pass the constraints object to the setConstraints() method of the layout manager.

Example 6–6: GridBagLayoutExample.java

```
import java.applet.*;
import java.awt.*;

public class GridBagLayoutExample extends Applet {
  public void init() {
    // Create and specify a layout manager
    this.setLayout(new GridBagLayout());

    // Create a constraints object, and specify some default values
    GridBagConstraints c = new GridBagConstraints();
    c.fill = GridBagConstraints.BOTH;   // components grow in both dimensions
    c.insets = new Insets(5,5,5,5);     // 5-pixel margins on all sides
```

Graphical User Interfaces

Example 6-6: GridBagLayoutExample.java (continued)

```
    // Create and add a bunch of buttons, specifying different grid
    // position, and size for each.
    // Give the first button a resize weight of 1.0 and all others
    // a weight of 0.0.  The first button will get all extra space.
    c.gridx = 0; c.gridy = 0; c.gridwidth = 4; c.gridheight=4;
    c.weightx = c.weighty = 1.0;
    this.add(new Button("Button #1"), c);

    c.gridx = 4; c.gridy = 0; c.gridwidth = 1; c.gridheight=1;
    c.weightx = c.weighty = 0.0;
    this.add(new Button("Button #2"), c);

    c.gridx = 4; c.gridy = 1; c.gridwidth = 1; c.gridheight=1;
    this.add(new Button("Button #3"), c);

    c.gridx = 4; c.gridy = 2; c.gridwidth = 1; c.gridheight=2;
    this.add(new Button("Button #4"), c);

    c.gridx = 0; c.gridy = 4; c.gridwidth = 1; c.gridheight=1;
    this.add(new Button("Button #5"), c);

    c.gridx = 2; c.gridy = 4; c.gridwidth = 1; c.gridheight=1;
    this.add(new Button("Button #6"), c);

    c.gridx = 3; c.gridy = 4; c.gridwidth = 2; c.gridheight=1;
    this.add(new Button("Button #7"), c);

    c.gridx = 1; c.gridy = 5; c.gridwidth = 1; c.gridheight=1;
    this.add(new Button("Button #8"), c);

    c.gridx = 3; c.gridy = 5; c.gridwidth = 1; c.gridheight=1;
    this.add(new Button("Button #9"), c);
  }
}
```

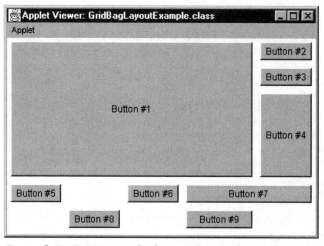

Figure 6-7: Components laid out with a GridBagLayout

Hardcoded Layout

All AWT containers have a default layout manager. If you set this manager to `null`, however, you can arrange components within a container however you like. You do this by calling the `setBounds()` method of each component, or, in Java 1.0, by calling the now deprecated `reshape()` method. Note that this technique does not work if any layout manager is specified because the layout manager resizes and repositions all of the components in a container.

Before using this technique, you should understand that there are a number of good reasons not to hardcode component sizes and positions. First, since components have a platform-dependent look and feel, they may have different sizes on different platforms. Similarly, fonts differ somewhat from platform to platform and this can affect the sizes of components. And finally, hardcoding component sizes and positions doesn't allow for customization (using the user's preferred font, for example) or internationalization (translating text in your GUI into other languages).

Nevertheless, there may be times when layout management becomes frustrating enough that you resort to hardcoded component sizes and positions. Example 6-7 is a simple program that does this; it is pictured in Figure 6-8. Note that this example overrides the `getPreferredSize()` method to report the preferred size of the container. This is functionality that is usually provided by the layout manager. In the absence of a manager, we must determine the preferred size of the container ourselves. `getPreferredSize()` is not actually necessary when the container is an `Applet`, as it is here, because an applet has a fixed size assigned by the Web browser or applet viewer. If we were hardcoding the positions of components within a `Panel`, however, the `getPreferredSize()` method would be very important.

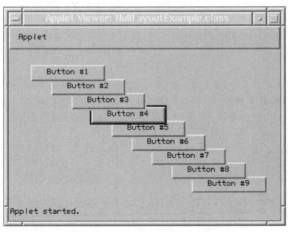

Figure 6–8: Hardcoded component positions

Example 6-7: NullLayoutExample.java

```java
import java.applet.*;
import java.awt.*;

public class NullLayoutExample extends Applet {
  public void init() {
    // Get rid of the default layout manager.
    // We'll arrange the components ourself.
    this.setLayout(null);
    for(int i = 1; i <= 9; i++) {
      Button b = new Button("Button #" + i);
      b.setBounds(i*26, i*18, 100, 25); // use reshape() in Java 1.1
      this.add(b);
    }
  }
  public Dimension getPreferredSize() { return new Dimension(350, 225); }
}
```

Creating Custom Layout Managers

When none of the pre-defined AWT layout managers is appropriate for the GUI you want to implement, you have the option of writing your own custom layout manager. This is actually easier to do that it might seem. The primary method of interest is layoutContainer(), which the container calls when it wants the components it contains to be laid out. This method should loop through the components contained in that container and set the size and position of each one, using set-Bounds() in Java 1.1 or reshape() in Java 1.0. This method may call preferred-Size() on each component to determine the size it would like to be.

The other important method is preferredLayoutSize(). This method should return the preferred size of the container. Typically this is the size required to arrange all of the components at their preferred sizes. The minimumLayoutSize() method is similar, in that it should return the minimum allowable size for the container. Finally, if your layout manager is interested in constraints specified when the add() method is called to add a component to a container, it can define the addLayoutComponent() method.

Example 6-8 is an implementation of the LayoutManager2 interface that arranges components in a column. Unlike a one-column GridLayout, however, this layout manager does not force all components to be the same size. Figure 6-9 shows some components arranged using this custom layout manager.

Example 6-8: ColumnLayout.java

```java
import java.awt.*;

/**
 * This LayoutManager arranges the components into a column.
 * Components are always given their preferred size.
 *
 * When you create a ColumnLayout, you may specify four values:
 *   margin_height -- how much space to leave on top and bottom
 *   margin_width -- how much space to leave on left and right
 *   spacing -- how much vertical space to leave between items
 *   alignment -- the horizontal position of the components:
```

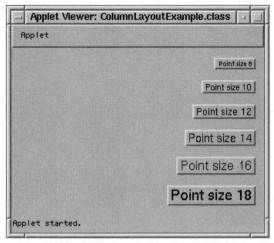

Figure 6-9: Component laid out with a custom layout manager

Example 6-8: ColumnLayout.java (continued)

```
*        ColumnLayout.LEFT -- left-justify the components
*        ColumnLayout.CENTER -- horizontally center the components
*        ColumnLayout.RIGHT -- right-justify the components
*
* You never call the methods of a ColumnLayout object.  Just create one
* and make it the layout manager for your container by passing it to
* the addLayout() method of the Container object.
*/
public class ColumnLayout implements LayoutManager2 {
  protected int margin_height;
  protected int margin_width;
  protected int spacing;
  protected int alignment;

  // Constants for the alignment argument to the constructor.
  public static final int LEFT = 0;
  public static final int CENTER = 1;
  public static final int RIGHT = 2;

  /** The constructor.  See comment above for meanings of these arguments */
  public ColumnLayout(int margin_height, int margin_width,
                      int spacing, int alignment)  {
    this.margin_height = margin_height;
    this.margin_width = margin_width;
    this.spacing = spacing;
    this.alignment = alignment;
  }

  /** A default constructor that creates a ColumnLayout using 5-pixel
   *  margin width and height, 5-pixel spacing, and left alignment */
  public ColumnLayout() { this(5, 5, 5, LEFT); }

  /** The method that actually performs the layout.  Called by the Container */
  public void layoutContainer(Container parent) {
    Insets insets = parent.getInsets();
```

Example 6-8: ColumnLayout.java (continued)

```
        Dimension parent_size = parent.getSize();
        Component kid;
        int nkids = parent.getComponentCount();
        int x0 = insets.left + margin_width;
        int x;
        int y = insets.top + margin_height;

        for(int i = 0; i < nkids; i++) {
          kid = parent.getComponent(i);
          if (!kid.isVisible()) continue;
          Dimension pref = kid.getPreferredSize();
          switch(alignment) {
          default:
          case LEFT:   x = x0; break;
          case CENTER: x = x0 + (parent_size.width - pref.width)/2; break;
          case RIGHT:  x = parent_size.width-insets.right-margin_width-pref.width;
                       break;
          }
          kid.setBounds(x, y, pref.width, pref.height);
          y += pref.height + spacing;
        }
    }

    /** The Container calls this to find out how big the layout should to be */
    public Dimension preferredLayoutSize(Container parent) {
      return layoutSize(parent, 1);
    }
    /** The Container calls this to find out how big the layout must be */
    public Dimension minimumLayoutSize(Container parent) {
      return layoutSize(parent, 2);
    }
    /** The Container calls this to find out how big the layout can be */
    public Dimension maximumLayoutSize(Container parent) {
      return layoutSize(parent, 3);
    }

    protected Dimension layoutSize(Container parent, int sizetype) {
      int nkids = parent.getComponentCount();
      Dimension size = new Dimension(0,0);
      Insets insets = parent.getInsets();
      int num_visible_kids = 0;

      // Compute maximum width and total height of all visible kids
      for(int i = 0; i < nkids; i++) {
        Component kid = parent.getComponent(i);
        Dimension d;
        if (!kid.isVisible()) continue;
        num_visible_kids++;
        if (sizetype == 1) d = kid.getPreferredSize();
        else if (sizetype == 2) d = kid.getMinimumSize();
        else d = kid.getMaximumSize();
        if (d.width > size.width) size.width = d.width;
        size.height += d.height;
      }

      // Now add in margins and stuff
      size.width += insets.left + insets.right + 2*margin_width;
      size.height += insets.top + insets.bottom + 2*margin_height;
```

Example 6–8: ColumnLayout.java (continued)

```
    if (num_visible_kids > 1)
      size.height += (num_visible_kids - 1) * spacing;
    return size;
  }

  // Other LayoutManager(2) methods that are unused by this class
  public void addLayoutComponent(String constraint, Component comp) {}
  public void addLayoutComponent(Component comp, Object constraint) {}
  public void removeLayoutComponent(Component comp) {}
  public void invalidateLayout(Container parent) {}
  public float getLayoutAlignmentX(Container parent) { return 0.5f; }
  public float getLayoutAlignmentY(Container parent) { return 0.5f; }
}
```

Frames

Most of the examples we've seen so far in this book have been applets. An applet is a subclass of the Panel container, and therefore implicitly has a display area in which it can draw graphics or display a GUI. If a standalone application wants to display graphics or implement a GUI, it must explicitly create its own window, which is done with the Frame object.

Because a Frame represents a top-level window, it behaves somewhat differently than other AWT components. In order to actually make a Frame appear on the screen, you must call its show() method. But before making a window appear, you should set its size. There are two ways to do this. One is to call setSize() (or resize() in Java 1.0) to set an explicit size. The other technique is to call pack(). This method does several things, but essentially, it queries the preferred size of the window, and sets its size to that value. If a Frame contains GUI components, pack() is probably the best way to set its size. If the frame is just used for drawing, or contains some kind of custom component with no preferred size, you'll have to use setSize() to explicitly set a size for the window.

Example 6-9 shows our simple Scribble applet, modified so that it can also be run as a standalone application. Note the use of the anonymous inner class to catch WindowEvent.WINDOW_CLOSING event types. This event signals that the user has requested that the window be closed in some platform-dependent way (such as typing **Alt-F4** on a Windows system). If we did not handle this event, there would be no way to exit the application.

Example 6-9: StandaloneScribble.java

```
import java.applet.*;
import java.awt.*;
import java.awt.event.*;

/** An applet that can also run as a standalone application */
public class StandaloneScribble extends Applet {
  /**
   * The main() method.  If this program is invoked as an application, this
   * method will create the necessary window, add the applet to it, and
   * call init(), below.  Note that Frame uses a PanelLayout by default.
   */
```

Example 6-9: StandaloneScribble.java (continued)

```
public static void main(String[] args) {
  Frame f = new Frame();                          // Create a window
  Applet a = new StandaloneScribble();            // Create the applet panel
  f.add(a, "Center");                             // Add applet to window
  a.init();                                       // Initialize the applet
  f.setSize(400, 400);                            // Set the size of the window
  f.show();                                       // Make the window visible
  f.addWindowListener(new WindowAdapter() {       // Handle window close requests
    public void windowClosing(WindowEvent e) { System.exit(0); }
  });
}


/**
 * The init() method.  If the program is invoked as an applet, the browser
 * allocates screen space for it and calls this method to set things up
 */
public void init() {
  // Define, instantiate and register a MouseListener object
  this.addMouseListener(new MouseAdapter() {
    public void mousePressed(MouseEvent e) {
      lastx = e.getX();
      lasty = e.getY();
    }
  });

  // Define, instantiate and register a MouseMotionListener object
  this.addMouseMotionListener(new MouseMotionAdapter() {
    public void mouseDragged(MouseEvent e) {
      Graphics g = getGraphics();
      int x = e.getX(), y = e.getY();
      g.setColor(Color.black);
      g.drawLine(lastx, lasty, x, y);
      lastx = x; lasty = y;
    }
  });

  // Create a clear button
  Button b = new Button("Clear");
  // Define, instantiate, and register a listener to handle button presses
  b.addActionListener(new ActionListener() {
    public void actionPerformed(ActionEvent e) {  // clear the scribble
      Graphics g = getGraphics();
      g.setColor(getBackground());
      g.fillRect(0, 0, getSize().width, getSize().height);
    }
  });
  // And add the button to the applet
  this.add(b);
}

protected int lastx, lasty;  // Coordinates of last mouse click
}
```

A Closeable Frame

When you create a Frame, you are creating a platform-dependent native window that appears to the user like all other application windows on his or her system. This window probably contains a close control of some sort, or provides some other method (such as **Alt-F4**) by which the user can ask that the window be closed. Because a Frame appears just like all other native windows, it should behave like them. It is poor programming practice not to register a Window-Listener object to react to the windowClosing() event. However, registering this listener for every Frame you create can become tedious. Example 6-10 shows a solution. This CloseableFrame subclass of Frame is a WindowListener, and closes itself when its windowClosing() method is invoked. You may find this class useful in your own GUI-based Java applications.

Example 6-10: CloseableFrame.java

```java
import java.awt.*;
import java.awt.event.*;

/**
 * This class is a convenient subclass of Frame that knows how to
 * handled the WindowClosing event generated when the user requests
 * that the window be closed.  By default it simply closes itself,
 * which makes it useful for things like modeless dialogs that can be
 * closed without affecting the rest of the application.  Subclasses
 * of CloseableFrame can override the windowClosing() method if they
 * want to perform additional actions.  Applications that use the
 * CloseableFrame class for a main window may want to exit when a
 * CloseableFrame actually closes.  They can do this by overriding
 * windowClosed() or by registering a separate WindowListener to
 * receive the windowClosed() event.
 **/
public class CloseableFrame extends Frame implements WindowListener {
  // There are two versions of the constructor.  Both register the Frame
  // as its own WindowListener object
  public CloseableFrame() { this.addWindowListener(this); }
  public CloseableFrame(String title) {
    super(title);
    this.addWindowListener(this);
  }

  // These are the methods of the WindowListener object.  Only
  // windowClosing() is implemented
  public void windowClosing(WindowEvent e) { this.dispose(); }
  public void windowOpened(WindowEvent e) {}
  public void windowClosed(WindowEvent e) {}
  public void windowIconified(WindowEvent e) {}
  public void windowDeiconified(WindowEvent e) {}
  public void windowActivated(WindowEvent e) {}
  public void windowDeactivated(WindowEvent e) {}
}
```

Menus

An important features of the `Frame` class is that it is the only AWT container that can display a menubar. Java 1.1 adds popup menus to the AWT's menuing capabilities; these menus are not restricted to `Frame` objects; they can be displayed over any container or component.

Creating both pulldown and popup menus is remarkably straightforward. The first step in creating pulldown menus is to create a `MenuBar` object and display it in a `Frame` by calling the `setMenuBar()` method of the frame. The next step is to create the necessary menu panes, which are represented by `Menu` objects, and add them to the menubar with its `add()` method. On systems that support tear-off menus, a simple flag to the `Menu()` constructor specifies whether the menu should be a tear-off or not. If one of your menus is a **Help** menu, you should also pass it to the `setHelpMenu()` method to indicate this fact—on some platforms, the **Help** menu is treated specially. Finally, you create `MenuItem` and `CheckboxMenuItem` objects and add them to each menu pane by calling the `add()` method of the appropriate `Menu` object.

Creating a popup menu is even simpler. First you create a `PopupMenu` object and then add `MenuItem` and `CheckboxMenuItem` objects to it, just as you would add them to a pulldown menu pane. You must associate your popup menu with the component or container it is going to pop up over by passing it to the `add()` method of that component. Finally, you must arrange for your popup menu to "pop up" when the appropriate event arrives. You make the menu appear by calling its `show()` method; you can test for the appropriate platform-dependent event with the `isPopupTrigger()` method of the `MouseEvent` class.

Event handling for menus is also simple. `MenuItem` behaves much like `Button` does, and `CheckboxMenuItem` is much like `Checkbox`. In Java 1.0, you can handle menu events in the `action()` method of a `Frame`. In Java 1.1, you handle menu events by registering an event listener object—often registering the same object for all of the items in a menu.

Example 6-11 adds menus to the code shown in Example 6-9. When run as an applet, the program displays a popup menu. When run as a standalone application, however, it displays pulldown menus instead.

Example 6–11: MenuScribble.java

```
import java.applet.*;
import java.awt.*;
import java.awt.event.*;

/** An applet with a popup menu or an application with pulldown menus */
public class MenuScribble extends Applet implements ActionListener {
    /**
     * The main() method.  If this program is invoked as an application, this
     * method will create a window and pulldown menu system for it.
     */
    public static void main(String[] args) {
        Frame f = new Frame();                          // Create a window
        MenuScribble applet = new MenuScribble();       // Create the applet panel
        f.add(applet, "Center");                        // Add applet to window
        applet.init();                                  // Initialize the applet
```

Example 6–11: MenuScribble.java (continued)

```
    // Create a menubar and tell the frame about it
    MenuBar menubar = new MenuBar();
    f.setMenuBar(menubar);

    // Create three pulldown menus for the menubar
    Menu file = new Menu("File");
    Menu colors = new Menu("Colors");
    Menu help = new Menu("Help");

    // Add the menus to the bar, and treat Help menu specially.
    menubar.add(file);
    menubar.add(colors);
    menubar.add(help);
    menubar.setHelpMenu(help);

    // Add two items, with a keyboard shortcuts to the File menu
    MenuItem clear = new MenuItem("Clear", new MenuShortcut(KeyEvent.VK_C));
    clear.addActionListener(applet);   // Say who's listening for the events
    clear.setActionCommand("clear");   // A detail to go along with the events
    file.add(clear);                   // Add item to menu pane
    MenuItem quit = new MenuItem("Quit", new MenuShortcut(KeyEvent.VK_Q));
    quit.addActionListener(applet);
    quit.setActionCommand("quit");
    file.add(quit);

    // Add items to the other two menus, this time using a  convenience
    // method defined below.  Note use of new anonymous array syntax.
    createMenuItems(colors, applet,
                    new String[] { "Red", "Green", "Blue", "Black" },
                    new String[] { "red", "green", "blue", "black" },
                    new int[] { KeyEvent.VK_R, KeyEvent.VK_G,
                                KeyEvent.VK_B, KeyEvent.VK_L });
    createMenuItems(help, applet,
                    new String[] { "About" }, new String[] {"about"},
                    new int[] { KeyEvent.VK_A });

    // Handle window close requests
    f.addWindowListener(new WindowAdapter() {
      public void windowClosing(WindowEvent e) { System.exit(0); }
    });

    f.setSize(400, 400);    // Set the size of the window
    f.show();               // Finally, pop the window up.
}

/**
 * The init() method.  If the program is invoked as an applet, the browser
 * allocates screen space for it and calls this method to set things up.
 * If running as an applet, this method creates a popup menu and adds
 * it to the applet.
 */
public void init() {
  // If we are not in a frame (i.e. we are an applet), create a popup menu
  if (!(this.getParent() instanceof Frame)) {
    // Create the popup menu
    popup = new PopupMenu("File");
    // Add items to it using the convenience routine below
    createMenuItems(popup, this,
```

Example 6-11: MenuScribble.java (continued)

```
                         new String[] {"Clear", "Red", "Green", "Blue", "Black"},
                         new String[] {"clear", "red", "green", "blue", "black"},
                         new int[] { KeyEvent.VK_C, KeyEvent.VK_R, KeyEvent.VK_G,
                                     KeyEvent.VK_B, KeyEvent.VK_L });
    // Add the popup menu to the component it will appear over.
    this.add(popup);
  }

  // Define, instantiate and register the Listener objects for scribbling
  this.addMouseListener(new MouseAdapter() {
    public void mousePressed(MouseEvent e) {
      lastx = e.getX(); lasty = e.getY();
    }
  });
  this.addMouseMotionListener(new MouseMotionAdapter() {
    public void mouseDragged(MouseEvent e) {
      Graphics g = getGraphics();
      int x = e.getX(), y = e.getY();
      g.setColor(color);                   // draw with the specified color
      g.drawLine(lastx, lasty, x, y);
      lastx = x; lasty = y;
    }
  });
}

/**
 * This is the convenience routine for adding menu items to a menu pane.
 * It works for pulldown or popup menu panes, since PopupMenu extends Menu.
 */
protected static void createMenuItems(Menu pane, ActionListener listener,
                                      String[] labels, String[] commands,
                                      int[] shortcuts) {
  for(int i = 0; i < labels.length; i++) {
    MenuItem mi = new MenuItem(labels[i]);
    mi.addActionListener(listener);
    if ((commands != null) && (commands[i] != null))
      mi.setActionCommand(commands[i]);
    if ((shortcuts != null) && (shortcuts[i] != 0))
      mi.setShortcut(new MenuShortcut(shortcuts[i]));
    pane.add(mi);
  }
}

/**
 * This method is required to make the popup menu, if any, pop up.  It
 * uses the low-level Java 1.1 event handling mechanism to test all mouse
 * events (except mouse motion events) to see if they are the platform-
 * dependent popup menu trigger.  If so, it calls show() to pop the
 * popup up.  If not, it passes the event to the superclass version of
 * this method so that it is dispatched as usual and can be passed to
 * the listener object registered by the init method for scribbling.
 */
public void processMouseEvent(MouseEvent e) {
  if ((popup != null) && e.isPopupTrigger())
    popup.show(this, e.getX(), e.getY());
  else super.processMouseEvent(e);
}
```

Example 6-11: MenuScribble.java (continued)

```
/**
 * This is the method defined by the ActionListener interface. All
 * the menu item commands are handled here because the applet was specified
 * as the listener for all menu items. Note the use of getActionCommand()
 * to determine the command string registered with the individual items.
 */
public void actionPerformed(ActionEvent e) {
  String cmd = e.getActionCommand();
  if (cmd.equals("quit")) System.exit(0);    // Don't do this in an applet
  else if (cmd.equals("clear")) clear();     // defined below
  else if (cmd.equals("about")) /* not yet implemented */ ;
  else if (cmd.equals("red")) color = Color.red;
  else if (cmd.equals("green")) color = Color.green;
  else if (cmd.equals("blue")) color = Color.blue;
  else if (cmd.equals("black")) color = color.black;
}

/** Clear the applet area.  Used by actionPerformed() above */
protected void clear() {
  Graphics g = this.getGraphics();
  g.setColor(this.getBackground());
  g.fillRect(0, 0, this.getSize().width, this.getSize().height);
}

// Here are the instance variables for this program
protected int lastx, lasty;        // Coordinates of last mouse click
protected Color color = Color.black; // Current drawing color
protected PopupMenu popup;
}
```

Dialogs

As we've seen, the Frame class is suitable for top-level application windows with menubars. Dialog boxes also appear in windows of their own, but they typically do not have menubars, and often appear in somewhat restricted windows. On some platforms, for example, dialog box windows do not have resize handles. Because of the distinction between these types of windows, dialog boxes in Java are implemented using the Dialog class. When you create a Dialog, you must specify the Frame that it is associated with. You must also specify whether it should be a modal or non-modal dialog. Modal dialogs block input to the rest of the application until they are dismissed.

To create a custom dialog for an applet or application in Java 1.0, you have to subclass Dialog because of the requirements of the Java 1.0 event model. In Java 1.1, however, you can create custom dialogs without subclassing. Creating a GUI within a dialog box is just like creating a GUI within a Frame, except that you can't use pulldown menus.

While many applications need to display one or two custom dialogs, most applications repeatedly need to display certain simple types of dialog boxes. One of these is the "information dialog" that simply displays a message to the user and sits there until the user dismisses it. Example 6-12 shows how you can write a reusable Dialog subclass that does just this. A dialog box produced with this class is pictured in Figure 6-10.

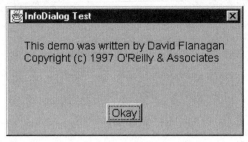

Figure 6-10: A simple information dialog

The InfoDialog() constructor lets you specify the message to be displayed. Once the dialog is created, you pop it up by calling show(). The dialog has a single button, which pops the dialog down when clicked. Note the use of a BorderLayout layout manager and a nested Panel that uses a FlowLayout in order to center the button at the bottom of the dialog window. The MultiLineLabel class used by this code is a custom component that is developed in Example 6-14. Note that this example uses the deprecated Java 1.0 event model so that it is useful with both Java 1.0 and Java 1.1 applets and applications. The action() method responds to button clicks by calling hide() on the Dialog to pop it down and calling dispose() to free up the native window resource associated with it. Once dispose() has been called, the Dialog (or Frame) cannot be used again. The main() method is a simple test program that demonstrates how the dialog class might be used.

Example 6-12: InfoDialog.java

```java
import java.awt.*;

public class InfoDialog extends Dialog {
    protected Button button;          // The okay button of the dialog
    protected MultiLineLabel label;   // The message displayed by the dialog

    public InfoDialog(Frame parent, String title, String message) {
        // Create a non-modal dialog with the specified title and parent
        super(parent, title, false);

        // Create and use a BorderLayout manager with 15 pixel spacing
        this.setLayout(new BorderLayout(15, 15));

        // Create the message component and add it to the window
        // MultiLineLabel is a custom component defined later in this chapter
        label = new MultiLineLabel(message, 20, 20);
        this.add("Center", label);

        // Create an Okay button in a Panel; add the Panel to the window
        // Use a FlowLayout to center the button in the panel and give it margins.
        // Note the nested use of containers and layout managers.
        button = new Button("Okay");
        Panel p = new Panel();
        p.setLayout(new FlowLayout(FlowLayout.CENTER, 15, 15));
        p.add(button);
        this.add("South", p);
```

Example 6-12: InfoDialog.java (continued)

```
    // Set the dialog size to the preferred size of its components
    this.pack();
  }

  // Pop down the window when the button is clicked.  Note 1.0 event model
  public boolean action(Event e, Object arg) {
    if (e.target == button) {
      this.hide();      // Pop the dialog down
      this.dispose();   // Destroy it.  Cannot be shown again after disposed
      return true;
    }
    else return false;
  }

  /**
   * A main method that demonstrates how to use this class, and allows testing
   */
  public static void main(String[] args) {
    // Create, size, and show a frame because dialogs require a frame parent.
    Frame f = new Frame("InfoDialog Test");
    f.resize(100, 100);  // Use setSize() in Java 1.1
    f.show();

    // Create an instance of InfoDialog, with title and message specified
    InfoDialog d = new InfoDialog(f, "InfoDialog Test",
                        "This demo was written by David Flanagan\n" +
                        "Copyright (c) 1997 O'Reilly & Associates");

    // And pop it up.  It will pop itself down automatically.
    d.show();
  }
}
```

A Dialog with User Response

Another commonly used type of dialog box displays a message to the user and asks for a simple **Yes/No/Cancel** response. Example 6-13 shows a subclass of Dialog that can be used to display this sort of dialog and get the user's response. Figure 6-11 shows a sample dialog created with this class.

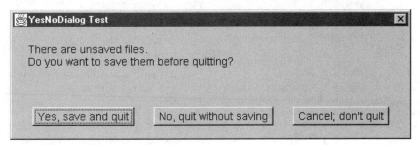

Figure 6-11: A yes-or-no dialog

This example uses the Java 1.1 event model, and does some fairly sophisticated things with it. Because the dialog must return the user's response to the question it displays, it generates an ActionEvent, just as a button does. For this reason, it has addActionListener() and removeActionListener() methods, which are implemented quite easily with the help of the AWTEventMulticaster class. The dialog can display up to three buttons. The action listener for these buttons makes a copy of the ActionEvent generated by the button, substitutes the dialog for the button as the event "source," and passes the event on to the listeners on its own list. The event sent to a listener registered on the dialog has an "action command" of "yes," "no," or "cancel," depending on which of the three buttons was clicked. The main() method is a simple application that demonstrates the use of the class.

Example 6–13: YesNoDialog.java

```java
import java.awt.*;
import java.awt.event.*;

public class YesNoDialog extends Dialog {
    public YesNoDialog(Frame parent, String title, String message,
                       String yes_label, String no_label, String cancel_label)
    {
        // Create a modal dialog with the specified title and parent
        super(parent, title, true);

        // Specify a LayoutManager for it
        this.setLayout(new BorderLayout(15, 15));

        // Put the message label in the middle of the window.
        // Note: MultiLineLabel is a custom component defined later in the chapter
        this.add("Center", new MultiLineLabel(message, 20, 20));

        // Create an action listener for use by the buttons of the dialog.
        // When a button is pressed, this listener first closes the dialog box.
        // Then, it passes the event on to the listeners registered for the
        // dialog box, after changing the event source from the individual button
        // to the dialog box itself.  Since events are immutable, it must create
        // a new ActionEvent object in order to change the source.  It passes
        // this new event to the listeners by calling actionPerformed() on the
        // AWTEventMulticaster object stored in the listeners field (see below).
        ActionListener listener = new ActionListener() {
            public void actionPerformed(ActionEvent e) {
                YesNoDialog.this.dispose();   // pop down dialog
                if (listeners != null)        // notify all registered listeners
                    listeners.actionPerformed(new ActionEvent(YesNoDialog.this,
                                                   e.getID(),
                                                   e.getActionCommand()));
            }
        };

        // Create a panel for the dialog buttons and put it at the bottom
        // of the dialog.  Specify a FlowLayout layout manager for it.
        Panel buttonbox = new Panel();
        buttonbox.setLayout(new FlowLayout(FlowLayout.CENTER, 25, 15));
        this.add("South", buttonbox);

        // Create each specified button, specifying the action listener
        // and action command for each, and adding them to the buttonbox
        if (yes_label != null) {              // if a label was specified...
```

Example 6-13: YesNoDialog.java (continued)

```
    Button yes = new Button(yes_label);       //   create button
    yes.setActionCommand("yes");              //   set action command
    yes.addActionListener(listener);          //   set listener
    buttonbox.add(yes);                       //   add button to the panel
  }
  if (no_label != null) {
    Button no = new Button(no_label);
    no.setActionCommand("no");
    no.addActionListener(listener);
    buttonbox.add(no);
  }
  if (cancel_label != null) {
    Button cancel = new Button(cancel_label);
    cancel.setActionCommand("cancel");
    cancel.addActionListener(listener);
    buttonbox.add(cancel);
  }

  // Finally, set the dialog to its preferred size.
  this.pack();
}

/** This field will hold a list of registered ActionListeners, thanks
 *  to the magic of AWTEventMulticaster */
protected ActionListener listeners = null;

/** Register an action listener to be notified when a button is pressed
 *  AWTEventMulticaster makes this easy. */
public void addActionListener(ActionListener l) {
  listeners = AWTEventMulticaster.add(listeners, l);
}

/** Remove an action listener from our list of interested listeners */
public void removeActionListener(ActionListener l) {
  listeners = AWTEventMulticaster.remove(listeners, l);
}

/**
 * A main method that demonstrates how to use this class, and allows testing
 */
public static void main(String[] args) {
  // Create, size, and show a frame because dialogs require a frame parent.
  Frame f = new Frame("YesNoDialog Test");
  f.setSize(100, 100);
  f.show();

  // Create an instance of InfoDialog, with title and message specified
  YesNoDialog d =
    new YesNoDialog(f, "YesNoDialog Test",
                    "There are unsaved files.\n" +
                    "Do you want to save them before quitting?",
                    "Yes, save and quit",
                    "No, quit without saving",
                    "Cancel; don't quit");

  // Register an action listener for the dialog.  This one just prints
  // the results out to the console.
  d.addActionListener(new ActionListener() {
```

*Graphical
User Interfaces*

Example 6-13: YesNoDialog.java (continued)

```
    public void actionPerformed(ActionEvent e) {
      System.out.println("The user pressed: " + e.getActionCommand());
    }
  });

  // Now pop the dialog up.  It will pop itself down automatically.
  d.show();
  }
}
```

Custom Components

The previous two examples have shown how to create Dialog subclasses that are useful, reusable components. In this sense, the InfoDialog and YesNoDialog classes are "custom components." Both of these examples have used a MultiLineLabel class that displays multiple static lines of text, which is something that the AWT Label class cannot do. The code for MultiLineLabel is shown in Example 6-14. This is what is usually meant by the phrase "custom component"—a class that has its own paint() method to draw itself and handles its own events (if it handles any events) at a low-level.

Much of the code in this example is taken up with the mechanics of breaking the label into separate lines and measuring the size of each of those lines. The most important code, however, is in several required methods that make any component work correctly. First, there is the paint() method, of course. All components (including applets) use this method to display themselves on the screen. Second, the getPreferredSize() and getMinimumSize() methods return the preferred and minimum sizes for the component. These methods must be implemented so that layout managers can correctly lay the component out. (Note, though, that for compatibility with Java 1.0, this example defines the deprecated preferredSize() and minimumSize() methods instead.)

MultiLineLabel extends Canvas, which is a blank component intended primarily for subclassing. When a component is a subclass of Canvas, it is typically given its own native window in the underlying window system. In Java 1.1, however, it is possible to define "lightweight" custom components by extending Component instead of Canvas. A lightweight component does not have its own native window in the underlying window system.

Example 6-14: MultiLineLabel.java

```
import java.awt.*;
import java.util.*;

/**
 * A custom component that displays multiple lines of text with specified
 * margins and alignment.  In Java 1.1, we could extend Component instead
 * of Canvas, making this a more efficient "Lightweight component"
 */
public class MultiLineLabel extends Canvas {
  // User-specified attributes
  protected String label;              // The label, not broken into lines
```

Example 6-14: MultiLineLabel.java (continued)

```java
  protected int margin_width;          // Left and right margins
  protected int margin_height;         // Top and bottom margins
  protected int alignment;             // The alignment of the text.
  public static final int LEFT = 0, CENTER = 1, RIGHT = 2; // alignment values
  // Computed state values
  protected int num_lines;             // The number of lines
  protected String[] lines;            // The label, broken into lines
  protected int[] line_widths;         // How wide each line is
  protected int max_width;             // The width of the widest line
  protected int line_height;           // Total height of the font
  protected int line_ascent;           // Font height above baseline
  protected boolean measured = false;  // Have the lines been measured?

  // Here are five versions of the constructor
  public MultiLineLabel(String label, int margin_width,
                        int margin_height, int alignment) {
    this.label = label;                // Remember all the properties
    this.margin_width = margin_width;
    this.margin_height = margin_height;
    this.alignment = alignment;
    newLabel();                        // Break the label up into lines
  }
  public MultiLineLabel(String label, int margin_width, int margin_height) {
    this(label, margin_width, margin_height, LEFT);
  }
  public MultiLineLabel(String label, int alignment) {
    this(label, 10, 10, alignment);
  }
  public MultiLineLabel(String label) { this(label, 10, 10, LEFT); }
  public MultiLineLabel() { this(""); }

  // Methods to set and query the various attributes of the component
  // Note that some query methods are inherited from the superclass.
  public void setLabel(String label) {
    this.label = label;
    newLabel();            // Break the label into lines
    measured = false;      // Note that we need to measure lines
    repaint();             // Request a redraw
  }
  public void setFont(Font f) {
    super.setFont(f);      // tell our superclass about the new font
    measured = false;      // Note that we need to remeasure lines
    repaint();             // Request a redraw
  }
  public void setForeground(Color c) {
    super.setForeground(c);  // tell our superclass about the new color
    repaint();               // Request a redraw (size is unchanged)
  }
  public void setAlignment(int a) { alignment = a; repaint(); }
  public void setMarginWidth(int mw) { margin_width = mw; repaint(); }
  public void setMarginHeight(int mh) { margin_height = mh; repaint(); }
  public String getLabel() { return label; }
  public int getAlignment() { return alignment; }
  public int getMarginWidth() { return margin_width; }
  public int getMarginHeight() { return margin_height; }

  /**
   * This method is called by a layout manager when it wants to
```

Example 6-14: MultiLineLabel.java (continued)

```
 * know how big we'd like to be.  In Java 1.1, getPreferredSize() is
 * the preferred version of this method.  We use this deprecated version
 * so that this component can interoperate with 1.0 components.
 */
public Dimension preferredSize() {
  if (!measured) measure();
  return new Dimension(max_width + 2*margin_width,
                       num_lines * line_height + 2*margin_height);
}

/**
 * This method is called when the layout manager wants to know
 * the bare minimum amount of space we need to get by.
 * For Java 1.1, we'd use getMinimumSize().
 */
public Dimension minimumSize() { return preferredSize(); }

/**
 * This method draws the label (same method that applets use).
 * Note that it handles the margins and the alignment, but that
 * it doesn't have to worry about the color or font--the superclass
 * takes care of setting those in the Graphics object we're passed.
 */
public void paint(Graphics g) {
  int x, y;
  Dimension size = this.size();  // use getSize() in Java 1.1
  if (!measured) measure();
  y = line_ascent + (size.height - num_lines * line_height)/2;
  for(int i = 0; i < num_lines; i++, y += line_height) {
    switch(alignment) {
    default:
    case LEFT:   x = margin_width; break;
    case CENTER: x = (size.width - line_widths[i])/2; break;
    case RIGHT:  x = size.width - margin_width - line_widths[i]; break;
    }
    g.drawString(lines[i], x, y);
  }
}

/** This internal method breaks a specified label up into an array of lines.
 *  It uses the StringTokenizer utility class. */
protected synchronized void newLabel() {
  StringTokenizer t = new StringTokenizer(label, "\n");
  num_lines = t.countTokens();
  lines = new String[num_lines];
  line_widths = new int[num_lines];
  for(int i = 0; i < num_lines; i++) lines[i] = t.nextToken();
}

/** This internal method figures out how the font is, and how wide each
 *  line of the label is, and how wide the widest line is. */
protected synchronized void measure() {
  FontMetrics fm = this.getToolkit().getFontMetrics(this.getFont());
  line_height = fm.getHeight();
  line_ascent = fm.getAscent();
  max_width = 0;
  for(int i = 0; i < num_lines; i++) {
    line_widths[i] = fm.stringWidth(lines[i]);
```

Example 6-14: MultiLineLabel.java (continued)

```
        if (line_widths[i] > max_width) max_width = line_widths[i];
    }
    measured = true;
  }
}
```

Putting It All Together

We began this chapter with a discussion of the basic steps required to assemble a GUI and a list of the components provided by the AWT. Figure 6-1 and Figure 6-2 showed an example GUI that used all of the standard components from `java.awt`. Example 6-15 lists the code used to create that GUI. It shows how to create almost all of the standard components, and how to use the Java 1.1 event model to respond to the events they generate. The example also makes use of some of the classes developed in this chapter. It uses the `ColumnLayout` layout manager, the `MultiLineLabel` component, and the `InfoDialog` and `YesNoDialog` dialogs. It is a good, practical example of how to put all the pieces together and create a moderately-sized GUI.

Example 6-15: AllComponents.java

```java
import java.awt.*;
import java.awt.event.*;

/** A program that uses all the standard AWT components */
public class AllComponents extends Frame implements ActionListener {
  TextArea textarea;  // Events messages will be displayed here.

  /** Create the whole GUI, and set up event listeners */
  public AllComponents(String title) {
    super(title);  // set frame title.

    // Arrange to detect window close events
    this.addWindowListener(new WindowAdapter() {
      public void windowClosing(WindowEvent e) { System.exit(0); }
    });

    // Set a default font
    this.setFont(new Font("SansSerif", Font.PLAIN, 12));

    // Create the menubar.  Tell the frame about it.
    MenuBar menubar = new MenuBar();
    this.setMenuBar(menubar);

    // Create the file menu.  Add to menubar.
    Menu file = new Menu("File");
    menubar.add(file);

    // Create two items for the file menu, setting their label, shortcut,
    // action command and listener.  Add them to File menu.
    // Note that we use the frame itself as the action listener
    MenuItem open = new MenuItem("Open", new MenuShortcut(KeyEvent.VK_O));
    open.setActionCommand("open");
    open.addActionListener(this);
    file.add(open);
```

Example 6–15: AllComponents.java (continued)

```
MenuItem quit = new MenuItem("Quit", new MenuShortcut(KeyEvent.VK_Q));
quit.setActionCommand("quit");
quit.addActionListener(this);
file.add(quit);

// Create Help menu; add an item; add to menubar
// Display the help menu in a special reserved place.
Menu help = new Menu("Help");
menubar.add(help);
menubar.setHelpMenu(help);

// Create and add an item to the Help menu
MenuItem about = new MenuItem("About", new MenuShortcut(KeyEvent.VK_A));
about.setActionCommand("about");
about.addActionListener(this);
help.add(about);

// Now that we've done the menu, we can begin work on the contents of
// the frame.  Assign a BorderLayout manager with margins for this frame.
this.setLayout(new BorderLayout(10, 10));

// Create two panels to contain two columns of components.  Use our custom
// ColumnLayout layout manager for each.  Add them on the west and
// center of the frame's border layout
Panel column1 = new Panel();
column1.setLayout(new ColumnLayout(5, 10, 2, ColumnLayout.LEFT));
this.add(column1, "West");
Panel column2 = new Panel();
column2.setLayout(new ColumnLayout(5, 10, 2, ColumnLayout.LEFT));
this.add(column2, "Center");

// Create a panel to contain the buttons at the bottom of the window
// Give it a FlowLayout layout manager, and add it along the south border
Panel buttonbox = new Panel();
buttonbox.setLayout(new FlowLayout(FlowLayout.CENTER, 100, 10));
this.add(buttonbox, "South");

// Create pushbuttons and add them to the buttonbox
Button okay = new Button("Okay");
Button cancel = new Button("Cancel");
buttonbox.add(okay);
buttonbox.add(cancel);

// Handle events on the buttons
ActionListener buttonlistener = new ActionListener() {
  public void actionPerformed(ActionEvent e) {
    textarea.append("You clicked: " +
                    ((Button)e.getSource()).getLabel() + "\n");
  }
};
okay.addActionListener(buttonlistener);
cancel.addActionListener(buttonlistener);

// Now start filling the left column.
// Create a 1-line text field and add to left column, with a label
TextField textfield = new TextField(15);
column1.add(new Label("Name:"));
column1.add(textfield);
```

Example 6-15: AllComponents.java (continued)

```
// Handle events on the TextField
textfield.addActionListener(new ActionListener() {
  public void actionPerformed(ActionEvent e) {
    textarea.append("Your name is: " +
                    ((TextField)e.getSource()).getText() + "\n");
  }
});
textfield.addTextListener(new TextListener() {
  public void textValueChanged(TextEvent e) {
    textarea.append("You have typed: " +
                    ((TextField)e.getSource()).getText() + "\n");
  }
});

// Create a dropdown list or option menu of choices
Choice choice = new Choice();
choice.addItem("red");
choice.addItem("green");
choice.addItem("blue");
column1.add(new Label("Favorite color:"));
column1.add(choice);

// Handle events on this choice
choice.addItemListener(new ItemListener() {
  public void itemStateChanged(ItemEvent e) {
    textarea.append("Your favorite color is: " + e.getItem() + "\n");
  }
});

// Create checkboxes, and group them in a CheckboxGroup to give them
// "radio button" behavior.
CheckboxGroup checkbox_group = new CheckboxGroup();
Checkbox[] checkboxes = new Checkbox[3];
checkboxes[0] = new Checkbox("vanilla", checkbox_group, false);
checkboxes[1] = new Checkbox("chocolate", checkbox_group, true);
checkboxes[2] = new Checkbox("strawberry", checkbox_group, false);
column1.add(new Label("Favorite flavor:"));
for(int i = 0; i < checkboxes.length; i++) column1.add(checkboxes[i]);

// Handle events on the checkboxes
ItemListener checkbox_listener = new ItemListener() {
  public void itemStateChanged(ItemEvent e) {
    textarea.append("Your favorite flavor is: " +
                    ((Checkbox)e.getItemSelectable()).getLabel() + "\n");
  }
};
for(int i = 0; i < checkboxes.length; i++)
  checkboxes[i].addItemListener(checkbox_listener);

// Create a list of choices.
List list = new List(4, true);
list.addItem("Java"); list.addItem("C"); list.addItem("C++");
list.addItem("Smalltalk"); list.addItem("Lisp");
list.addItem("Modula-3"); list.addItem("Forth");
column1.add(new Label("Favorite languages:"));
column1.add(list);
```

Example 6-15: AllComponents.java (continued)

```java
// Handle events on this list
list.addItemListener(new ItemListener() {
  public void itemStateChanged(ItemEvent e) {
    textarea.append("Your favorite languages are: ");
    String[] languages = ((List)e.getItemSelectable()).getSelectedItems();
    for(int i = 0; i < languages.length; i++) {
      if (i > 0) textarea.append(",");
      textarea.append(languages[i]);
    }
    textarea.append("\n");
  }
});

// Create a multi-line text area in column 2
textarea = new TextArea(6, 40);
textarea.setEditable(false);
column2.add(new Label("Messages"));
column2.add(textarea);

// Create a scrollpane that displays portions of a larger component
ScrollPane scrollpane = new ScrollPane();
scrollpane.setSize(300, 150);
column2.add(new Label("Scrolling Window"));
column2.add(scrollpane);

// Create a custom MultiLineLabel with a really big font and make it
// a child of the ScrollPane container
String message =
  "/**************************************************\n" +
  " * AllComponents.java                            *\n" +
  " * Written by David Flanagan                     *\n" +
  " * Copyright (c) 1997 by O'Reilly & Associates   *\n" +
  " *                                               *\n" +
  " **************************************************/\n";
MultiLineLabel biglabel = new MultiLineLabel(message);
biglabel.setFont(new Font("Monospaced", Font.BOLD + Font.ITALIC, 24));
scrollpane.add(biglabel);
}

/** This is the action listener method that the menu items invoke */
public void actionPerformed(ActionEvent e) {
  String command = e.getActionCommand();
  if (command.equals("quit")) {
    YesNoDialog d = new YesNoDialog(this, "Really Quit?",
                                    "Are you sure you want to quit?",
                                    "Yes", "No", null);
    d.addActionListener(new ActionListener() {
      public void actionPerformed(ActionEvent e) {
        if (e.getActionCommand().equals("yes")) System.exit(0);
        else textarea.append("Quit not confirmed\n");
      }
    });
    d.show();
  }
  else if (command.equals("open")) {
    FileDialog d = new FileDialog(this, "Open File", FileDialog.LOAD);
    d.show();  // display the dialog and block until answered
    textarea.append("You selected file: " + d.getFile() + "\n");
```

Example 6-15: AllComponents.java (continued)

```
            d.dispose();
        }
        else if (command.equals("about")) {
            InfoDialog d = new InfoDialog(this, "About",
                                "This demo was written by David Flanagan\n" +
                                "Copyright (c) 1997 O'Reilly & Associates");
            d.show();
        }
    }

    public static void main(String[] args) {
        Frame f = new AllComponents("AWT Demo");
        f.pack();
        f.show();
    }
}
```

Exercises

6-1. Write an applet that displays a red circle centered within the display area and a row of buttons along the bottom of the flow area. The buttons should be labelled **Left**, **Right**, **Up**, and **Down**. You'll probably want to use BorderLay-out and FlowLayout layout managers to achieve this layout. When the user clicks on any of the four buttons, move the red circle a few pixels in the indicated direction.

6-2. Modify the applet you developed in Exercise 6-1 so that it creates its own Frame and runs as a standalone program. Add a simple pulldown menu system that contains a **Quit** option to exit the program.

6-3. Modify the program from Exercise 6-2 so that it displays a column of radio buttons along the right edge of the window. Each button should be labelled with the name of a color. When the user selects a button, the color of the circle should change to the specified color.

6-4. Modify the program from Exercise 6-3 so that it uses a Choice component to list the color choices available, instead of radio buttons. Place the Choice component along the bottom of the applet display area, in the same row as the buttons

6-5. Modify the program once again, so that it makes the color choices available in a popup menu.

6-6. Using the ColumnLayout layout manager as a guide, write a RowLayout layout manager that has similar behavior. Test it by using it in place of the FlowLay-out layout manager you used in one of the previous exercises.

6-7. Write a subclass of Dialog that displays a modal dialog box that allows the user to select a font. The dialog should allow the user to select one of the standard Java font families, one of the four standard font styles, and one of 4 to 8 point sizes. It should display a preview of the font the user has selected. It should include **Ok** and **Cancel** buttons that the user can use to dismiss the dialog. The class you define should include a getFont() method that returns a `Font` object selected by the user. It should also have a method named `was-Cancelled()` that returns `true` if the user clicked the **Cancel** button instead of clicking the **Ok** button.

CHAPTER 7

Data Transfer

Java 1.1 added inter-application data transfer capabilities to the AWT with the classes and interfaces in the java.awt.datatransfer package. In Java 1.1, this package is limited to cut-and-paste, but a future release of Java will also support the drag-and-drop data transfer metaphor. This chapter demonstrates how you can add simple and not-so-simple cut-and-paste facilities to a Java application.

An Overview of Cut-and-Paste

Before we begin studying data transfer examples, it is important to understand the data transfer and cut-and-paste architecture used by java.awt.datatransfer. The DataFlavor class is perhaps the most central class in the package. It represents the type of data to be transferred. Every data flavor consists of a human-readable name and a data type specification. The data type can be specified in one of two ways: with a Java Class object or with a MIME type string. These two ways of specifying the data type reflect two different ways of transferring the data. When the data type is specified as a class object, objects of that type are transferred using the object serialization mechanism (which is discussed in Chapter 13, *Object Serialization*). In Example 7-2, for example, the DataFlavor is specified using the Class object for java.util.Vector. This means that data is transferred as a serialized Vector object. It also means that the DataFlavor object has an implicit MIME type of:

```
application/x-java-serialized-object; class=java.util.Vector
```

The data type of a DataFlavor can also be specified as a MIME type. In this case, data is transferred through a stream—the recipient of the data receives a Reader stream from which it can read textual data. In this case, the recipient usually has to parse the data according to the rules of the specified MIME type.

The Transferable interface is another important piece of the AWT data transfer picture. This interface specifies methods that must be implemented by any object that wants to make data available for transfer. One of its methods returns an array of all the DataFlavor types it can use to transfer its data. Another method checks whether the Transferable object supports a given flavor. The most important method, getTransferData(), actually returns the data in a format appropriate for the requested DataFlavor.

While DataFlavor and Transferable provide the underlying infrastructure for data transfer, it is the Clipboard class and ClipboardOwner interface that support the cut-and-paste style of data transfer. A typical cut-and-paste scenario works like this:

- When the user issues a command to "copy" or "cut" something, the initiating application first obtains the system Clipboard object by calling the get-SystemClipboard() method of the Toolkit object. Next, it creates a Transferable object that represents the data to be transferred. Finally, it passes this transferable object to the clipboard by calling the setContents() method of the clipboard. The initiating application must also pass an object that implements the ClipboardOwner interface to setContents(). By doing so, it becomes the "clipboard owner," and, therefore, must maintain its Transferable object until it ceases to be the clipboard owner.

- When the user issues a command to "paste," the receiving application first obtains the system Clipboard object in the same way that the initiating application did. Then, it calls the getContents() method of the system clipboard to receive the Transferable object stored there. Now it can use the methods defined by the Transferable interface to choose a DataFlavor for the data transfer and actually transfer the data.

- When the user copies or cuts some other piece of data, a new data transfer is initiated, and the new initiating application (it may be the same one) becomes the new clipboard owner. The previous owner is notified that it is no longer the clipboard owner when the system invokes the lostOwnership() method of the ClipboardOwner object specified in the initiating call to setContents().

Note that untrusted applets are not allowed to work with the system clipboard because there might be sensitive data on it from other applications. This means that applets cannot participate in inter-application cut-and-paste. Instead, an applet must create a private clipboard object that it can use for intra-applet data transfer.

Simple String Cut-and-Paste

Example 7-1 is a simple program, StringCutAndPaste, that demonstrates how to add String cut-and-paste capabilities to a program. It relies on the predefined data flavor, DataFlavor.stringFlavor, and on the StringSelection class, which implements both the Transferable and ClipboardOwner interfaces. Because it can use the StringSelection object, this example is a relatively simple one. The code of interest is in the cut() and paste() methods at the end of the example.

Example 7–1: StringCutAndPaste.java

```
import java.awt.*;
import java.awt.datatransfer.*;
import java.awt.event.*;
```

Example 7-1: StringCutAndPaste.java (continued)

```
/**
 * This program demonstrates how to add string cut-and-paste capabilities
 * to an application.
 **/
public class StringCutAndPaste extends Frame implements ActionListener
{
  /**
   * The main method creates a frame, arranges to handle its closing,
   * packs it and pops it up.
   **/
  public static void main(String[] args) {
    Frame f = new StringCutAndPaste();
    f.addWindowListener(new WindowAdapter() {
      public void windowClosing(WindowEvent e) { System.exit(0); }
    });
    f.pack();
    f.show();
  }

  /** The text field that holds the text that is cut or pasted */
  TextField field;

  /**
   * The constructor builds a very simple test GUI, and registers this object
   * as the ActionListener for the buttons
   **/
  public StringCutAndPaste() {
    this.setFont(new Font("SansSerif", Font.PLAIN, 14));  // Use a nice font

    // Set up the Cut button
    Button cut = new Button("Cut");
    cut.addActionListener(this);
    cut.setActionCommand("cut");
    this.add(cut, "West");

    // Set up the Paste button
    Button paste = new Button("Paste");
    paste.addActionListener(this);
    paste.setActionCommand("paste");
    this.add(paste, "East");

    // Set up the text field that they both operate on
    field = new TextField();
    this.add(field, "North");
  }

  /**
   * Clicking on one of the buttons invokes this method, which in turn
   * invokes either the cut() or the paste() method
   **/
  public void actionPerformed(ActionEvent e) {
    String cmd = e.getActionCommand();
    if (cmd.equals("cut")) cut();
    else if (cmd.equals("paste")) paste();
  }

  /**
   * This method takes the current contents of the text field, creates a
```

Example 7-1: StringCutAndPaste.java (continued)

```
 * StringSelection object to represent that string, and puts the
 * StringSelection onto the clipboard
 **/
public void cut() {
  // Get the currently displayed value
  String s = field.getText();

  // Create a StringSelection object to represent it.
  // This is a big convenience, because StringSelection implements both
  // the Transferable interface and the ClipboardOwner.  We don't have
  // to deal with either of them.
  StringSelection ss = new StringSelection(s);

  // Now set the StringSelection object as the contents of the clipboard
  // Also set it as the owner of the clipboard.
  this.getToolkit().getSystemClipboard().setContents(ss, ss);
}

/**
 * This method does the reverse.  It gets the contents of the clipboard,
 * then asks for them to be converted to a string, then displays the
 * string.
 **/
public void paste() {
  // Get the clipboard
  Clipboard c = this.getToolkit().getSystemClipboard();

  // Get the contents of the clipboard, as a Transferable object
  Transferable t = c.getContents(this);

  // Ask for the transferable data in string form, using the predefined
  // string DataFlavor.  Then display that string in the field.
  try {
    String s = (String) t.getTransferData(DataFlavor.stringFlavor);
    field.setText(s);
  }
  // If anything goes wrong with the transfer, just beep and do nothing.
  catch (Exception e) {
    this.getToolkit().beep();
    return;
  }
 }
}
```

Custom Cut-and-Paste

While the ability to cut-and-paste strings is important, most interesting applications of cut-and-paste involve transfering other, more complex, data types. Example 7-2 is a program that shows how you can do this. It is a version of the Scribble program we've seen many other times in this book. This version of the program adds a popup menu that contains **Copy**, **Cut**, and **Paste** items. When a scribble is cut and then pasted, an entire Vector of Line objects is transferred.

The example is moderately long, but don't let that put you off. Much of the code is used simply to set up the application; only about a third of it is directly related to cut-and-paste. The example creates a custom DataFlavor object to represent the

Vector flavor of the data it transfers. The most interesting methods are copy() and paste(). They rely on the nested SimpleSelection class that provides a custom implementation of the Transferable and ClipboardOwner interfaces. The scribble window created by the application has a pulldown menu that allows the user to create additional copies of the window, as shown in Figure 7-1.

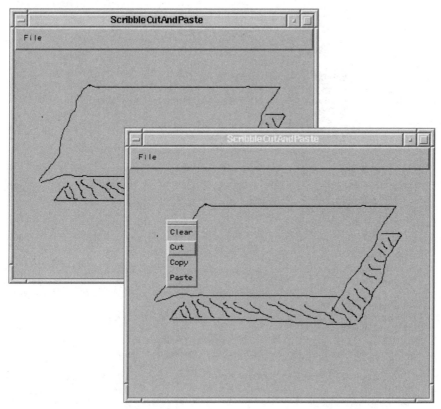

Figure 7-1: Two ScribbleCutAndPaste windows

Creating multiple windows allows you to test cutting and pasting of scribble data between windows. The example uses the system clipboard, so that scribbles should be able to be pasted between entirely separate instances of the Scribble-CutAndPaste application (i.e., between instances running in separate Java virtual machines). Unfortunately, however, this does not work in Java 1.1. Although this behavior is undocumented, Java 1.1 apparently only supports inter-application cut-and-paste for the pre-defined DataFlavor.stringFlavor and Data-Flavor.textFlavor data flavors. Custom types like the one used in Example 7-2 do not correctly interface with the system clipboard.[*]

---

[*] Even worse, on Windows platforms, you cannot use the system clipboard with custom types at all. To fix this program to work on Windows systems, you need to use a local clipboard. Add a class variable to the ScribblePanel class to represent the clipboard. Then change copy() and paste() so that they use the local clipboard instead of the system clipboard.

Example 7-2: ScribbleCutAndPaste.java

```java
import java.awt.*;
import java.awt.event.*;
import java.awt.datatransfer.*;  // Clipboard, Transferable, DataFlavor, etc.
import java.util.Vector;         // To store the scribble in

/**
 * This class demonstrates how to implement cut-and-paste of data
 * other than strings.  It is a variant of the Scribble program we've
 * seen so much.  Only about a third of this code is directly cut-and-paste
 * code.  The rest is support code to make this an interesting example
 **/
public class ScribbleCutAndPaste extends Frame {
  /** A very simple main() method for our program. */
  public static void main(String[] args) { new ScribbleCutAndPaste(); }

  /**
   * Remember # of open windows so we can quit when the last one is closed
   * We support multiple windows so that we can cut-and-paste among them.
   **/
  protected static int num_windows = 0;

  /** Create a Frame, Menu, and ScrollPane for the scribble component */
  public ScribbleCutAndPaste() {
    super("ScribbleCutAndPaste");            // Create the window
    num_windows++;                           // Count it

    // Create scribble area and add to the frame
    ScribblePanel scribble = new ScribblePanel(this, 400, 300);
    this.add(scribble, "Center");

    // Set up a menubar
    MenuBar menubar = new MenuBar();         // Create menubar
    this.setMenuBar(menubar);                // Add it to the frame
    Menu file = new Menu("File");            // Create a File menu
    menubar.add(file);                       // Add to menubar

    // Create three menu items, with menu shortcuts, and add to the menu
    MenuItem n, c, q;
    file.add(n = new MenuItem("New Window", new MenuShortcut(KeyEvent.VK_N)));
    file.add(c = new MenuItem("Close Window",new MenuShortcut(KeyEvent.VK_W)));
    file.addSeparator();
    file.add(q = new MenuItem("Quit", new MenuShortcut(KeyEvent.VK_Q)));

    // Create and register action listener objects for the three menu items
    n.addActionListener(new ActionListener() {     // Open a new window
      public void actionPerformed(ActionEvent e) { new ScribbleCutAndPaste(); }
    });
    c.addActionListener(new ActionListener() {     // Close this window
      public void actionPerformed(ActionEvent e) { close(); }
    });
    q.addActionListener(new ActionListener() {     // Quit the program
      public void actionPerformed(ActionEvent e) { System.exit(0); }
    });

    // Another event listener, this one to handle window close requests
    this.addWindowListener(new WindowAdapter() {
      public void windowClosing(WindowEvent e) { close(); }
    });
```

Example 7–2: ScribbleCutAndPaste.java (continued)

```
       // Set the window size and pop it up
       this.pack();
       this.show();
    }

    /** Close a window.  If this is the last open window, just quit. */
    void close() {
       if (--num_windows == 0) System.exit(0);
       else this.dispose();
    }

    /**
     * This class is a custom component that supports scribbling.  It also has
     * a popup menu that provides access to cut-and-paste facilities.
     **/
    static class ScribblePanel extends Canvas implements ActionListener {
       protected short last_x, last_y;              // Coordinates of last click
       protected Vector lines = new Vector(256,256); // Store the scribbles
       protected int width, height;                 // The preferred size
       protected PopupMenu popup;                    // The popup menu
       protected Frame frame;                        // The frame we are within

       /** This constructor requires a Frame and a desired size */
       public ScribblePanel(Frame frame, int width, int height) {
          this.frame = frame;
          this.width = width;
          this.height = height;

          // We handle scribbling with low-level events, so we must specify
          // which events we are interested in.
          this.enableEvents(AWTEvent.MOUSE_EVENT_MASK);
          this.enableEvents(AWTEvent.MOUSE_MOTION_EVENT_MASK);

          // Create the popup menu.
          String[] labels = new String[] {   "Clear", "Cut", "Copy", "Paste" };
          String[] commands = new String[] { "clear", "cut", "copy", "paste" };
          popup = new PopupMenu();                   // Create the menu
          for(int i = 0; i < labels.length; i++) {
             MenuItem mi = new MenuItem(labels[i]);   // Create a menu item
             mi.setActionCommand(commands[i]);        // Set its action command
             mi.addActionListener(this);              // And its action listener
             popup.add(mi);                           // Add item to the popup menu
          }
          // Finally, register the popup menu with the component it appears over
          this.add(popup);
       }

       /**
        * Specifies how big the component would like to be.  It always returns the
        * preferred size passed to the ScribblePanel() constructor
        **/
       public Dimension getPreferredSize() {return new Dimension(width, height);}

       /** This is the ActionListener method invoked by the popup menu items */
       public void actionPerformed(ActionEvent event) {
          String command = event.getActionCommand();
          if (command.equals("clear")) clear();
          else if (command.equals("cut")) cut();
```

Example 7-2: ScribbleCutAndPaste.java (continued)

```java
    else if (command.equals("copy")) copy();
    else if (command.equals("paste")) paste();
}

/** Draw all the saved lines of the scribble */
public void paint(Graphics g) {
  for(int i = 0; i < lines.size(); i++) {
    Line l = (Line)lines.elementAt(i);
    g.drawLine(l.x1, l.y1, l.x2, l.y2);
  }
}

/**
 * This is the low-level event-handling method called on mouse events
 * that do not involve mouse motion.  It handles posting the popup menu
 * and also initiates scribbles
 **/
public void processMouseEvent(MouseEvent e) {
  if (e.isPopupTrigger())                            // If popup trigger,
    popup.show(this, e.getX(), e.getY());            // Pop up the menu
  else if (e.getID() == MouseEvent.MOUSE_PRESSED) {  // Otherwise
    last_x = (short)e.getX(); last_y = (short)e.getY(); // Save position
  }
  else super.processMouseEvent(e);  // Pass other event types on
}

/**
 * This method is called for mouse motion events.  It adds a line to the
 * scribble, both on the screen and in the saved representation
 **/
public void processMouseMotionEvent(MouseEvent e) {
  if (e.getID() == MouseEvent.MOUSE_DRAGGED) {
    Graphics g = getGraphics();                      // Object to draw with
    g.drawLine(last_x, last_y, e.getX(), e.getY());  // Draw this line
    lines.addElement(new Line(last_x, last_y,        // And save it, too.
                          (short) e.getX(), (short)e.getY()));
    last_x = (short) e.getX();  // Remember current mouse coordinates
    last_y = (short) e.getY();
  }
  else super.processMouseMotionEvent(e);  // Important!
}

/** Clear the scribble.  Invoked by popup menu */
void clear() {
  lines.removeAllElements();   // Throw out the saved scribble
  repaint();                   // And redraw everything.
}

/**
 * The DataFlavor used for our particular type of cut-and-paste data.
 * This one will transfer data in the form of a serialized Vector object.
 * Note that in Java 1.1.1, this works intra-application, but not between
 * applications.  Java 1.1.1 inter-application data transfer is limited to
 * the pre-defined string and text data flavors.
 **/
public static final DataFlavor dataFlavor =
    new DataFlavor(Vector.class, "ScribbleVectorOfLines");
```

Example 7–2: ScribbleCutAndPaste.java (continued)

Data Transfer

```
/**
 * Copy the current scribble and store it in a SimpleSelection object
 * (defined below).  Then put that object on the clipboard for pasting.
 **/
public void copy() {
  // Get system clipboard
  Clipboard c = this.getToolkit().getSystemClipboard();
  // Copy and save the scribble in a Transferable object
  SimpleSelection s = new SimpleSelection(lines.clone(), dataFlavor);
  // Put that object on the clipboard
  c.setContents(s, s);
}

/** Cut is just like a copy, except we erase the scribble afterwards */
public void cut() { copy(); clear();  }

/**
 * Ask for the Transferable contents of the system clipboard.
 * Then ask that Transferable object for the scribble data it represents.
 * If either step fails, beep!
 **/
public void paste() {
  Clipboard c = this.getToolkit().getSystemClipboard(); // Get clipboard
  Transferable t = c.getContents(this);                 // Get its contents
  if (t == null) {              // If there is nothing to paste, beep
    this.getToolkit().beep();
    return;
  }
  try {
    // Ask for clipboard contents to be converted to our data flavor.
    // This will throw an exception if our flavor is not supported.
    Vector newlines = (Vector) t.getTransferData(dataFlavor);
    // Add all those pasted lines to our scribble.
    for(int i = 0; i < newlines.size(); i++)
      lines.addElement(newlines.elementAt(i));
    // And redraw the whole thing
    repaint();
  }
  catch (UnsupportedFlavorException e) {
    this.getToolkit().beep();   // If clipboard has some other type of data
  }
  catch (Exception e) {
    this.getToolkit().beep();   // Or if anything else goes wrong...
  }
}

/**
 * This nested class implements the Transferable and ClipboardOwner
 * interfaces used in data transfer.  It is a simple class that remembers
 * a selected object and makes it available in only one specified flavor.
 * It would be useful for transferring other types of data, too.
 **/
static class SimpleSelection implements Transferable, ClipboardOwner {
  protected Object selection;    // The data to be transferred
  protected DataFlavor flavor;   // The one data flavor supported

  /** The constructor.  Just initialize some fields */
  public SimpleSelection(Object selection, DataFlavor flavor) {
```

Example 7-2: ScribbleCutAndPaste.java (continued)

```
        this.selection = selection;  // Specify data
        this.flavor = flavor;        // Specify flavor
    }

    /** Return the list of supported flavors.  Just one in this case */
    public DataFlavor[] getTransferDataFlavors() {
      return new DataFlavor[] { flavor };
    }

    /** Check whether we support a specified flavor */
    public boolean isDataFlavorSupported(DataFlavor f) {
      return f.equals(flavor);
    }

    /** If the flavor is right, transfer the data (i.e. return it) */
    public Object getTransferData(DataFlavor f)
         throws UnsupportedFlavorException {
          if (f.equals(flavor)) return selection;
          else throw new UnsupportedFlavorException(f);
    }

    /**
     * This is the ClipboardOwner method.  Called when the data is no
     * longer on the clipboard.  In this case, we don't need to do much.
     **/
    public void lostOwnership(Clipboard c, Transferable t) {
      selection = null;
    }
  }

  /**
   * A class to store the coordinates of one scribbled line.
   * The complete scribble is stored as a Vector of these objects
   **/
  static class Line {
    public short x1, y1, x2, y2;
    public Line(short x1, short y1, short x2, short y2) {
      this.x1 = x1; this.y1 = y1; this.x2 = x2; this.y2 = y2;
    }
  }
}
```

Exercises

7-1. Recall Exercise 5-3, in which you wrote an applet that draws circles where the user clicks the mouse. Modify this exercise so that it runs as a standalone program, can display multiple windows, and supports cut-and-paste. Use Example 7-2 as a model. Remember that because of the incomplete implementation of cut-and-paste in Java 1.1, cut-and-paste may only work between windows of the same application, not between separate applications.

7-2. It is often useful for an application to support data transfer using multiple formats of data. For example, if you cut a list of circles from one application and attempt to paste them into a text editor, it would be useful if the circles application converted the data to some textual format. Modify the program from Exercise 7-1 to add the ability to transfer data using the pre-defined `DataFlavor.stringFlavor` flavor. When the list of circles is requested as a string, you should return a string like the following: "2 Circles, centered at (100, 123), (34, 278)".

7–3. Recall that in Java 1.1, inter-application cut-and-paste does not work for data flavors other than simple strings. Modify your program from Exercise 7-1 or 7-2 (or modify Example 7-2) so that it supports inter-application cut-and-paste using strings. That is, when data is cut, convert it into some compact string representation for transfer. When that string is transferred and pasted, parse it and convert it back into its original form.

CHAPTER 8

Input/Output

This chapter demonstrates many of the input/output capabilities of the `java.io` package. The examples here show you how to:

- Read and write files

- List directories and obtain file size and date information

- Use various Java stream classes

- Define customized stream subclasses

I/O is used in most programs, so you should find the examples here quite useful. The techniques introduced in this chapter are also used in other places in this book. We'll see many examples that use streams for input and output in Chapter 9, *Networking*, and we'll see a specialized kind of I/O in Chapter 13, *Object Serialization*.

Files and Streams

One of the commonly used classes in the `java.io` package is `File`. This class is somewhat misleadingly named, for it represents a filename (or directory name), rather than a file itself. Because files (and directories) have different naming conventions under different operating systems, Java provides the `File` class to try to encapsulate and hide some of those differences. The `File` class also defines various methods for operating on files as a whole: deleting files, creating directories, listing directories, querying the size and modification time of a file, and so on.

While the `File` class provides methods to manipulate directories and the files within those directories, it does not provide any methods that manipulate the contents of the files. In other words, it doesn't provide any way to read or write the bytes or characters that are contained in the files. In Java, sequential file I/O is performed through a stream abstraction. (Random-access file I/O is performed with the `RandomAccessFile` class, but sequential I/O is much more common.)

A *stream* is simply an object from which data can be read sequentially or to which data can be written sequentially. The bulk of the java.io package is stream classes: there are 40 of them. InputStream and OutputStream and their respective subclasses are objects for reading and writing streams of bytes, while Reader and Writer and their subclasses (all new in Java 1.1) are objects for reading and writing streams of Unicode characters. In addition to these stream classes, the java.util.zip package defines another eight byte input and output streams for data compression and decompression. Table 8-1 through Table 8-4 summarize the stream classes available in java.io and java.util.zip.

Table 8-1: Byte Input Streams

Byte Input Stream	Description
BufferedInputStream	Reads a buffer of bytes from an InputStream, and then returns bytes from the buffer, making small reads more efficient.
ByteArrayInputStream	Reads bytes sequentially from an array.
CheckedInputStream	This java.util.zip class computes a checksum of the bytes it reads from an InputStream.
DataInputStream	Reads binary representations of Java primitive types from an InputStream.
FileInputStream	Reads bytes sequentially from a file.
FilterInputStream	The superclass of byte input stream filter classes.
GZIPInputStream	This java.util.zip class uncompresses GZIP-compressed bytes it reads from an InputStream.
InflaterInputStream	The superclass of GZIPInputStream and ZipInputStream.
InputStream	The superclass of all byte input streams.
LineNumberInputStream	This class is deprecated in Java 1.1; use LineNumberReader instead.
ObjectInputStream	Reads binary representations of Java objects and primitive values from a byte stream. This class is used for the deserialization of objects.
PipedInputStream	Reads bytes written to the PipedOutputStream to which it is connected. Used in multi-threaded programs.
PushbackInputStream	Adds a fixed-size "pushback buffer" to an input stream, so that bytes can be "unread." Useful with some parsers.
SequenceInputStream	Reads bytes sequentially from two or more input streams, as if they were a single stream.
StringBufferInputStream	This class is deprecated in Java 1.1; use StringReader instead.
ZipInputStream	This java.util.zip class uncompresses entries in a ZIP file.

Table 8-2: Character Input Streams

Character Input Stream	Description
BufferedReader	Reads a buffer of characters from a Reader, and then returns characters from the buffer, making small reads more efficient.
CharArrayReader	Reads characters sequentially from an array.
FileReader	Reads characters sequentially from a file. An InputStreamReader subclass that reads from an automatically-created FileInputStream.
FilterReader	The superclass of character input stream filter classes.
InputStreamReader	Reads characters from a byte input stream. Converts bytes to characters using the encoding of the default locale, or a specified encoding.
LineNumberReader	Reads lines of text and keeps track of how many have been read.
PipedReader	Reads characters written to the PipedWriter to which it is connected. Used in multi-threaded programs.
PushbackReader	Adds a fixed-size "pushback buffer" to a Reader, so that characters can be "unread." Useful with some parsers.
Reader	The superclass of all character input streams.
StringReader	Reads characters sequentially from a string.

Table 8-3: Byte Output Streams

Byte Output Stream	Description
BufferedOutputStream	Buffers byte output for efficiency; writes to an OutputStream only when the buffer fills up.
ByteArrayOutputStream	Writes bytes sequentially into an array.
CheckedOutputStream	This java.util.zip class computes a checksum of the bytes it writes to an OutputStream.
DataOutputStream	Writes binary representations of Java primitive types to an OutputStream.
DeflaterOutputStream	The superclass of GZIPOutputStream and ZipOutputStream.
FileOutputStream	Writes bytes sequentially to a file.
FilterOutputStream	The superclass of all byte output stream filters.
GZIPOutputStream	This java.util.zip class outputs a GZIP-compressed version of the bytes written to it.

Table 8–3: Byte Output Streams (continued)

Byte Output Stream	Description
ObjectOutputStream	Writes binary representations of Java objects and primitive values to an OutputStream. Used for the serialization of objects.
OutputStream	The superclass of all byte output streams.
PipedOutputStream	Writes bytes to the PipedInputStream to which it is connected. Used in multi-threaded programs.
PrintStream	Writes a textual representation of Java objects and primitive values. Deprecated except for use by the standard output stream System.out in Java 1.1. In other contexts, use PrintWriter instead.
ZipOutputStream	This java.util.zip class compresses entries in a ZIP file.

Table 8–4: Character Output Streams

Character Output Stream	Description
BufferedWriter	Buffers output for efficiency; writes characters to a Writer only when the buffer fills up.
CharArrayWriter	Writes characters sequentially into an array.
FileWriter	Writes characters sequentially to a file. A subclass of OutputStreamWriter that automatically creates a FileOutputStream.
FilterWriter	The superclass of all character output stream filters.
OutputStreamWriter	Writes characters to a byte output stream. Converts characters to bytes using the encoding of the default locale, or a specified encoding.
PipedWriter	Writes characters to the PipedReader to which it is connected. Used in multi-threaded programs.
PrintWriter	Writes textual representations of Java objects and primitive values to a Writer.
StringWriter	Writes characters sequentially into an internally-created StringBuffer.
Writer	The superclass of all character output streams.

Working with Files

Example 8-1 is a relatively short program that deletes a file or directory specified on the command line. It demonstrates a number of the methods of the File class—methods that operate on a file (or directory) as a whole, but not on its contents. Other useful File methods include getParent(), length(), mkdir(), and renameTo().

Example 8-1: Delete.java

```java
import java.io.*;

/**
 * This class is a static method delete() and a standalone program that
 * deletes a specified file or directory.
 **/
public class Delete {
  /**
   * This is the main() method of the standalone program.  After checking
   * it arguments, it invokes the Delete.delete() method to do the deletion
   **/
  public static void main(String[] args) {
    if (args.length != 1) {      // Check command-line arguments
      System.err.println("Usage: java Delete <file or directory>");
      System.exit(0);
    }
    // Call delete() and display any error messages it throws.
    try { delete(args[0]); }
    catch (IllegalArgumentException e) { System.err.println(e.getMessage()); }
  }

  /**
   * The static method that does the deletion.  Invoked by main(), and designed
   * for use by other programs as well.  It first makes sure that the
   * specified file or directory is deleteable before attempting to delete it.
   * If there is a problem, it throws an IllegalArgumentException.
   */
  public static void delete(String filename) {
    // Create a File object to represent the filename
    File f = new File(filename);
    // Make sure the file or directory exists and isn't write protected
    if (!f.exists()) fail("Delete: no such file or directory: " + filename);
    if (!f.canWrite()) fail("Delete: write protected: " + filename);
    // If it is a directory, make sure it is empty
    if (f.isDirectory()) {
      String[] files = f.list();
      if (files.length > 0) fail("Delete: directory not empty: " + filename);
    }
    // If we passed all the tests, then attempt to delete it
    boolean success = f.delete();
    // And throw an exception if it didn't work for some (unknown) reason.
    // For example, because of a bug with Java 1.1.1 on Linux,
    // directory deletion always fails
    if (!success) fail("Delete: deletion failed");
  }

  /** A convenience method to throw an exception */
  protected static void fail(String msg) throws IllegalArgumentException {
    throw new IllegalArgumentException(msg);
  }
}
```

Copying File Contents

Example 8-2 shows a program that copies the contents of a specified file to another. This example uses the File class, much as Example 8-1 did, to check that the source file exists, that the destination is writable, and so on. But it also introduces the use of streams to work with the contents of files. It uses a FileInput-Stream to read the bytes of the source file and a FileOutputStream to copy those bytes to the destination file.

The copy() method implements the functionality of the program. This method is heavily commented, so that you can follow the steps it takes. First, it performs a surprisingly large number of checks to verify that the copy request is a legitimate one. If all those tests succeed, it then creates a FileInputStream to read bytes from the source and a FileOutputStream to write those bytes to the destination. Notice the use of a byte array buffer to store bytes during the copy. Pay particular attention to the short while loop that actually performs the copy. The combination of assignment and testing in the condition of the while loop is a useful idiom that occurs frequently in I/O programming. Also notice the finally statement that is used to ensure that the streams are properly closed before the program exits.

This program uses streams to do more than read from and write to files, however. Before overwriting an existing file, this example asks for user confirmation. It demonstrates how to read lines of text with a BufferedReader that reads individual characters from an InputStreamReader, which in turn reads bytes from System.in (an InputStream), which itself reads keystrokes from the user's keyboard. Additionally, the program displays textual output with System.out and System.err, which are both instances of PrintStream.

The static FileCopy.copy() method can be called directly by any program. The FileCopy class also provides a main() method, however, so that it can be used as a standalone program.

Example 8-2: FileCopy.java

```
import java.io.*;

/**
 * This class is a standalone program to copy a file, and also defines a
 * static copy() method that other programs can use to copy files.
 **/
public class FileCopy {
  /** The main() method of the standalone program.  Calls copy(). */
  public static void main(String[] args) {
    if (args.length != 2)     // Check arguments
      System.err.println("Usage: java FileCopy <source file> <destination>");
    else {
      // Call copy() to do the copy, and display any error messages it throws.
      try { copy(args[0], args[1]); }
      catch (IOException e) { System.err.println(e.getMessage()); }
    }
  }

  /**
   * The static method that actually performs the file copy.
   * Before copying the file, however, it performs a lot of tests to make
```

Example 8-2: FileCopy.java (continued)

```
  * sure everything is as it should be.
  */
 public static void copy(String from_name, String to_name) throws IOException{
   File from_file = new File(from_name);  // Get File objects from Strings
   File to_file = new File(to_name);

   // First make sure the source file exists, is a file, and is readable.
   if (!from_file.exists())
     abort("FileCopy: no such source file: " + from_name);
   if (!from_file.isFile())
     abort("FileCopy: can't copy directory: " + from_name);
   if (!from_file.canRead())
     abort("FileCopy: source file is unreadable: " + from_name);
   // If the destination is a directory, use the source file name
   // as the destination file name
   if (to_file.isDirectory())
     to_file = new File(to_file, from_file.getName());

   // If the destination exists, make sure it is a writeable file
   // and ask before overwriting it.  If the destination doesn't
   // exist, make sure the directory exists and is writeable.
   if (to_file.exists()) {
     if (!to_file.canWrite())
       abort("FileCopy: destination file is unwriteable: " + to_name);
     // Ask whether to overwrite it
     System.out.print("Overwrite existing file " + to_file.getName() +
                      "? (Y/N): ");
     System.out.flush();
     // Get the user's response.
     BufferedReader in=new BufferedReader(new InputStreamReader(System.in));
     String response = in.readLine();
     // Check the response.  If not a Yes, abort the copy.
     if (!response.equals("Y") && !response.equals("y"))
       abort("FileCopy: existing file was not overwritten.");
   }
   else {
     // if file doesn't exist, check if directory exists and is writeable.
     // If getParent() returns null, then the directory is the current dir.
     // so look up the user.dir system property to find out what that is.
     String parent = to_file.getParent();  // Get the destination directory
     if (parent == null) parent = System.getProperty("user.dir"); // or CWD
     File dir = new File(parent);           // Convert it to a file.
     if (!dir.exists())
       abort("FileCopy: destination directory doesn't exist: " + parent);
     if (dir.isFile())
       abort("FileCopy: destination is not a directory: " + parent);
     if (!dir.canWrite())
       abort("FileCopy: destination directory is unwriteable: " + parent);
   }

   // If we've gotten this far, then everything is okay.
   // So we copy the file, a buffer of bytes at a time.
   FileInputStream from = null;  // Stream to read from source
   FileOutputStream to = null;   // Stream to write to destination
   try {
     from = new FileInputStream(from_file);  // Create input stream
     to = new FileOutputStream(to_file);     // Create output stream
     byte[] buffer = new byte[4096];         // A buffer to hold file contents
```

Example 8-2: FileCopy.java (continued)

```
  int bytes_read;                          // How many bytes in buffer
  // Read a chunk of bytes into the buffer, then write them out,
  // looping until we reach the end of the file (when read() returns -1).
  // Note the combination of assignment and comparison in this while
  // loop. This is a common I/O programming idiom.
  while((bytes_read = from.read(buffer)) != -1) // Read bytes until EOF
    to.write(buffer, 0, bytes_read);       //   write bytes
  }
  // Always close the streams, even if exceptions were thrown
  finally {
    if (from != null) try { from.close(); } catch (IOException e) { ; }
    if (to != null) try { to.close(); } catch (IOException e) { ; }
  }
}

/** A convenience method to throw an exception */
private static void abort(String msg) throws IOException {
  throw new IOException(msg);
}
}
```

Input/Output

Reading and Displaying Text Files

Example 8-3 combines the use of the File class and I/O streams with the GUI techniques we saw in Chapter 6, *Graphical User Interfaces*. This FileViewer class reads the contents of a file and displays it in an AWT TextArea component. It is pictured in Figure 8-1.

The FileViewer constructor concerns itself mainly with the mechanics of setting up the necessary GUI. There are some interesting uses of the File object at the end of this constructor, however. The heart of this example is the setFile() method. This is where the file contents are loaded and displayed. Because the file contents are to be displayed in a TextArea component, we make the legitimate assumption that the file contains characters, and use a character input stream, a FileReader, instead of the byte input stream used in the FileCopy program of Example 8-2. setFile() uses the length() method of File to determine the size of the file, and then loops until it has read all of the characters in the file into one large buffer. Once again, we use a finally clause to ensure that the FileReader stream is properly closed.

The actionPerformed() method handles GUI events. If the user clicks on the **Open File** button, this method creates a FileDialog object to prompt for a new file to display. Note how the default directory is set before the dialog is displayed and then retrieved after the user makes a selection. This is possible because the show() method actually blocks until the user selects a file and dismisses the dialog.

The FileViewer class is designed to be used by other classes. It also has its own main() method, however, so that it can be run as a standalone program.

Example 8-3: FileViewer.java

```
import java.awt.*;
import java.awt.event.*;
```

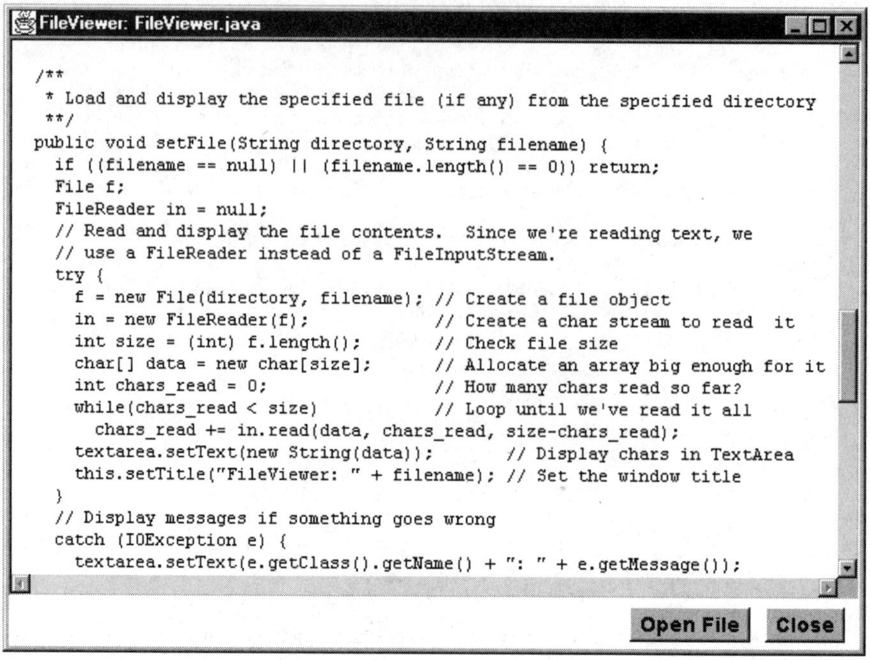

```
FileViewer: FileViewer.java                                      _ □ ✕
/**
 * Load and display the specified file (if any) from the specified directory
 **/
public void setFile(String directory, String filename) {
  if ((filename == null) || (filename.length() == 0)) return;
  File f;
  FileReader in = null;
  // Read and display the file contents.  Since we're reading text, we
  // use a FileReader instead of a FileInputStream.
  try {
    f = new File(directory, filename); // Create a file object
    in = new FileReader(f);            // Create a char stream to read  it
    int size = (int) f.length();       // Check file size
    char[] data = new char[size];      // Allocate an array big enough for it
    int chars_read = 0;                // How many chars read so far?
    while(chars_read < size)           // Loop until we've read it all
      chars_read += in.read(data, chars_read, size-chars_read);
    textarea.setText(new String(data));       // Display chars in TextArea
    this.setTitle("FileViewer: " + filename); // Set the window title
  }
  // Display messages if something goes wrong
  catch (IOException e) {
    textarea.setText(e.getClass().getName() + ": " + e.getMessage());

                                              Open File    Close
```

Figure 8–1: A FileViewer window

Example 8–3: FileViewer.java (continued)

```
import java.io.*;

/**
 * This class creates and displays a window containing a TextArea,
 * in which the contents of a text file are displayed.
 **/
public class FileViewer extends CloseableFrame implements ActionListener {
  String directory; // The default directory to display in the FileDialog
  TextArea textarea; // The area to display the file contents into

  /** Convenience constructor: file viewer starts out blank */
  public FileViewer() { this(null, null); }
  /** Convenience constructor: display file from current directory */
  public FileViewer(String filename) { this(null, filename); }

  /**
   * The real constructor.  Create a FileViewer object to display the
   * specified file from the specified directory
   **/
  public FileViewer(String directory, String filename) {
    super();  // Create the (closeable) frame

    // Create a TextArea to display the contents of the file in
    textarea = new TextArea("", 24, 80);
    textarea.setFont(new Font("MonoSpaced", Font.PLAIN, 12));
    textarea.setEditable(false);
    this.add("Center", textarea);
```

Example 8-3: FileViewer.java (continued)

```
      // Create a bottom panel to hold a couple of buttons in
      Panel p = new Panel();
      p.setLayout(new FlowLayout(FlowLayout.RIGHT, 10, 5));
      this.add(p, "South");

      // Create the buttons and arrange to handle button clicks
      Font font = new Font("SansSerif", Font.BOLD, 14);
      Button openfile = new Button("Open File");
      Button close = new Button("Close");
      openfile.addActionListener(this);
      openfile.setActionCommand("open");
      openfile.setFont(font);
      close.addActionListener(this);
      close.setActionCommand("close");
      close.setFont(font);
      p.add(openfile);
      p.add(close);

      this.pack();

      // Figure out the directory, from filename or current dir, if necessary
      if (directory == null) {
        File f;
        if ((filename != null) && (f = new File(filename)).isAbsolute()) {
          directory = f.getParent();
          filename = f.getName();
        }
        else directory = System.getProperty("user.dir");
      }

      this.directory = directory;     // Remember the directory, for FileDialog
      setFile(directory, filename);   // Now load and display the file
    }

    /**
     * Load and display the specified file (if any) from the specified directory
     **/
    public void setFile(String directory, String filename) {
      if ((filename == null) || (filename.length() == 0)) return;
      File f;
      FileReader in = null;
      // Read and display the file contents.  Since we're reading text, we
      // use a FileReader instead of a FileInputStream.
      try {
        f = new File(directory, filename); // Create a file object
        in = new FileReader(f);            // Create a char stream to read  it
        int size = (int) f.length();       // Check file size
        char[] data = new char[size];      // Allocate an array big enough for it
        int chars_read = 0;                // How many chars read so far?
        while(chars_read < size)           // Loop until we've read it all
          chars_read += in.read(data, chars_read, size-chars_read);
        textarea.setText(new String(data));        // Display chars in TextArea
        this.setTitle("FileViewer: " + filename); // Set the window title
      }
      // Display messages if something goes wrong
      catch (IOException e) {
        textarea.setText(e.getClass().getName() + ": " + e.getMessage());
        this.setTitle("FileViewer: " + filename + ": I/O Exception");
```

Example 8–3: FileViewer.java (continued)

```
  }
  // Always be sure to close the input stream!
  finally { try { if (in != null) in.close(); } catch (IOException e) {} }
}

/**
 * Handle button clicks
 **/
public void actionPerformed(ActionEvent e) {
  String cmd = e.getActionCommand();
  if (cmd.equals("open")) {           // If user clicked "Open" button
    // Create a file dialog box to prompt for a new file to display
    FileDialog f = new FileDialog(this, "Open File", FileDialog.LOAD);
    f.setDirectory(directory);        // Set the default directory
    f.show();                         // Display dialog and wait for response
    directory = f.getDirectory();     // Remember new default directory
    setFile(directory, f.getFile());  // Load and display selection
    f.dispose();                      // Get rid of the dialog box
  }
  else if (cmd.equals("close"))       // If user clicked "Close" button
    this.dispose();                   //    then close the window
}

/**
 * The FileViewer can be used by other classes, or it can be
 * used standalone with this main() method.
 **/
static public void main(String[] args) throws IOException {
  // Create a FileViewer object
  Frame f = new FileViewer((args.length == 1)?args[0]:null);
  // Arrange to exit when the FileViewer window closes
  f.addWindowListener(new WindowAdapter() {
    public void windowClosed(WindowEvent e) { System.exit(0); }
  });
  // And pop the window up
  f.show();
  }
}
```

Listing Directory and File Information

Just as the FileViewer class of Example 8-3 displays the contents of a file in a TextArea component, the FileLister class, shown in Example 8-4, displays the contents of a directory in a List component. When you select a file or directory name from the list, it displays information (size, modification date, etc.) about the file or directory in a TextField component. When you double-click on a directory, the contents of that directory are displayed. When you double-click on a file, it displays the contents of the file in a FileViewer object. Figure 8-2 shows a FileLister window.

The GUI mechanics of making the FileLister work form a large part of this example. The listDirectory() method lists the contents of a directory, using an optionally specified FilenameFilter object passed to the FileLister() constructor. This object defines an accept() method that is called for every entry in a directory to determine whether it should be listed. listDirectory() also calls the

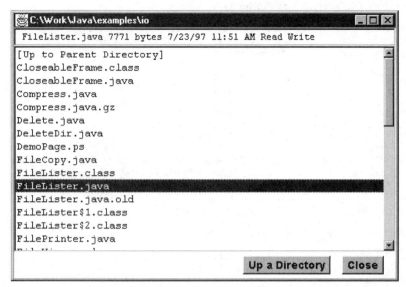

Figure 8-2: A FileLister window

`Sorter.sort()` method developed in Chapter 2, *Object, Classes, and Interfaces*, to sort the directory entries into alphabetical order.

The `itemStateChanged()` method is invoked when an item in the list is selected. It obtains information about the file or directory and displays it. The `action-Performed()` method is another event listener method. This one is invoked when the user clicks either of the `Button` objects, or double-clicks on an item in the list. If the user double-clicks on a directory, the program lists the contents of that directory. If the user double-clicks on a file, however, it creates and display a `FileViewer` window to list the contents of the file.

Like the `FileViewer` class, the `FileLister` can be used by other classes, or it can be invoked as a standalone program. If you invoke it standalone, it lists the contents of the current directory. You can also invoke it with an optional directory name to see the contents of that directory. Using the optional `-e` flag followed by a file extension causes the program to filter the list of files and only display the ones that have the specified extension. Note how the `main()` method parses the command-line arguments, and uses an anonymous class to implement the `File-nameFilter` interface.

Example 8-4: FileLister.java

```java
import java.awt.*;
import java.awt.event.*;
import java.io.*;
import java.text.DateFormat;
import java.util.Date;

/**
 * This class creates and displays a window containing a list of
 * files and sub-directories in a specified directory.  Clicking on an
```

Example 8-4: FileLister.java (continued)

```
 * entry in the list displays more information about it. Double-clicking
 * on an entry displays it, if a file, or lists it if a directory.
 * An optionally-specified FilenameFilter filters the displayed list.
 **/
public class FileLister extends CloseableFrame
                        implements ActionListener, ItemListener {
  private List list;                    // To display the directory contents in
  private TextField details;            // To display detail info in.
  private Panel buttons;                // Holds the buttson
  private Button up, close;             // The Up and Close buttons
  private File currentDir;              // The directory currently listed
  private FilenameFilter filter;        // An optional filter for the directory
  private String[] files;               // The directory contents
  private DateFormat dateFormatter =    // To display dates and time correctly
     DateFormat.getDateTimeInstance(DateFormat.SHORT, DateFormat.SHORT);

  /**
   * Constructor: create the GUI, and list the initial directory.
   **/
  public FileLister(String directory, FilenameFilter filter) {
    super("File Lister");               // Create the window
    this.filter = filter;               // Save the filter, if any

    list = new List(12, false);         // Set up the list
    list.setFont(new Font("MonoSpaced", Font.PLAIN, 14));
    list.addActionListener(this);
    list.addItemListener(this);

    details = new TextField();          // Set up the details area
    details.setFont(new Font("MonoSpaced", Font.PLAIN, 12));
    details.setEditable(false);

    buttons = new Panel();              // Set up the button box
    buttons.setLayout(new FlowLayout(FlowLayout.RIGHT, 15, 5));
    buttons.setFont(new Font("SansSerif", Font.BOLD, 14));

    up = new Button("Up a Directory"); // Set up the two buttons
    close = new Button("Close");
    up.addActionListener(this);
    close.addActionListener(this);

    buttons.add(up);                    // Add buttons to button box
    buttons.add(close);

    this.add(list, "Center");           // Add stuff to the window
    this.add(details, "North");
    this.add(buttons, "South");
    this.setSize(500, 350);

    listDirectory(directory);           // And now list the initial directory.
  }

  /**
   * This method uses the list() method to get all entries in a directory
   * and then displays them in the List component.
   **/
  public void listDirectory(String directory) {
    // Convert the string to a File object, and check that the dir exists
```

Example 8-4: FileLister.java (continued)

```java
File dir = new File(directory);
if (!dir.isDirectory())
  throw new IllegalArgumentException("FileLister: no such directory");

// Get the (filtered) directory entries
files = dir.list(filter);
// And sort them.
Sorter.sort(files);

// Remove any old entries in the list, and add the new ones
list.removeAll();
list.addItem("[Up to Parent Directory]");  // A special case entry
for(int i = 0; i < files.length; i++) list.addItem(files[i]);

// Display directory name in window titlebar and in the details box
this.setTitle(directory);
details.setText(directory);

// Remember this directory for later.
currentDir = dir;
}

/**
 * This ItemListener method uses various File methods to obtain information
 * about a file or directory. Then it displays that info in the details box.
 **/
public void itemStateChanged(ItemEvent e) {
  int i = list.getSelectedIndex() - 1;       // minus 1 for Up To Parent entry
  if (i < 0) return;
  String filename = files[i];                // Get the selected entry
  File f = new File(currentDir, filename);   // Convert to a File
  if (!f.exists())                           // Confirm that it exists
    throw new IllegalArgumentException("FileLister: " +
                                       "no such file or directory");

  // Get the details about the file or directory, concatenate to a string
  String info = filename;
  if (f.isDirectory()) info += File.separator;
  info += " " + f.length() + " bytes ";
  info += dateFormatter.format(new java.util.Date(f.lastModified()));
  if (f.canRead()) info += " Read";
  if (f.canWrite()) info += " Write";

  // And display the details string
  details.setText(info);
}

/**
 * This ActionListener method is invoked when the user double-clicks on an
 * entry or clicks on one of the buttons.  If they double-click on a file,
 * create a FileViewer to display that file.  If they double-click on a
 * directory, call the listDirectory() method to display that directory
 **/
public void actionPerformed(ActionEvent e) {
  if (e.getSource() == close) this.dispose();
  else if (e.getSource() == up) { up(); }
  else if (e.getSource() == list) {  // Double click on an item
    int i = list.getSelectedIndex(); // Check which item
```

Example 8-4: FileLister.java (continued)

```
      if (i == 0) up();                      // Handle first Up To Parent item
      else {                                 // Otherwise, get filename
        String name = files[i-1];
        File f = new File(currentDir, name);  // Convert to a File
        String fullname = f.getAbsolutePath();
        if (f.isDirectory()) listDirectory(fullname);  // List a directory
        else new FileViewer(fullname).show();          // or display a file
      }
    }
  }

  /** A convenience method to display the contents of the parent directory */
  protected void up() {
    String parent = currentDir.getParent();
    if (parent == null) return;
    listDirectory(parent);
  }

  /** A convenience method used by main() */
  public static void usage() {
    System.out.println("Usage: java FileLister [directory_name] " +
                       "[-e file_extension]");
    System.exit(0);
  }

  /**
   * A main() method so FileLister can be run standalone.
   * Parse command line arguments and create the FileLister object.
   * If an extension is specified, create a FilenameFilter for it.
   * If no directory is specified, use the current directory.
   */
  public static void main(String args[]) throws IOException {
    FileLister f;
    FilenameFilter filter = null;  // The filter, if any
    String directory = null;       // The specified dir, or the current dir

    // Loop through args array, parsing arguments
    for(int i = 0; i < args.length; i++) {
      if (args[i].equals("-e")) {
        if (++i >= args.length) usage();
        final String suffix = args[i];  // final for use in anon. class below

        // This class is a simple FilenameFilter.  It defines the
        // accept() method required to determine whether a specified
        // file should be listed.  A file will be listed if its name
        // ends with the specified extension, or if it is a directory.
        filter = new FilenameFilter() {
          public boolean accept(File dir, String name) {
            if (name.endsWith(suffix)) return true;
            else return (new File(dir, name)).isDirectory();
          }
        };
      }
      else {
        if (directory != null) usage();  // If dir already specified, fail.
        else directory = args[i];
      }
    }
```

Example 8-4: FileLister.java (continued)

```
      // if no directory specified, use the current directoy
      if (directory == null) directory = System.getProperty("user.dir");
      // Create the FileLister object, with directory and filter specified.
      f = new FileLister(directory, filter);
      // Arrange for the application to exit when the FileLister window closes
      f.addWindowListener(new WindowAdapter() {
        public void windowClosed(WindowEvent e) { System.exit(0); }
      });
      // And pop up the FileLister.
      f.show();
    }
}
```

Compressing Files and Directories

Example 8-5 demonstrates an interesting application of stream classes: compressing files and directories. The classes of interest in this example are not actually part of the java.io package, but instead are part of the java.util.zip package, which is new in Java 1.1. The Compress class defines two static methods, gzip-File(), which compresses a file using GZIP compression format, and zipDirectory(), which compresses the files (but not directories) in a directory using the ZIP archive and compression format. gzipFile() uses the GZIPOutputStream class, while zipDirectory() uses the ZipOutputStream and ZipEntry classes, all from java.util.zip.

This example demonstrates the versatility of the stream classes and and shows again how streams can be wrapped around one another so that the output of one stream becomes the input of another. This technique makes it possible to achieve a great variety of effects. Notice again the while loop in both methods that does the actual copying of data from source file to compressed file. These methods do not attempt to handle exceptions; instead they just pass them on to the caller, which is often exactly the right thing to do.

Compress is meant to be used as a utility class by other programs, so it does not itself include a main() method. The example does include a nested Compress.Test class, however, and this nested class has a main() method that can be used to test the gzipFile() and zipDirectory() methods.

Example 8-5: Compress.java

```
import java.io.*;
import java.util.zip.*;

/**
 * This class defines two static methods for gzipping files and zipping
 * directories.  It also defines a demonstration program as a nested class.
 **/
public class Compress {
  /** Gzip the contents of the from file and save in the to file. */
  public static void gzipFile(String from, String to) throws IOException {
    // Create stream to read from the from file
    FileInputStream in = new FileInputStream(from);
    // Create stream to compress data and write it to the to file.
```

Example 8-5: Compress.java (continued)

```java
    GZIPOutputStream out = new GZIPOutputStream(new FileOutputStream(to));
    // Copy bytes from one stream to the other
    byte[] buffer = new byte[4096];
    int bytes_read;
    while((bytes_read = in.read(buffer)) != -1)
      out.write(buffer, 0, bytes_read);
    // And close the streams
    in.close();
    out.close();
  }

  /** Zip the contents of the directory, and save it in the zipfile */
  public static void zipDirectory(String dir, String zipfile)
      throws IOException, IllegalArgumentException {
    // Check that the directory is a directory, and get its contents
    File d = new File(dir);
    if (!d.isDirectory())
      throw new IllegalArgumentException("Compress: not a directory:  " + dir);
    String[] entries = d.list();
    byte[] buffer = new byte[4096];  // Create a buffer for copying
    int bytes_read;

    // Create a stream to compress data and write it to the zipfile
    ZipOutputStream out = new ZipOutputStream(new FileOutputStream(zipfile));

    // Loop through all entries in the directory
    for(int i = 0; i < entries.length; i++) {
      File f = new File(d, entries[i]);
      if (f.isDirectory()) continue;                // Don't zip sub-directories
      FileInputStream in = new FileInputStream(f); // Stream to read file
      ZipEntry entry = new ZipEntry(f.getPath());  // Make a ZipEntry
      out.putNextEntry(entry);                      // Store entry in zipfile
      while((bytes_read = in.read(buffer)) != -1)  // Copy bytes to zipfile
        out.write(buffer, 0, bytes_read);
      in.close();                                   // Close input stream
    }
    // When we're done with the whole loop, close the output stream
    out.close();
  }

  /**
   * This nested class is a test program that demonstrates the use of the
   * static methods defined above.
   **/
  public static class Test {
    /**
     * Compress a specified file or directory.  If no destination name is
     * specified, append .gz to a file name or .zip to a directory name
     **/
    public static void main(String args[]) throws IOException {
      if ((args.length != 1) && (args.length != 2)) {  // check arguments
        System.err.println("Usage: java Compress$Test <from> [<to>]");
        System.exit(0);
      }
      String from = args[0], to;
      File f = new File(from);
      boolean directory = f.isDirectory();    // Is it a file or directory?
      if (args.length == 2) to = args[1];
```

Example 8-5: Compress.java (continued)

```
    else {                              // If destination not specified
      if (directory) to = from + ".zip"; //   use a .zip suffix
      else to = from + ".gz";           //   or a .gz suffix
    }

    if ((new File(to)).exists()) { // Make sure not to overwrite anything
      System.err.println("Compress: won't overwrite existing file: " + to);
      System.exit(0);
    }

    // Finally, call one of the methods defined above to do the work.
    if (directory) Compress.zipDirectory(from, to);
    else Compress.gzipFile(from, to);
  }
 }
}
```

Input/Output

Filtering Character Streams

The FilterReader is an abstract class that defines a "null filter"—it reads characters from a specified Reader and returns them with no modification. In other words, FilterReader defines no-op implementations of all the Reader methods. A subclass must override at least the two read() methods to perform whatever sort of filtering is necessary. Some subclasses may override other methods as well. Example 8-6 shows RemoveHTMLReader, which is a custom subclass of Filter-Reader that reads HTML text from a stream and filters out all of the HTML tags from the text it returns.

In our example, we implement the HTML tag filtration in the three-argument version of read(), and then implement the no-argument version in terms of that more complicated version. The example includes a static Test class with a main() method that shows how you might use the RemoveHTMLReader class.

Note that we could also have defined a RemoveHTMLWriter class by performing the same filtration in a FilterWriter subclass. To filter byte streams instead of character stream, we would subclass FilterInputStream and FilterOutputStream. This is only one example of a filter stream. Other possibilities include streams that count the number of characters or bytes processed, convert characters to upper case, extract URLs, perform search-and-replace operations, convert UNIX-style LF line terminators to Windows-style CRLF line terminators, and so on.

Example 8-6: RemoveHTMLReader.java

```java
import java.io.*;

/**
 * A simple FilterReader that strips HTML tags out of a stream of characters.
 * It isn't perfect: it doesn't know about <XMP> tags, for example, within
 * which '<' and '>' aren't to be interpreted as tags.  It will also strip
 * '<' and '>' characters (and anything in between) out of plain text files.
 * For this reason, it should only be used with properly formatted HTML input.
 **/
public class RemoveHTMLReader extends FilterReader {
  /** A trivial constructor.  Just initialze our superclass */
```

Example 8–6: RemoveHTMLReader.java (continued)

```java
public RemoveHTMLReader(Reader in) { super(in); }

boolean intag = false;     // Used to remember whether we are "inside" a tag

/**
 * This is the implementation of the no-op read() method of FilterReader.
 * It calls in.read() to get a buffer full of characters, then strips
 * out the HTML tags. (in is a protected field of the superclass).
 **/
public int read(char[] buf, int from, int len) throws IOException {
  int numchars = 0;           // how many characters have been read
  // Loop, because we might read a bunch of characters, then strip them
  // all out, leaving us with zero characters to return.
  while (numchars == 0) {
    numchars = in.read(buf, from, len);     // Read characters
    if (numchars == -1) return -1;          // Check for EOF and handle it.
    // Loop through the characters we read, stripping out HTML tags.
    // Characters not in tags are copied over any previous tags in the buffer
    int last = from;                        // Index of last non-HTML char
    for(int i = from; i < from + numchars; i++) {
      if (!intag) {                         // If not in an HTML tag
        if (buf[i] == '<') intag = true;    //   check for start of a tag
        else buf[last++] = buf[i];          //   and copy the character
      }
      else if (buf[i] == '>') intag = false; // Else, check for end of tag
    }
    numchars = last - from;   // Figure out how many characters remain
  }                           // And if it is more than zero characters
  return numchars;            // Then return that number.
}


/**
 * This is another no-op read() method we have to implement.  We
 * implement it in terms of the method above.  Our superclass implements
 * the remaining read() methods in terms of these two.
 **/
public int read() throws IOException {
  char[] buf = new char[1];
  int result = read(buf, 0, 1);
  if (result == -1) return -1;
  else return (int)buf[0];
}

/** This class defines a main() method to test the RemoveHTMLReader */
public static class Test {
  /** The test program: read a text file, strip HTML, print to console */
  public static void main(String[] args) {
    try {
      if (args.length != 1)
        throw new IllegalArgumentException("Wrong number of arguments");
      // Create a stream to read from the file and strip tags from it
      BufferedReader in =
        new BufferedReader(new RemoveHTMLReader(new FileReader(args[0])));
      // Read line by line, printing lines to the console
      String line;
      while((line = in.readLine()) != null)
        System.out.println(line);
```

Example 8-6: RemoveHTMLReader.java (continued)

```
      in.close();  // Close the stream.
    }
    catch(Exception e) {
      System.err.println(e);
      System.err.println("Usage: java RemoveHTMLReader$Test <filename>");
    }
  }
 }
}
```

Filtering Lines of Text

Example 8-7 defines `GrepReader`, another custom input stream. This one reads lines of text from a specified `Reader` and only returns those lines that contain a specified substring. In this way, it works like the UNIX *fgrep* command—it performs a "grep" or search. `GrepReader` performs filtering, but it filters text a line at a time, rather than a character at a time, so we extend `BufferedReader` instead of `FilterReader`.

The code for this example is straightforward, and it includes a nested `Test` class with a `main()` method that demonstrates the use of the `GrepReader` stream. You might invoke this test program like this:

```
% java GrepReader\$Test needle haystack.txt
```

Example 8-7: GrepReader.java

```java
import java.io.*;

/**
 * This class is a BufferedReader that filters out all lines that
 * do not contain the specified pattern.
 **/
public class GrepReader extends BufferedReader {
  String pattern;  // The string we are going to be matching.

  /** Pass the stream to our superclass, and remember the pattern ourself */
  public GrepReader(Reader in, String pattern) {
    super(in);
    this.pattern = pattern;
  }

  /**
   * This is the filter: call our superclass's readLine() to get the
   * actual lines, but only return lines that contain the pattern.
   * When the superclass readLine() returns null (EOF), we return null.
   **/
  public final String readLine() throws IOException {
    String line;
    do { line = super.readLine(); }
    while ((line != null) && line.indexOf(pattern) == -1);
    return line;
  }

  /**
   * This class demonstrates the use of the GrepReader class.
```

Example 8– 7: GrepReader.java (continued)

```
 * It prints the lines of a file that contain a specified substring.
 **/
public static class Test {
  public static void main(String args[]) {
    try {
      if (args.length != 2)
        throw new IllegalArgumentException("Wrong number of arguments");
      GrepReader in = new GrepReader(new FileReader(args[1]), args[0]);
      String line;
      while((line = in.readLine()) != null) System.out.println(line);
      in.close();
    }
    catch (Exception e) {
      System.err.println(e);
      System.out.println("Usage: java GrepReader$Test <pattern> <file>");
    }
  }
}
}
```

A Custom HTML Output Stream

The Java 1.1 class libraries do not include an HTML parser or an HTML displayer. This is unfortunate because HTML has become a very common document format. Applets do run within a Web browser, however, so it seems logical that there should be some way to use the HTML display capabilities of the browser from within an applet.

Example 8-8 shows a custom output stream named HTMLWriter that provides exactly this capability. It is designed for use by applets running in Netscape Navigator 4.0 or later. When a new HTMLWriter stream is created, it communicates with the Web browser using JavaScript commands and tells the browser to open a new window. Then, when HTML-formatted text is written to this stream, it passes that text, through JavaScript, to the new Web browser window, which parses and displays it. This class relies on Navigator's LiveConnect technology and the netscape.javascript.JSObject class, and is therefore dependent on the Netscape platform.

Note the implementation of the write() and close() methods, and the no-op implementation of the flush() method. These are the three abstract methods of Writer that must be implemented by every concrete subclass. Note also the closeWindow() method that this class adds.

You are not expected to understand the JSObject class or the JavaScript commands sent to the browser through it. If you are interested in learning about these things, I recommend my JavaScript book, *JavaScript: The Definitive Guide*, also published by O'Reilly & Associates.

The example includes a nested applet class named Test that demonstrates how to use the HTMLWriter class. This applet reads a URL specified in an applet parameter (i.e., with a <PARAM> tag) and creates an HTMLWriter to display the contents of that URL. You can test out this applet with an HTML tag like the following:

```
<APPLET CODE="HTMLWriter$Test.class" WIDTH=10 HEIGHT=10 MAYSCRIPT>
  <PARAM NAME="url" VALUE="HTMLWriter.java">
</APPLET>
```

Note the MAYSCRIPT attribute of the <APPLET> tag. This gives the Java applet permission to invoke JavaScript commands in the browser. The <PARAM> tag specifies the value of the parameter named url—the URL of the file the applet will display.

Example 8–8: HTMLWriter.java

```
import java.io.*;
import java.net.*;
import java.applet.Applet;
import netscape.javascript.JSObject;    // A special class we need

/**
 * An output stream that sends HTML text to a newly created web browser window.
 * It relies on the netscape.javascript.JSObject class to send JavaScript
 * commands to the Web browser, and only works for applets running in
 * the Netscape Navigator Web browser.
 **/
public class HTMLWriter extends Writer {
  JSObject main_window;          // the initial browser window
  JSObject window;               // the new window we create
  JSObject document;             // the document of that new window
  static int window_num = 0;     // used to give each new window a unique name

  /**
   * When you create a new HTMLWriter, it pops up a new, blank, Web browser
   * window to display the output in.  You must specify the applet
   * (this specifies the main browser window) and the desired size
   * for the new window.
   **/
  public HTMLWriter(Applet applet, int width, int height) {
    // Verify that we can find the JSObject class we need.  Warn if not.
    try { Class c = Class.forName("netscape.javascript.JSObject"); }
    catch (ClassNotFoundException e) {
      throw new NoClassDefFoundError("HTMLWriter requires " +
                                "Netscape Navigator 4.0 or higher");
    }

    // Get a reference to the main browser window from the applet.
    main_window = JSObject.getWindow(applet);

    // Create a new window to display output in.
    window = (JSObject)
      main_window.eval("self.open(''," +
                  "'HTMLWriter" + window_num++ + "'," +
                  "'menubar,status,resizable,scrollbars," +
                  "width=" + width + ",height=" + height + "')");

    // Obtain the Document object of this new window, and open it.
    document = (JSObject) window.getMember("document");
    document.call("open", null);
  }

  /**
   * This is the write() method required for all Writer subclasses.
   * Writer defines all its other write() methods in terms of this one.
   **/
```

Example 8-8: HTMLWriter.java (continued)

```java
public void write(char[] buf, int offset, int length) {
  // If no window or document, do nothing.   This occurs if the stream
  // has been closed, or if the code is not running in Navigator.
  if ((window == null) || (document == null)) return;
  // If the window has been closed by the user, do nothing
  if (((Boolean)window.getMember("closed")).booleanValue()) return;
  // Otherwise, create a string from the specified bytes
  String s = new String(buf, offset, length);
  // And pass it to the JS document.write() method to output the HTML
  document.call("write", new String[] { s });
}

/**
 * There is no general way to force JavaScript to flush all pending output,
 * so this method does nothing.  To flush, output a <P> tag or some other
 * HTML tag that forces a line break in the output.
 **/
public void flush() {}

/**
 * When the stream is closed, close the JavaScript Document object
 * (But don't close the window yet.)
 **/
public void close() { document.call("close", null); document = null; }

/**
 * If the browser window is still open, close it.
 * This method is unique to HTMLWriter.
 **/
public void closeWindow() {
  if (document != null) close();
  if (!((Boolean)window.getMember("closed")).booleanValue())
    window.call("close", null);
  window = null;
}

/** A finalizer method to close the window in case we forget. */
public void finalize() { closeWindow(); }

/**
 * This nested class is an applet that demonstrates the use of HTMLWriter.
 * It reads the contents of the URL specified in its url parameter and
 * writes them out to an HTMLWriter stream.  It will only work in
 * Netscape 4.0 or later.  It requires an <APPLET> tag like this:
 *   <APPLET CODE="HTMLWriter$Test.class" WIDTH=10 HEIGHT=10 MAYSCRIPT>
 *   <PARAM NAME="url" VALUE="HTMLWriter.java">
 *   </APPLET>
 * Note that MAYSCRIPT attribute.  It is required to enable the applet
 * to invoke JavaScript.
 **/
public static class Test extends Applet {
  HTMLWriter out;
  /** When the applet starts, read and display specified URL */
  public void init() {
    try {
      // Get the URL specified in the <PARAM> tag
      URL url = new URL(this.getDocumentBase(), this.getParameter("url"));
      // Get a stream to read its contents
```

Example 8-8: HTMLWriter.java (continued)

```
        Reader in = new InputStreamReader(url.openStream());
        // Create an HTMLWriter stream for out output
        out = new HTMLWriter(this, 400, 200);
        // Read buffers of characters and output them to the HTMLWriter
        char[] buffer = new char[4096];
        int numchars;
        while((numchars = in.read(buffer)) != -1)
          out.write(buffer, 0, numchars);
        // Close the streams
        in.close();
        out.close();
      }
      catch (IOException e) {}
    }
    /** When the applet terminates, close the window we created */
    public void destroy() { out.closeWindow(); }
  }
}
```

A Custom Hardcopy Stream

Most of the custom stream examples we've seen so far merely filter data and pass it on. The data still comes from the same basic source, a file, or goes to the same basic sink, the console. Example 8-9 defines an entirely new sink for data, the HardcopyWriter stream. This class uses the PrintJob class of the java.awt package to format, paginate, and print the text that is passed to it. Figure 8-3 shows a sample of the output from this stream.

The implementation of HardcopyWriter is a fairly long one. Much of it, however, is involved with manipulating PrintJob, Font, and other java.awt classes. You may want to study those portions of the example for a refresher on what we covered in Chapter 4, *Graphics*. From an I/O standpoint, the most interesting pieces of HardcopyWriter are the write(), flush() and close() methods. As we saw with Example 8-8, these are the three abstract methods of Writer that subclasses must implement. HardcopyWriter adds the additional methods pagebreak() and setFontStyle().

The public HardcopyWriter methods use synchronized statements to acquire a lock on the lock object inherited from the Writer subclass. Example 8-8 did not do this, which means that the HTMLWriter stream it defined is not safe for use by multiple threads. As an aside, you may have noticed that none of the methods of the standard Reader and Writer classes are synchronized, although many of the methods of InputStream and OutputStream classes are. This is because the Reader and Writer classes acquire their locks internally, as we do in this example, for a slight improvement in efficiency over the technique used by InputStream and OutputStream.

The HardcopyWriter() constructor includes a workaround for a bug on Windows platforms. On these platforms, the PrintJob object does not properly report the page size and resolution, so those values must be obtained in some other way. Also note that this constructor method throws a PrintCanceledException if the user clicks the **Cancel** button in the print dialog box (in other words, if

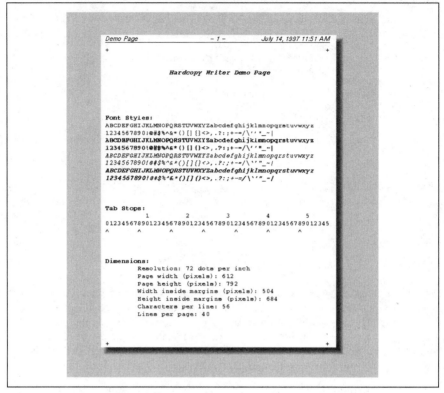

Figure 8–3: Output of HardcopyWriter

`Toolkit.getPrintJob()` returns `null`). `PrintCanceledException` is defined as a nested class within `HardcopyWriter`.

The example includes a nested `PrintFile` program that reads a specified text file and sends it to a `HardcopyWriter` stream. In order to do this, it must create an empty `Frame` and display it temporarily, since the `HardcopyWriter` constructor requires a `Frame` argument. (The constructor requires a `Frame` because the `Toolkit.getPrintJob()` method requires one). The frame must actually be visible when the `HardcopyWriter()` constructor is called, or a `NullPointerException` results.

The example also includes a nested `Demo` class that, when run as a standalone program, prints the demonstration page shown in Figure 8-3.

Example 8–9: HardcopyWriter.java

```java
import java.awt.*;
import java.awt.event.*;
import java.io.*;
import java.text.*;
import java.util.*;
```

Example 8-9: HardcopyWriter.java (continued)

```java
/**
 * A character output stream that sends output to a printer.
 **/
public class HardcopyWriter extends Writer {
  // These are the instance variables for the class
  protected PrintJob job;                    // The PrintJob object in use
  protected Graphics page;                   // Graphics object for current page
  protected String jobname;                  // The name of the print job
  protected int fontsize;                    // Point size of the font
  protected String time;                     // Current time (appears in header)
  protected Dimension pagesize;              // Size of the page (in dots)
  protected int pagedpi;                     // Page resolution in dots per inch
  protected Font font, headerfont;           // Body font and header font
  protected FontMetrics metrics;             // Metrics for the body font
  protected FontMetrics headermetrics;       // Metrics for the header font
  protected int x0, y0;                      // Upper-left corner inside margin
  protected int width, height;               // Size (in dots) inside margins
  protected int headery;                     // Baseline of the page header
  protected int charwidth;                   // The width of each character
  protected int lineheight;                  // The height of each line
  protected int lineascent;                  // Offset of font baseline
  protected int chars_per_line;              // Number of characters per line
  protected int lines_per_page;              // Number of lines per page
  protected int charnum = 0, linenum = 0;    // Current column and line position
  protected int pagenum = 0;                 // Current page number

  // A field to save state between invocations of the write() method
  private boolean last_char_was_return = false;

  // A static variable that holds user preferences between print jobs
  protected static Properties printprops = new Properties();

  /**
   * The constructor for this class has a bunch of arguments:
   * The frame argument is required for all printing in Java.
   * The jobname appears left justified at the top of each printed page.
   * The font size is specified in points, as on-screen font sizes are.
   * The margins are specified in inches (or fractions of inches).
   **/
  public HardcopyWriter(Frame frame, String jobname, int fontsize,
                        double leftmargin, double rightmargin,
                        double topmargin, double bottommargin)
       throws HardcopyWriter.PrintCanceledException
  {
    // Get the PrintJob object with which we'll do all the printing.
    // The call is synchronized on the static printprops object, which
    // means that only one print dialog can be popped up at a time.
    // If the user clicks Cancel in the print dialog, throw an exception.
    Toolkit toolkit = frame.getToolkit();    // get Toolkit from Frame
    synchronized(printprops) {
      job = toolkit.getPrintJob(frame, jobname, printprops);
    }
    if (job == null)
      throw new PrintCanceledException("User cancelled print request");

    pagesize = job.getPageDimension();       // query the page size
    pagedpi = job.getPageResolution();       // query the page resolution
```

Example 8–9: HardcopyWriter.java (continued)

```java
    // Bug Workaround:
    // On windows, getPageDimension() and getPageResolution don't work, so
    // we've got to fake them.
    if (System.getProperty("os.name").regionMatches(true,0,"windows",0,7)) {
      // Use screen dpi, which is what the PrintJob tries to emulate, anyway
      pagedpi = toolkit.getScreenResolution();
      System.out.println(pagedpi);
      // Assume a 8.5" x 11" page size.  A4 paper users have to change this.
      pagesize = new Dimension((int)(8.5 * pagedpi), 11*pagedpi);
      System.out.println(pagesize);
      // We also have to adjust the fontsize.  It is specified in points,
      // (1 point = 1/72 of an inch) but Windows measures it in pixels.
      fontsize = fontsize * pagedpi / 72;
      System.out.println(fontsize);
      System.out.flush();
    }

    // Compute coordinates of the upper-left corner of the page.
    // I.e. the coordinates of (leftmargin, topmargin).  Also compute
    // the width and height inside of the margins.
    x0 = (int)(leftmargin * pagedpi);
    y0 = (int)(topmargin * pagedpi);
    width = pagesize.width - (int)((leftmargin + rightmargin) * pagedpi);
    height = pagesize.height - (int)((topmargin + bottommargin) * pagedpi);

    // Get body font and font size
    font = new Font("Monospaced", Font.PLAIN, fontsize);
    metrics = toolkit.getFontMetrics(font);
    lineheight = metrics.getHeight();
    lineascent = metrics.getAscent();
    charwidth = metrics.charWidth('0');   // Assumes a monospaced font!

    // Now compute columns and lines will fit inside the margins
    chars_per_line = width / charwidth;
    lines_per_page = height / lineheight;

    // Get header font information
    // And compute baseline of page header: 1/8" above the top margin
    headerfont = new Font("SansSerif", Font.ITALIC, fontsize);
    headermetrics = toolkit.getFontMetrics(headerfont);
    headery = y0 - (int)(0.125 * pagedpi) -
      headermetrics.getHeight() + headermetrics.getAscent();

    // Compute the date/time string to display in the page header
    DateFormat df = DateFormat.getDateTimeInstance(DateFormat.LONG,
                                                   DateFormat.SHORT);
    df.setTimeZone(TimeZone.getDefault());
    time = df.format(new Date());

    this.jobname = jobname;                // save name
    this.fontsize = fontsize;              // save font size
  }

  /**
   * This is the write() method of the stream.  All Writer subclasses
   * implement this.  All other versions of write() are variants of this one
   **/
```

Example 8-9: HardcopyWriter.java (continued)

```java
public void write(char[] buffer, int index, int len) {
  synchronized(this.lock) {
    // Loop through all the characters passed to us
    for(int i = index; i < index + len; i++) {
      // If we haven't begun a page (or a new page), do that now.
      if (page == null) newpage();

      // If the character is a line terminator, then begin new line,
      // unless it is a \n immediately after a \r.
      if (buffer[i] == '\n') {
        if (!last_char_was_return) newline();
        continue;
      }
      if (buffer[i] == '\r') {
        newline();
        last_char_was_return = true;
        continue;
      }
      else last_char_was_return = false;

      // If it some other non-printing character, ignore it.
      if (Character.isWhitespace(buffer[i]) &&
          !Character.isSpaceChar(buffer[i]) && (buffer[i] != '\t')) continue;

      // If no more characters will fit on the line, start a new line.
      if (charnum >= chars_per_line) {
        newline();
        if (page == null) newpage();  // and start a new page, if necessary
      }

      // Now print the character:
      // If it is a space, skip one space, without output.
      // If it is a tab, skip the necessary number of spaces.
      // Otherwise, print the character.
      // It is inefficient to draw only one character at a time, but
      // because our FontMetrics don't match up exactly to what the
      // printer uses we need to position each character individually.
      if (Character.isSpaceChar(buffer[i])) charnum++;
      else if (buffer[i] == '\t') charnum += 8 - (charnum % 8);
      else {
        page.drawChars(buffer, i, 1,
                       x0 + charnum * charwidth,
                       y0 + (linenum*lineheight) + lineascent);
        charnum++;
      }
    }
  }
}

/**
 * This is the flush() method that all Writer subclasses must implement.
 * There is no way to flush a PrintJob without prematurely printing the
 * page, so we don't do anything.
 **/
public void flush() { /* do nothing */ }

/**
 * This is the close() method that all Writer subclasses must implement.
```

Example 8-9: HardcopyWriter.java (continued)

```java
 * Print the pending page (if any) and terminate the PrintJob.
 */
public void close() {
  synchronized(this.lock) {
    if (page != null) page.dispose();   // Send page to the printer
    job.end();                          // Terminate the job
  }
}


/**
 * Set the font style.  The argument should be one of the font style
 * constants defined by the java.awt.Font class.  All subsequent output
 * will be in that style.  This method relies on all styles of the
 * Monospaced font having the same metrics.
 **/
public void setFontStyle(int style) {
  synchronized (this.lock) {
    // Try to set a new font, but restore current one if it fails
    Font current = font;
    try { font = new Font("Monospaced", style, fontsize); }
    catch (Exception e) { font = current; }
    // If a page is pending, set the new font.  Otherwise newpage() will.
    if (page != null) page.setFont(font);
  }
}

/** End the current page.  Subsequent output will be on a new page. */
public void pageBreak() { synchronized(this.lock) { newpage(); } }

/** Return the number of columns of characters that fit on the page */
public int getCharactersPerLine() { return this.chars_per_line; }

/** Return the number of lines that fit on a page */
public int getLinesPerPage() { return this.lines_per_page; }

/** This internal method begins a new line */
protected void newline() {
  charnum = 0;                        // Reset character number to 0
  linenum++;                          // Increment line number
  if (linenum >= lines_per_page) {    // If we've reached the end of the page
    page.dispose();                   //    send page to printer
    page = null;                      //    but don't start a new page yet.
  }
}

/** This internal method begins a new page and prints the header. */
protected void newpage() {
  page = job.getGraphics();                     // Begin the new page
  linenum = 0; charnum = 0;                     // Reset line and char number
  pagenum++;                                    // Increment page number
  page.setFont(headerfont);                     // Set the header font.
  page.drawString(jobname, x0, headery);        // Print job name left justified

  String s = "- " + pagenum + " -";             // Print the page number centered.
  int w = headermetrics.stringWidth(s);
  page.drawString(s, x0 + (this.width - w)/2, headery);
```

Example 8-9: HardcopyWriter.java (continued)

```
    w = headermetrics.stringWidth(time);       // Print date right justified
    page.drawString(time, x0 + width - w, headery);

    // Draw a line beneath the header
    int y = headery + headermetrics.getDescent() + 1;
    page.drawLine(x0, y, x0+width, y);

    // Set the basic monospaced font for the rest of the page.
    page.setFont(font);
}

/**
 * This is the exception class that the HardcopyWriter constructor
 * throws when the user clicks "Cancel" in the print dialog box.
 **/
public static class PrintCanceledException extends Exception {
    public PrintCanceledException(String msg) { super(msg); }
}

/**
 * A program that prints the specified file using HardcopyWriter
 **/
public static class PrintFile {
    public static void main(String[] args) {
        try {
            if (args.length != 1)
                throw new IllegalArgumentException("Wrong number of arguments");
            FileReader in = new FileReader(args[0]);
            HardcopyWriter out = null;
            Frame f = new Frame("PrintFile: " + args[0]);
            f.setSize(200, 50);
            f.show();
            try { out = new HardcopyWriter(f, args[0], 10, .75, .75, .75, .75); }
            catch (HardcopyWriter.PrintCanceledException e) { System.exit(0); }
            f.setVisible(false);
            char[] buffer = new char[4096];
            int numchars;
            while((numchars = in.read(buffer)) != -1)
                out.write(buffer, 0, numchars);
            out.close();
        }
        catch (Exception e) {
            System.err.println(e);
            System.err.println("Usage: java HardcopyWriter$PrintFile <filename>");
            System.exit(1);
        }
        System.exit(0);
    }
}

/**
 * A program that prints a demo page using HardcopyWriter
 **/
public static class Demo extends Frame implements ActionListener {
    /** The main method of the program.  Create a test window and display it */
    public static void main(String[] args) { Frame f = new Demo();  f.show(); }
```

Example 8-9: HardcopyWriter.java (continued)

```java
// Buttons used in this program
protected Button print, quit;

/** Constructor for the test program's window. */
public Demo() {
  super("HardcopyWriter Test");           // Call frame constructor
  Panel p = new Panel();                  // Add a panel to the frame
  this.add(p, "Center");                  // Center it
  p.setFont(new Font("SansSerif",         // Set a default font
                     Font.BOLD, 18));
  print = new Button("Print Test Page"); // Create a Print button
  quit = new Button("Quit");              // Create a Quit button
  print.addActionListener(this);          // Specify that we'll handle
  quit.addActionListener(this);           //   button presses
  p.add(print);                           // Add the buttons to the panel
  p.add(quit);
  this.pack();                            // Set the size of everything
}

/** Handle the button presses */
public void actionPerformed(ActionEvent e) {
  Object o = e.getSource();
  if (o == quit) System.exit(0);
  else if (o == print) printDemoPage();
}

/** Print the demo page */
public void printDemoPage() {
  // Create the HardcopyWriter, using a 10 point font and 3/4" margins.
  HardcopyWriter hw;
  try { hw=new HardcopyWriter(this, "Demo Page", 14, .75, .75, .75, .75); }
  catch (HardcopyWriter.PrintCanceledException e) { return; }

  // Send output to it through a PrintWriter stream
  PrintWriter out = new PrintWriter(hw);

  // Figure out the size of the page
  int rows = hw.getLinesPerPage(), cols = hw.getCharactersPerLine();

  // Mark upper left and upper-right corners
  out.print("+"); for(int i=0;i<cols-2;i++) out.print(" "); out.print("+");

  // Display a title
  hw.setFontStyle(Font.BOLD + Font.ITALIC);
  out.println("\n\n\n\t\tHardcopy Writer Demo Page\n\n\n\n\n");

  // Demonstrate font styles
  hw.setFontStyle(Font.BOLD);
  out.println("Font Styles:");
  int[] styles = { Font.PLAIN,Font.BOLD,Font.ITALIC,Font.ITALIC+Font.BOLD};
  for(int i = 0; i < styles.length; i++) {
    hw.setFontStyle(styles[i]);
    out.println("ABCDEFGHIJKLMNOPQRSTUVWXYZabcdefghijklmnopqrstuvwxyz");
    out.println("1234567890!@#$%^&*()[]{}<>,.?:;+-=/\\'`\"_~|");
  }
  hw.setFontStyle(Font.PLAIN);
  out.println("\n\n");
```

Example 8-9: HardcopyWriter.java (continued)

```
        // Demonstrate tab stops
        hw.setFontStyle(Font.BOLD);
        out.println("Tab Stops:");
        hw.setFontStyle(Font.PLAIN);
        out.println("          1         2         3         4         5");
        out.println("0123456789012345678901234567890123456789012345");
        out.println("^\t^\t^\t^\t^\t^\t^\t^");
        out.println("\n\n");

        // Output some information about page dimensions and resolution
        hw.setFontStyle(Font.BOLD);
        out.println("Dimensions:");
        hw.setFontStyle(Font.PLAIN);
        out.println("\tResolution: " + hw.pagedpi + " dots per inch");
        out.println("\tPage width (pixels): " + hw.pagesize.width);
        out.println("\tPage height (pixels): " + hw.pagesize.height);
        out.println("\tWidth inside margins (pixels): " + hw.width);
        out.println("\tHeight inside margins (pixels): " + hw.height);
        out.println("\tCharacters per line: " + cols);
        out.println("\tLines per page: " + rows);

        // Skip down to the bottom of the page
        for(int i = 0; i < rows-37; i++) out.println();
        // And mark the lower left and lower right
        out.print("+"); for(int i=0;i<cols-2;i++) out.print(" "); out.print("+");

        // Close the output stream, forcing the page to be printed
        out.close();
    }
  }
}
```

Input/Output

Exercises

8-1. Write a program named Head that prints out the first 10 lines of each file specified on the command line.

8-2. Write a corresponding program named Tail that prints out the last 10 lines of each file specified on the command line.

8-3. Write a program that counts and reports the number of lines, words, and characters in a specified file. Use static methods of the java.lang.Character class to determine whether a given character is a space (and therefore the boundary between two words).

8-4. Write a program that adds up and reports the size of all files in a specified directory. It should recursively scan any subdirectories, summing and reporting the size of the files that they contain, and incorporate those directory sizes into its final output.

8-5. Write a program that lists all of the files and subdirectories in a specified directory, along with their sizes and modification dates. By default, the output should be sorted by name. If invoked with the -s option, however, output should be sorted by size from largest to smallest. If invoked with the -d option, output should be sorted by date, from most recent to least. Use the Sorter class developed in Chapter 2 to help with sorting.

8-6. Write a program named Uncompress that uncompresses files and directories compressed by the Compress example in this chapter.

8-7. Modify Example 7-2 so that it can save its scribbles to a file and later read them back from the file. Use a FileDialog to ask the user for a filename. Use DataOutputStream and DataInputStream to write and read the user's scribbles in binary format.

8-8. Write a subclass of OutputStream named TeeOutputStream that acts like a T joint in a pipe—the stream sends its output to two different output streams, specified when the TeeOutputStream is created. Write a simple test program that uses two TeeOutputStream objects to send text read from System.in to System.out and to two different test files.

8-9. Write a simple subclass of Reader named TestReader that returns the same character (a character passed to the constructor) over and over. The stream should never reach EOF. Write a trivial subclass of Writer named NullWriter that simply discards any output sent to it. Streams like these are occasionally useful for testing and other purposes. Write a test program that reads from the TestReader and sends its output to a PrintWriter wrapped around a NullWriter.

CHAPTER 9

Networking

The examples in this chapter demonstrate Java's networking capabilities at a number of different levels of abstraction. They show you how to:

- Use the URL class to parse URLs and download the network resources specified by a URL

- Use the URLConnection class to gain more control over the downloading of network resources

- Write client programs that use the Socket class to communicate over the Net

- Use the Socket and ServerSocket classes to write servers

- Send and receive low-overhead datagram packets

Downloading the Contents of a URL

Example 9-1 shows how you can download the network resource referred to by a URL using the URL class. This class serves mainly to represent and parse URLs, but also has several important methods for downloading URLs. The most high-level of these methods is getContent(), which downloads the content of a URL, parses it, and returns the parsed object. This method relies on special "content handlers" having been installed to perform the parsing. By default, the JDK has content handlers for plain text and for several common image formats. When you call the get-Content() method of a URL object that refers to a plain text or GIF or JPEG image file, the method returns a String or Image object. This method is much less useful with other data types, however. If it does not know how to handle the data type, it simply returns an InputStream so that you can read and parse the data yourself.

Example 9-1 does not use the getContent() method. Instead, it calls openStream() to return an InputStream from which the contents of the URL can be downloaded. This InputStream is connected, through the network, to the remote resource named by the URL, but the URL class hides all the details of setting up this connection. (In fact, the connection is set up by a "protocol handler" class; the JDK has default handlers for the most common network protocols, including *http:*, *ftp:*, *gopher:* and *file:*.)

Example 9-1 is a simple standalone program that downloads the contents of a specified URL and saves it in a file or writes it to the console. You'll note that most of this program looks like it belongs in Chapter 8, *Input/Output*. In fact, as we'll see in this and other examples in this chapter, almost all networking involves the use of the I/O techniques we learned about in that chapter.

Example 9–1: GetURL.java

```java
import java.io.*;
import java.net.*;

/**
 * This simple program uses the URL class and its openStream() method to
 * download the contents of a URL and copy them to a file or to the console.
 **/
public class GetURL {
  public static void main(String[] args) {
    InputStream in = null;
    OutputStream out = null;
    try {
      // Check the arguments
      if ((args.length != 1) && (args.length != 2))
        throw new IllegalArgumentException("Wrong number of arguments");

      // Set up the streams
      URL url = new URL(args[0]);     // Create the URL
      in = url.openStream();          // Open a stream to it
      if (args.length == 2)           // Get an appropriate output stream
        out = new FileOutputStream(args[1]);
      else out = System.out;

      // Now copy bytes from the URL to the output stream
      byte[] buffer = new byte[4096];
      int bytes_read;
      while((bytes_read = in.read(buffer)) != -1)
        out.write(buffer, 0, bytes_read);
    }
    // On exceptions, print error message and usage message.
    catch (Exception e) {
      System.err.println(e);
      System.err.println("Usage: java GetURL <URL> [<filename>]");
    }
    finally {  // Always close the streams, no matter what.
      try { in.close();  out.close(); } catch (Exception e) {}
    }
  }
}
```

Using a URLConnection

The URLConnection class is used to establish a connection to a· URL. The openStream() method of URL that we used in Example 9-1 is merely a convenience method that creates a URLConnection object and calls its getInputStream() method. By using a URLConnection object directly, instead of relying on

---

openStream(), you have much more control over the process of downloading the contents of a URL.

Example 9-2 is a simple program that shows how to use a URLConnection to obtain the content type, size, last-modified date, and other information about the resource referred to by a URL. If the URL uses the HTTP protocol, it also demonstrates how to use the HttpURLConnection subclass to obtain additional information about the connection.

Note the use of the java.util.Date class to convert a timestamp (a long that contains the number of milliseconds since midnight, January 1, 1970 GMT) to a human-readable date and time string.

Example 9-2: GetURLInfo.java

```java
import java.net.*;
import java.io.*;
import java.util.Date;

/**
 * A class that displays information about a URL.
 **/
public class GetURLInfo {
  /** Use the URLConnection class to get info about the URL */
  public static void printinfo(URL url) throws IOException {
    URLConnection c = url.openConnection();  // Get URLConnection from the URL
    c.connect();                             // Open a connection to the URL

    // Display some information about the URL contents
    System.out.println("  Content Type: " + c.getContentType());
    System.out.println("  Content Encoding: " + c.getContentEncoding());
    System.out.println("  Content Length: " + c.getContentLength());
    System.out.println("  Date: " + new Date(c.getDate()));
    System.out.println("  Last Modified: " + new Date(c.getLastModified()));
    System.out.println("  Expiration: " + new Date(c.getExpiration()));

    // If it is an HTTP connection, display some additional information.
    if (c instanceof HttpURLConnection) {
      HttpURLConnection h = (HttpURLConnection) c;
      System.out.println("  Request Method: " + h.getRequestMethod());
      System.out.println("  Response Message: " + h.getResponseMessage());
      System.out.println("  Response Code: " + h.getResponseCode());
    }
  }

  /** Create a URL object, call printinfo() to display information about it. */
  public static void main(String[] args) {
    try { printinfo(new URL(args[0])); }
    catch (Exception e) {
      System.err.println(e);
      System.err.println("Usage: java GetURLInfo <url>");
    }
  }
}
```

Sending Email Through a URLConnection

As mentioned above, Java includes support for different URL protocols through "protocol handlers" that are implemented internally to the JDK. In the Java 1.1 version of the JDK, these handlers include support for the *mailto:* protocol. Example 9-3 shows a program that uses a *mailto:* URL to send email. The program prompts the user to enter the sender, recipient or recipients, subject, and body of the message, and then creates an appropriate *mailto:* URL and obtains a URLConnection object for it. The program uses the setDoInput() and setDoOutput() methods to specify that it is writing data to the URLConnection. It obtains the appropriate stream with getOutputStream() and then writes the message headers and body to that stream, closing the stream when the message body is complete. The program uses the user.name system property and the InetAddress class to attempt to create a valid return address for the sender of the email, though this does not actually work correctly on all platforms.

In order for the *mailto:* protocol handler to send mail, it must know what computer, or "mailhost," to send it to. By default, it attempts to send it to the machine on which it is running. Some computers, particularly UNIX machines on intranets, work as mailhosts, so this works fine. Other computers, such as PCs connected to the Internet by a dialup connection, have to explicitly specify a mailhost on the command line. If your Internet service provider has the domain name *isp.net*, then the appropriate mailhost is often *mail.isp.net*. If you specify a mailhost, it is stored in the system property mail.host, which is read by the internal *mailto:* protocol handler.

Example 9-3: SendMail.java

```
import java.io.*;
import java.net.*;

/**
 * This program sends e-mail using a mailto: URL
 **/
public class SendMail {
  public static void main(String[] args) {
    try {
      // If the user specified a mailhost, tell the system about it.
      if (args.length >= 1) System.getProperties().put("mail.host", args[0]);

      // A Reader stream to read from the console
      BufferedReader in = new BufferedReader(new InputStreamReader(System.in));

      // Ask the user for the from, to, and subject lines
      System.out.print("From: ");
      String from = in.readLine();
      System.out.print("To: ");
      String to = in.readLine();
      System.out.print("Subject: ");
      String subject = in.readLine();

      // Establish a network connection for sending mail
      URL u = new URL("mailto:" + to);       // Create a mailto: URL
      URLConnection c = u.openConnection();  // Create a URLConnection for it
      c.setDoInput(false);                   // Specify no input from this URL
      c.setDoOutput(true);                   // Specify we'll do output
```

Example 9-3: SendMail.java (continued)

```
        System.out.println("Connecting...");    // Tell the user what's happening
        System.out.flush();                      // Tell them right now
        c.connect();                             // Connect to mail host
        PrintWriter out =                        // Get output stream to mail host
          new PrintWriter(new OutputStreamWriter(c.getOutputStream()));

        // Write out mail headers.  Don't let users fake the From address
        out.println("From: \"" + from + "\" <" +
                    System.getProperty("user.name") + "@" +
                    InetAddress.getLocalHost().getHostName() + ">");
        out.println("To: " + to);
        out.println("Subject: " + subject);
        out.println();  // blank line to end the list of headers

        // Now ask the user to enter the body of the message
        System.out.println("Enter the message. " +
                           "End with a '.' on a line by itself.");
        // Read message line by line and send it out.
        String line;
        for(;;) {
          line = in.readLine();
          if ((line == null) || line.equals(".")) break;
          out.println(line);
        }

        // Close the stream to terminate the message
        out.close();
        // Tell the user it was successfully sent.
        System.out.println("Message sent.");
        System.out.flush();
      }
    catch (Exception e) {  // Handle any exceptions, print error message.
      System.err.println(e);
      System.err.println("Usage: java SendMail [<mailhost>]");
    }
  }
}
```

Connecting to a Web Server

Example 9-4 is a program, HttpClient, that downloads the contents of a URL from a Web server and writes it to a file or to the console. It behaves just like the GetURL program from Example 9-1 does. Despite the similarity in behavior, however, the implementation of these two programs is entirely different. While GetURL relies on the URL class (and the content handlers it uses) to handle protocol details, HttpClient connects directly to a Web server, and communicates with it using the HTTP protocol. (It uses an old and extremely simple version of the protocol, which keeps the program very simple.) As a consequence, HttpClient is restricted to downloading URLs that use the *http:* protocol. It cannot handle *ftp:* or other network protocols. Note that HttpClient does use the URL class, but only to represent a URL and to parse it, not to connect to it.

The main point of interest in this example is the introduction of the Socket class, which is used to create a stream-based network connection between a client and a server. To create a network connection to another host, you simply create a Socket, specifying the desired host and port. If there is a program (a server) running on the specified host and listening for connections on the specified port, then the Socket() constructor returns a Socket object to you that you can use to communicate with the server. (If there is not a server listening on the specified host and port, or if anything goes wrong—and many things can go wrong with networking—the Socket() constructor throws an exception).

If you are not familiar with hosts and ports, think of the host as a post office and the port as a post-office box. Just as a post office has many different post-office boxes, any host on the network can run many different servers at a time. Different servers use different ports as their address, and to establish a connection, you must specify both the correct host and the correct port. Many services have standard default ports. Web servers run on port 80, POP email servers run on port 110, and so on.

Once you have a Socket object, you are connected, across the network, to a server. The getInputStream() method of the socket returns an InputStream that you can use to read bytes from the server, and getOutputStream() returns an OutputStream that you can use to write bytes to the server. This is exactly what the HttpClient program does. It establishes a connection to the Web server, sends an HTTP GET request to the server through the output stream of the socket, and then reads the server's response through the input stream of the socket.

Example 9–4: HttpClient.java

```java
import java.io.*;
import java.net.*;

/**
 * This program connects to a Web server and downloads the specified URL
 * from it.  It uses the HTTP protocol directly.
 **/
public class HttpClient {
  public static void main(String[] args) {
    try {
      // Check the arguments
      if ((args.length != 1) && (args.length != 2))
        throw new IllegalArgumentException("Wrong number of arguments");

      // Get an output stream to write the URL contents to
      OutputStream to_file;
      if (args.length == 2) to_file = new FileOutputStream(args[1]);
      else to_file = System.out;

      // Now use the URL class to parse the user-specified URL into
      // its various parts: protocol, host, port, filename.  Check the protocol
      URL url = new URL(args[0]);
      String protocol = url.getProtocol();
      if (!protocol.equals("http"))
        throw new IllegalArgumentException("URL must use 'http:' protocol");
      String host = url.getHost();
      int port = url.getPort();
      if (port == -1) port = 80;  // if no port, use the default HTTP port
      String filename = url.getFile();
```

Example 9-4: HttpClient.java (continued)

```
      // Open a network socket connection to the specified host and port
      Socket socket = new Socket(host, port);
      // Get input and output streams for the socket
      InputStream from_server = socket.getInputStream();
      PrintWriter to_server =
        new PrintWriter(new OutputStreamWriter(socket.getOutputStream()));

      // Send the HTTP GET command to the Web server, specifying the file.
      // This uses an old and very simple version of the HTTP protocol
      to_server.println("GET " + filename + "\n");
      to_server.flush();   // Send it right now!

      // Now read the server's response, and write it to the file
      byte[] buffer = new byte[4096];
      int bytes_read;
      while((bytes_read = from_server.read(buffer)) != -1)
        to_file.write(buffer, 0, bytes_read);

      // When the server closes the connection, we close our stuff
      socket.close();
      to_file.close();
    }
    catch (Exception e) {    // Report any errors that arise
      System.err.println(e);
      System.err.println("Usage: java HttpClient <URL> [<filename>]");
    }
  }
}
```

A Simple Web Server

Example 9-5 shows a very simple Web server, HttpMirror. Instead of returning a requested file, however, this server simply "mirrors" the request back to the client as its reply. This can be useful when debugging Web clients, and can be interesting if you are just curious about the details of HTTP client requests. To run the program, you specify the port that it should listen on as an argument. For example, I can run the server on the host *oxymoron.ora.com* like this:

```
oxymoron% java HttpMirror 4444
```

Then, in my Web browser, I can load *http://oxymoron.ora.com:4444/testing.html*. The server ignores the request for the file *testing.html*, but it echoes back the request that my Web browser sent. It might look something like this:

```
GET /testing.html HTTP/1.0
Connection: Keep-Alive
User-Agent: Mozilla/3.01Gold (X11; I; Linux 2.0.18 i486)
Host: 127.0.0.1:4444
Accept: image/gif, image/x-xbitmap, image/jpeg, image/pjpeg, */*
```

The main new feature introduced in Example 9-5 is the ServerSocket class. This class is used by a server, or any other program, that wants to sit and wait for a connection request from a client. When you create a ServerSocket, you specify the port to listen on. To connect to a client, call the accept() method of the ServerSocket. This method blocks until a client attempts to connect to the port that the ServerSocket is listening on. When such a connection attempt occurs, the ServerSocket establishes a connection to the client and returns a Socket object that can be used to communicate with the client. Your code can then call the get-InputStream() and getOutputStream() methods of the socket to get streams for reading bytes from the client and for writing bytes to the client.

Note that the ServerSocket is not used for communication between the server and its client; it is only used to wait for and establish the connection to the client. Typically a single ServerSocket object is used over and over again to establish connections to any number of clients.

Example 9-5 is quite straightforward. It creates a ServerSocket and calls its accept() method, as outlined above. When a client connects, it sets up the streams, and then sends some HTTP headers to the client telling it that the request has been received successfully and that the reply is text/plain data. Next, it reads all the HTTP headers of the client's request and sends them back to the client as the body of its reply. When it reads a blank line from the client, this indicates the end of the client's headers, so it closes the connection.

Note that the body of the HttpMirror program is a big infinite loop. It connects to a client, handles the request, and then loops and waits for another client connection. Although this simple server works perfectly well for the testing purposes for which it is designed, there is one flaw in it: it is a single-threaded server and can only talk to one client at a time. Later in this chapter, we'll see examples of servers that use multiple threads and can maintain connections to any number of clients.

Example 9–5: HttpMirror.java

```java
import java.io.*;
import java.net.*;

/**
 * This program is a very simple Web server.  When it receives a HTTP request
 * it sends the request back as the reply.  This can be of interest when
 * you want to see just what a Web client is requesting, or what data is
 * being sent when a form is submitted, for example.
 **/
public class HttpMirror {
  public static void main(String args[]) {
    try {
      // Get the port to listen on
      int port = Integer.parseInt(args[0]);
      // Create a ServerSocket to listen on that port.
      ServerSocket ss = new ServerSocket(port);
      // Now enter an infinite loop, waiting for connections and handling them.
      for(;;) {
        // Wait for a client to connect.  The method will block, and when it
        // returns the socket will be already connected to the client
        Socket client = ss.accept();
        // Get input and output streams to talk to the client from the socket
        BufferedReader in =
          new BufferedReader(new InputStreamReader(client.getInputStream()));
        PrintWriter out =
          new PrintWriter(new OutputStreamWriter(client.getOutputStream()));

        // Start sending our reply, using the HTTP 1.0 protocol
        out.println("HTTP/1.0 200 ");          // Version & status code
```

Example 9–5: HttpMirror.java (continued)

```
      out.println("Content-Type: text/plain");    // The type of data we send
      out.println();                              // End of response headers
      out.flush();

      // Now, read the HTTP request from the client, and send it right
      // back to the client as part of the body of our response.
      // The client doesn't disconnect, so we never get an EOF.
      // It does sends an empty line at the end of the headers, though.
      // So when we see the empty line, we stop reading.  This means we
      // don't mirror the contents of POST requests, for example.
      String line;
      while((line = in.readLine()) != null) {
        if (line.length() == 0) break;
        out.println(line);
      }

      // Close the streams and socket, breaking the connection to the client
      out.close();
      in.close();
      client.close();
    } // Loop again, waiting for the next connection
  }
  // If anything goes wrong, print an error message
  catch (Exception e) {
    System.err.println(e);
    System.err.println("Usage: java HttpMirror <port>");
  }
}
}
```

A Proxy Server

Example 9-6 shows another network server: a simple, single-threaded proxy server. A proxy server is one that acts as a proxy for some other real server. When a client connects to a proxy server, the proxy forwards the client's requests to the real server, and then forwards the server's responses to the client. To the client, the proxy looks like the server. To the real server, the proxy looks like a client.

Why bother with a proxy server at all? Why can't a client just connect directly to the real server? First and foremost, there are firewall-related reasons to use proxy servers. There are also interesting filtering applications of such servers—a sophisticated proxy Web server might strip advertising out of the Web pages it downloads, for example. There is yet another reason to use proxy servers that arises when using Java networking capabilities with applets, as the following scenario makes clear.

Suppose that I have developed a nifty new server that runs on my computer *oxymoron.ora.com*. Now I write an applet client for my service, and make the applet available on the Web by publishing it on the *www.ora.com* Web server. Right away there is a problem. Applet security restrictions only allow an applet to establish network connections to one host: the host from which it was downloaded. So my applet client downloaded from *www.ora.com* cannot communicate to my incredibly useful server on *oxymoron.ora.com*. What can I do? The system administrator won't allow me to install my new server on *www.ora.com* and my manager won't authorize the purchase of a commercial Web server for my desktop workstation *oxymoron*. So instead, I run a simple proxy server, like the one in Example 9-6, on *oxymoron*. I set it up so that it listens for connections on port 4444 and acts as a proxy for the Web server running on port 80 of *www.ora.com*. I publish my applet at *http://www.ora.com/staff/david/nifty.html*, but tell people to load it from *http://oxymoron.ora.com:4444/staff/david/nifty.html*.[*] This solves the problem. As far as the applet is concerned, it has been loaded from *oxymoron.ora.com*, so it can connect to my nifty service running on that host.

There are not really any new features in Example 9-6. It is an interesting example because it combines the features of both client and server into one program. When studying this code, remember that the proxy server mediates the connection between a client and a server. It acts like a server to the client, and acts like a client to the server. `SimpleProxyServer` is a single-threaded server—it can only handle one client connection at a time. Nevertheless, you'll notice that it does use a thread (implemented in an anonymous inner class) so that the proxy can transfer data from client to server and from server to client at the same time. In this example, the main thread reads bytes from the server and sends them to the client. A separate thread is used to read bytes from the client and send them to the server.

Example 9–6: SimpleProxyServer.java

```
import java.io.*;
import java.net.*;

/**
 * This class implements a simple single-threaded proxy server.
 **/
public class SimpleProxyServer {
  /** The main method parses arguments and passes them to runServer */
  public static void main(String[] args) throws IOException {
    try {
      // Check the number of arguments
      if (args.length != 3)
        throw new IllegalArgumentException("Wrong number of arguments.");

      // Get the command-line arguments: the host and port we are proxy for
      // and the local port that we listen for connections on
      String host = args[0];
      int remoteport = Integer.parseInt(args[1]);
      int localport = Integer.parseInt(args[2]);
      // Print a start-up message
      System.out.println("Starting proxy for " + host + ":" + remoteport +
                         " on port " + localport);
      // And start running the server
      runServer(host, remoteport, localport);   // never returns
    }
    catch (Exception e) {
      System.err.println(e);
      System.err.println("Usage: java SimpleProxyServer " +
                         "<host> <remoteport> <localport>");
    }
  }
```

---

[*] This is a fictitious example—these URLs don't really do anything!

Example 9-6: SimpleProxyServer.java (continued)

```
/**
 * This method runs a single-threaded proxy server for
 * host:remoteport on the specified local port.  It never returns.
 **/
public static void runServer(String host, int remoteport, int localport)
     throws IOException {
  // Create a ServerSocket to listen for connections with
  ServerSocket ss = new ServerSocket(localport);

  // Create buffers for client-to-server and server-to-client communication.
  // We make one final so it can be used in an anonymous class below.
  // Note the assumptions about the volume of traffic in each direction...
  final byte[] request = new byte[1024];
  byte[] reply = new byte[4096];

  // This is a server that never returns, so enter an infinite loop.
  while(true) {
    // Variables to hold the sockets to the client and to the server.
    Socket client = null, server = null;
    try {
      // Wait for a connection on the local port
      client = ss.accept();

      // Get client streams.  Make them final so they can
      // be used in the anonymous thread below.
      final InputStream from_client = client.getInputStream();
      final OutputStream to_client= client.getOutputStream();

      // Make a connection to the real server
      // If we cannot connect to the server, send an error to the
      // client, disconnect, then continue waiting for another connection.
      try { server = new Socket(host, remoteport); }
      catch (IOException e) {
        PrintWriter out = new PrintWriter(new OutputStreamWriter(to_client));
        out.println("Proxy server cannot connect to " + host + ":" +
                    remoteport + ":\n" + e);
        out.flush();
        client.close();
        continue;
      }

      // Get server streams.
      final InputStream from_server = server.getInputStream();
      final OutputStream to_server = server.getOutputStream();

      // Make a thread to read the client's requests and pass them to the
      // server.  We have to use a separate thread because requests and
      // responses may be asynchronous.
      Thread t = new Thread() {
        public void run() {
          int bytes_read;
          try {
            while((bytes_read = from_client.read(request)) != -1) {
              to_server.write(request, 0, bytes_read);
              to_server.flush();
            }
          }
          catch (IOException e) {}
```

Example 9-6: SimpleProxyServer.java (continued)

```
              // the client closed the connection to us, so  close our
              // connection to the server.  This will also cause the
              // server-to-client loop in the main thread exit.
              try {to_server.close();} catch (IOException e) {}
          }
        };

        // Start the client-to-server request thread running
        t.start();

        // Meanwhile, in the main thread, read the server's responses
        // and pass them back to the client.  This will be done in
        // parallel with the client-to-server request thread above.
        int bytes_read;
        try {
          while((bytes_read = from_server.read(reply)) != -1) {
            to_client.write(reply, 0, bytes_read);
            to_client.flush();
          }
        }
        catch(IOException e) {}

        // The server closed its connection to us, so close our
        // connection to our client.  This will make the other thread exit.
        to_client.close();
      }
      catch (IOException e) { System.err.println(e); }
      // Close the sockets no matter what happens each time through the loop.
      finally {
        try {
          if (server != null) server.close();
          if (client != null) client.close();
        }
        catch(IOException e) {}
      }
    }
  }
}
```

Networking with Applets

As described above, untrusted applets have a strict restriction placed on the kind of networking they can do. They are only allowed to connect to, and accept connections from, the one host from which they were loaded. No other networking is allowed. This still leaves open some interesting applet networking possibilities, though, and Example 9-7 illustrates one of them.

finger is a program and network service that used to be run on almost all UNIX machines. It allows a client to connect over the network and obtain a list of the users who are logged on to another system. It may also allow a client to obtain detailed information (such as telephone numbers) for individual users. Nowadays, with heightened security concerns, many UNIX machines do not provide this service.

The applet shown in Example 9-7 is a client for the *finger* service. Suppose that I'm an old UNIX hacker, and I think that the *finger* service is a great thing. I run the *finger* server on my workstation, and I encourage my friends to use it to find out when I'm logged on. Unfortunately, my friends work on PCs, so they don't have access to the old-fashioned, text-based *finger* client that all UNIX machines have. The Who applet in Example 9-7 solves this problem. It connects to the appropriate port on my host and tells them whether I'm logged on or not. Of course, for this to work, the applet has to be served from my host as well. I might use the SimpleProxyServer program from Example 9-6 to make my computer into a proxy Web server. (Or, of course, I could use SimpleProxyServer to set up a proxy *finger* server for my host on the host that runs the Web server.)

If your system does not run the *finger* server itself, trying this applet out may be a little tricky. What you can do is find some host out on the Net that does provide the *finger* service. (I've used *rtfm.mit.edu*, for example.) Then use SimpleProxy-Server to run a local proxy for that finger server and run the applet locally on your machine. You'll have to modify the applet slightly to make it connect to the desired proxy port, instead of the reserved finger port 79, however.

Example 9-7: Who.java

```java
import java.applet.*;
import java.awt.*;
import java.awt.event.*;
import java.io.*;
import java.net.*;

/**
 * This applet connects to the "finger" server on the host
 * it was served from to determine who is currently logged on.
 * Because it is an untrusted applet, it can only connect to the host
 * from which it came.  Since web servers do not usually run finger
 * servers themselves, this applet will often be used in conjunction
 * with a proxy server, to serve it from some other host that does run
 * a finger server.
 **/
public class Who extends Applet implements ActionListener, Runnable {
  Button who;  // The button in the applet
  /**
   * The init method just creates a button to display in the applet.
   * When the user clicks the button, we'll check who is logged on.
   **/
  public void init() {
    who = new Button("Who?");
    who.setFont(new Font("SansSerif", Font.PLAIN, 14));
    who.addActionListener(this);
    who.setActionCommand("who");
    this.add(who);
  }

  /**
   * When the button is clicked, start a thread that will connect to
   * the finger server and display who is logged on
   **/
  public void actionPerformed(ActionEvent e) {
    if (e.getActionCommand().equals("who")) new Thread(this).start();
  }
```

Example 9–7: Who.java (continued)

```java
/**
 * This is the method that does the networking and displays the results.
 * It is implemented as the body of a separate thread because it might
 * take some time to complete, and applet methods need to return promptly.
 **/
public void run() {
    // Disable the button so we don't get multiple queries at once...
    who.setEnabled(false);

    // Create a window to display the output in
    Frame f = new CloseableFrame("Who's Logged On: Connecting...");
    TextArea t = new TextArea(10, 80);
    t.setFont(new Font("MonoSpaced", Font.PLAIN, 10));
    f.add(t, "Center");
    f.pack();
    f.show();

    // Find out  who's logged on
    Socket s = null;
    PrintWriter out = null;
    BufferedReader in = null;
    try {
        // Connect to port 79 (the standard finger port) on the host
        // that the applet was loaded from.
        String hostname = this.getCodeBase().getHost();
        s = new Socket(hostname, 79);
        // Set up the streams
        out = new PrintWriter(new OutputStreamWriter(s.getOutputStream()));
        in = new BufferedReader(new InputStreamReader(s.getInputStream()));

        // Send a blank line to the finger server, telling it that we want
        // a listing of everyone logged on instead of information about an
        // individual user.
        out.println();
        out.flush();     // Send it now!

        // Now read the server's response and display it in the textarea
        String line;
        while((line = in.readLine()) != null) {
            t.append(line);
            t.append("\n");
        }
        f.setTitle("Who's Logged On: " + hostname);
    }
    // If something goes wrong, we'll just display the exception message
    catch (IOException e) {
        t.append(e.toString());
        f.setTitle("Who's Logged On: Error");
    }
    // And finally, don't forget to close the streams!
    finally { try {in.close(); out.close(); s.close();} catch(Exception e){} }

    // And enable the button again
    who.setEnabled(true);
  }
}
```

A Generic Client

The HttpClient class of Example 9-4 was a special-purpose client. Example 9-8 defines a class, GenericClient, that can serve as a client for a variety of servers. When you run this program, it connects to the host and port you have specified on the command line. From that point on, it simply sends the text you type to the server, and then outputs the text the server sends in response to the console.

You can use GenericClient to download files from a Web server by sending a simple HTTP protocol GET command, as HttpClient does. For big files, however, the server's output scrolls by too quickly for this to be useful. GenericClient is more useful for text-based interactive protocols. The Post Office Protocol (POP) is such a protocol. You can use GenericClient to preview any mail you have waiting for you at your ISP (or elsewhere). An interaction, using GenericClient, with a POP server might look like this code. The lines in bold are those typed by the user.

```
oxymoron% java GenericClient mail.isp.net 110
Connected to mail.isp.net/208.99.99.251:110
+OK QUALCOMM Pop server derived from UCB (version 2.1.4-R3) at mail.isp.net
starting.
user djf
+OK Password required for djf.
pass notrealpassword
+OK djf has 3 message(s) (2861 octets).
retr 3
+OK 363 octets
Received: from obsidian.ora.com (obsidian.ora.com [207.144.66.251])
        by mail.isp.net (8.8.5/8.8.5) with SMTP id RAA11654
        for djf@isp.net; Wed, 25 Jun 1997 17:01:50 -0400 (EDT)
Date: Wed, 25 Jun 1997 17:01:50 -0400 (EDT)
Message-Id: <199706252101.RAA11654@mail.isp.net>
From: "Paula Ferguson" <pf@ora.com>
To: djf@isp.net
Subject: testing

This is a test...
dele 3
+OK Message 3 has been deleted.
quit
+OK Pop server at mail.isp.net signing off.
Connection closed by server.
oxymoron%
```

The GenericClient class is fairly similar in structure to the SimpleProxyServer class shown in Example 9-6. Like SimpleProxyServer, GenericClient uses an anonymous second thread. This thread transfers data from server to client in parallel with the main thread, which transfers data from client to server. By using two threads, user input and server output can occur asynchronously, which, in fact, it does in some protocols. The only complication in GenericClient is that the two threads must have different priorities, because on some operating systems a thread cannot write to the console while another thread of the same priority is blocked waiting to read from the console.

Example 9-8: GenericClient.java

```java
import java.io.*;
import java.net.*;

/**
 * This program connects to a server at a specified host and port.
 * It reads text from the console and sends it to the server.
 * It reads text from the server and sends it to the console.
 **/
public class GenericClient {
  public static void main(String[] args) throws IOException {
    try {
      // Check the number of arguments
      if (args.length != 2)
        throw new IllegalArgumentException("Wrong number of arguments");

      // Parse the host and port specifications
      String host = args[0];
      int port = Integer.parseInt(args[1]);

      // Connect to the specified host and port
      Socket s = new Socket(host, port);

      // Set up streams for reading from and writing to the server.
      // The from_server stream is final for use in the anonymous class below
      final Reader from_server = new InputStreamReader(s.getInputStream());
      PrintWriter to_server =
        new PrintWriter(new OutputStreamWriter(s.getOutputStream()));

      // Set up streams for reading from and writing to the console
      // The to_user stream is final for use in the anonymous class below.
      BufferedReader from_user =
        new BufferedReader(new InputStreamReader(System.in));
      final PrintWriter to_user =
        new PrintWriter(new OutputStreamWriter(System.out));

      // Tell the user that we've connected
      to_user.println("Connected to " + s.getInetAddress() + ":"+ s.getPort());
      to_user.flush();

      // Create a thread that gets output from the server and displays
      // it to the user.  We use a separate thread for this so that we can
      // receive asynchronous output
      Thread t = new Thread() {
        public void run() {
          char[] buffer = new char[1024];
          int chars_read;
          try {
            while((chars_read = from_server.read(buffer)) != -1) {
              to_user.write(buffer, 0, chars_read);
              to_user.flush();
            }
          }
          catch (IOException e) { to_user.println(e); }

          // When the server closes the connection, the loop above will end.
          // Tell the user what happened, and call System.exit(), causing
          // the main thread to exit along with this one.
          to_user.println("Connection closed by server.");
```

Example 9–8: GenericClient.java (continued)

```
          to_user.flush();
          System.exit(0);
        }
      };

      // We set the priority of the server-to-user thread above to be one
      // level higher than the main thread.  We shouldn't have to do this, but
      // on some operating systems, output sent to the console doesn't appear
      // when a thread at the same priority level is blocked waiting for
      // input from the console.
      t.setPriority(Thread.currentThread().getPriority() + 1);

      // Now start the server-to-user thread
      t.start();

      // And in parallel, read the user's input and pass it on to the server.
      String line;
      while((line = from_user.readLine()) != null) {
        to_server.println(line);
        to_server.flush();
      }

      // If the user types a Ctrl-D (Unix) or Ctrl-Z (Windows) to end their
      // input, we'll get and EOF, and the loop above will exit.  When this
      // happens, we stop the server-to-user thread and close the socket.
      t.stop();
      s.close();
      to_user.println("Connection closed by client.");
      to_user.flush();
    }
    // If anything goes wrong, print an error message
    catch (Exception e) {
      System.err.println(e);
      System.err.println("Usage: java GenericClient <hostname> <port>");
    }
  }
}
```

A Generic Multi-Threaded Server

Example 9-9 is a long and fairly complex example. The Server class it defines is a
multi-threaded server that provides services defined by implementations of a
nested Server.Service interface. It can provide multiple services (defined by multiple Service objects) on multiple ports, and it has the ability to dynamically load
and instantiate Service classes and add (and remove) new services at runtime. It
logs its actions to a specified stream and limits the number of concurrent connections to a specified maximum.

The Server class uses a number of nested classes. The Server.Listener class is a
thread that waits for connections on a given port. There is one Listener object for
each service the Server is providing. The Server.ConnectionManager class manages the list of current connections to all services. There is one ConnectionManager
shared by all services. When a Listener gets a connection from a client, it passes
it to the ConnectionManager, which rejects it if the connection limit has been

reached. If the ConnectionManager does not reject a client, it creates a Server.Connection object to handle the connection. Connection is a Thread subclass, so each service can handle multiple connections at a time, making this a multi-threaded server. Each Connection object is passed a Service object and invokes its serve() method, which is what actually provides the service.

The Service interface is a nested member of the Server class; Server includes a number of implementations of this interface. Many of these implementations are trivial, demonstration services. The Control class, however, is a non-trivial Service. This service provides password-protected runtime access to the server, and allows a remote administrator to add and remove services, check the server status, and change the current connection limit.

Finally, the main() method of Server is a standalone program that creates and runs a Server. By specifying the -control argument on the command line, you can tell this program to create an instance of the Control service so that the server can be administered at runtime. Other arguments to this program specify the names of Service classes to be run and the ports that they should use. For example, you could start the server with a command like this:

```
% java Server -control mypassword 3000 Server\$Time 3001 \
              Server\$Reverse 3002 Server\$HTTPMirror 3003 \
              Server\$UniqueID 3004
```

This command starts the Control service on port 3000, the Server.Time service on 3001, the Server.Reverse service on 3002, the Server.HTTPMirror service on 3003, and the Server.UniqueID service on 3004. Once you have started the server program, you can use GenericClient (see Example 9-8) to connect to each of the services it provides. Using the Control service is the most interesting, of course.

The best way to understand the Server class and its nested classes and interfaces is to dive in and study the code. It is heavily commented. I recommend that you skim it, reading comments first, and then go back through and study each class in detail.

Example 9–9: Server.java

```
import java.io.*;
import java.net.*;
import java.util.*;

/**
 * This class is a generic framework for a flexible, multi-threaded server.
 * It listens on any number of specified ports, and, when it receives a
 * connection on a port, passes input and output streams to a specified Service
 * object which provides the actual service.  It can limit the number of
 * concurrent connections, and logs activity to a specified stream.
 **/
public class Server {
  /**
   * A main() method for running the server as a standalone program.
   * The command-line arguments to the program should be pairs of servicenames
   * and port numbers.  For each pair, the program will dynamically load the
   * named Service class, instantiate it, and tell the server to provide that
   * Service on the specified port.  The special -control argument should be
   * followed by a password and port, and will start special server control
```

Example 9-9: Server.java (continued)

```
 * service running on the specified port, protected by the specified
 * password.
 **/
public static void main(String[] args) {
  try {
    if (args.length < 2)  // Check number of arguments
      throw new IllegalArgumentException("Must start at least one service");

    // Create a Server object that uses standard out as its log and
    // has a limit of ten concurrent connections at once.
    Server s = new Server(System.out, 10);

    // Parse the argument list
    int i = 0;
    while(i < args.length) {
      if (args[i].equals("-control")) {    // Handle the -control argument
        i++;
        String password = args[i++];
        int port = Integer.parseInt(args[i++]);
        s.addService(new Control(s, password), port);  // add control service
      }
      else {
        // Otherwise start a named service on the specified port.
        // Dynamically load and instantiate a class that implements Service.
        String serviceName = args[i++];
        Class serviceClass = Class.forName(serviceName); // dynamic load
        Service service = (Service)serviceClass.newInstance(); // instantiate
        int port = Integer.parseInt(args[i++]);
        s.addService(service, port);
      }
    }
  }
  catch (Exception e) { // Display a message if anything goes wrong
    System.err.println("Server: " + e);
    System.err.println("Usage: java Server [-control <password> <port>] " +
                       "[<servicename> <port> ... ]");
    System.exit(1);
  }
}

// This is the state for the server
ConnectionManager connectionManager; // The ConnectionManager object
Hashtable services;                  // The current services and their ports
ThreadGroup threadGroup;             // The threadgroup for all our threads
PrintWriter logStream;               // Where we send our logging output to

/**
 * This is the Server() constructor.  It must be passed a stream
 * to send log output to (may be null), and the limit on the number of
 * concurrent connections.  It creates and starts a ConnectionManager
 * thread which enforces this limit on connections.
 **/
public Server(OutputStream logStream, int maxConnections) {
  setLogStream(logStream);
  log("Starting server");
  threadGroup = new ThreadGroup("Server");
  connectionManager = new ConnectionManager(threadGroup, maxConnections);
  connectionManager.start();
```

Example 9-9: Server.java (continued)

```
   services = new Hashtable();
}

/**
 * A public method to set the current logging stream.  Pass null
 * to turn logging off
 **/
public void setLogStream(OutputStream out) {
  if (out != null) logStream = new PrintWriter(new OutputStreamWriter(out));
  else logStream = null;
}

/** Write the specified string to the log */
protected synchronized void log(String s) {
  if (logStream != null) {
    logStream.println("[" + new Date() + "] " + s);
    logStream.flush();
  }
}
/** Write the specified object to the log */
protected void log(Object o) { log(o.toString()); }


/**
 * This method makes the server start providing a new service.
 * It runs the specified Service object on the specified port.
 **/
public void addService(Service service, int port) throws IOException {
  Integer key = new Integer(port);  // the hashtable key
  // Check whether a service is already on that port
  if (services.get(key) != null)
    throw new IllegalArgumentException("Port " + port + " already in use.");
  // Create a Listener object to listen for connections on the port
  Listener listener = new Listener(threadGroup, port, service);
  // Store it in the hashtable
  services.put(key, listener);
  // Log it
  log("Starting service " + service.getClass().getName() +
      " on port " + port);
  // Start the listener running.
  listener.start();
}


/**
 * This method makes the server stop providing a service on a port.
 * It does not terminate any pending connections to that service, merely
 * causes the server to stop accepting new connections
 **/
public void removeService(int port) {
  Integer key = new Integer(port);  // hashtable key
  // Look up the Listener object for the port in the hashtable of services
  final Listener listener = (Listener) services.get(key);
  if (listener == null) return;
  // Ask the listener to stop
  listener.pleaseStop();
  // Remove it from the hashtable
  services.remove(key);
  // And log it.
```

Example 9-9: Server.java (continued)

```
    log("Stopping service " + listener.service.getClass().getName() +
        " on port " + port);
}

/**
 * This nested Thread subclass is a "listener".  It listens for connections
 * on a specified port (using a ServerSocket) and when it gets a connection
 * request, it calls a method of the ConnectionManager to accept (or reject)
 * the connection.  There is one Listener for each Service being provided
 * by the Server.  The Listener passes the Server object to the
 * ConnectionManager, but doesn't do anything with it itself.
 */
public class Listener extends Thread {
  ServerSocket listen_socket;    // The socket we listen for connections on
  int port;                      // The port we're listening on
  Service service;               // The service to provide on that port
  boolean stop = false;          // Whether we've been asked to stop

  /**
   * The Listener constructor creates a thread for itself in the specified
   * threadgroup.  It creates a ServerSocket to listen for connections
   * on the specified port.  It arranges for the ServerSocket to be
   * interruptible, so that services can be removed from the server.
   **/
  public Listener(ThreadGroup group, int port, Service service)
        throws IOException {
    super(group, "Listener:" + port);
    listen_socket = new ServerSocket(port);
    // give the socket a non-zero timeout so accept() can be interrupted
    listen_socket.setSoTimeout(600000);
    this.port = port;
    this.service = service;
  }

  /** This is the nice way to get a Listener to stop accepting connections */
  public void pleaseStop() {
    this.stop = true;      // set the stop flag
    this.interrupt();      // and make the accept() call stop blocking
  }

  /**
   * A Listener is a Thread, and this is its body.
   * Wait for connection requests, accept them, and pass the socket on
   * to the ConnectionManager object of this server
   **/
  public void run() {
    while(!stop) {          // loop until we're asked to stop.
      try {
        Socket client = listen_socket.accept();
        connectionManager.addConnection(client, service);
      }
      catch (InterruptedIOException e) {}
      catch (IOException e) {log(e);}
    }
  }
}
```

Example 9–9: Server.java (continued)

```java
/**
 * This nested class  manages client connections for the server.
 * It maintains a list of current connections and enforces the
 * maximum connection limit.  It creates a separate thread (one per
 * server) that sits around and wait()s to be notify()'d that a connection
 * has terminated.  When this happens, it updates the list of connections.
 **/
public class ConnectionManager extends Thread {
  int maxConnections;  // The maximum number of allowed connections
  Vector connections;  // The current list of connections

  /**
   * Create a ConnectionManager in the specified thread group to enforce
   * the specified maximum connection limit.  Make it a daemon thread so
   * the interpreter won't wait around for it to exit.
   **/
  public ConnectionManager(ThreadGroup group, int maxConnections) {
    super(group, "ConnectionManager");
    this.setDaemon(true);
    this.maxConnections = maxConnections;
    connections = new Vector(maxConnections);
    log("Starting connection manager.  Max connections: " + maxConnections);
  }

  /**
   * This is the method that Listener objects call when they accept a
   * connection from a client.  It either creates a Connection object
   * for the connection and adds it to the list of current connections,
   * or, if the limit on connections has been reached, it closes the
   * connection.
   **/
  synchronized void addConnection(Socket s, Service service) {
    // If the connection limit has been reached
    if (connections.size() >= maxConnections) {
      try {
        PrintWriter out = new PrintWriter(s.getOutputStream());
        // Then tell the client it is being rejected.
        out.println("Connection refused; " +
                    "server has reached maximum number of clients.");
        out.flush();
        // And close the connection to the rejected client.
        s.close();
        // And log it, of course
        log("Connection refused to " + s.getInetAddress().getHostAddress() +
            ":" + s.getPort() + ": max connections reached.");
      } catch (IOException e) {log(e);}
    }
    else {  // Otherwise, if the limit has not been reached
      // Create a Connection thread to handle this connection
      Connection c = new Connection(s, service);
      // Add it to the list of current connections
      connections.addElement(c);
      // Log this new connection
      log("Connected to " + s.getInetAddress().getHostAddress() +
          ":" + s.getPort() + " on port " + s.getLocalPort() +
          " for service " + service.getClass().getName());
      // And start the Connection thread running to provide the service
      c.start();
```

Example 9-9: Server.java (continued)

```
    }
  }

  /**
   * A Connection object calls this method just before it exits.
   * This method uses notify() to tell the ConnectionManager thread
   * to wake up and delete the thread that has exited.
   **/
  public synchronized void endConnection() { this.notify(); }

  /** Change the current connection limit */
  public synchronized void setMaxConnections(int max) { maxConnections=max; }

  /**
   * Output the current list of connections to the specified stream.
   * This method is used by the Control service defined below.
   **/
  public synchronized void printConnections(PrintWriter out) {
    for(int i = 0; i < connections.size(); i++) {
      Connection c = (Connection)connections.elementAt(i);
      out.println("CONNECTED TO " +
                  c.client.getInetAddress().getHostAddress() + ":" +
                  c.client.getPort() + " ON PORT " + c.client.getLocalPort()+
                  " FOR SERVICE " + c.service.getClass().getName());
    }
  }

  /**
   * The ConnectionManager is a thread, and this is the body of that
   * thread.  While the ConnectionManager methods above are called by other
   * threads, this method is run in its own thread.  The job of this thread
   * is to keep the list of connections up to date by removing connections
   * that are no longer alive.  It uses wait() to block until notify()'d by
   * the endConnection() method.
   **/
  public void run() {
    while(true) {  // infinite loop
      // Check through the list of connections, removing dead ones
      for(int i = 0; i < connections.size(); i++) {
        Connection c = (Connection)connections.elementAt(i);
        if (!c.isAlive()) {
          connections.removeElementAt(i);
          log("Connection to " + c.client.getInetAddress().getHostAddress() +
            ":" + c.client.getPort() + " closed.");
        }
      }
      // Now wait to be notify()'d that a connection has exited
      // When we wake up we'll check the list of connections again.
      try { synchronized(this) { this.wait(); } }
      catch(InterruptedException e) {}
    }
  }
}

/**
 * This class is a subclass of Thread that handles an individual connection
 * between a client and a Service provided by this server.  Because each
 * such connection has a thread of its own, each Service can have multiple
```

Networking

Example 9-9: Server.java (continued)

```
 * connections pending at once.  Despite all the other threads in use, this
 * is the key feature that makes this a multi-threaded server implementation.
 **/
public class Connection extends Thread {
  Socket client;      // The socket to talk to the client through
  Service service;    // The service being provided to that client

  /**
   * This constructor just saves some state and calls the superclass
   * constructor to create a thread to handle the connection.  Connection
   * objects are created by Listener threads.  These threads are part of
   * the server's ThreadGroup, so all Connection threads are part of that
   * group, too.
   **/
  public Connection(Socket client, Service service) {
    super("Server.Connection:" + client.getInetAddress().getHostAddress() +
          ":" + client.getPort());
    this.client = client;
    this.service = service;
  }

  /**
   * This is the body of each and every Connection thread.
   * All it does is pass the client input and output streams to the
   * serve() method of the specified Service object.  That method
   * is responsible for reading from and writing to those streams to
   * provide the actual service.  Recall that the Service object has been
   * passed from the Server.addService() method to a Listener object
   * to the ConnectionManager.addConnection() to this Connection object,
   * and is now finally getting used to provide the service.
   * Note that just before this thread exits it calls the
   * ConnectionManager.endConnection() method to wake up the
   * ConnectionManager thread so that it can remove this Connection
   * from its list of active connections.
   **/
  public void run() {
    try {
      InputStream in = client.getInputStream();
      OutputStream out = client.getOutputStream();
      service.serve(in, out);
    }
    catch (IOException e) {log(e);}
    finally { connectionManager.endConnection(); }
  }
}

/**
 * Here is the Service interface that we have seen so much of.
 * It defines only a single method which is invoked to provide the service.
 * serve() will be passed an input stream and an output stream to the client.
 * It should do whatever it wants with them, and should close them before
 * returning.
 *
 * All connections through the same port to this service share a single
 * Service object.  Thus, any state local to an individual connection must
 * be stored in local variables within the serve() method.  State that should
 * be global to all connections on the same port should be stored in
 * instance variables of the Service class.  If the same Service is running
```

Example 9-9: Server.java (continued)

```
 * on more than one port, there will typically be different Service instances
 * for each port.  Data that should be global to all connections on any port
 * should be stored in static variables.
 *
 * Note that implementations of this interface must have a no-argument
 * constructor if they are to be dynamically instantiated by the main()
 * method of the Server class.
 **/
public interface Service {
  public void serve(InputStream in, OutputStream out) throws IOException;
}

/**
 * A very simple service.  It displays the current time on the server
 * to the client, and closes the connection.
 **/
public static class Time implements Service {
  public void serve(InputStream i, OutputStream o) throws IOException {
    PrintWriter out = new PrintWriter(new OutputStreamWriter(o));
    out.println(new Date());
    out.close();
    i.close();
  }
}

/**
 * This is another example service.  It reads lines of input from the
 * client, and sends them back, reversed.  It also displays a welcome
 * message and instructions, and closes the connection when the user
 * enters a '.' on a line by itself.
 **/
public static class Reverse implements Service {
  public void serve(InputStream i, OutputStream o) throws IOException {
    BufferedReader in = new BufferedReader(new InputStreamReader(i));
    PrintWriter out =
      new PrintWriter(new BufferedWriter(new OutputStreamWriter(o)));
    out.println("Welcome to the line reversal server.");
    out.println("Enter lines.  End with a '.' on a line by itself");
    for(;;) {
      out.print("> ");
      out.flush();
      String line = in.readLine();
      if ((line == null) || line.equals(".")) break;
      for(int j = line.length()-1; j >= 0; j--)
        out.print(line.charAt(j));
      out.println();
    }
    out.close();
    in.close();
  }
}

/**
 * This service is an HTTP mirror, just like the HttpMirror class
 * implemented earlier in this chapter.  It echos back the client's
 * HTTP request
 **/
public static class HTTPMirror implements Service {
```

Example 9–9: Server.java (continued)

```java
  public void serve(InputStream i, OutputStream o) throws IOException {
    BufferedReader in = new BufferedReader(new InputStreamReader(i));
    PrintWriter out = new PrintWriter(new OutputStreamWriter(o));
    out.println("HTTP/1.0 200 ");
    out.println("Content-Type: text/plain");
    out.println();
    String line;
    while((line = in.readLine()) != null) {
      if (line.length() == 0) break;
      out.println(line);
    }
    out.close();
    in.close();
  }
}

/**
 * This service demonstrates how to maintain state across connections
 * by saving it in instance variables and using synchronized access to
 * those variables.  It maintains a count of how many clients have connected
 * and tells each client what number it is
 **/
public static class UniqueID implements Service {
  public int id=0;
  public synchronized int nextId() { return id++; }
  public void serve(InputStream i, OutputStream o) throws IOException {
    PrintWriter out = new PrintWriter(new OutputStreamWriter(o));
    out.println("You are client #: " + nextId());
    out.close();
    i.close();
  }
}

/**
 * This is a non-trivial service.  It implements a command-based protocol
 * that gives password-protected runtime control over the operation of the
 * server.  See the main() method of the Server class to see how this
 * service is started.
 *
 * The recognized commands are:
 *   password:   give password; authorization is required for most commands
 *   add:        dynamically add a named service on a specified port
 *   remove:     dynamically remove the service running on a specified port
 *   max:        change the current maximum connection limit.
 *   status:     display current services, connections, and connection limit
 *   help:       display a help message
 *   quit:       disconnect
 *
 * This service displays a prompt, and sends all of its output to the user
 * in capital letters.  Only one client is allowed to connect to this service
 * at a time.
 **/
public static class Control implements Service {
  Server server;              // The server we control
  String password;            // The password we require
  boolean connected = false;  // Whether a client is already connected to us
```

Example 9-9: Server.java (continued)

```
/**
 * Create a new Control service.  It will control the specified Server
 * object, and will require the specified password for authorization
 * Note that this Service does not have a no argument constructor, which
 * means that it cannot be dynamically instantiated and added as the other,
 * generic services above can be.
 **/
public Control(Server server, String password) {
  this.server = server;
  this.password = password;
}


/**
 * This is the serve method that provides the service.  It reads a line
 * the client, and uses java.util.StringTokenizer to parse it into
 * commands and arguments.  It does various things depending on the
 * command.
 **/
public void serve(InputStream i, OutputStream o) throws IOException {
  // Setup the streams
  BufferedReader in = new BufferedReader(new InputStreamReader(i));
  PrintWriter out = new PrintWriter(new OutputStreamWriter(o));
  String line;
  boolean authorized = false;  // Has the user has given the password yet?
  int num;

  // If there is already a client connected to this service, display a
  // message to this client and close the connection.  We use a
  // synchronized block to prevent a race condition.
  synchronized(this) {
    if (connected) {
      out.println("ONLY ONE CONTROL CONNECTION ALLOWED AT A TIME.");
      out.close();
      return;
    }
    else connected = true;
  }

  for(;;) {  // infinite loop
    out.print("> ");            // Display a prompt
    out.flush();                // Make it appear right away
    line = in.readLine();       // Get the user's input
    if (line == null) break;    // Quit if we get EOF.
    try {
      // Use a StringTokenizer to parse the user's command
      StringTokenizer t = new StringTokenizer(line);
      if (!t.hasMoreTokens()) continue;  // if input was blank line
      // Get the first word of the input and convert to lower case
      String command = t.nextToken().toLowerCase();
      // Now compare it to each of the possible commands, doing the
      // appropriate thing for each command
      if (command.equals("password")) {       // Password command
        String p = t.nextToken();             // Get the next word of input
        if (p.equals(this.password)) {        // Does it equal the password
          out.println("OK");                  // Say so
          authorized = true;                  // Grant authorization
        }
        else out.println("INVALID PASSWORD"); // Otherwise fail
```

Example 9-9: Server.java (continued)

```
    }
    else if (command.equals("add")) {        // Add Service command
      // Check whether password has been given
      if (!authorized) out.println("PASSWORD REQUIRED");
      else {
        // Get the name of the service and try to dynamically load
        // and instantiate it.  Exceptions will be handled below
        String serviceName = t.nextToken();
        Class serviceClass = Class.forName(serviceName);
        Service service;
        try { service = (Service) serviceClass.newInstance(); }
        catch (NoSuchMethodError e) {
          throw new IllegalArgumentException("Service must have a " +
                                          "no-argument constructor");
        }
        int port = Integer.parseInt(t.nextToken());
        // If no exceptions occurred, add the service
        server.addService(service, port);
        out.println("SERVICE ADDED");        // acknowledge
      }
    }
    else if (command.equals("remove")) {    // Remove service command
      if (!authorized) out.println("PASSWORD REQUIRED");
      else {
        int port = Integer.parseInt(t.nextToken());  // get port
        server.removeService(port);       // remove the service on it
        out.println("SERVICE REMOVED"); // acknowledge
      }
    }
    else if (command.equals("max")) {        // Set max connection limit
      if (!authorized) out.println("PASSWORD REQUIRED");
      else {
        int max = Integer.parseInt(t.nextToken());        // get limit
        server.connectionManager.setMaxConnections(max); // set limit
        out.println("MAX CONNECTIONS CHANGED");          // acknowledge
      }
    }
    else if (command.equals("status")) {    // Status Display command
      if (!authorized) out.println("PASSWORD REQUIRED");
      else {
        // Display a list of all services currently running
        Enumeration keys = server.services.keys();
        while(keys.hasMoreElements()) {
          Integer port = (Integer) keys.nextElement();
          Listener listener = (Listener)server.services.get(port);
          out.println("SERVICE " + listener.service.getClass().getName()+
                    " ON PORT " + port);
        }
        // Display a list of all current connections
        server.connectionManager.printConnections(out);
        // Display the current connection limit
        out.println("MAX CONNECTIONS: " +
                    server.connectionManager.maxConnections);
      }
    }
    else if (command.equals("help")) {            // Help command
      // Display command syntax.  Password not required
      out.println("COMMANDS:\n" +
```

Example 9–9: Server.java (continued)

```
                        "\tpassword <password>\n" +
                        "\tadd <service> <port>\n" +
                        "\tremove <port>\n" +
                        "\tmax <max-connections>\n" +
                        "\tstatus\n" +
                        "\thelp\n" +
                        "\tquit");
            }
            else if (command.equals("quit")) break;    // Quit command. Exit.
            else out.println("UNRECOGNIZED COMMAND"); // Unknown command error
        }
        catch (Exception e) {
            // If an exception occurred during the command, print an error
            // message, then output details of the exception.
            out.println("EXCEPTION WHILE PARSING OR EXECUTING COMMAND:");
            out.println(e);
        }
    }
    // Finally, when the loop command loop ends, close the streams
    // and set our connected flag to false so that other clients can
    // now connect.
    out.close();
    in.close();
    connected = false;
    }
  }
}
```

A Multi-Threaded Proxy Server

Example 9-6 demonstrated how to write a simple, single-threaded proxy server. Example 9-10 uses the Server class and Server.Service interface defined in Example 9-9 to implement a multi-threaded proxy server. It demonstrates how you can use the generic Server class to implement your own custom servers without using the main() method of Server. The body of the nested Proxy class (which is what implements the Service interface) is reminiscent of the SimpleProxyServer class, but creates two anonymous threads instead of just one. The main thread uses the join() method of the Thread class to wait for these two anonymous threads to finish.

Example 9–10: ProxyServer.java

```
import java.io.*;
import java.net.*;

/**
 * This class uses the Server class to provide a multi-threaded server
 * framework for a relatively simple proxy service.  The main() method
 * starts up the server.  The nested Proxy class implements the
 * Server.Service interface and provides the proxy service.
 **/
public class ProxyServer {
  /**
   * Create a Server object, and add Proxy service objects to it to provide
   * proxy service as specified by the command-line arguments.
   **/
```

Example 9-10: ProxyServer.java (continued)

```java
public static void main(String[] args) {
  try {
    // Check number of args.  Must be a multiple of 3 and > 0.
    if ((args.length == 0) || (args.length % 3 != 0))
      throw new IllegalArgumentException("Wrong number of arguments");

    // Create the Server object
    Server s = new Server(null, 12); // log stream, max connections

    // Loop through the arguments parsing (host, remoteport, localport)
    // tuples.  Create an appropriate Proxy object, and add it to the server
    int i = 0;
    while(i < args.length) {
      String host = args[i++];
      int remoteport = Integer.parseInt(args[i++]);
      int localport = Integer.parseInt(args[i++]);
      s.addService(new Proxy(host, remoteport), localport);
    }
  }
  catch (Exception e) {  // Print an error message if anything goes wrong.
    System.err.println(e);
    System.err.println("Usage: java ProxyServer " +
                       "<host> <remoteport> <localport> ...");
    System.exit(1);
  }
}

/**
 * This is the class that implements the proxy service.  The serve() method
 * will be called when the client has connected.  At that point, it must
 * establish a connection to the server, and then transfer bytes back and
 * forth between client and server.  For symmetry, this class implements
 * two very similar threads as anonymous classes.  One thread copies bytes
 * from client to server, and the other copies them from server to client.
 * The thread that invoke the serve() method creates and starts these
 * threads, then just sits and waits for them to exit.
 **/
public static class Proxy implements Server.Service {
  String host;
  int port;

  /** Remember the host and port we are a proxy for */
  public Proxy(String host, int port) {
    this.host = host;
    this.port = port;
  }

  /** The server invokes this method when a client connects. */
  public void serve(InputStream in, OutputStream out) {
    // These are some sockets we'll use.  They are final so they can be used
    // by the anonymous classes defined below.
    final InputStream from_client = in;
    final OutputStream to_client = out;
    final InputStream from_server;
    final OutputStream to_server;

    // Try to establish a connection to the specified server and port
    // and get sockets to talk to it.  Tell our client if we fail.
```

Example 9-10: ProxyServer.java (continued)

```java
Socket server;
try {
  server = new Socket(host, port);
  from_server = server.getInputStream();
  to_server = server.getOutputStream();
}
catch (Exception e) {
  PrintWriter pw = new PrintWriter(new OutputStreamWriter(out));
  pw.println("Proxy server could not connect to " + host + ":" + port);
  pw.flush();
  pw.close();
  try { in.close(); } catch (IOException ex) {}
  return;
}

// Create an array to hold two Threads.  It is declared final so that
// it can be used by the anonymous classes below.  We use an array
// instead of two variables because given the structure of this program
// two variables would not work if declared final.
final Thread[] threads = new Thread[2];

// Define and create a thread to transmit bytes from client to server
Thread c2s = new Thread() {
  public void run() {
    byte[] buffer = new byte[2048];
    int bytes_read;
    try {
      while((bytes_read = from_client.read(buffer)) != -1) {
        to_server.write(buffer, 0, bytes_read);
        to_server.flush();
      }
    }
    catch (IOException e) {}

    // if the client closed its stream to us, we close our stream
    // to the server.  First, stop the other thread
    threads[1].stop();
    try { to_server.close(); } catch (IOException e) {}
  }
};

// Define and create a thread to copy bytes from server to client.
Thread s2c = new Thread() {
  public void run() {
    byte[] buffer = new byte[2048];
    int bytes_read;
    try {
      while((bytes_read = from_server.read(buffer)) != -1) {
        to_client.write(buffer, 0, bytes_read);
        to_client.flush();
      }
    }
    catch (IOException e) {}

    // if the server closed its stream to us, we close our stream
    // to the client.  First, stop the other thread, though.
    threads[0].stop();
    try { to_client.close(); } catch (IOException e) {}
```

Example 9–10: ProxyServer.java (continued)

```
      }
    };

    // Store the threads into the final threads[] array, so that the
    // anonymous classes can refer to each other.
    threads[0] = c2s; threads[1] = s2c;

    // start the threads
    c2s.start(); s2c.start();

    // Wait for them to exit
    try { c2s.join(); s2c.join(); } catch (InterruptedException e) {}
  }
 }
}
```

Sending Datagrams

Now that we've throughly covered the possibilities of networking with sockets and streams, we'll examine how low-level networking can be done using datagrams and packets. Example 9-11 and Example 9-12 show how you can implement simple network communication using datagrams. Datagram communication is sometimes called "UDP," for Unreliable Datagram Protocol. Sending datagrams is fast, but the tradeoff is that that they are not guaranteed to reach their destination. In addition, multiple datagrams are not guaranteed to travel to their destination by the same route or to arrive at their destination in the order in which they were sent. Datagrams are useful when you want low-overhead communication of non-critical data and when a stream model of communication is not necessary. For example, you might implement a multi-user chat server for a local-area network using datagrams.

To send and receive datagrams, you use the DatagramPacket and DatagramSocket classes. These objects are created and initialized differently depending on whether they are being used to send or receive datagrams. Example 9-11 shows how to send a datagram, while Example 9-12 shows how to receive a datagram and how to find out who sent it.

To send a datagram, you first create a DatagramPacket, specifying the data to be sent, the length of the data, the host that it is to be sent to, and the port on that host where it is to be sent. You then use the send() method of a DatagramSocket to send the packet. The DatagramSocket is a generic one, created with no arguments. It can be reused to send any packet to any address and port.

Example 9–11: UDPSend.java

```
import java.io.*;
import java.net.*;

/**
 * This class sends the specified text or file as a datagram to the
 * specified port of the specified host.
 **/
public class UDPSend {
```

Example 9-11: UDPSend.java (continued)

```java
public static void main(String args[]) {
  try {
    // Check the number of arguments
    if (args.length < 3)
      throw new IllegalArgumentException("Wrong number of arguments");

    // Parse the arguments
    String host = args[0];
    int port = Integer.parseInt(args[1]);

    // Figure out the message to send.
    // If the third argument is -f, then send the contents of the file
    // specified as the fourth argument.  Otherwise, concatenate the
    // third and all remaining arguments and send that.
    byte[] message;
    if (args[2].equals("-f")) {
      File f = new File(args[3]);
      int len = (int)f.length();    // figure out how big the file is
      message = new byte[len];       // create a buffer big enough
      FileInputStream in = new FileInputStream(f);
      int bytes_read = 0, n;
      do {                           // loop until we've read it all
        n = in.read(message, bytes_read, len-bytes_read);
        bytes_read += n;
      } while((bytes_read < len) && (n != -1));
    }
    else { // Otherwise, just combine all the remaining arguments.
      String msg = args[2];
      for (int i = 3; i < args.length; i++) msg += " " + args[i];
      message = msg.getBytes();
    }

    // Get the internet address of the specified host
    InetAddress address = InetAddress.getByName(host);

    // Initialize a datagram packet with data and address
    DatagramPacket packet = new DatagramPacket(message, message.length,
                                               address, port);

    // Create a datagram socket, send the packet through it, close it.
    DatagramSocket dsocket = new DatagramSocket();
    dsocket.send(packet);
    dsocket.close();
  }
  catch (Exception e) {
    System.err.println(e);
    System.err.println("Usage: java UDPSend <hostname> <port> <msg>...\n" +
                       "    or: java UDPSend <hostname> <port> -f <file>");
  }
}
}
```

Networking

Receiving Datagrams

Example 9-12 is a program that sits and waits to receive datagrams. When it receives them, it prints out the contents of the datagram and the name of the host that sent it.

To receive a datagram, you must first create a DatagramSocket that listens on a particular port of the local host. This socket can only be used to receive packets sent to that particular port. Then, you must create a DatagramPacket with a byte buffer into which datagram data is stored. Finally, you call the Datagram-Socket.receive() method to wait for a datagram to arrive on the specified port. When it does, the data it contains is transferred into the specified buffer, and receive() returns. If the datagram contains more bytes than fit into the specified buffer, the extra bytes are discarded. When a datagram arrives, receive() also stores the host and port that the datagram was sent from into the packet.

Example 9-12: UDPReceive.java

```java
import java.io.*;
import java.net.*;

/**
 * This program waits to receive datagrams sent the specified port.
 * When it receives one, it displays the sending host and prints the
 * contents of the datagram as a string.  Then it loops and waits again.
 **/
public class UDPReceive {
  public static void main(String args[]) {
    try {
      if (args.length != 1)
        throw new IllegalArgumentException("Wrong number of arguments");

      // Get the port from the command line
      int port = Integer.parseInt(args[0]);

      // Create a socket to listen on the port.
      DatagramSocket dsocket = new DatagramSocket(port);

      // Create a buffer to read datagrams into.  If anyone sends us a
      // packet containing more than will fit into this buffer, the excess
      // will simply be discarded!
      byte[] buffer = new byte[2048];

      // Now loop forever, waiting to receive packets and printing them out.
      for(;;) {
        // Create a packet with an empty buffer to receive data
        DatagramPacket packet = new DatagramPacket(buffer, buffer.length);

        // Wait to receive a datagram
        dsocket.receive(packet);

        // Convert the contents to a string, and display them
        String msg = new String(buffer, 0, packet.getLength());
        System.out.println(packet.getAddress().getHostName() + ": " + msg);
      }
    }
    catch (Exception e) {
```

Example 9-12: UDPReceive.java (continued)

```
        System.err.println(e);
        System.err.println("Usage: java UDPReceive <port>");
      }
    }
  }
}
```

Exercises

9-1. Using the URLConnection techniques demonstrated in Example 9-2, write a program that prints the modification date of a specified URL.

9-2. Modify the HttpClient program of Example 9-4 so that it uses a newer version of the HTTP protocol. To do this, you have to send a somewhat more complicated GET request to the Web server. Use the HttpMirror program of Example 9-5 to find out what form this request should take. HTTP versions 1.0 and later add a version number to the GET request and follow the GET line with a number of header lines followed by a blank line that serves to terminate the request.

For this exercise, the only header you need to include is the User-Agent line, which should identify the Web client that you are using. Since you are writing your own Web client, you can give it any name you like! Be sure to follow your GET request and User-Agent header with a blank line, or the Web server will keep waiting for more headers and will never respond to your request. When you get this program working, you should notice that Web servers respond differently to requests from it than they did to requests from the original HttpClient program. When a client requests data using HTTP 1.0 or 1.1, the server sends a version number, a status code, and a number of response header lines before it sends the actual requested file.

9-3. Write a simple server that reports the current time (in textual form) to any client that connects. Use Example 9-5, HttpMirror, as a framework for your server. This server should simply output the current time and close the connection, without reading anything from the client. You need to choose a port number that your service will listen on. Use the GenericClient program of Example 9-8 to connect to this port and test your program. Alternatively, use the HttpClient program of Example 9-4 to test your program. To do this, you need to encode the appropriate port number into the URL. HttpClient sends an extraneous GET request to the time server, but it still displays the server's response.

9-4. In the discussion of Example 9-8, GenericClient, there is an example of using that program to communicate with a POP (Post Office Protocol) server to retrieve email. The POP protocol is a simple one; a little experimentation with GenericClient should allow you to figure out how it works. (Be careful not to delete any important email!)

For this exercise, write a client program named Checkmail that uses the POP protocol to check a user's mail. It should output the number of messages that are waiting to be retreived and display the From line of each message.

This client should *not* use the POP dele command to delete mail messages from the server; it should simply display a summary of the messages waiting to be retrieved. In order to read mail messages, this client has to know the hostname of the POP server and has to send a username and password to the server. Your program may obtain the hostname, username, and password from the command line, or by prompting the user, but should ideally get this information by reading a configuration file. Consider using a java.util.Properties object to implement such a configuration file.

9-5. Write a simple Web server that responds to GET requests like those generated by the program you wrote in Exercise 9-2. You may want to use Example 9-5, HttpMirror, as a framework for your server. Alternatively, you can implement your server as a Service subclass for use with the Server program developed in Example 9-9.

Your server should use the HTTP 1.0 protocol, or a later version. This means that ther server expects GET requests to be followed by header lines and terminated by a blank line. And it means that the responses to GET requests should begin with a version number and status code. This status line is followed by header lines, which are terminated with a blank line. The content of the response follows the blank line. Use the client you wrote in Exercise 9-2 to experiment with existing Web servers to see how they respond to various GET requests.

The Web server you write should be started with a directory specified on the command line, and should serve files relative to this directory. When a client requests a file in or beneath the directory, the server should return the contents of the file, but should first output Content-Type, Content-Length, and Last-Modified header lines. For this exercise, assume that files with an extension of *.html* or *.htm* have a content type of text/html, and that all other files are text/plain. If a client requests a file that does not exist, your server should return an appropriate error code and message. Again, use the client you developed in Exercise 9-2 to figure out how existing Web servers respond to requests for non-existent files.

9-6. Modify the UDPSend and UDPReceive programs of Examples 9-11 and 9-12 so that UDPReceive sends an acknowledgment when it receives a datagram, and so that UDPSend does not exit until it receives the acknowledgment. The acknowledgment should itself be a datagram, and can contain any data you desire. (You could use the checksum classes of the java.util.zip package, for example, to compute a checksum of the received data and send this back in the acknowledgment packet.)

CHAPTER 10

Threads

The use of threads is basic to the Java programming model; it is not possible to confine a discussion of them to just one chapter. We used threads in Chapter 3, *Applets*, to perform animations. And we made heavy use of threads in Chapter 9, *Networking*, to write network servers that can talk to more than one client at a time. The examples in this chapter demonstrate some additional uses of threads.

Threads and Thread Groups

Every Java Thread belongs to some ThreadGroup and may be constrained and controlled through the methods of that ThreadGroup. Similarly, every ThreadGroup is itself contained in some "parent" ThreadGroup. Thus, there is a hierarchy of thread groups and the threads they contain. Example 10-1 is a ThreadLister class, with a public listAllThreads() method that displays this hierarchy by listing all threads and thread groups currently running on the Java interpreter. This method displays the name and priority of each thread, as well as other information about threads and thread groups. Example 10-1 also contains a nested Applet subclass that displays the threads running in the Java virtual machine of a Web browser. Figure 10-1 shows the output of this applet.

The listAllThreads() method uses the Thread static method currentThread() to obtain the current thread, and then uses getThreadGroup() to find the thread group of that thread. It then uses the ThreadGroup.getParent() method to move through the thread group hierarchy until it finds the "root" thread group, the thread group that contains all other threads and thread groups.

listAllThreads() then calls the private ThreadLister.printGroupInfo() method to display the contents of the root thread group, and to recursively display the contents of all thread groups it contains. printGroupInfo(), and the printThread-Info() method it calls, use various Thread and ThreadGroup methods to obtain information about the threads and their groups. Note that the isDaemon() method returns whether a thread is a "daemon thread" or not. Daemon threads are

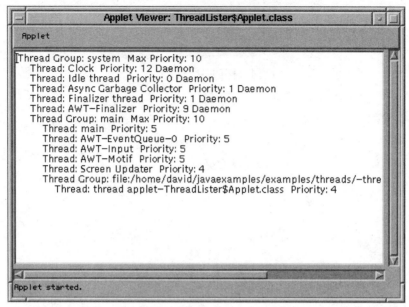

Figure 10–1: A thread-listing applet

background threads that are not expected to exit. The Java interpreter exits when all non-daemon threads have quit.

The ThreadLister class has a main() method so that it can be run as a standalone program. It is more interesting, of course, to invoke the listAllThreads() method from within another program or applet—and it can also help you to diagnose problems you are having with threads.

Example 10–1: ThreadLister.java

```java
import java.io.*;

/**
 * This class contains a useful static method for listing all threads
 * and threadgroups in the VM.  It also has a simple main() method so it
 * can be run as a standalone program.
 **/
public class ThreadLister {
  /** Display information about a thread. */
  private static void printThreadInfo(PrintWriter out, Thread t,
                                      String indent) {
    if (t == null) return;
    out.println(indent + "Thread: " + t.getName() +
            "  Priority: " + t.getPriority() +
            (t.isDaemon()?" Daemon":"") +
            (t.isAlive()?"":" Not Alive"));
  }

  /** Display info about a thread group and its threads and groups */
  private static void printGroupInfo(PrintWriter out, ThreadGroup g,
                                     String indent) {
```

Example 10–1: ThreadLister.java (continued)

```
    if (g == null) return;
    int num_threads = g.activeCount();
    int num_groups = g.activeGroupCount();
    Thread[] threads = new Thread[num_threads];
    ThreadGroup[] groups = new ThreadGroup[num_groups];

    g.enumerate(threads, false);
    g.enumerate(groups, false);

    out.println(indent + "Thread Group: " + g.getName() +
                "  Max Priority: " + g.getMaxPriority() +
                (g.isDaemon()?" Daemon":""));

    for(int i = 0; i < num_threads; i++)
      printThreadInfo(out, threads[i], indent + "    ");
    for(int i = 0; i < num_groups; i++)
      printGroupInfo(out, groups[i], indent + "    ");
  }

  /** Find the root thread group and list it recursively */
  public static void listAllThreads(PrintWriter out) {
    ThreadGroup current_thread_group;
    ThreadGroup root_thread_group;
    ThreadGroup parent;

    // Get the current thread group
    current_thread_group = Thread.currentThread().getThreadGroup();

    // Now go find the root thread group
    root_thread_group = current_thread_group;
    parent = root_thread_group.getParent();
    while(parent != null) {
      root_thread_group = parent;
      parent = parent.getParent();
    }

    // And list it, recursively
    printGroupInfo(out, root_thread_group, "");
  }

  /**
   * The main() method:  just print the list of threads to the console
   **/
  public static void main(String[] args) {
    PrintWriter out = new PrintWriter(new OutputStreamWriter(System.out));
    ThreadLister.listAllThreads(out);
    out.flush();
  }

  /**
   * This nested class is a simple applet that displays the output of
   * ThreadLister.listAllThreads() when run from an the start() method of
   * an applet.  The output from an applet is typically different than the
   * output when run from a standalone program.
   **/
  public static class Applet extends java.applet.Applet {
    java.awt.TextArea textarea;  // Where to display the output.
```

Example 10-1: ThreadLister.java (continued)

```
  /** Create a text area to put our listing in */
  public void init() {
    textarea = new java.awt.TextArea();
    this.setLayout(new java.awt.BorderLayout());
    this.add("Center", textarea);
  }

  /** When the applet starts, list all the threads */
  public void start() {
    StringWriter sout = new StringWriter();   // Capture listing in a string
    PrintWriter out = new PrintWriter(sout);
    ThreadLister.listAllThreads(out);
    out.flush();
    textarea.setText(sout.toString());        // Display the listing
  }
}
}
```

Deadlock

Multi-threaded programming requires a programmer to take special care in several areas. For example, if multiple threads can be changing the state of an object at the same time, you must typically use synchronized methods, or the synchronized statement, to ensure that only one thread changes the object's state at a time. If you do not, two threads could end up overwriting each other's edits, leaving the object in an inconsistent state.

Unfortunately, using synchronization can itself raise problems. Thread synchronization involves acquiring an exclusive "lock." Only the one thread that currently holds the lock can execute the synchronized code. When a program uses more than one lock, however, a situation known as "deadlock" can arise. Deadlock occurs when two or more threads are all waiting to acquire a lock that is currently held by one of the other waiting threads. Because each thread is waiting to acquire a lock, it will never release the lock or locks it already holds. And this means that none of the waiting threads will ever acquire the lock they are waiting for. The situation is a total impasse. All of the threads involved come to a halt, and the program cannot continue.

Example 10-2 is a simple program that creates a deadlock situation in which two threads attempt to acquire locks on two different resources. It is pretty easy to see how deadlock can arise in this simple program. It might not be as clear, however, if there were synchronized methods involved, instead of a simple symmetrical set of synchronized statements. More complicated situations also arise with multiple threads and multiple resources. In general, the problem of deadlock is a deep and nasty one. One good technique for preventing it, however, is for all threads to always acquire all the locks they need in the same order.

Example 10-2: Deadlock.java

```
/**
 * This is a demonstration of how NOT to write multi-threaded programs.
 * It is a program that purposely causes deadlock between two threads that
 * are both trying to acquire locks for the same two resources.
```

Example 10–2: Deadlock.java (continued)

```
 * To avoid this sort of deadlock when locking multiple resources, all threads
 * should always acquire their locks in the same order.
 **/
public class Deadlock {
  public static void main(String[] args) {
    // These are the two resource objects we'll try to get locks for
    final Object resource1 = "resource1";
    final Object resource2 = "resource2";
    // Here's the first thread.  It tries to lock resource1 then resource2
    Thread t1 = new Thread() {
      public void run() {
        // Lock resource 1
        synchronized(resource1) {
          System.out.println("Thread 1: locked resource 1");

          // Pause for a bit, simulating some file I/O or something.
          // Basically, we just want to give the other thread a chance to
          // run.  Threads and deadlock are asynchronous things, but we're
          // trying to force deadlock to happen here...
          try { Thread.sleep(50); } catch (InterruptedException e) {}

          // Now wait 'till we can get a lock on resource 2
          synchronized(resource2) {
            System.out.println("Thread 1: locked resource 2");
          }
        }
      }
    };

    // Here's the second thread.  It tries to lock resource2 then resource1
    Thread t2 = new Thread() {
      public void run() {
        // This thread locks resource 2 right away
        synchronized(resource2) {
          System.out.println("Thread 2: locked resource 2");

          // Then it pauses, for the same reason as the first thread does
          try { Thread.sleep(50); } catch (InterruptedException e) {}

          // Then it tries to lock resource1.  But wait!  Thread 1 locked
          // resource1, and won't release it 'till it gets a lock on
          // resource2.  This thread holds the lock on resource2, and won't
          // release it 'till it gets resource1.  We're at an impasse. Neither
          // thread can run, and the program freezes up.
          synchronized(resource1) {
            System.out.println("Thread 2: locked resource 1");
          }
        }
      }
    };

    // Start the two threads. If all goes as planned, deadlock will occur,
    // and the program will never exit.
    t1.start();
    t2.start();
  }
}
```

Threads

Pipes

The `PipedReader` and `PipedWriter` classes of `java.io` allow separate threads to read and write data from and to each other. Example 10-3 shows one way that you might make use of this capability. It is a long and complicated example, so you should study it carefully.

The code in this example allows you to set up UNIX-style "pipes"—data flows from a source, through any number of filters, and then into a sink. For example, the source might be a file, the filter might be one that performs a search-and-replace operation on the data, and the sink might be another file or the `System.out` stream. The source, filters, and sink of a pipe are all implemented as separate threads, which means that they work independently of each other, running when data is available to be read in the pipe, and blocking when there is no data available.

The `Pipes` class is merely a placeholder for a collection of nested classes that implement our pipe system. `Pipe` is a subclass of `Thread` that implements the basic pipe connection functionality. `ReaderPipeSource` is a `Pipe` subclass that uses an arbitrary `Reader` as the source of data for a pipe. Similarly, `WriterPipeSink` is a `Pipe` subclass that uses an arbitrary `Writer` as a data sink for a pipe.

The `PipeFilter` class is a simple class that makes it a little easier to write classes that act as filters in pipes. The only thing this abstract class leaves out is a `filter()` method. The example defines three concrete subclasses of `PipeFilter`: `GrepFilter`, `Rot13Filter`, and `UnicodeToASCIIFilter`. Each performs a different filtering operation on data.

The best place to start studying this example is with the `Pipes.Test` class at the beginning. The `main()` method of this test program shows how all the other classes are used: it demonstrates the creation of a source, four filters, and a sink. It connects them to each other, starts them, and lets them perform their various tasks.

Example 10–3: Pipes.java

```
import java.io.*;

/**
 * This Pipes class serves to group a number of pipe classes and interfaces.
 * It has no fields or methods of its own; its only members are static
 * classes and interfaces.
 **/
public class Pipes {
  /**
   * This class contains a test program for the pipe classes below.
   * It also demonstrates how you typically use these pipes classes.
   * It is basically another implementation of a Unix-like grep command.
   * Note that it frivolously passes the output of the grep filter through
   * two rot13 filters (which, combined, leave the output unchanged).
   * Then it converts non-ASCII characters to their \U Unicode encodings.
   *
   * With the pipe infrastructure defined below, it is easy to define
   * new filters and create pipes to perform many useful operations.
   * Other filter possibilities include sorting lines, removing
```

Example 10-3: Pipes.java (continued)

```
 * duplicate lines, and doing search-and-replace.
 **/
public static class Test {
  /** This is the test program for our pipes infrastructure */
  public static void main(String[] args) throws IOException {
    // Check the command-line arguments
    if (args.length != 2) {
      System.out.println("Usage: java Pipe$Test <pattern> <filename>");
      System.exit(0);
    }

    // Create a Reader to read data from, and a Writer to send data to.
    Reader in = new BufferedReader(new FileReader(args[1]));
    Writer out = new BufferedWriter(new OutputStreamWriter(System.out));

    // Now build up the pipe, starting with the sink, and working
    // backwards, through various filters, until we reach the source
    WriterPipeSink sink = new WriterPipeSink(out);
    PipeFilter filter4 = new UnicodeToASCIIFilter(sink);
    PipeFilter filter3 = new Rot13Filter(filter4);
    PipeFilter filter2 = new Rot13Filter(filter3);
    PipeFilter filter1 = new GrepFilter(filter2, args[0]);
    ReaderPipeSource source = new ReaderPipeSource(filter1, in);

    // Start the pipe -- start each of the threads in the pipe running.
    // This call returns quickly, since the each component of the pipe
    // is its own thread
    System.out.println("Starting pipe...");
    source.startPipe();

    // Wait for the pipe to complete
    try { source.joinPipe(); } catch (InterruptedException e) {}
    System.out.println("Done.");
  }
}

/**
 * A Pipe is a kind of thread that is connected to another (possibly null)
 * thread, known as its "sink". If it has a sink, it creates a PipedWriter
 * stream through which it can write characters to that sink. It connects
 * its PipedWriter stream to a corresponding PipedReader stream in the sink.
 * It asks the sink to create and return such a PipedReader stream by calling
 * the getReader() method of the sink.
 *
 * In once sense, a Pipe is just a linked list of threads, and the Pipe
 * class defines operations that operate on the whole chain of threads,
 * rather than a single thread.
 **/
public static abstract class Pipe extends Thread {
  protected Pipe sink = null;
  protected PipedWriter out = null;
  protected PipedReader in = null;

  /**
   * Create a Pipe and connect it to the specified Pipe
   **/
  public Pipe(Pipe sink) throws IOException {
    this.sink = sink;
```

Threads

Example 10–3: Pipes.java (continued)

```
    out = new PipedWriter();
    out.connect(sink.getReader());
}

/**
 * This constructor is for creating terminal Pipe threads--i.e. those
 * sinks that are at the end of the pipe, and are not connected to any
 * other threads.
 **/
public Pipe() { super(); }

/**
 * This protected method requests a Pipe threads to create and return
 * a PipedReader thread so that another Pipe thread can connect to it.
 **/
protected PipedReader getReader() {
  if (in == null) in = new PipedReader();
  return in;
}

/**
 * This and the following methods provide versions of basic Thread methods
 * that operate on the entire pipe of threads.
 * This one calls start() on all threads in sink-to-source order.
 **/
public void startPipe() {
  if (sink != null) sink.startPipe();
  this.start();
}

/** Call resume() on all threads in the pipe, in sink-to-source order */
public void resumePipe() {
  if (sink != null)  sink.resumePipe();
  this.resume();
}

/** Call stop() on all threads in the pipe, in source-to-sink order */
public void stopPipe() {
  this.stop();
  if (sink != null) sink.stopPipe();
}

/** Call suspend() on all threads in the pipe, in source-to-sink order */
public void suspendPipe() {
  this.suspend();
  if (sink != null) sink.suspendPipe();
}

/** Wait for all threads in the pipe to terminate */
public void joinPipe() throws InterruptedException {
  if (sink != null) sink.joinPipe();
  this.join();
}
}

/**
 * This class is a source of data for a pipe of threads.  It connects to
 * a sink, but cannot serve as a sink for any other Pipe.  That is, it must
```

Example 10–3: Pipes.java (continued)

```
 * always be at the beginning, or "source" of the pipe. For this class,
 * the source of data is the specified Reader object (such as a FileReader).
 **/
public static class ReaderPipeSource extends Pipe {
  protected Reader in;  // The Reader we take data from

  /**
   * To create a ReaderPipeSource, specify the Reader that data comes from
   * and the Pipe sink that it should be sent to.
   **/
  public ReaderPipeSource(Pipe sink, Reader in)
      throws IOException {
    super(sink);
    this.in = in;
  }

  /**
   * This is the thread body. When the pipe is started, this method copies
   * characters from the Reader into the pipe
   **/
  public void run() {
    try {
      char[] buffer = new char[1024];
      int chars_read;
      while((chars_read = in.read(buffer)) != -1)
        out.write(buffer, 0, chars_read);
    }
    catch (IOException e) {}
    // When done with the data, close the Reader and the pipe
    finally { try { in.close(); out.close(); } catch (IOException e) {} }
  }

  /**
   * This method overrides the getReader() method of Pipe. Because this
   * is a source thread, this method should never be called. To make sure
   * that it is never called, we throw an Error if it is.
   **/
  protected PipedReader getReader() {
    throw new Error("Can't connect to a ReaderPipeSource!");
  }
}

/**
 * This class is a sink for data from a pipe of threads. It can be connected
 * to by other Pipe, but its constructor is not passed a Pipe sink for it
 * to connect to. That is, it must always be at the end or "sink" of a
 * pipe. It writes the characters into a specified Writer (such as a
 * FileWriter).
 **/
public static class WriterPipeSink extends Pipe {
  protected Writer out;  // The stream to write data to

  /**
   * To create a WriterPipeSink, just specify what Writer characters
   * from the pipe should be written to
   **/
  public WriterPipeSink(Writer out) throws IOException {
    super();  // Create a terminal Pipe with no sink attached.
```

Example 10-3: Pipes.java (continued)

```
    this.out = out;
  }

  /**
   * This is the thread body for this sink.  When the pipe is started, it
   * copies characters from the pipe into the specified Writer.
   **/
  public void run() {
    try {
      char[] buffer = new char[1024];
      int chars_read;
      while((chars_read = in.read(buffer)) != -1)
        out.write(buffer, 0, chars_read);
    }
    catch (IOException e) {}
    // When done with the data, close the pipe and flush the Writer
    finally { try {in.close(); out.flush(); } catch (IOException e) {} }
  }
}

/**
 * This abstract class simplifies (somewhat) the task of writing a
 * filter pipe--i.e. one that reads data from one Pipe thread, filters
 * it somehow, and writes the results to some other Pipe.
 **/
public static abstract class PipeFilter extends Pipe {
  public PipeFilter(Pipe sink) throws IOException { super(sink); }

  public void run() {
    try { filter(in, out); }
    catch (IOException e) {}
    finally { try { in.close(); out.close(); } catch (IOException e) {} }
  }

  /** The method that subclasses must implement to do the filtering */
  abstract public void filter(Reader in, Writer out) throws IOException;
}

/**
 * This is concrete implementation of the PipeFilter interface.
 * It uses the GrepReader we defined elsewhere to do the filtering.
 **/
public static class GrepFilter extends PipeFilter {
  protected String pattern;   // The string to grep for.

  /**
   * Create a GrepFilter, will search its input for the specified pattern
   * and send the results to the specified Pipe.
   **/
  public GrepFilter(Pipe sink, String pattern)
        throws IOException {
    super(sink);
    this.pattern = pattern;
  }

  /**
   * Do the filtering, using a GrepReader to filter lines read from
   * the Reader, and using a PrintWriter to send those lines back out
```

Example 10-3: Pipes.java (continued)

```
   * to the Writer.
   **/
  public void filter(Reader in, Writer out) throws IOException {
    GrepReader gr = new GrepReader(new BufferedReader(in), pattern);
    PrintWriter pw = new PrintWriter(out);
    String line;
    while((line = gr.readLine()) != null) pw.println(line);
  }
}

/**
 * This is another implementation of Filter.  It implements the
 * trivial rot13 cipher on the letters A-Z and a-z.  Rot-13 "rotates"
 * ASCII letters 13 characters through the alphabet.
 **/
public static class Rot13Filter extends PipeFilter {
  /** Constructor just calls superclass */
  public Rot13Filter(Pipe sink) throws IOException { super(sink); }

  /** Filter characters from in to out */
  public void filter(Reader in, Writer out) throws IOException {
    char[] buffer = new char[1024];
    int chars_read;

    while((chars_read = in.read(buffer)) != -1) { // read a batch of chars
      // Apply rot-13 to each character, one at a time
      for(int i = 0; i < chars_read; i++) {
        if ((buffer[i] >= 'a') && (buffer[i] <= 'z')) {
          buffer[i] = (char) ('a' + ((buffer[i]-'a') + 13) % 26);
        }
        if ((buffer[i] >= 'A') && (buffer[i] <= 'Z')) {
          buffer[i] = (char) ('A' + ((buffer[i]-'A') + 13) % 26);
        }
      }
      out.write(buffer, 0, chars_read);                 // write the batch of chars
    }
  }
}

/**
 * This class is a Filter that accepts arbitrary Unicode characters as input
 * and outputs non-ASCII characters with their \U Unicode encodings
 **/
public static class UnicodeToASCIIFilter extends PipeFilter {
  /** Constructor just calls superclass */
  public UnicodeToASCIIFilter(Pipe sink) throws IOException {
    super(sink);
  }

  /**
   * Read characters from the reader, one at a time (using a BufferedReader
   * for efficiency).  Output printable ASCII characters unfiltered.  For
   * other characters, output the \U Unicode encoding.
   **/
  public void filter(Reader r, Writer w) throws IOException {
    BufferedReader in = new BufferedReader(r);
    PrintWriter out = new PrintWriter(new BufferedWriter(w));
    int c;
```

Threads

Example 10-3: Pipes.java (continued)

```
      while((c = in.read()) != -1) {
        // Just output ASCII characters
        if (((c >= ' ') && (c <= '~')) || (c=='\t') || (c=='\n') || (c=='\r'))
          out.write(c);
        // And encode the others
        else {
          String hex = Integer.toHexString(c);
          switch (hex.length()) {
            case 1:  out.print("\\u000" + hex); break;
            case 2:  out.print("\\u00" + hex); break;
            case 3:  out.print("\\u0" + hex); break;
            default: out.print("\\u" + hex); break;
          }
        }
      }
      out.flush();  // flush the output buffer we create
    }
  }
}
```

Exercises

10-1. The Server class in Example 9-9 is a multi-threaded, multi-service network server. It demonstrates important networking techniques, but it also makes heavy use of threads. One particular feature of this program is that it creates a ThreadGroup to contain all the threads it creates. Modify this example so that in addition to creating this one master thread group, it also creates nested thread groups for each of the individual services it provides. Place the thread for each individual client connection within the thread group for its service. Also, modify the program so that each service can have a thread priority specified, and use this priority value when creating connection threads. You will probably want to store the thread group and priority for each service as fields of the nested Listener class.

10-2. Example 10-2 demonstrates how deadlock can occur when two threads each attempt to obtain a lock held by the other. Modify the example to create deadlock among three threads each trying to acquire a lock held by one of the other threads.

10-3. Example 10-2 uses the synchronized statement to demonstrate deadlock. Write a similar program that causes two threads to deadlock, but use synchronized methods instead of the synchronized statement. This sort of deadlock is a little more subtle and harder to detect.

CHAPTER 11

Java Beans

The JavaBeans API provides a framework for defining reusable, embeddable, modular software components. The JavaBeans Specification includes the following definition of a bean: "a reusable software component that can be manipulated visually in a builder tool." As you can see, this is a rather loose definition; beans can take a variety of forms. At the simplest level, individual AWT components (in Java 1.1) are all beans, while at a much higher level, an embeddable spreadsheet application might also function as a bean. Most beans, however, will probably fall somewhere between these two extremes.

One of the goals of the JavaBeans model is interoperability with similar component frameworks. So, for example, a native Windows program can, with an appropriate bridge or wrapper object, use a Java bean as if it were a COM or ActiveX component. The details of this sort of interoperability are beyond the scope of this chapter, however.

Beans can be used at three levels, by three different categories of programmers:

- If you are developing GUI editors, application builders, or other "beanbox" tools, you need the JavaBeans API to manipulate beans within these tools. *beanbox* is the name of the sample bean manipulation program provided by Sun in its Beans Development Kit (BDK). The term is a useful one, and I'll use it to describe any kind of graphical design tool or application builder that manipulates beans.

- If you are writing actual beans, you need the JavaBeans API to write code that can be used in any conforming beanbox.

- If you are writing applications that use beans developed by other programmers, or using a beanbox tool to combine those beans into an application, you do not actually need to be familiar with the JavaBeans API. You only need to be familiar with the documentation for individual beans that you are using.

This chapter explains how to use the JavaBeans API at the second level, or in other words, it describes how to write beans. It covers the following topics.

- Basic bean concepts and terminology

- Requirements for the simplest beans

- Packaging beans in JAR files

- Providing additional information about beans with the BeanInfo class

- Defining property editors to allow custom editing of bean properties

- Defining bean customizers to allow customization of an entire bean

- The various naming conventions and requirements imposed by the JavaBeans model

Bean Basics

We begin our discussion of beans with some basic concepts and terminology. Any object that conforms to certain basic rules can be a bean; there is no Bean class that all beans are required to subclass. Many beans are AWT components, but it is also quite possible, and often useful, to write "invisible" beans that do not have an on-screen appearance. (Just because a bean does not have an on-screen appearance in a finished application does not mean that it won't be visually manipulated by a beanbox tool, however.)

A bean exports properties, events, and methods. A *property* is a piece of the bean's internal state that can be programmatically set and queried, usually through a standard pair of get and set accessor methods. A bean may generate *events* in the same way that an AWT component, such as a Button, generates ActionEvent events. The JavaBeans API uses the same event model as the Java 1.1 AWT does. See Chapter 5, *Events*, for a full discussion of this model. A bean defines an event by providing methods for adding and removing event listener objects from a list of interested listeners for that event. Finally, the *methods* exported by a bean are simply any public methods defined by the bean, excluding those methods used to get and set property values and register and remove event listeners.

In addition to the regular sort of properties described above, the JavaBeans API also provides support for "indexed properties," "bound properties," and "constrained properties." An indexed property is any property that has an array value and for which the bean provides methods to get and set individual elements of the array, as well as methods to get and set the entire array. A bound property is one that sends out a notification event when its value changes, while a constrained property is one that sends out a notification event when its value changes and allows the change to be vetoed by listeners.

Because Java allows dynamic loading of classes, beanbox programs can load arbitrary beans. The beanbox tool determines the properties, events, and methods a bean supports by using an "introspection" mechanism based on the java.lang.reflect reflection mechanism for obtaining information about the members of a class. A bean can also provide an auxiliary BeanInfo class that provides additional information about the bean. The `BeanInfo` class provides this additional information in the form of a number of `FeatureDescriptor` objects, each one describing a single feature of the bean. `FeatureDescriptor` has a number of subclasses: `BeanDescriptor`, `PropertyDescriptor`, `IndexedProperty-Descriptor`, `EventSetDescriptor`, `MethodDescriptor`, and `ParameterDescriptor`.

One of the primary tasks of a beanbox application is to allow the user to customize a bean by setting property values. A beanbox defines "property editors" for commonly used property types, such as numbers, strings, fonts, and colors. If a bean has properties of more complicated types, however, it may need to define a `PropertyEditor` class that enables the beanbox to let the user set values for that property.

In addition, a complex bean may not be satisfied with the property-by-property customization mechanism provided by most beanboxes. Such a bean may want to define a `Customizer` class, which creates a graphical interface that allows the user to configure a bean in some useful way. A particularly complex bean may even define customizers that serve as "wizards" that guide the user step-by-step through the customization process.

A Simple Bean

As noted above, the AWT components in Java 1.1 can all function as beans. When you write a custom GUI component, it is not difficult to make it function as a bean as well. Example 11-1 shows the definition of the custom component, `Multi-LineLabel`, that we developed in Chapter 6, *Graphical User Interfaces*, to display labels that contain more that one line of text. This component is also a bean.

What makes this component a bean is that all of its properties have `get` and `set` accessor methods. Because `MultiLineLabel` does not respond to user input in any way, it does not define any events, so there are no event listener registration methods required. Although it is not a formal requirement for a bean, most beanboxes attempt to instantiate a bean by invoking its no-argument constructor. Thus, a bean should define a constructor that expects no arguments.

Example 11-1: MultiLineLabel.java

```
package oreilly.beans.yesno;
import java.awt.*;
import java.util.*;

/**
 * A custom component that displays multiple lines of text with specified
 * margins and alignment.  In Java 1.1, we could extend Component instead
 * of Canvas, making this a more efficient "Lightweight component"
 */
public class MultiLineLabel extends Canvas {
    // User-specified attributes
    protected String label;           // The label, not broken into lines
    protected int margin_width;       // Left and right margins
    protected int margin_height;      // Top and bottom margins
    protected int alignment;          // The alignment of the text.
    public static final int LEFT = 0, CENTER = 1, RIGHT = 2; // alignment values
```

Example 11-1: MultiLineLabel.java (continued)

```java
// Computed state values
protected int num_lines;            // The number of lines
protected String[] lines;           // The label, broken into lines
protected int[] line_widths;        // How wide each line is
protected int max_width;            // The width of the widest line
protected int line_height;          // Total height of the font
protected int line_ascent;          // Font height above baseline
protected boolean measured = false; // Have the lines been measured?

// Here are five versions of the constructor.
public MultiLineLabel(String label, int margin_width,
                      int margin_height, int alignment) {
  this.label = label;               // Remember all the properties.
  this.margin_width = margin_width;
  this.margin_height = margin_height;
  this.alignment = alignment;
  newLabel();                       // Break the label up into lines.
}
public MultiLineLabel(String label, int margin_width, int margin_height) {
  this(label, margin_width, margin_height, LEFT);
}
public MultiLineLabel(String label, int alignment) {
  this(label, 10, 10, alignment);
}
public MultiLineLabel(String label) { this(label, 10, 10, LEFT); }
public MultiLineLabel() { this(""); }

// Methods to set and query the various attributes of the component.
// Note that some query methods are inherited from the superclass.
public void setLabel(String label) {
  this.label = label;
  newLabel();               // Break the label into lines.
  measured = false;         // Note that we need to measure lines.
  repaint();                // Request a redraw.
}
public void setFont(Font f) {
  super.setFont(f);         // Tell our superclass about the new font.
  measured = false;         // Note that we need to remeasure lines.
  repaint();                // Request a redraw.
}
public void setForeground(Color c) {
  super.setForeground(c);   // Tell our superclass about the new color.
  repaint();                // Request a redraw (size is unchanged).
}
public void setAlignment(int a) { alignment = a; repaint(); }
public void setMarginWidth(int mw) { margin_width = mw; repaint(); }
public void setMarginHeight(int mh) { margin_height = mh; repaint(); }
public String getLabel() { return label; }
public int getAlignment() { return alignment; }
public int getMarginWidth() { return margin_width; }
public int getMarginHeight() { return margin_height; }

/**
 * This method is called by a layout manager when it wants to
 * know how big we'd like to be.  In Java 1.1, getPreferredSize() is
 * the preferred version of this method.  We use this deprecated version
 * so that this component can interoperate with 1.0 components.
 */
```

Example 11-1: MultiLineLabel.java (continued)

```java
public Dimension preferredSize() {
  if (!measured) measure();
  return new Dimension(max_width + 2*margin_width,
                       num_lines * line_height + 2*margin_height);
}
/**
 * This method is called when the layout manager wants to know
 * the bare minimum amount of space we need to get by.
 * For Java 1.1, we'd use getMinimumSize().
 */
public Dimension minimumSize() { return preferredSize(); }

/**
 * This method draws the label (same method that applets use).
 * Note that it handles the margins and the alignment, but that
 * it doesn't have to worry about the color or font--the superclass
 * takes care of setting those in the Graphics object we're passed.
 */
public void paint(Graphics g) {
  int x, y;
  Dimension size = this.size();  // use getSize() in Java 1.1
  if (!measured) measure();
  y = line_ascent + (size.height - num_lines * line_height)/2;
  for(int i = 0; i < num_lines; i++, y += line_height) {
    switch(alignment) {
    default:
    case LEFT:   x = margin_width; break;
    case CENTER: x = (size.width - line_widths[i])/2; break;
    case RIGHT:  x = size.width - margin_width - line_widths[i]; break;
    }
    g.drawString(lines[i], x, y);
  }
}
/** This internal method breaks a specified label up into an array of lines.
 *  It uses the StringTokenizer utility class. */
protected synchronized void newLabel() {
  StringTokenizer t = new StringTokenizer(label, "\n");
  num_lines = t.countTokens();
  lines = new String[num_lines];
  line_widths = new int[num_lines];
  for(int i = 0; i < num_lines; i++) lines[i] = t.nextToken();
}

/** This internal method figures out how the font is, and how wide each
 *  line of the label is, and how wide the widest line is. */
protected synchronized void measure() {
  FontMetrics fm = this.getToolkit().getFontMetrics(this.getFont());
  line_height = fm.getHeight();
  line_ascent = fm.getAscent();
  max_width = 0;
  for(int i = 0; i < num_lines; i++) {
    line_widths[i] = fm.stringWidth(lines[i]);
    if (line_widths[i] > max_width) max_width = line_widths[i];
  }
  measured = true;
}
}
```

Packaging a Bean

To prepare a bean for use in a beanbox, you must package it up in a JAR file, along with any other classes or resource files it requires. (JAR files are "Java archives"; they were introduced in Chapter 3, *Applets*.) Because a single bean can have many auxiliary files, and because a JAR file can contain multiple beans, the manifest of the JAR file must define which of the JAR file entries are beans. You create a JAR file with the c option to the *jar* command. When you use the m option in conjunction with c, it tells *jar* to read a partial manifest file that you specify. *jar* uses the information in your partially-specified manifest file when creating the complete manifest for the JAR file. To identify a class file as a bean, you simply add the following line to the file's manifest entry:

```
Java-Bean: True
```

So, to package up the MultiLineLabel class in a JAR file, you must first create a manifest "stub" file. Create a file, perhaps named *manifest*, with the following contents:

```
Name: oreilly/beans/yesno/MultiLineLabel.class
Java-Bean: True
```

Note that the forward slashes in the manifest file should not be changed to backward slashes on Windows systems. The format of the JAR manifest file requires forward slashes to separate directories regardless of the platform. Having created this partial manifest file, we can now go ahead and create the JAR file:

```
% jar cfm MultiLineLabel.jar manifest oreilly/beans/yesno/MultiLineLabel.class
```

(On a Windows system, you do need to replace forward slashes with backslashes in this command line.) If this bean required auxiliary files, we would specify them on the end of the *jar* command line, along with the class file for the bean.

Installing a Bean

The procedure for installing a bean depends entirely upon the beanbox tool that you are using. For the *beanbox* tool shipped with the BDK, all you need to do is to copy the bean's JAR file into the *jars/* directory within the BDK directory. Once you have done this, the bean appears on the palette of beans everytime you start up the application. Alternatively, you can also load a bean's JAR file at runtime by selecting the **Load JAR** option from the **File** menu of *beanbox*.

A More Complex Bean

Example 11-2 shows another bean, YesNoDialog. This bean creates a dialog box that displays a simple message to the user and asks the user to respond by clicking the **Yes**, **No**, or **Cancel** button. Figure 11-1 shows the bean being manipulated in Sun's *beanbox* tool and also shows a dialog displayed by the bean.

The YesNoDialog bean uses a custom AnswerEvent type to notify AnswerListener objects when the user has dismissed the dialog by clicking on one of its three buttons. This new event class and listener interface are defined in the next section.

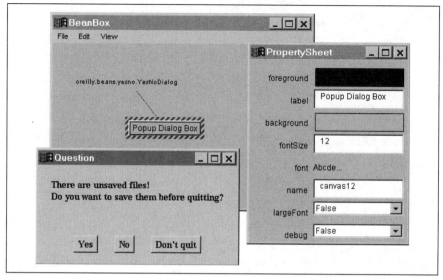

Figure 11–1: The YesNoDialog bean in the beanbox

Note that `YesNoDialog` is a subclass of `Object`, not `Dialog`. This is a result of the requirement for a bean to have a no-argument constructor. Because all dialog boxes must be associated with a `Frame`, `Dialog` does not have a no-argument constructor, which means that subclasses of `Dialog` cannot have meaningful no-argument constructors, either. As a result, `YesNoDialog` defers creation of its window and associated GUI components until it is actually popped up with the `display()` method. Another *beanbox* shortcoming is that it only recognizes methods with no arguments.[*] For this reason, the `display()` method has no arguments, so no `Frame` can be specified through that method either. Since a parent `Frame` cannot be specified, `YesNoDialog` cannot create a `Dialog` object, and instead simulates a dialog box with a `Frame` window. An alternative to this solution would be to define a bean property through which the required `Frame` could be specified.

Since `YesNoDialog` is not a subclass of `Component`, it defines its own properties and accessor methods for fonts and colors; normally these would be inherited from `Component`. Since this bean is not a `Component` subclass, it is an "invisible" bean that does not have a graphical representation of its own. (It pops up a window when the `display()` method is called, but that is not the same as having a graphical representation that appears within another window.) Different tools treat invisible beans differently. *beanbox* simply displays the classname of invisible beans.

Notice that `YesNoDialog` does not use any classes from the `java.beans` package. One of the surprising things about beans is that they typically do not have to use any classes from this package. As we'll see in later sections, it is the auxiliary classes that are shipped with a bean that make heavy use of that package.

---

[*] The *beanbox* tool shipped with the February 1997 version of the BDK has a number of shortcomings. In part, this is due to the fact that the BDK is a new technology and not as stable or robust as the JDK. It is also because *beanbox* is intended as a test environment, not an actual programmer's tool.

Example 11-2: YesNoDialog.java

```java
package oreilly.beans.yesno;        // Put this bean in its own private package.
import java.awt.*;
import java.awt.event.*;
import java.util.*;

public class YesNoDialog {
  // Properties of the bean.
  protected String message, title;
  protected String yesLabel, noLabel, cancelLabel;
  protected int alignment;
  protected Font font = new Font("Serif", Font.PLAIN, 12);
  protected Color background = SystemColor.control;
  protected Color foreground = SystemColor.controlText;

  // Constants for the alignment property.
  public static final int LEFT = MultiLineLabel.LEFT;
  public static final int RIGHT = MultiLineLabel.RIGHT;
  public static final int CENTER = MultiLineLabel.CENTER;

  // Methods to query all of the bean properties.
  public String getMessage() { return message; }
  public String getTitle() { return title; }
  public String getYesLabel() { return yesLabel; }
  public String getNoLabel() { return noLabel; }
  public String getCancelLabel() { return cancelLabel; }
  public int getAlignment() { return alignment; }
  public Font getFont() { return font; }
  public Color getBackground() { return background; }
  public Color getForeground() { return foreground; }

  // Methods to set all of the bean properties.
  public void setMessage(String m) { message = m; }
  public void setTitle(String t) { title=t; }
  public void setYesLabel(String l) { yesLabel = l; }
  public void setNoLabel(String l) { noLabel = l; }
  public void setCancelLabel(String l) { cancelLabel = l; }
  public void setAlignment(int a) { alignment = a; }
  public void setFont(Font f) { font = f; }
  public void setBackground(Color bg) { background = bg; }
  public void setForeground(Color fg) { foreground = fg; }

  /** This field holds a list of registered ActionListeners.
   *  Vector is internally synchronized to prevent race conditions */
  protected Vector listeners = new Vector();

  /** Register an action listener to be notified when a button is pressed */
  public void addAnswerListener(AnswerListener l) {
    listeners.addElement(l);
  }

  /** Remove an Answer listener from our list of interested listeners */
  public void removeAnswerListener(AnswerListener l) {
    listeners.removeElement(l);
  }

  /** Send an event to all registered listeners */
  public void fireEvent(AnswerEvent e) {
    // Make a copy of the list and fire the events using that copy.
```

Example 11-2: YesNoDialog.java (continued)

```
    // This means that listeners can be added or removed from the original
    // list in response to this event.  We ought to be able to just use an
    // enumeration for the vector, but that doesn't copy the list internally.
    Vector list = (Vector) listeners.clone();
    for(int i = 0; i < list.size(); i++) {
      AnswerListener listener = (AnswerListener)list.elementAt(i);
      switch(e.getID()) {
      case AnswerEvent.YES: listener.yes(e); break;
      case AnswerEvent.NO:  listener.no(e); break;
      case AnswerEvent.CANCEL: listener.cancel(e); break;
      }
    }
  }

  /** The no-argument bean constructor, with default property values */
  public YesNoDialog() {
    this("Question", "Your\nMessage\nHere", "Yes", "No", "Cancel", LEFT);
  }

  /** A constructor for programmers using this class "by hand" */
  public YesNoDialog(String title, String message,
                     String yesLabel, String noLabel, String cancelLabel,
                     int alignment) {
    this.title = title;
    this.message = message;
    this.yesLabel = yesLabel;
    this.noLabel = noLabel;
    this.cancelLabel = cancelLabel;
    this.alignment = alignment;
  }

  /** This method makes the bean display the dialog box */
  public void display() {
    // Create a frame with the specified title.  It would be nice to
    // use a Dialog, but that needs to be passed a Frame argument, and
    // the BDK beanbox tool only seems to work with no-argument methods.
    final Frame frame = new Frame(title);

    // Specify a LayoutManager for it.
    frame.setLayout(new BorderLayout(15, 15));

    // Specify font and colors, if any are specified.
    if (font != null) frame.setFont(font);
    if (background != null) frame.setBackground(background);
    if (foreground != null) frame.setForeground(foreground);

    // Put the message label in the middle of the window.
    frame.add("Center", new MultiLineLabel(message, 20, 20, alignment));

    // Create an action listener for use by the buttons of the dialog.
    // When a button is pressed, this listener first closes the dialog box.
    // Then, it creates an AnswerEvent object that corresponds to the
    // button that was pressed, and send that new event to all registered
    // listeners, using the fireEvent() method defined above.
    ActionListener listener = new ActionListener() {
      public void actionPerformed(ActionEvent e) {
        frame.dispose();    // pop down window
        if (listeners != null) {    // notify any registered listeners
```

Java Beans

Example 11-2: YesNoDialog.java (continued)

```
            String cmd = e.getActionCommand();
            int type;
            if (cmd.equals("yes")) type = AnswerEvent.YES;
            else if (cmd.equals("no")) type = AnswerEvent.NO;

            else type = AnswerEvent.CANCEL;
            fireEvent(new AnswerEvent(YesNoDialog.this, type));
        }
    }
};

// Create a panel for the dialog buttons and put it at the bottom
// of the dialog.  Specify a FlowLayout layout manager for it.
Panel buttonbox = new Panel();
buttonbox.setLayout(new FlowLayout(FlowLayout.CENTER, 25, 15));
frame.add("South", buttonbox);

// Create each specified button, specifying the action listener
// and action command for each, and adding them to the buttonbox
if ((yesLabel != null) && (yesLabel.length() > 0)) {
  Button yes = new Button(yesLabel);        // Create button.
  yes.setActionCommand("yes");              // Set action command.
  yes.addActionListener(listener);          // Set listener.
  buttonbox.add(yes);                       // Add button to the panel.
}
if ((noLabel != null) && (noLabel.length() > 0)) {
  Button no = new Button(noLabel);
  no.setActionCommand("no");
  no.addActionListener(listener);
  buttonbox.add(no);
}
if ((cancelLabel != null) && (cancelLabel.length() > 0)) {
  Button cancel = new Button(cancelLabel);
  cancel.setActionCommand("cancel");
  cancel.addActionListener(listener);
  buttonbox.add(cancel);
}

// Finally, set the dialog to its preferred size and display it.
frame.pack();
frame.show();
}

/**
 * A main method that demonstrates how to use this class, and allows testing
 */
public static void main(String[] args) {
  // Create an instance of InfoDialog, with title and message specified:
  YesNoDialog d =
    new YesNoDialog("YesNoDialog Test",
                    "There are unsaved files.\n" +
                    "Do you want to save them before quitting?",
                    "Yes, save and quit",
                    "No, quit without saving",
                    "Cancel; don't quit",
                    YesNoDialog.CENTER);
```

Example 11–2: YesNoDialog.java (continued)

```
    // Register an action listener for the dialog.  This one just prints
    // the results out to the console.
    d.addAnswerListener(new AnswerListener() {
      public void yes(AnswerEvent e) { System.out.println("Yes"); }
      public void no(AnswerEvent e) { System.out.println("No"); }
      public void cancel(AnswerEvent e) { System.out.println("Cancel"); }
    });

    // Now pop the dialog up.  It will pop itself down automatically.
    d.display();
  }
}
```

Custom Events

Beans can use the standard AWT event types defined in the java.awt.event package, but they do not have to. Our YesNoDialog class defines its own event type, AnswerEvent. Defining a new event class is really quite simple; AnswerEvent is shown in Example 11-3.

Example 11–3: AnswerEvent.java

```
package oreilly.beans.yesno;

public class AnswerEvent extends java.util.EventObject {
  protected int id;
  public static final int YES = 0, NO = 1, CANCEL = 2;
  public AnswerEvent(Object source, int id) {
    super(source);
    this.id = id;
  }
  public int getID() { return id; }
}
```

Along with the AnswerEvent class, YesNoDialog also defines a new type of event listener interface, AnswerListener, that defines the methods that must be implemented by any object that wants to receive notification from a YesNoDialog. The definition of AnswerListener is shown in Example 11-4.

Example 11–4: AnswerListener.java

```
package oreilly.beans.yesno;

public interface AnswerListener extends java.util.EventListener {
  public void yes(AnswerEvent e);
  public void no(AnswerEvent e);
  public void cancel(AnswerEvent e);
}
```

Specifying Bean Information

The YesNoDialog class itself and the AnswerEvent and AnswerListener classes it relies on are all a required part of our bean. When an application that uses the bean is shipped, it has to include all three of these class files. There are other

Java Beans

kinds of classes, however, that are often bundled with a bean that are not intended for use by the application developer. These classes are used by the beanbox tool that manipulates the bean. The bean class itself does not refer to any of these auxiliary beanbox classes, so it is not dependent on them and they do not have to be shipped with the bean in finished products.

The first of these optional, auxiliary classes is a BeanInfo class. As explained earlier, a beanbox discovers the properties, events, and methods exported by a bean through "introspection" based on the Java Reflection API. A bean developer who wants to provide additional information about a bean, or who wants to refine the (somewhat rough) information available through introspection, should define a class that implements the BeanInfo interface to provide that information. A BeanInfo class typically subclasses SimpleBeanInfo, which provides a no-op implementation of the BeanInfo interface. When you only want to override one or two methods, it is easier to subclass SimpleBeanInfo than to implement BeanInfo directly. Beanbox tools rely on a naming convention in order to find the BeanInfo class for a given bean: a BeanInfo class should have the same name as the bean, with the string "BeanInfo" appended. Example 11-5 shows an implementation of the YesNoDialogBeanInfo class.

This BeanInfo class specifies a number of pieces of information for our bean:

- An icon that can be used to represent the bean.

- A BeanDescriptor object, which includes a reference to a Customizer class for the bean. We'll see an implementation of this class later in the chapter.

- A list of the supported properties of the bean, along with a short description of each one. Some beanbox tools (but not Sun's *beanbox*) display these strings to the user in some useful way.

- A method that returns the most commonly customized property of the bean— this is called the "default" property.

- References to PropertyEditor classes for two of the properties. We'll see implementations of these property editor classes later in the chapter.

- A list of the methods supported by the bean, again with a short description of each one.

Besides specifying this information, a BeanInfo class can also provide information about the events it generates and specify a default event. The various Feature-Descriptor objects used to provide information about such things as properties and methods can also include other information not provided by YesNo-DialogBeanInfo, such as a localized display name that is distinct from the programmatic name.

Example 11–5: YesNoDialogBeanInfo.java

```
package oreilly.beans.yesno;
import java.beans.*;
import java.lang.reflect.*;
import java.awt.*;
```

Example 11-5: YesNoDialogBeanInfo.java (continued)

```java
/** The BeanInfo class for the YesNoDialog bean */
public class YesNoDialogBeanInfo extends SimpleBeanInfo {

  /** Return an icon for the bean.  We should really check the kind argument
   *  to see what size icon the beanbox wants, but since we only have one
   *  icon to offer, we just return it and let the beanbox deal with it */
  public Image getIcon(int kind) {
    return loadImage("YesNoDialogIcon.gif");
  }

  /** Return a descriptor for the bean itself.  It specifies a customizer
   *  for the bean class.  We could also add a description string here */
  public BeanDescriptor getBeanDescriptor() {
    return new BeanDescriptor(YesNoDialog.class, YesNoDialogCustomizer.class);
  }

  /** This is a convenience routine for creating PropertyDescriptor objects */
  public static PropertyDescriptor property(String name, String description)
       throws IntrospectionException
  {
    PropertyDescriptor p = new PropertyDescriptor(name, YesNoDialog.class);
    p.setShortDescription(description);
    return p;
  }

  /** This method returns an array of PropertyDescriptor objects that specify
   *  additional information about the properties supported by the bean.
   *  By explicitly specifying property descriptors, we are able to provide
   *  simple help strings for each property; these would not be available to
   *  the beanbox through simple introspection.  We are also able to register
   *  special property editors for two of the properties
   */
  public PropertyDescriptor[] getPropertyDescriptors() {
    try {
      PropertyDescriptor[] props = {
        property("title", "The string that appears in the dialog title bar"),
        property("message", "The string that appears in the dialog body"),
        property("yesLabel", "The label for the 'Yes' button, if any"),
        property("noLabel", "The label for the 'No' button, if any"),
        property("cancelLabel", "The label for the 'Cancel' button, if any"),
        property("alignment", "The alignment of the message text"),
        property("font", "The font to use for message and buttons"),
        property("background", "The background color for the dialog"),
        property("foreground", "The text color for message and buttons")
      };

      props[1].setPropertyEditorClass(YesNoDialogMessageEditor.class);
      props[5].setPropertyEditorClass(YesNoDialogAlignmentEditor.class);

      return props;
    }
    catch (IntrospectionException e) {return super.getPropertyDescriptors(); }
  }

  /** The message property is most often customized; make it the default */
  public int getDefaultPropertyIndex() { return 1; }
```

Example 11–5: YesNoDialogBeanInfo.java (continued)

```
/** This is a convenience method for creating MethodDescriptors.  Note that
 *  it assumes we are talking about methods with no arguments */
public static MethodDescriptor method(String name, String description)
      throws NoSuchMethodException, SecurityException {
  Method m = YesNoDialog.class.getMethod(name, new Class[] {});
  MethodDescriptor md = new MethodDescriptor(m);
  md.setShortDescription(description);
  return md;
}

/** This method returns an array of method descriptors for the supported
 * methods of a bean. This allows us to provide useful description strings,
 * but it also allows us to filter out non-useful methods like wait()
 * and notify() that the bean inherits and which might otherwise be
 * displayed by the beanbox.
 */
public MethodDescriptor[] getMethodDescriptors() {
  try {
    MethodDescriptor[] methods = {
      method("display", "Pop up the dialog; make it visible")
    };
    return methods;
  }
  catch (Exception e) {
    return super.getMethodDescriptors();
  }
}
}
```

Defining a Simple Property Editor

A bean can also provide an auxiliary PropertyEditor for use by a beanbox tool. PropertyEditor is a flexible interface that allows a bean to tell a beanbox how to display and edit the values of certain types of properties.

A beanbox tool always provides simple property editors for common property types, such as strings, numbers, fonts, and colors. If your bean has properties of a non-standard type, however, you should register a property editor for that type. The easiest way to "register" a property editor is through a simple naming convention. If your type is defined by the class *X*, the editor for it should be defined in the class *X*Editor. Alternatively, you can register a property editor by calling the PropertyEditorManager.registerEditor() method, probably from the constructor of your BeanInfo class. If you call this method from the bean itself, the bean then depends on the property editor class, so the editor has to be bundled with the bean in applications, which is not desirable.

In our YesNoDialog example, we don't define any new data types, but we still have two individual properties that need custom editors. In this case, we register the property editors for individual properties by specifying them in the Property-Descriptor objects returned by the getPropertyDescriptors() method of our BeanInfo class.

The PropertyEditor interface can seem confusing at first. Its methods allow you to define three techniques for displaying the value of a property and two techniques for allowing the user to edit the value of a property. The value of a property can be displayed:

- *As a string.* If you define the getAsText() method, a beanbox can convert a property to a string and display that string to the user.

- *As an enumerated value.* If a property can only take on values from a fixed set of values, you can define the getTags() method to allow a beanbox to display a dropdown menu of allowed values for the property.

- *In a graphical display.* If you define paintValue(), a beanbox can ask the property editor to display the value using some natural graphical format, such as a color swatch for colors. You also need to define isPaintable() to specify that a graphical format is supported.

The two editing techniques are:

- *String editing.* If you define the setAsText() method, a beanbox knows it can simply have the user type a value into a text field and pass that value to setAsText(). If your property editor defines getTags(), it should also define setAsText() so that a beanbox can set the property value using the individual tag values.

- *Custom editing.* If your property editor defines getCustomEditor(), a beanbox can call it to obtain some kind of AWT component that can be displayed in a dialog box and serve as a custom editor for the property. You also need to define supportsCustomEditor() to specify that custom editing is supported.

The setValue() method of a PropertyEditor is called to specify the current value of the property. It is this value that should be converted to a string or graphical representation by getAsText() or paintValue().

A property editor must maintain a list of event listeners that are interested in changes to the value of the property. The addPropertyChangeListener() and removePropertyChangeListener() methods are standard event listener registration and removal methods. When a property editor changes the value of a property, either through setAsText() or through a custom editor, it must send a Property-ChangeEvent to all registered listeners.

PropertyEditor defines the getJavaInitializationString() for use by beanbox tools that generate Java code. This method should return a fragment of Java code that can be used to initialize a variable to the current property value.

Finally, a class that implements the PropertyEditor interface must have a no-argument constructor, so that it can be dynamically loaded and instantiated by a beanbox.

Most property editors can be much simpler than this detailed description would suggest. In many cases, you can subclass PropertyEditorSupport instead of implementing the PropertyEditor interface directly. This useful class provides no-op implementations of most PropertyEditor methods. It also implements the methods for adding and removing event listeners.

A property that has an enumerated value requires a simple property editor. The alignment property of the YesNoDialog bean is an example of this common type of property. The property is defined as an int, but it has only three legal values, defined by the constants LEFT, CENTER, and RIGHT. By default, a beanbox only knows that the property is an int, so it displays the property as a number and allows the user to enter any integer as a property value. Instead, we would like the beanbox display one of the strings "left," "center," or "right" as the value, and allow the user to choose from these values when setting the property. This can be done with the getTags() and setAsText() methods of a property editor, as shown in Example 11-6.

This example creates the YesNoDialogAlignmentEditor class, which is registered as a PropertyEditor for the alignment property by the YesNoDialogBeanInfo class shown in Example 11-5. The property editor subclasses PropertyEditorSupport, so it is relatively short. Notice that it passes Integer objects in the calls to set-Value() that are made from the setAsText() method. You need to use wrapper objects for any primitive-type properties. The use of the Integer class is also apparent in the definition of getJavaInitializationString(). The setValue() method of PropertyEditorSupport handles notifying registered PropertyChange-Listener objects about changes in the value of the property, so this simple property editor does not need to be aware of the existence of such listeners.

Example 11-6: YesNoDialogAlignmentEditor.java

```
package oreilly.beans.yesno;
import java.beans.*;
import java.awt.*;

public class YesNoDialogAlignmentEditor extends PropertyEditorSupport {
  // These two methods allow the property to be edited in a dropdown list.
  // Return the list of value names for the enumerated type.
  public String[] getTags() {
    return new String[] { "left", "center", "right" };
  }

  // Convert each of those value names into the actual value.
  public void setAsText(String s) {
    if (s.equals("left")) setValue(new Integer(YesNoDialog.LEFT));
    else if (s.equals("center")) setValue(new Integer(YesNoDialog.CENTER));
    else if (s.equals("right")) setValue(new Integer(YesNoDialog.RIGHT));
    else throw new IllegalArgumentException(s);
  }

  // This is an important method for code generation.
  public String getJavaInitializationString() {
    switch(((Number)getValue()).intValue()) {
    default:
    case YesNoDialog.LEFT:   return "oreilly.beans.yesno.YesNoDialog.LEFT";
    case YesNoDialog.CENTER: return "oreilly.beans.yesno.YesNoDialog.CENTER";
    case YesNoDialog.RIGHT:  return "oreilly.beans.yesno.YesNoDialog.RIGHT";
    }
  }
}
```

Defining a Complex Property Editor

There is another `YesNoDialog` property value that requires a property editor. The `message` property of `YesNoDialog` can specify a multi-line message to be displayed in the dialog. This property requires a property editor because the *beanbox* program does not distinguish between single-line and multi-line string types; the `TextField` objects it uses for text input do not allow the user to enter multiple lines of text. For this reason, we define the `YesNoDialogMessageEditor` class and register it with the `PropertyDescriptor` for the message property, as shown in Example 11-5.

Example 11-7 shows the definition of this property editor. This is a more complex editor that supports the creation of a custom editor component and graphical display of the value. Note that this example implements `PropertyEditor` directly. `getCustomEditor()` returns an editor component for multi-line strings. Figure 11-2 shows this custom editor placed within a dialog box created by the *beanbox* program. Note that the **Done** button in this figure is part of the *beanbox* dialog, not part of the property editor itself.

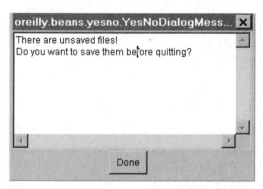

Figure 11-2: A custom property editor dialog

The `paintValue()` method is responsible for displaying the value of the `message` property. This multi-line value does not typically fit in the small rectangle of screen space allowed for the property, so `paintValue()` displays instructions for popping up the custom editor, which allows the user to inspect and edit the property value. (This example relies on the click-to-edit behavior of the *beanbox* program; the `paintValue()` method may not make sense when the bean is used in other beanbox tools.)

Example 11-7: YesNoDialogMessageEditor.java

```
package oreilly.beans.yesno;
import java.beans.*;
import java.awt.*;
import java.awt.event.*;

/**
 * This class is a custom editor for the message property of the
 * YesNoDialog bean.  It is necessary because the default editor for
```

Example 11-7: YesNoDialogMessageEditor.java (continued)

```
 * properties of type String does not allow multi-line strings
 * to be entered.
 */
public class YesNoDialogMessageEditor implements PropertyEditor {
  protected String value;  // The value we will be editing.

  public void setValue(Object o) {  value = (String) o; }
  public Object getValue() { return value; }
  public void setAsText(String s) { value = s; }
  public String getAsText() { return value; }
  public String[] getTags() { return null; }  // not enumerated; no tags

  // Say that we allow custom editing.
  public boolean supportsCustomEditor() { return true; }

  // Return the custom editor.  This just creates and returns a TextArea
  // to edit the multi-line text.  But it also registers a listener on the
  // text area to update the value as the user types and to fire the
  // property change events that property editors are required to fire.
  public Component getCustomEditor() {
    final TextArea t = new TextArea(value);
    t.setSize(300, 150); // TextArea doesn't have a preferred size, so set one
    t.addTextListener(new TextListener() {
      public void textValueChanged(TextEvent e) {
        value = t.getText();
        listeners.firePropertyChange(null, null, null);
      }
    });
    return t;
  }

  // Visual display of the value, for use with the custom editor.
  // Just print some instructions and hope they fit in the in the box.
  // This could be more sophisticated.
  public boolean isPaintable() { return true; }
  public void paintValue(Graphics g, Rectangle r) {
    g.setClip(r);
    g.drawString("Click to edit...", r.x+5, r.y+15);
  }

  // Important method for code generators.  Note that it
  // ought to add any necessary escape sequences.
  public String getJavaInitializationString() { return "\"" + value + "\""; }

  // This code uses the PropertyChangeSupport class to maintain a list of
  // listeners interested in the edits we make to the value.
  protected PropertyChangeSupport listeners = new PropertyChangeSupport(this);
  public void addPropertyChangeListener(PropertyChangeListener l) {
    listeners.addPropertyChangeListener(l);
  }
  public void removePropertyChangeListener(PropertyChangeListener l) {
    listeners.removePropertyChangeListener(l);
  }
}
```

Defining a Bean Customizer

A bean may want to provide some way for the user of a beanbox program to customize its properties other than by setting them one at a time. A bean can do this by creating a Customizer class for itself, and registering the customizer class with the BeanDescriptor object returned by its BeanInfo class, as in Example 11-5.

A customizer must be some kind of AWT component that is suitable for display in a dialog box created by the beanbox. Therefore, a customizer class is typically a subclass of Panel. In addition, a customizer must implement the Customizer interface. This interface consists of methods for adding and removing property change event listeners and a setObject() method that the beanbox calls to tell the customizer what bean object it is customizing. Whenever the user makes a change to the bean through the customizer, the customizer sends a PropertyChangeEvent to any interested listeners. Finally, like a property editor, a customizer must have a no-argument constructor, so it can easily be instantiated by a beanbox.

Example 11-8 shows a customizer for our YesNoDialog bean. This customizer displays a panel that has the same layout as a YesNoDialog, but it substitutes a TextArea object for the message display and three TextField objects for the three buttons that the dialog can display. These text entry areas allow the user to enter values for the message, yesLabel, noLabel, and cancelLabel properties. Figure 11-3 shows this customizer panel displayed within a dialog box created by the *beanbox* program. Again, note that the **Done** button is part of the *beanbox* dialog, not part of the customizer itself.

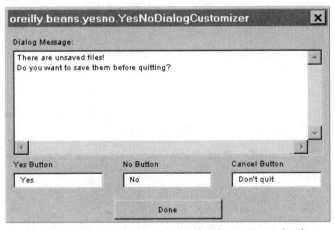

Figure 11-3: The customizer dialog for the YesNoDialog bean

Example 11-8: YesNoDialogCustomizer.java

```
package oreilly.beans.yesno;

import java.awt.*;
import java.awt.event.*;
import java.beans.*;
```

Example 11-8: YesNoDialogCustomizer.java (continued)

```
/**
 * This class is a customizer for the YesNoDialog bean.  It displays a
 * TextArea and three TextFields where the user can enter the dialog message
 * and the labels for each of the three buttons.  It does not allow the
 * dialog title or other resources to be set.
 */
public class YesNoDialogCustomizer extends Panel
                                   implements Customizer, TextListener
{
  protected YesNoDialog bean;                    // The bean being customized
  protected TextComponent message, fields[];  // Components used by customizer

  // Default constructor: YesNoDialogCustomizer() { super(); }

  // The bean box calls this method to tell us what object to customize.
  // This method will always be called before the customizer is displayed,
  // so it is safe to create the customizer GUI here.
  public void setObject(Object o) {
    bean = (YesNoDialog)o;   // save the object we're customizing

    // Put a label at the top of the panel.
    this.setLayout(new BorderLayout());
    this.add(new Label("Enter the message to appear in the dialog:"), "North");

    // And a big text area below it for entering the dialog message.
    message = new TextArea(bean.getMessage());
    message.addTextListener(this);
    // TextAreas don't know how big they want to be.  You must tell them.
    message.setSize(400, 200);
    this.add(message, "Center");

    // Then add a row of textfields for entering the button labels.
    Panel buttonbox = new Panel();                      // The row container
    buttonbox.setLayout(new GridLayout(1, 0, 25, 10)); // Equally spaced items
    this.add(buttonbox, "South");                       // Put row on bottom

    // Now go create three TextFields to put in this row.  But actually
    // position a Label above each, so create an container for each
    // TextField+Label combination.
    fields = new TextComponent[3];          // Array of TextFields.
    String[] labels = new String[] {        // Labels for each.
      "Yes Button Label", "No Button Label", "Cancel Button Label"};
    String[] values = new String[] {        // Initial values of each.
      bean.getYesLabel(), bean.getNoLabel(), bean.getCancelLabel()};
    for(int i = 0; i < 3; i++) {
      Panel p = new Panel();                       // Create a container.
      p.setLayout(new BorderLayout());             // Give it a BorderLayout.
      p.add(new Label(labels[i]), "North");        // Put a label on the top.
      fields[i] = new TextField(values[i]);        // Create the text field.
      p.add(fields[i], "Center");                  // Put it below the label.
      fields[i].addTextListener(this);             // Set the event listener.
      buttonbox.add(p);                            // Add container to row.
    }
  }
```

Example 11–8: YesNoDialogCustomizer.java (continued)

```
// Add some space around the outside of the panel.
public Insets getInsets() { return new Insets(10, 10, 10, 10); }

// This is the method defined by the TextListener interface.  Whenever the
// user types a character in the TextArea or TextFields, this will get
// called.  It updates the appropriate property of the bean and fires a
// property changed event, as all customizers are required to do.
// Note that we are not required to fire an event for every keystroke.
// Instead we could include an "Apply" button that would make all the
// changes at once, with a single property changed event.
public void textValueChanged(TextEvent e) {
  TextComponent t = (TextComponent)e.getSource();
  String s = t.getText();
  if (t == message) bean.setMessage(s);
  else if (t == fields[0]) bean.setYesLabel(s);
  else if (t == fields[1]) bean.setNoLabel(s);
  else if (t == fields[2]) bean.setCancelLabel(s);
  listeners.firePropertyChange(null, null, null);
}

// This code uses the PropertyChangeSupport class to maintain a list of
// listeners interested in the edits we make to the bean.
protected PropertyChangeSupport listeners = new PropertyChangeSupport(this);
public void addPropertyChangeListener(PropertyChangeListener l) {
  listeners.addPropertyChangeListener(l);
}
public void removePropertyChangeListener(PropertyChangeListener l) {
  listeners.removePropertyChangeListener(l);
}
}
```

Naming Patterns and Conventions

As we've seen, beanbox programs may rely on introspection of a bean to determine the list of properties, events, and methods it supports. In order for this to work, bean developers must follow a set of standard naming conventions, sometimes referred to as JavaBeans "design patterns." These patterns specify, for example, that the getter and setter accessor methods for a property should begin with get and set.

Not all of the patterns are absolute requirements. If a bean has accessor methods with different names, it is possible to use a PropertyDescriptor object, specified in a BeanInfo class, to specify the accessor methods for the property. Note, however, that although an accessor method name is not required to follow the pattern, the method is required to have the exact type signature specified by the pattern.

Table 11-1 lists the design patterns for bean properties, events, and methods. It also lists other conventions and requirements that you should keep in mind when developing beans.

Java Beans

Table 11-1: Java Bean Patterns

Beans

class name:	Any
superclass:	Any
constructor:	Must have a no-argument constructor, or a serialized template file
packaging:	JAR file manifest entry specifies `Java-Bean: True`

Properties (property *p* of type *T*)

getter:	`public T getP()`
setter:	`public void setP(T value)`

Boolean Properties (property *p* of type boolean)

getter:	`public boolean getP()` *or*
	`public boolean isP()`
setter:	`public void setP`

Indexed Properties (property *p* of type *T*[ ])

array getter:	`public T[] getP()`
array setter:	`public void setP(T[] value)`
element getter:	`public T getP(int index)`
element setter:	`public void setP(int index, T value)`

Bound Properties (property *p* of type *T*)

getter:	Same as regular property
setter:	Same as regular property
listeners:	One event listener list for all bound properties of a bean
listener registration:	`public void addPropertyChangeListener` `(PropertyChangeListener l)`
listener removal:	`public void removePropertyChangeListener` `(PropertyChangeListener l)`

Constrained Properties (property *p* of type *T*)

getter:	Same as regular property
setter:	`public void setP(T value)` `throws PropertyVetoException`
listeners:	One event listener list for all constrained properties of a bean
listener registration:	`public void addVetoableChangeListener` `(VetoableChangeListener l)`
listener removal:	`public void removeVetoableChangeListener` `(VetoableChangeListener l)`

Events (event named *E*)

event class name:	`EEvent`
listener name:	`EListener`
listener methods:	`public void methodname(EEvent e)`
listener registration:	`public void addEListener(EListener l)`
listener removal:	`public void removeEListener(EListener l)`

Table 11-1: Java Bean Patterns (continued)

Unicast Events (event named *E* only one listener allowed)

listener registration:	public void add*E*Listener(*E*Listener l) throws TooManyListenersException
listener removal:	public void remove*E*Listener(*E*Listener l)

Methods

method name:	Any
method args:	Any; some tools only recognize no-argument methods

BeanInfo Classes (for bean *B*)

class name:	*B*BeanInfo

Property Editors (for properties of type *T*)

class name:	*T*Editor
constructor:	Must have a no-argument constructor

Property Editors (for individual properties)

class name:	Any; register via PropertyDescriptor
constructor:	Must have a no-argument constructor

Customizers (for bean *B*)

class name:	Any; register via BeanDescriptor (*B*Customizer by convention)
superclass:	Must be a component; typically extends Panel
constructor:	Must have a no-argument constructor

Documentation File (for bean *B*)

default docs:	*B*.html
localized docs:	*locale/B*.html

Exercises

11-1. Example 3-3, and a number of other examples throughout Chapters 3, 4, 5, and 6, define versions of a scribble applet. Choose one of these examples, preferably a simpler one, like Example 3-3, and modify it so that it is an AWT component instead of an applet. As an AWT component, it should be suitable for use as a Java bean. To do this, you need to extend Panel, Canvas, or Container instead of extending Applet. You might want to give the class a getPreferredSize() method that specifies fixed screen dimensions for the bean. Give the class an erase() method that erases any scribbles currently displayed by the component. Finally, be sure to give it a no-argument constructor, so that it can be instantiated by a beanbox. Package the bean in a JAR file, as described in this chapter, and install it in a beanbox application of your choice to demonstrate that it works.

11-2. Modify your Scribble bean so that it has color and line width properties that specify the color and width of the lines used for the scribbles. (Note that you have to approximate wide lines by drawing multiple thin lines next to each other.) Re-package the bean and test the properties in a beanbox.

11-3.   An application that uses a Scribble bean might be interested in being notified each time the user completes a single stroke of the scribble (i.e., each time the user clicks, drags, and then releases the mouse). For example, an application might make an off-screen copy of the scribble after each stroke so that it could implement an undo facility. In order to provide this kind of notification, the Scribble bean has to support a "stroke" event. Define a simple StrokeEvent class and StrokeListener interface. Modify the Scribble bean so that it allows registration and removal of StrokeListener objects, and so that it notifies all registered listeners each time a stroke of the scribble is complete. Regenerate the bean's JAR file so that it includes the StrokeEvent and StrokeListener class files.

11-4.   Define a BeanInfo subclass for the Scribble bean. This class should provide information about the erase() method, the color and width properties, and the stroke event defined by the bean. The BeanInfo class should use the FeatureDescriptor.setShortDescription() method to provide simple descriptive strings for the bean itself, and for its method, properties, and event.

CHAPTER 12

Reflection

The Reflection API allows a Java program to inspect and manipulate itself; it comprises the much-expanded Class class in java.lang and the java.lang.reflect package, which represents the members of a class with Method, Constructor, and Field objects.

Reflection can be used to obtain information about a class and its members. This is the technique that the JavaBeans "introspection" mechanism uses to determine the properties, events, and methods that are supported by a bean, for example. Reflection can also be used to manipulate objects in Java. You can use the Field class to query and set the values of fields, the Method class to invoke methods, and the Constructor class to create new objects. The examples in this chapter demonstrate both techniques for using the Reflection API.

In addition to the examples in this chapter, the Java Reflection API is also used by an example in Chapter 16, *Database Access with SQL.*

Obtaining Class and Member Information

Example 12-1 shows a program that uses the Class, Constructor, Field, and Method classes to display information about a specified class. The program's output is similar to the class synopses that appear in *Java in a Nutshell.* (You might notice that the names of method arguments are not shown; argument names are not stored in class files, so they are not available through the Reflection API.)

Here is the output from using ShowClass on itself:

```
% java ShowClass ShowClass
public class ShowClass extends java.lang.Object {
  // Constructors
   public ShowClass();
  // Fields
  // Methods
   public static void main(java.lang.String[]);
```

```
      public static void print_class(java.lang.Class);
      public static java.lang.String typename(java.lang.Class);
      public static java.lang.String modifiers(int);
      public static void print_field(java.lang.reflect.Field);
      public static void print_method_or_constructor(java.lang.reflect.Member);
    }
```

The code for this example is quite straightforward. It uses the Class.forName()
method to dynamically load the named class, and then calls various methods of
Class object to look up the superclass, interfaces, and members of the class. The
example uses Constructor, Field, and Method objects to obtain information about
each member of the class.

Example 12–1: ShowClass.java

```
import java.lang.reflect.*;

/** A program that displays a class synopsis for the named class */
public class ShowClass {
  /** The main method.  Print info about the named class */
  public static void main(String[] args) throws ClassNotFoundException {
    Class c = Class.forName(args[0]);
    print_class(c);
  }

  /** Display the modifiers, name, superclass and interfaces of a class
   *  or interface. Then go and list all constructors, fields, and methods. */
  public static void print_class(Class c)
  {
    // Print modifiers, type (class or interface), name and superclass.
    if (c.isInterface()) {
      // The modifiers will include the "interface" keyword here...
      System.out.print(Modifier.toString(c.getModifiers()) +  c.getName());
    }
    else if (c.getSuperclass() != null)
      System.out.print(Modifier.toString(c.getModifiers()) + " class " +
                       c.getName() +
                       " extends " + c.getSuperclass().getName());
    else
      System.out.print(Modifier.toString(c.getModifiers()) + " class " +
                       c.getName());

    // Print interfaces or super-interfaces of the class or interface.
    Class[] interfaces = c.getInterfaces();
    if ((interfaces != null) && (interfaces.length > 0)) {
      if (c.isInterface()) System.out.println(" extends ");
      else System.out.print(" implements ");
      for(int i = 0; i < interfaces.length; i++) {
        if (i > 0) System.out.print(", ");
        System.out.print(interfaces[i].getName());
      }
    }

    System.out.println(" {");                   // Begin class member listing.

    // Now look up and display the members of the class.
    System.out.println(" // Constructors");
    Constructor[] constructors = c.getDeclaredConstructors();
    for(int i = 0; i < constructors.length; i++)       // Display constructors.
      print_method_or_constructor(constructors[i]);
```

Example 12-1: ShowClass.java (continued)

```
  System.out.println(" // Fields");
  Field[] fields = c.getDeclaredFields();          // Look up fields.
  for(int i = 0; i < fields.length; i++)           // Display them.
    print_field(fields[i]);

  System.out.println(" // Methods");
  Method[] methods = c.getDeclaredMethods();        // Look up methods.
  for(int i = 0; i < methods.length; i++)           // Display them.
    print_method_or_constructor(methods[i]);

  System.out.println("}");                // End class member listing.
}

/** Return the name of an interface or primitive type, handling arrays. */
public static String typename(Class t) {
  String brackets = "";
  while(t.isArray()) {
    brackets += "[]";
    t = t.getComponentType();
  }
  return t.getName() + brackets;
}

/** Return a string version of modifiers, handling spaces nicely. */
public static String modifiers(int m) {
  if (m == 0) return "";
  else return Modifier.toString(m) + " ";
}

/** Print the modifiers, type, and name of a field */
public static void print_field(Field f) {
  System.out.println("  " +
                     modifiers(f.getModifiers()) +
                     typename(f.getType()) + " " + f.getName() + ";");
}

/** Print the modifiers, return type, name, parameter types and exception
 *  type of a method or constructor.  Note the use of the Member interface
 *  to allow this method to work with both Method and Constructor objects */
public static void print_method_or_constructor(Member member) {
  Class returntype=null, parameters[], exceptions[];
  if (member instanceof Method) {
    Method m = (Method) member;
    returntype = m.getReturnType();
    parameters = m.getParameterTypes();
    exceptions = m.getExceptionTypes();
  } else {
    Constructor c = (Constructor) member;
    parameters = c.getParameterTypes();
    exceptions = c.getExceptionTypes();
  }

  System.out.print("  " + modifiers(member.getModifiers()) +
                   ((returntype!=null)? typename(returntype)+" " : "") +
                   member.getName() + "(");
  for(int i = 0; i < parameters.length; i++) {
    if (i > 0) System.out.print(", ");
    System.out.print(typename(parameters[i]));
```

Reflection

Example 12–1: ShowClass.java (continued)

```
    }
    System.out.print(")");
    if (exceptions.length > 0) System.out.print(" throws ");
    for(int i = 0; i < exceptions.length; i++) {
      if (i > 0) System.out.print(", ");
      System.out.print(typename(exceptions[i]));
    }
    System.out.println(";");
  }
}
```

Invoking a Named Method

Example 12-2 demonstrates another use of the Reflection API. This `Universal-ActionListener` object uses reflection to invoke a named method of a specified object, passing another optionally specified object as an argument. It does this in the framework of the `ActionListener` interface, so that it can serve as an action listener within a Java 1.1 GUI. By using the reflection capabilities of the `UniversalActionListener`, a program can avoid having to create a lot of trivial `ActionListener` implementations to handle action events. The `main()` method at the end of this example is a simple test GUI that demonstrates how you could use the `UniversalActionListener` object. Contrast it with the anonymous class event-handling techniques demonstrated in Chapter 5, *Events.*

Java does not allow methods to be passed directly as data values, but the Reflection API makes it possible for methods passed by name to be invoked indirectly. Note that this technique is not particularly efficient. For asynchronous event handling in a GUI, though, it is certainly efficient enough: indirect method invocation through the Reflection API will always be much faster than the response time required by the limits of human perception. Invoking a method by name is not an appropriate technique, however, when repetitive, synchronous calls are required. Thus, you should not use this technique for passing a comparison method to a sorting routine or passing a filename filter to a directory listing method. In cases like these, you should use the standard technique of implementing a class that contains the desired method and passing an instance of the class to the appropriate routine.

Example 12–2: UniversalActionListener.java

```
import java.awt.event.*;
import java.lang.reflect.*;
import java.awt.*;    // Only used for the test program below.

public class UniversalActionListener implements ActionListener {
  protected Object target;
  protected Object arg;
  protected Method m;

  public UniversalActionListener(Object target, String methodname, Object arg)
      throws NoSuchMethodException, SecurityException
  {
    this.target = target;                      // Save the target object.
    this.arg = arg;                            // And method argument.
```

Example 12-2: UniversalActionListener.java (continued)

```
  // Now look up and save the Method to invoke on that target object
  Class c, parameters[];
  c = target.getClass();                       // The Class object.
  if (arg == null) parameters = new Class[0];  // Method parameter.
  else parameters = new Class[] { arg.getClass() };
  m = c.getMethod(methodname, parameters);     // Find matching method.
}

public void actionPerformed(ActionEvent event) {
  Object[] arguments;
  if (arg == null) arguments = new Object[0];  // Set up arguments.
  else arguments = new Object[] { arg };
  try { m.invoke(target, arguments); }         // And invoke the method.
  catch (IllegalAccessException e) {           // Should never happen.
    System.err.println("UniversalActionListener: " + e);
  } catch (InvocationTargetException e) {      // Should never happen.
    System.err.println("UniversalActionListener: " + e);
  }
}

// A simple test program for the UniversalActionListener
public static void main(String[] args) throws NoSuchMethodException {
  Frame f = new Frame("UniversalActionListener Test");// Create window.
  f.setLayout(new FlowLayout());               // Set layout manager.
  Button b1 = new Button("tick");              // Create buttons.
  Button b2 = new Button("tock");
  Button b3 = new Button("Close Window");
  f.add(b1); f.add(b2); f.add(b3);             // Add them to window.

  // Specify what the buttons do.  Invoke a named method with
  // the UniversalActionListener object.
  b1.addActionListener(new UniversalActionListener(b1, "setLabel", "tock"));
  b1.addActionListener(new UniversalActionListener(b2, "setLabel", "tick"));
  b1.addActionListener(new UniversalActionListener(b3, "hide", null));
  b2.addActionListener(new UniversalActionListener(b1, "setLabel", "tick"));
  b2.addActionListener(new UniversalActionListener(b2, "setLabel", "tock"));
  b2.addActionListener(new UniversalActionListener(b3, "show", null));
  b3.addActionListener(new UniversalActionListener(f, "dispose", null));

  f.pack();                                    // Set window size.
  f.show();                                    // And pop it up.
  }
}
```

Exercises

12-1. Write a program that takes the name of a Java class as a command line argument and uses the Class class to print out all the superclasses of that class. For example, if invoked with the argument "java.awt.Applet", the program prints the following: `java.lang.Object   java.awt.Component java.awt.Container java.awt.Panel`.

12-2. Modify the program you wrote for Exercise 12-1 so that it prints out all of the interfaces implemented by a specified class or by any of its superclasses. Be sure to check for the case of classes that implement interfaces that extend other interfaces. For example, if a class implements java.awt.LayoutManager2, both the LayoutManager2 interface and Layout-Manager, its "superinterface," should be listed.

12-3. Modify the UniversalActionListener class of Example 12-2 so that in addition to invoking a named method of an object, it can also set the value of a named field of an object. If the second argument to the UniversalAction-Listener() constructor is not the name of a method, check to see if it is the name of a field instead. If it is, the actionPerformed() method should set that field of the *target* object to the *arg* value.

CHAPTER 13

Object Serialization

Object serialization is one of the important new features of Java 1.1. Despite its importance, however, serialization is done with a very simple API. This chapter demonstrates several uses of serialization. In addition to the examples shown here, there also examples that use serialization in Chapter 15, *Remote Method Invocation*, and Chapter 17, *Security and Cryptography*.

Simple Serialization

Objects are serialized with the ObjectOutputStream and they are deserialized with the ObjectInputStream. Both of these classes are part of the java.io package, and they function, in many ways, like DataOutputStream and DataInputStream because they define the same methods for writing and reading binary representations of Java primitive types to and from streams. What ObjectOutputStream and ObjectInputStream add, however, is the ability to write and read non-primitive object and array values to and from a stream.

An object is serialized by passing it to the writeObject() method of an ObjectOutputStream. This writes out the values of all of its fields, including private fields and fields inherited from superclasses. The values of primitive fields are simply written to the stream as they would be with a DataOutputStream. When a field in an object refers to another object, an array, or a string, however, the writeObject() method is invoked recursively to serialize that object as well. If that object (or an array element) refers to another object, writeObject() is again invoked recursively. Thus, a single call to writeObject() may result in an entire "object graph" being serialized. When two or more objects each refer to the other, the serialization algorithm is careful to only output each object once—writeObject() cannot enter infinite recursion.

Deserializing an object simply follows the reverse of this process. An object is read from a stream of data by calling the readObject() method of an ObjectInput-

Stream. This re-creates the object in the state it was in when serialized. If the object refers to other objects, they are recursively deserialized as well.

This ability to serialize an entire graph of objects and read those objects back in later is a very powerful feature that hides itself in two simple looking methods. Example 13-1 uses object serialization, but unless you pay attention, you might miss the crucial writeObject() and readObject() calls! Serialization is used in this Scribble example to give the program an automatic file format for saving the user's scribbles.

The main points of interest in Example 13-1 are the save() and load() methods. In save(), note the creation of the ObjectOutputStream and the use of the write-Object() method. The corresponding load() method simply reverses the streams to read the scribble back in. Also note the use of a GZIPOutputStream (from java.util.zip) to compress the serialized object data before writing it to disk.

Example 13-1: SerializedScribble.java

```
import java.awt.*;              // ScrollPane, PopupMenu, MenuShortcut, etc.
import java.awt.event.*;        // New event model.
import java.io.*;               // Object serialization streams.
import java.util.zip.*;         // Data compression/decompression streams.
import java.util.Vector;        // To store the scribble in.

/**
 * This class demonstrates the use of object serialization to provide
 * a file format for saving application state.  It saves a user's scribbles
 * as a compressed, serialized Vector of Line objects.
 **/
public class SerializedScribble extends Frame {
  /** A very simple main() method for our program. */
  public static void main(String[] args) { new SerializedScribble(); }

  /** Create a Frame, Menu, and Scribble component */
  public SerializedScribble() {
    super("SerialziedScribble");               // Create the window.

    final Scribble scribble;
    scribble = new Scribble(this, 300, 300); // Create a bigger scribble area.
    this.add(scribble, "Center");            // Add it to the ScrollPane.

    MenuBar menubar = new MenuBar();          // Create a menubar.
    this.setMenuBar(menubar);                 // Add it to the frame.
    Menu file = new Menu("File");             // Create a File menu.
    menubar.add(file);                        // Add to menubar.

    // Create three menu items, with menu shortcuts, and add to the menu.
    MenuItem load, save, quit;
    file.add(load = new MenuItem("Load"));
    file.add(save = new MenuItem("Save"));
    file.addSeparator();                      // Put a separator in the menu
    file.add(quit = new MenuItem("Quit"));

    // Create and register action listener objects for the three menu items.
    load.addActionListener(new ActionListener() {     // Open a new window
      public void actionPerformed(ActionEvent e) { scribble.load(); }
    });
```

Example 13-1: SerializedScribble.java (continued)

```
    save.addActionListener(new ActionListener() {      // Close this window.
      public void actionPerformed(ActionEvent e) { scribble.save(); }
    });
    quit.addActionListener(new ActionListener() {      // Quit the program.
      public void actionPerformed(ActionEvent e) { System.exit(0); }
    });

    // Another event listener, this one to handle window close requests.
    this.addWindowListener(new WindowAdapter() {
      public void windowClosing(WindowEvent e) { System.exit(0); }
    });

    // Set the window size and pop it up.
    this.pack();
    this.show();
  }

  /**
   * This class is a custom component that supports scribbling.  Note that
   * it extends Component rather than Canvas, making it "lightweight."
   **/
  static class Scribble extends Component {
    protected short last_x, last_y;             // Coordinates of last click.
    protected Vector lines = new Vector(256,256); // Store the scribbles.
    protected int width, height;                // The preferred size.
    protected Frame frame;                       // The frame we are within.

    /** This constructor requires a Frame and a desired size */
    public Scribble(Frame frame, int width, int height) {
      this.frame = frame;
      this.width = width;
      this.height = height;

      // We handle scribbling with low-level events, so we must specify
      // which events we are interested in.
      this.enableEvents(AWTEvent.MOUSE_EVENT_MASK);
      this.enableEvents(AWTEvent.MOUSE_MOTION_EVENT_MASK);
    }

    /**
     * Specifies big the component would like to be.  It always returns the
     * preferred size passed to the Scribble() constructor
     **/
    public Dimension getPreferredSize() {return new Dimension(width, height);}

    /** Draw all the saved lines of the scribble */
    public void paint(Graphics g) {
      for(int i = 0; i < lines.size(); i++) {
        Line l = (Line)lines.elementAt(i);
        g.drawLine(l.x1, l.y1, l.x2, l.y2);
      }
    }

    /**
     * This is the low-level event-handling method called on mouse events
     * that do not involve mouse motion.
     **/
    public void processMouseEvent(MouseEvent e) {
```

Example 13-1: SerializedScribble.java (continued)

```
    if (e.getID() == MouseEvent.MOUSE_PRESSED) {
      last_x = (short)e.getX(); last_y = (short)e.getY(); // Save position.
    }
    else super.processMouseEvent(e);  // Pass other event types on.
  }

  /**
   * This method is called for mouse motion events.  It adds a line to the
   * scribble, on screen, and in the saved representation
   **/
  public void processMouseMotionEvent(MouseEvent e) {
    if (e.getID() == MouseEvent.MOUSE_DRAGGED) {
      Graphics g = getGraphics();                        // Object to draw with.
      g.drawLine(last_x, last_y, e.getX(), e.getY()); // Draw this line
      lines.addElement(new Line(last_x, last_y,         // and save it, too.
                                (short) e.getX(), (short)e.getY()));
      last_x = (short) e.getX();   // Remember current mouse coordinates.
      last_y = (short) e.getY();
    }
    else super.processMouseMotionEvent(e);   // Important!
  }

  /**
   * Prompt the user for a filename, and save the scribble in that file.
   * Serialize the vector of lines with an ObjectOutputStream.
   * Compress the serialized objects with a GZIPOutputStream.
   * Write the compressed, serialized data to a file with a FileOutputStream.
   * Don't forget to flush and close the stream.
   **/
  public void save() {
    // Create a file dialog to query the user for a filename.
    FileDialog f = new FileDialog(frame, "Save Scribble", FileDialog.SAVE);
    f.show();                            // Display the dialog and block.
    String filename = f.getDirectory() + f.getFile();   // Get response
    if (filename != null) {             // If user didn't click "Cancel".
      try {
        // Create the necessary output streams to save the scribble.
        FileOutputStream fos = new FileOutputStream(filename);// Save to file
        GZIPOutputStream gzos = new GZIPOutputStream(fos);   // Compressed
        ObjectOutputStream out = new ObjectOutputStream(gzos);// Save objects
        out.writeObject(lines);         // Write the entire Vector of scribbles
        out.flush();                    // Always flush the output.
        out.close();                    // And close the stream.
      }
      // Print out exceptions.  We should really display them in a dialog...
      catch (IOException e) { System.out.println(e); }
    }
  }

  /**
   * Prompt for a filename, and load a scribble from that file.
   * Read compressed, serialized data with a FileInputStream.
   * Uncompress that data with a GZIPInputStream.
   * Deserialize the vector of lines with a ObjectInputStream.
   * Replace current data with new data, and redraw everything.
   **/
  public void load() {
    // Create a file dialog to query the user for a filename.
```

Example 13-1: SerializedScribble.java (continued)

```
    FileDialog f = new FileDialog(frame, "Load Scribble", FileDialog.LOAD);
    f.show();                         // Display the dialog and block.
    String filename = f.getDirectory() + f.getFile();    // Get response
    if (filename != null) {           // If user didn't click "Cancel".
      try {
        // Create necessary input streams
        FileInputStream fis = new FileInputStream(filename);// Read from file
        GZIPInputStream gzis = new GZIPInputStream(fis);    // Uncompress
        ObjectInputStream in = new ObjectInputStream(gzis); // Read objects
        // Read in an object.  It should be a vector of scribbles
        Vector newlines = (Vector)in.readObject();
        in.close();                   // Close the stream.
        lines = newlines;             // Set the Vector of lines.
        repaint();                    // And redisplay the scribble.
      }
      // Print out exceptions.  We should really display them in a dialog...
      catch (Exception e) { System.out.println(e); }
    }
  }

  /**
   * A class to store the coordinates of one scribbled line.
   * The complete scribble is stored as a Vector of these objects
   **/
  static class Line implements Serializable {
    public short x1, y1, x2, y2;
    public Line(short x1, short y1, short x2, short y2) {
      this.x1 = x1; this.y1 = y1; this.x2 = x2; this.y2 = y2;
    }
  }
}
}
```

Custom Serialization

Not every piece of program state can, or should, be serialized. Some things, like FileDescriptor objects, are inherently platform-specific or virtual-machine-dependent. If a FileDescriptor were serialized, it would have no meaning when deserialized in a different virtual machine. For this reason, and also for important security reasons, not all objects can be serialized.

Only classes that implement the Serializable or Externalizable interface can be written to or read from an object stream. Serializable is a marker interface, like Cloneable: it doesn't define any methods and serves only to specify whether an object is allowed to be serialized. The Externalizable interface does define methods, and is used by objects that want advanced control over the way they are written and read. We'll see more about Externalizable objects later in this chapter. It is worth noting at this point that Component implements Serializable, which means that all AWT components can be serialized.

Even when an object is serializable, it may not make sense for it to serialize all of its state. For example, in the Scribble example shown in Example 13-1, the last_x and last_y fields store the current position of the mouse and only contain valid data while the user has a mouse button pressed. The values of these fields will never be of interest (or use) when such an object is deserialized, so there is no need to bother saving the values of these fields as part of the Scribble object's state. To tell the serialization mechanism that a field should not be saved, simply declare it transient:

```
protected transient short last_x, last_y; // Temporary fields for mouse pos.
```

The transient modifier keyword has always been a legal part of the Java language, but it was not assigned any meaning until Java 1.1.

There are also situations where a field is not transient—i.e., it does contain an important part of an object's state—but for some reason it cannot be successfully serialized. One example is a custom AWT component that computes its preferred size based on the size of the text it displays. Because fonts have slight size variations from platform to platform, this pre-computed preferred size will not be valid if the component is serialized on one type of platform and deserialized on another. Since the preferred size fields will not be valid when deserialized, they should be declared transient, so that they don't take up space in the serialized object. But in this case, their values should be re-computed when the object is deserialized.

A class can define custom serialization and deserialization behavior for its objects by implementing writeObject() and readObject() methods. Suprisingly, these methods are not defined by any interface. The methods must be declared private, which is also suprising if you think about it, as they are called from outside of the class during serialization and deserialization. If a class defines these methods, the appropriate one is invoked by the ObjectOutputStream or ObjectInputStream when an object is serialized or deserialized.

For example, our custom component might define a readObject() method to give it an opportunity to re-compute its preferred size upon deserialization. The method might look like this:

```
private void readObject(ObjectInputStream in)
            throws IOException, ClassNotFoundException {
    in.defaultReadObject();      // Deserialize the component in the usual way.
    this.computePreferredSize(); // But then go recompute its size.
}
```

This method calls the defaultReadObject() method of the ObjectInputStream to deserialize the object as normal, and then takes care of the post-processing it needs to perform.

Example 13-2 is a more complete example of custom serialization. It shows a class that implements a growable array of numbers. This class defines a writeObject() method to do some pre-processing before being serialized and a readObject() method to do post-processing after deserialization.

Example 13-2: IntList.java

```
import java.io.*;

/** A simple class that implements a growable array or ints, and knows
 *  how to serialize itself as efficiently as a non-growable array. */
public class IntList implements Serializable
{
```

Example 13-2: IntList.java (continued)

```
private int[] nums = new int[8]; // An array to store the numbers.
private transient int size = 0;  // Index of next unused element of nums[].

/** Return an element of the array */
public int elementAt(int index) throws ArrayIndexOutOfBoundsException {
  if (index >= size) throw new ArrayIndexOutOfBoundsException(index);
  else return nums[index];
}

/** Add an int to the array, growing the array if necessary */
public void add(int x) {
  if (nums.length == size) resize(nums.length*2); // Grow array, if needed.
  nums[size++] = x;                               // Store the int in it.
}

/** An internal method to change the allocated size of the array */
protected void resize(int newsize) {
  int[] oldnums = nums;
  nums = new int[newsize];                   // Create a new array.
  System.arraycopy(oldnums, 0, nums, 0, size); // Copy array elements.
}

/** Get rid of unused array elements before serializing the array */
private void writeObject(ObjectOutputStream out) throws IOException {
  if (nums.length > size) resize(size);  // Compact the array.
  out.defaultWriteObject();              // Then write it out normally.
}

/** Compute the transient size field after deserializing the array */
private void readObject(ObjectInputStream in)
      throws IOException, ClassNotFoundException {
  in.defaultReadObject();                // Read the array normally.
  size = nums.length;                    // Restore the transient field.
}
}
```

Serialization and Class Versioning

When an object is serialized, some information about its class must obviously be serialized with it, so that the correct class file can be loaded when the object is deserialized. This information about the class is represented by the java.io.ObjectStreamClass class. It contains the fully-qualified name of the class and a version number. The version number is very important because an early version of a class may not be able to deserialize a serialized instance created by a later version of the same class. The version number of a class is stored in a constant long field named serialVersionUID. So, a class might declare its version number with a field like this:

```
static final long serialVersionUID = 280432937854755317L;
```

If a class does not define a serialVersionUID constant, the ObjectOutputStream automatically computes a unique version number for it by applying the Secure Hash Algorithm (SHA) to the name of the class, its interfaces, fields, and methods. In this case, any change to a field in a class or to a non-private method signature results in a change to the automatically-computed unique version number.

If you need to make minor changes to a class without breaking serialization compatibility, you should explicitly declare a serialVersionUID constant so that an updated and incompatible version number is not automatically generated. You can use the *serialver* program that is proided with the JDK to compute an initial value for this constant for the first version of your class. When you make minor, compatible changes to the class, leave the constant unchanged. Then, if you make larger changes that break serialization compatibility, run *serialver* again to generate an updated version number.

Serialized Applets

One of the uses of object serialization is for serialized applets. As of Java 1.1, the <APPLET> tag has a new attribute, OBJECT, that can be used in place of the CODE attribute to specify a serialized object file instead of a class file. When such an <APPLET> tag is encountered, the applet viewer or Web browser creates the applet by deserializing it.

The reason that this is interesting is that it allows an applet to be shipped in a pre-initialized state. The code for the applet need not even include the code that performed the initialization. For example, imagine a GUI builder tool that allows a programmer to build a GUI using a point-and-click interface. Such a tool could create a tree of AWT components within an Applet panel, and then serialize the applet, including all of the GUI components it contains. When deserialized, the applet would have a complete GUI, despite the fact that the applet's class file does not contain any code to create the GUI.

You can experiment with applet serialization with the JDK 1.1 *appletviewer* program. Start an applet running in *appletviewer* in the usual way. This loads the applet and runs its init() and start() methods. Next, select the **Stop** item from the menu to stop the applet. Now use the **Save** menu item to serialize the applet to a file. By convention, your serialized applet file should be given a *.ser* extension. If the applet refers to any non-serializable objects, you may not be able to serialize it. For example, you may encounter problems serializing applets that use threads or images.

Once you have serialized an applet, create an HTML file with an <APPLET> tag something like this:

```
<APPLET OBJECT="MyApplet.ser" WIDTH=400 HEIGHT=200></APPLET>
```

Finally, you can use *appletviewer* with this new HTML file. It should deserialize and display the applet. When created in this way, the applet's init() method is not called (since it was called before serialization), but its start() method is called (because the applet should have been stopped before serialization).

Advanced Serialization

The Object Serialization API also has some advanced features beyond those demonstrated above. One such feature is the Externalizable interface. If a class implements this interface, the ObjectInputStream and ObjectOutputStream classes use an object's readExternal() and writeExternal() methods to read and write its state from a stream. Most classes that want custom serialization behavior simply implement readObject() and writeObject() methods to do pre- and post-processing. Externalizable objects, on the other hand, take complete control over reading and writing their state. This interface is intended for objects that do not even want to use the basic serialized object data format used for all Serializable objects. A word processor object, for example, might "externalize" itself using its own native file format.

Another advanced serialization feature is the ability to register an ObjectInput-Validation object that can verify that an object graph has been deserialized in a consistent, valid state. Typically, the root of an object graph registers such a validation object by calling the registerValidation() method of the ObjectInput-Stream from its own custom readObject() method. Then, when the graph has been read completely, the validateObject() method of the ObjectInput-Validation object is called to perform whatever validity checks are necessary.

Finally, you may notice that ObjectOutputStream and ObjectInputStream have methods like annotateClass(), replaceObject(), resolveClass(), and resolve-Object(). These are intended for use by subclasses of the object streams that implement special kinds of object serialization behavior.

Exercises

13-1. Example 13-1 uses serialization to save application data to a file so it can later be restored. Another use for serialization is creating clones of objects. When you use the clone() method of Object, all the fields of the original object are copied to the clone object, but any objects the original object refers to are not copied. In other words, the clone() method performs a "shallow clone." When you serialize an object, however, all objects it refers to are also serialized, so upon deserialization, a "deep clone" is created.

For this exercise, modify Example 13-1 by adding a new **Clone** item to the **File** menu. When this item is selected, use serialization to create a "deep clone" of the entire GUI of the application. Call pack() and show() to make the cloned GUI visible. You may want to use ByteArrayOutputStream and ByteArrayInputStream to help perform this cloning operation.

13-2. When you clone a GUI as you did in Exercise 13-1, notice that the items in any cloned menus do not work. Take a look at the source code for the MenuItem class and see if you can determine why this is. (Hint: the menu item's event listeners are not being serialized. Why not?)

13-3. Use the *serialver* program to compute the serialization version number for the nested Line class used in Example 13-1. Explicitly add this version number to the class.

CHAPTER 14

Internationalization

Internationalization is the process of making a program flexible enough to run correctly in any "locale." The required corollary to internationalization is localization—the process of arranging for a program to run in a specific locale.

There are several distinct steps to the task of internationalization. Java 1.1 addresses these steps with several different mechanisms:

- A program must be able to read, write, and manipulate localized text. Java uses the Unicode character encoding, which by itself is a huge step towards internationalization. In addition, in Java 1.1 the InputStreamReader and OutputStreamWriter classes convert text from a locale-specific encoding to Unicode and from Unicode to a locale-specific encoding, respectively.

- A program must conform to local customs when displaying dates and times, formatting numbers, and sorting strings. Java addresses these issues with the classes in the new java.text package.

- A program must display all user-visible text in the local language. Translating the messages a program displays is always one of the main tasks in localizing a program. A more important task is writing the program so that all user-visible text is fetched at runtime, rather than hardcoded directly into the program. Java 1.1 facilitates this process with the ResourceBundle class and its subclasses in the java.util package.

This chapter discusses all three of these aspects of internationalization.

A Word About Locales

A locale represents a geographic, political, or cultural region. In Java 1.1, locales are represented by the java.util.Locale class. A locale is frequently defined by a language, which is represented by its standard lowercase two-letter code, such as en (English) or fr (French). Sometimes, however, language alone is not sufficient to uniquely specify a locale, and a country is added to the specification. A country is represented by an uppercase two-letter code. For example, the United States English locale (en_US) is distinct from the British English locale (en_GB), and the French spoken in Canada (fr_CA) is different from the French spoken in France (fr_FR). Occasionally, the scope of a locale is further narrowed with the addition of a system-dependent "variant" string.

The Locale class maintains a static default locale, which can be set and queried with Locale.setDefault() and Locale.getDefault(). Locale-sensitive methods in Java 1.1 typically come in two forms. One uses the default locale and the other uses a Locale object that is explicitly specified as an argument. A program can create and use any number of non-default Locale objects, although it is more common simply to rely on the default locale, which is inherited from the underlying default locale on the native platform. Locale-sensitive classes in Java often provide a method to query the list of locales that they support.

Finally, note that AWT components in Java 1.1 have a locale property, so it is possible for different components to use different locales. (Most components, however, are not locale-sensitive; they behave the same in any locale.)

Unicode

Java uses the Unicode character encoding. Java 1.0 used Unicode version 1.1, while Java 1.1 has adopted the newer Unicode 2.0 standard. Unicode is a 16-bit character encoding established by the Unicode Consortium, which describes the standard as follows (see *http://unicode.org*):

> The Unicode Worldwide Character Standard is a character coding system designed to support the interchange, processing, and display of the written texts of the diverse languages of the modern world. In addition, it supports classical and historical texts of many written languages.
>
> In its current version (2.0), the Unicode standard contains 38,885 distinct coded characters derived from 25 supported scripts. These characters cover the principal written languages of the Americas, Europe, the Middle East, Africa, India, Asia, and Pacifica.

In the canonical form of the Unicode encoding, which is what Java char and String types use, every character occupies two bytes. The Unicode characters \u0020 to \u007E are equivalent to the ASCII and ISO8859-1 (Latin-1) characters 0x20 through 0x7E. The Unicode characters \u00A0 to \u00FF are identical to the ISO8859-1 characters 0xA0 to 0xFF. Thus, there is a trivial mapping between Latin-1 and Unicode characters. A number of other portions of the Unicode encoding are based on pre-existing standards, such as ISO8859-5 (Cyrillic) and ISO8859-8 (Hebrew), though the mappings between these standards and Unicode may not be as trivial as the Latin-1 mapping.

Note that Unicode support is quite limited on many platforms. One of the difficulties with the use of Unicode is the poor availability of fonts to display all of the Unicode characters. Figure 14-1 shows the characters that are available on a typical configuration of the U.S. English Windows 95 platform. Note the special box glyph used to indicate undefined characters.

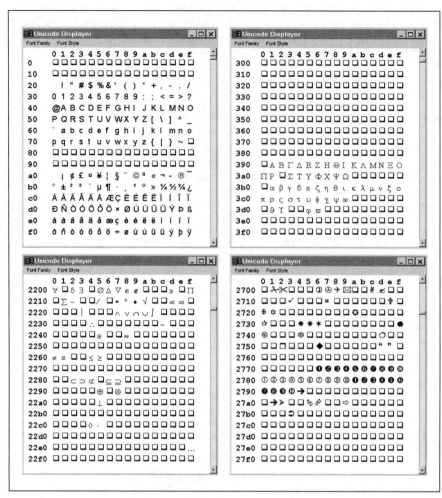

Figure 14-1: Some Unicode characters and their encodings

Example 14-1 lists code used to create the displays of Figure 14-1. This `Unicode-Display` program does not perform any sophisticated internationalization techniques to display Unicode glyphs. Despite the use of Unicode, this might be a better example of defining a custom AWT component than it is of internationalization.

Example 14-1: UnicodeDisplay.java

```
import java.awt.*;
import java.awt.event.*;

/**
 * This program displays Unicode glyphs using user-specified fonts
 * and font styles.
 **/
```

Example 14-1: UnicodeDisplay.java (continued)

```java
public class UnicodeDisplay extends Frame implements ActionListener
{
  int page = 0;
  UnicodePanel p;
  Scrollbar b;
  String fontfamily = "Serif";
  int fontstyle = Font.PLAIN;

  /**
   * This constructor creates the frame, menubar, and scrollbar
   * that work along with the UnicodePanel class, defined below
   **/
  public UnicodeDisplay(String name) {
    super(name);
    this.setLayout(new BorderLayout());
    p = new UnicodePanel();                  // Create the panel
    p.setBase((char)(page * 0x100));         // Initialize it
    this.add(p, "Center");                   // Center it

    // Create and set up a scrollbar, and put it on the right
    b = new Scrollbar(Scrollbar.VERTICAL, 0, 1, 0, 0xFF);
    b.setUnitIncrement(1);
    b.setBlockIncrement(0x10);
    b.addAdjustmentListener(new AdjustmentListener() {
      public void adjustmentValueChanged(AdjustmentEvent e) {
        page = e.getValue();
        p.setBase((char)(page * 0x100));
      }
    });
    this.add(b, "East");

    // Set things up so we respond to window close requests
    this.addWindowListener(new WindowAdapter() {
      public void windowClosing(WindowEvent e) {
        UnicodeDisplay.this.dispose();
        System.exit(0);
      }
    });

    // Handle Page Up and Page Down and the up and down arrow keys
    this.addKeyListener(new KeyAdapter() {
      public void keyPressed(KeyEvent e) {
        int code = e.getKeyCode();
        int oldpage = page;
        if ((code == KeyEvent.VK_PAGE_UP) || (code == KeyEvent.VK_UP)) {
          if (e.isShiftDown()) page -= 0x10;
          else page -= 1;
          if (page < 0) page = 0;
        }
        else if ((code == KeyEvent.VK_PAGE_DOWN) || (code==KeyEvent.VK_DOWN)) {
          if (e.isShiftDown()) page += 0x10;
          else page += 1;
          if (page > 0xff) page = 0xff;
        }
        if (page != oldpage) {                  // if anything has changed...
          p.setBase((char) (page * 0x100)); // update the display
          b.setValue(page);                     // and update scrollbar to match
        }
```

Example 14-1: UnicodeDisplay.java (continued)

```
    }
  });

  // Set up a menu system to change fonts.  Use a convenience method.
  MenuBar menubar = new MenuBar();
  this.setMenuBar(menubar);
  menubar.add(makemenu("Font Family",
                       new String[] {"Serif", "SansSerif", "Monospaced"},
                       this));
  menubar.add(makemenu("Font Style",
                       new String[]{"Plain", "Italic", "Bold", "BoldItalic"},
                       this));
}

/** This method handles the items in the menubars */
public void actionPerformed(ActionEvent e) {
  String cmd = e.getActionCommand();
  if (cmd.equals("Serif")) fontfamily = "Serif";
  else if (cmd.equals("SansSerif")) fontfamily = "SansSerif";
  else if (cmd.equals("Monospaced")) fontfamily = "Monospaced";
  else if (cmd.equals("Plain")) fontstyle = Font.PLAIN;
  else if (cmd.equals("Italic")) fontstyle = Font.ITALIC;
  else if (cmd.equals("Bold")) fontstyle = Font.BOLD;
  else if (cmd.equals("BoldItalic")) fontstyle = Font.BOLD + Font.ITALIC;
  p.setFont(fontfamily, fontstyle);
}

/** A convenience method to create a Menu from an array of items */
private Menu makemenu(String name, String[] itemnames,
                      ActionListener listener) {
  Menu m = new Menu(name);
  for(int i = 0; i < itemnames.length; i++) {
    MenuItem item = new MenuItem(itemnames[i]);
    item.addActionListener(listener);
    item.setActionCommand(itemnames[i]);  // okay here, though
    m.add(item);
  }
  return m;
}

/** The main() program just create a window, packs it, and shows it */
public static void main(String[] args) {
  UnicodeDisplay f = new UnicodeDisplay("Unicode Displayer");
  f.pack();
  f.show();
}

/**
 * This nested class is the one that displays one "page" of Unicode
 * glyphs at a time.  Each "page" is 256 characters, arranged into 16
 * rows of 16 columns each.
 **/
public static class UnicodePanel extends Canvas {
  protected char base;  // What character we start the display at
  protected Font font = new Font("serif", Font.PLAIN, 18);
  protected Font headingfont = new Font("monospaced", Font.BOLD, 18);
  static final int lineheight = 25;
  static final int charspacing = 20;
```

Example 14-1: UnicodeDisplay.java (continued)

```java
static final int x0 = 65;
static final int y0 = 40;

/** Specify where to begin displaying, and re-display */
public void setBase(char base) { this.base = base; repaint(); }

/** Set a new font name or style, and redisplay */
public void setFont(String family, int style) {
  this.font = new Font(family, style, 18);
  repaint();
}

/**
 * The paint() method actually draws the page of glyphs
 **/
public void paint(Graphics g) {
  int start = (int)base & 0xFFF0;  // Start on a 16-character boundary

  // Draw the headings in a special font
  g.setFont(headingfont);

  // Draw 0..F on top
  for(int i=0; i < 16; i++) {
    String s = Integer.toString(i, 16);
    g.drawString(s, x0 + i*charspacing, y0-20);
  }

  // Draw column down left.
  for(int i = 0; i < 16; i++) {
    int j = start + i*16;
    String s = Integer.toString(j, 16);
    g.drawString(s, 10, y0+i*lineheight);
  }

  // Now draw the characters
  g.setFont(font);
  char[] c = new char[1];
  for(int i = 0; i < 16; i++) {
    for(int j = 0; j < 16; j++) {
      c[0] = (char)(start + j*16 + i);
      g.drawChars(c, 0, 1, x0 + i*charspacing, y0 + j*lineheight);
    }
  }
}

/** Custom components like this one should always have this method */
public Dimension getPreferredSize() { return new Dimension(410, 430); }
}
}
```

Character Encodings

Text representation has traditionally been one of the most difficult problems of internationalization. Java 1.1, however, solves this problem quite elegantly and hides the difficult issues. Java uses Unicode internally, so it can represent essentially any character in any commonly used written language. As noted above, the remaining task is to convert Unicode to and from locale-specific encodings. Java 1.1 includes quite a few internal "byte-to-char" converters and "char-to-byte" converters that handle converting locale-specific character encodings to Unicode and vice versa. While the converters themselves are not public, they are accessed through the InputStreamReader and OutputStreamWriter classes, which are two of the new character streams included in the java.io package.

Any program can automatically handle locale-specific encodings simply by using these new character stream classes to do their textual input and output. (And in addition to automatic encoding conversion, the program also benefits from the greatly improved efficiency of these new classes over the byte streams of Java 1.0.)

Example 14-2 shows a simple program that works with character encodings. It converts a file from one specified encoding to another by converting from the first encoding to Unicode and then from Unicode to the second encoding. Note that most of the program is taken up with the mechanics of parsing argument lists, handling exceptions, and so on. Only a few lines are required to create the Input-StreamReader and OutputStreamWriter classes that perform the two halves of the conversion. Also note that exceptions are handled by calling Localized-Error.display(). This method is not part of the Java 1.1 API; it is a custom method shown in Example 14-7 at the end of this chapter.

Example 14-2: ConvertEncoding.java

```java
import java.io.*;

/** A program to convert from one character encoding to another */
public class ConvertEncoding {
  public static void main(String[] args) {
    String from = null, to = null;
    String infile = null, outfile = null;
    for(int i = 0; i < args.length; i++) {  // Parse command-line arguments.
      if (i == args.length-1) usage();       // All legal args require another.
      if (args[i].equals("-from")) from = args[++i];
      else if (args[i].equals("-to")) to = args[++i];
      else if (args[i].equals("-in")) infile = args[++i];
      else if (args[i].equals("-out")) outfile = args[++i];
      else usage();
    }

    try { convert(infile, outfile, from, to); }  // Attempt conversion.
    catch (Exception e) {                        // Handle possible exceptions.
      LocalizedError.display(e);  // Defined at the end of this chapter.
      System.exit(1);
    }
  }

  public static void usage() {
    System.err.println("Usage: java ConvertEncoding <options>\n" +
                       "Options:\n\t-from <encoding>\n\t-to <encoding>\n\t" +
                       "-in <file>\n\t-out <file>");
    System.exit(1);
  }

  public static void convert(String infile, String outfile,
                             String from, String to)
        throws IOException, UnsupportedEncodingException
```

Example 14–2: ConvertEncoding.java (continued)

```
  {
    // Set up byte streams.
    InputStream in;
    if (infile != null) in = new FileInputStream(infile);
    else in = System.in;
    OutputStream out;
    if (outfile != null) out = new FileOutputStream(outfile);
    else out = System.out;

    // Use default encoding if no encoding is specified.
    if (from == null) from = System.getProperty("file.encoding");
    if (to == null) to = System.getProperty("file.encoding");

    // Set up character streams.
    Reader r = new BufferedReader(new InputStreamReader(in, from));
    Writer w = new BufferedWriter(new OutputStreamWriter(out, to));

    // Copy characters from input to output.  The InputStreamReader converts
    // from the input encoding to Unicode, and the OutputStreamWriter converts
    // from Unicode to the output encoding.  Characters that cannot be
    // represented in the output encoding are output as '?'
    char[] buffer = new char[4096];
    int len;
    while((len = r.read(buffer)) != -1)   // Read a block of input.
      w.write(buffer, 0, len);            // And write it out.
    r.close();                            // Close the input.
    w.flush();                            // Flush and close output.
    w.close();
  }
}
```

Handling Local Customs

The second problem of internationalization is the task of following local customs and conventions in areas like date and time formatting. The java.text package defines classes to help with this duty.

The NumberFormat class is used to format numbers, monetary amounts, and percentages in a locale-dependent way for display to the user. This is necessary because different locales have different conventions for number formatting. For example, in France, a comma is used as a decimal separator instead of a period, as in many English speaking countries. A NumberFormat object can use the default locale or any locale you specify.

The DateFormat class is used to format dates and times in a locale-dependent way for display to the user. Different countries have different conventions. Should the month or day be displayed first? Should periods or colons be used to separate fields of the time? What are the names of the months in the language of the locale? A DateFormat object can simply use the default locale or it can use any locale you specify. The DateFormat class is used in conjunction with the TimeZone and Calendar classes of java.util. The TimeZone object tells the DateFormat what time zone the date should be interpreted in, while the Calendar object specifies how the date itself should be broken down into days, weeks, months, and years. Almost all locales use the standard GregorianCalendar.

The Collator class is used to compare strings in a locale-dependent way. This is necessary because different languages "alphabetize" strings in different ways (and some languages don't even use alphabets). In traditional Spanish, for example, the letters "ch" are treated as a single character that comes between "c" and "d" for the purposes of sorting. When you need to sort strings or search for a string within Unicode text, you should use a Collator object, either one created to work with the default locale or one created for a specified locale.

The BreakIterator class allows you to locate character, word, line, and sentence boundaries in a locale-dependent way. This is useful when you need to recognize such boundaries in Unicode text, like when you are implementing a word-wrapping algorithm.

Example 14-4 shows a class that uses the NumberFormat and DateFormat classes to display a hypothetical stock portfolio to the user following local conventions. The program uses various NumberFormat and DateFormat object to format (using the format() method) different types of numbers and dates. These Format objects all operate using the default locale, but could have been created with an explicitly specified locale. Example 14-3 shows the output of this program in American, Canadian, and French locales. Note the different treatment of dates, numbers, and monetary quantities in these three locales.

Example 14–3: Dates and Numbers Formatted for Three Locales

```
# American English locale (en_US)
Portfolio value at April 08, 1997 6:57:40 PM PDT:
Symbol  Shares  Bought On    At       Quote    Change
XXX     400     6/15/96      $11.90   $13.00   9%
YYY     1,100   9/14/96      $71.09   $27.25   -61%
ZZZ     6,000   6/27/91      $23.37   $89.12   281%

# Canadian English locale (en_CA)
Portfolio value at April 8, 1997 9:57:40 CDT PM:
Symbol  Shares  Bought On    At       Quote    Change
XXX     400     15/06/96     $11.90   $13.00   9%
YYY     1,100   14/09/96     $71.09   $27.25   -61%
ZZZ     6,000   27/06/91     $23.37   $89.12   281%

# French locale (fr_FR)
Portfolio value at 9 avril 1997 03:57:40 GMT+02:00:
Symbol  Shares  Bought On    At         Quote      Change
XXX     400     15/06/96     11,90 F    13,00 F    9%
YYY     1 100   14/09/96     71,09 F    27,25 F    -61%
ZZZ     6 000   27/06/91     23,37 F    89,12 F    281%
```

Example 14–4: Portfolio.java

```java
import java.text.*;
import java.util.Date;

/**
 * A partial implementation of a hypothetical stock portfolio class.
 * We use it only to demonstrate number and date internationalization.
 */
public class Portfolio {
  EquityPosition[] positions;
  Date lastQuoteTime = new Date();
```

Example 14–4: Portfolio.java (continued)

```
public void print() {
    // Obtain NumberFormat and DateFormat objects to format our data.
    NumberFormat number = NumberFormat.getInstance();
    NumberFormat price = NumberFormat.getCurrencyInstance();
    NumberFormat percent = NumberFormat.getPercentInstance();
    DateFormat shortdate = DateFormat.getDateInstance(DateFormat.SHORT);
    DateFormat fulldate = DateFormat.getDateTimeInstance(DateFormat.LONG,
                                                DateFormat.LONG);

    // Print some introductory data.
    System.out.println("Portfolio value at " +
                    fulldate.format(lastQuoteTime) + ":");
    System.out.println("Symbol\tShares\tBought On\tAt\t" +
                    "Quote\tChange");

    // Then display the table using the format() methods of the Format objects.
    for(int i = 0; i < positions.length; i++) {
        System.out.print(positions[i].name + "\t");
        System.out.print(number.format(positions[i].shares) + "\t");
        System.out.print(shortdate.format(positions[i].purchased) + "\t");
        System.out.print(price.format(positions[i].bought) + "\t");
        System.out.print(price.format(positions[i].current) + "\t");
        double change =
            (positions[i].current - positions[i].bought)/positions[i].bought;
        System.out.println(percent.format(change));
    }
}

static class EquityPosition {
    String name;            // Name of the stock.
    int shares;             // Number of shares held.
    Date purchased;         // When purchased.
    double bought, current; // Purchase price and current price (per share).
    EquityPosition(String n, int s, Date when, double then, double now) {
        name = n; shares = s; purchased = when; bought = then; current = now;
    }
}
}
```

Localizing User-Visible Messages

The third task of internationalization involves ensuring that there are no user-visible strings that are hardcoded in an application, instead of being looked up based on the locale. In Example 14-4, for example, the strings "Portfolio value", "Symbol", "Shares", and others are hardcoded in the application and appear in English, even when the program is run in the French locale. The only way to prevent this is to fetch all user-visible messages at runtime, and to translate every message into each of the languages that your application must support.

Java 1.1 helps you handle this task with the ResourceBundle class of the java.util package. This class represents a "bundle" of resources that can be looked up by name. You define a localized resource bundle for each locale you want to support, and Java takes care of loading the correct bundle for the default (or specified) locale. With the correct bundle loaded, you can look up the resources (typically strings) that your program needs at runtime.

Working with Resource Bundles

To define a bundle of localized resources, you create a subclass of `Resource-Bundle` and provide definitions for the `handleGetObject()` and `getKeys()` methods. `handleGetObject()` is passed the name of a resource; it should return an appropriate localized version of that resource. `getKeys()` should return an `Enumeration` object that gives the user a list of all resource names defined in the `ResourceBundle`. Instead of subclassing `ResourceBundle` directly, however, it is often easier to subclass `ListResourceBundle`. You can also simply provide a property file (see the `java.util.Properties` class) that `ResourceBundle.getBundle()` uses to create an instance of `PropertyResourceBundle`.

To use localized resources from a `ResourceBundle` in a program, you should first call the static `getBundle()` method, which dynamically loads and instantiates a `ResourceBundle`, as described below. The returned `ResourceBundle` has the name you specify and is appropriate for the specified locale (or for the default locale, if no locale is explicitly specified). Once you have obtained a `ResourceBundle` object with `getBundle()`, you use the `getObject()` method to look up resources by name. Note that there is a convenience method, `getString()`, that simply casts the value returned by `getObject()` to be a `String` object.

When you call `getBundle()`, you specify the base name of the desired `Resource-Bundle` and a desired locale (if you don't want to rely on the default locale). Recall that a `Locale` is specified with a two-letter language code, an optional two-letter country code, and an optional variant string. `getBundle()` looks for an appropriate `ResourceBundle` class for the locale by appending this locale information to the base name for the bundle. The method looks for an appropriate class with the following algorithm:

1. Search for a class with the following name:

   basename_language_country_variant

   If no such class is found, or no variant string is specified for the locale, it goes to the next step.

2. Search for a class with the following name:

   basename_language_country

   If no such class is found, or no country code is specified for the locale, it goes to the next step.

3. Search for a class with the following name:

   basename_language

   If no such class is found, it goes to the final step.

4. Search for a class which has the same name as the basename, or in other words, seach for a class with the following name:

   basename

   This represents a default resource bundle used by any locale that is not explicitly supported.

At each step in the above process, getBundle() checks first for a class file with the given name. If no class file is found, it uses the getResourceAsStream() method of ClassLoader to look for a Properties files with the same name as the class and a *.properties* extension. If such a properties file is found, its contents are used to create a Properties object and getBundle() instantiates and returns a PropertyResourceBundle that exports the properties in the Properties file through the ResourceBundle API.

If getBundle() cannot find a class or properties file for the specified locale in any of the four search steps above, it repeats the search using the default locale instead of the specified locale. If no appropriate ResourceBundle is found in this search either, getBundle() throws a MissingResourceException.

Any ResourceBundle object may have a parent ResourceBundle specified for it. When you look up a named resource in a ResourceBundle, getObject() first looks in the specified bundle, but if the named resource is not defined in that bundle, it recursively looks in the parent bundle. Thus, every ResourceBundle "inherits" the resources of its parent, and may choose to "override" some, or all, of these resources. (Note that we are using the terms "inherit" and "override" in a different sense than we do when talking about classes that inherit and override methods in their superclass.) What this means is that every ResourceBundle you define does not have to define every resource required by your application. For example, you might define a ResourceBundle of messages to display to French-speaking users. Then you might define a smaller and more specialized ResourceBundle that overrides a few of these messages so that they are appropriate for French-speaking users who live in Canada.

Your application is not required to find and set up the parent objects for the ResourceBundle objects it uses. The getBundle() method actually does this for you. When getBundle() finds an appropriate class or properties file as described above, it does not immediately return the ResourceBundle it has found. Instead, it continues through the remaining steps in the search process listed above, looking for less-specific class or properties files from which the ResourceBundle may "inherit" resources. If and when getBundle() finds these less-specific resource bundles, it sets them up as the appropriate ancestors of the original bundle. Only once it has checked all possibilities does it return the original ResourceBundle object that it created.

To continue the example begun above, when a program runs in Quebec, getBundle() might first find a small specialized ResourceBundle class that has only a few specific Quebecois resources. Next, it looks for a more general ResourceBundle that contains French messages and it sets this bundle as the parent of the original Quebecois bundle. Finally, getBundle() looks for (and probably finds) a class the defines a default set of resources, probably written in English (assuming that English is the native tongue of the original programmer). This default bundle is set as the parent of the French bundle (which makes it the grandparent of the Quebecois bundle). When the application looks up a named resource, the Quebecois bundle is searched first. If the resource is not defined there, then the French bundle is searched, and finally, any named resource not found in the French bundle is looked up in the default bundle.

ResourceBundle Example

Examining some code makes this discussion of resource bundles much clearer. Example 14-5 is a convenience routine for creating menu panes. Given a list of menu item names, it looks up labels and menu shortcuts for those named menu items in a resource bundle and creates a localized menu pane. The example has a simple test program attached.

Figure 14-2 shows the menus it creates in the American, British, and French locales. This program could not run, of course without localized resource bundles from which the localized menu labels are looked up.

Example 14-6 shows American, British, and French resource files used to create each of the menus shown in the figure.

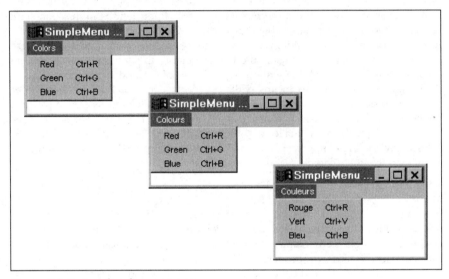

Figure 14-2: Localized menu panes

Example 14-5: SimpleMenu.java

```java
import java.awt.*;
import java.awt.event.*;
import java.util.Locale;
import java.util.ResourceBundle;
import java.util.MissingResourceException;

/** A convenience class to automatically create localized menu panes */
public class SimpleMenu {
    /** The convenience method that creates menu panes */
    public static Menu create(String bundlename,
                              String menuname, String[] itemnames,
                              ActionListener listener, boolean popup) {

        // Get the resource bundle used for this menu.
        ResourceBundle b = ResourceBundle.getBundle(bundlename);
```

Example 14–5: SimpleMenu.java (continued)

```
    // Get the menu title from the bundle.  Use name as default label.
    String menulabel;

    try { menulabel = b.getString(menuname + ".label"); }
    catch(MissingResourceException e) { menulabel = menuname; }

    // Create the menu pane.
    Menu m;
    if (popup) m = new PopupMenu(menulabel);
    else m = new Menu(menulabel);

    // For each named item in the menu.
    for(int i = 0; i < itemnames.length; i++) {
      // Look up the label for the item, using name as default.
      String itemlabel;
      try { itemlabel=b.getString(menuname + "." + itemnames[i] + ".label"); }
      catch (MissingResourceException e) { itemlabel = itemnames[i]; }

      // Look up a shortcut for the item, and create the menu shortcut, if any.
      String shortcut;
      try{shortcut = b.getString(menuname + "." + itemnames[i]+".shortcut"); }
      catch (MissingResourceException e) { shortcut = null; }
      MenuShortcut ms = null;
      if (shortcut != null) ms = new MenuShortcut(shortcut.charAt(0));

      // Create the menu item.
      MenuItem mi;
      if (ms != null) mi = new MenuItem(itemlabel, ms);
      else mi = new MenuItem(itemlabel);

      // Register an action listener and command for the item.
      if (listener != null) {
        mi.addActionListener(listener);
        mi.setActionCommand(itemnames[i]);
      }

      // Add the item to the menu.
      m.add(mi);
    }

    // Return the automatically created localized menu.
    return m;
  }

  /** A simple test program for the above code */
  public static void main(String[] args) {
    // Set the default locale based on the command-line args.
    if (args.length == 2) Locale.setDefault(new Locale(args[0], args[1]));

    Frame f = new Frame("SimpleMenu Test");  // Create a window.
    MenuBar menubar = new MenuBar();         // Create a menubar.
    f.setMenuBar(menubar);                   // Add menubar to window.

    // Create a menu using our convenience routine (and the default locale).
    Menu colors = SimpleMenu.create("Menus", "colors",
                              new String[] { "red", "green", "blue" },
                              null, false);
```

Example 14-5: SimpleMenu.java (continued)

```
        menubar.add(colors);          // Add the menu to the menubar.
        f.setSize(300, 150);          // Set the window size.
        f.show();                     // Pop the window up.
    }
}
```

This example does not stand alone. It relies on resource bundles to localize the menu. Example 14-6 shows three property files that serve as resource bundles for this example. Note that this single example listing actually contains the bodies of three separate files.

Example 14-6: Property Files as Resource Bundles

```
# The file Menus.properties is the default "Menus" resource bundle.
# As an American programmer, I made my own locale the default.
colors.label=Colors
colors.red.label=Red
colors.red.shortcut=R
colors.green.label=Green
colors.green.shortcut=G
colors.blue.label=Blue
colors.blue.shortcut=B

# This is the file Menus_en_GB.properties.  It is the resource bundle for
# British English.  Note that it overrides only a single resource definition
# and simply inherits the rest from the default (American) bundle.
colors.label=Colours

# This is the file Menus_fr.properties.  It is the resource bundle for all
# French-speaking locales.  It overrides most, but not all, of the resources
# in the default bundle.
colors.label=Couleurs
colors.red.label=Rouge
colors.green.label=Vert
colors.green.shortcut=V
colors.blue.label=Bleu
```

Formatted Messages

We've seen that in order to internationalize programs, you must place all user-visible messages into resource bundles. This is straightforward when the text to be localized consists of simple labels like those on buttons and menu items. It is trickier, however, with messages that are composed partially of static text and partially of dynamic values. For example, a compiler might have to display a message like "Error at line 5 of file 'hello.java'", in which the line number and filename are dynamic and locale-independent, while the rest of the message is static and needs to be localized.

The MessageFormat class of the java.text package helps tremendously with these types of messages. To use it, you store only the static parts of a message in the ResourceBundle and include special characters that indicate where the dynamic parts of the message are to be placed. For example, one resource bundle might contain the message: "Error at line {0} of file {1}." And another resource bundle might contain a "translation" that looks like this: "Erreur: {1}: {0}."

To use such a localized message, you create a MessageFormat object from the static part of the message, and then call its format() method, passing in an array of the values to be substituted. In this case, the array would contain an Integer object that specifies the line number and a String object that specifies the filename. The MessageFormat class knows about other Format classes defined in java.text. It creates and uses NumberFormat objects to format numbers and Date-Format objects to format dates and times. In addition, you can design messages that create ChoiceFormat objects to convert from numbers to strings—this is useful when working with enumerated types, such as numbers that correspond to month names, or when you need to use the singular or plural form of a word based on the value of some number.

Example 14-7 demonstrates this kind of MessageFormat usage. It is a convenience class with a single static method for the localized display of exception and error message. When invoked, the code attempts to load a ResourceBundle with the basename "Errors". If found, it looks up a message resource using the class name of the exception object that was passed. If such a resource is found, it is used to display the error message. An array of five values is passed to the format() method. The localized error message can include any or all of these arguments.

The LocalizedError.display() method defined in this example was used in Example 14-2 at the beginning of this chapter. Example 14-8 shows the default *Errors.properties* resource bundle used in conjunction with that example. Error message display for the program is nicely internationalized. Porting the program's error message to a new locale is simply a matter of translating (localizing) the *Errors.properties* file.

Example 14–7: LocalizedError.java

```
import java.text.*;
import java.io.*;
import java.util.*;

/**
 * A convenience class that can display a localized exception message
 * depending on the class of the exception.  It uses a MessageFormat,
 * and passes five arguments that the localized message may include:
 *    {0}: the message included in the exception or error.
 *    {1}: the full class name of the exception or error.
 *    {2}: a guess at what file the exception was caused by.
 *    {3}: a line number in that file.
 *    {4}: the current date and time.
 * Messages are looked up in a ResourceBundle with the basename
 * "Errors", using a the full class name of the exception object as
 * the resource name.  If no resource is found for a given exception
 * class, the superclasses are checked.
 */

public class LocalizedError {
  public static void display(Throwable error) {
    ResourceBundle bundle;
    // Try to get the resource bundle.
    // If none, print the error in a non-localized way.
    try { bundle = ResourceBundle.getBundle("Errors"); }
    catch (MissingResourceException e) {
```

Example 14-7: LocalizedError.java (continued)

```
        error.printStackTrace(System.err);
        return;
    }

    // Look up a localized message resource in that bundle, using the
    // classname of the error (or its superclasses) as the resource name.
    // If no resource was found, display the error without localization.
    String message = null;
    Class c = error.getClass();
    while((message == null) && (c != Object.class)) {
      try { message = bundle.getString(c.getName()); }
      catch (MissingResourceException e) { c = c.getSuperclass(); }
    }
    if (message == null) { error.printStackTrace(System.err);  return; }

    // Try to figure out the filename and line number of the
    // exception.  Output the error's stack trace into a string, and
    // use the heuristic that the first line number that appears in
    // the stack trace is after the first or  second colon.  We assume that
    // this stack frame is the first one the programmer has any control
    // over, and so report it as the location of the exception.
    String filename = "";
    int linenum = 0;
    try {
      StringWriter sw = new StringWriter();       // Output stream into a string.
      PrintWriter out = new PrintWriter(sw);      // PrintWriter wrapper.
      error.printStackTrace(out);                 // Print stacktrace.
      String trace = sw.toString();               // Get it as a string.
      int pos = trace.indexOf(':');               // Look for first colon.
      if (error.getMessage() != null)             // If the error has a message
        pos = trace.indexOf(':', pos+1);          // look for second colon.
      int pos2 = trace.indexOf(')', pos);         // Look for end of line number.
      linenum = Integer.parseInt(trace.substring(pos+1,pos2));  // Get linenum.
      pos2 = trace.lastIndexOf('(', pos);         // Back to start of filename.
      filename = trace.substring(pos2+1, pos);    // Get filename.
    }
    catch (Exception e) { ; }                     // Ignore exceptions.

    // Set up an array of arguments to use with the message
    String errmsg = error.getMessage();
    Object[] args = {
      ((errmsg!= null)?errmsg:""), error.getClass().getName(),
      filename, new Integer(linenum), new Date()
    };
    // Finally, display the localized error message, using
    // MessageFormat.format() to substitute the arguments into the message.
    System.out.println(MessageFormat.format(message, args));
  }
}
```

Example 14-8 shows the resource bundle properties file used to localize the set of possible error messages that could be thrown by the ConvertEncoding class shown at the beginning of this chapter. With a resource bundle like this, ConvertEncoding produces error messages like the following:

```
Error: Specified encoding not supported
        Error occurred at line 46 of file "ConvertEncoding.java"
        at 7:55:28 PM on 08-Apr-97
```

Example 14-8: A ResourceBundle Properties File with Localized Error Messages

```
#
# This is the file Errors.properties
# One property for each class of exceptions that our program might
# report.  Note the use of backslashes to continue long lines onto the
# next.  Also note the use of \n and \t for newlines and tabs
#
java.io.FileNotFoundException: \
Error: File "{0}" not found\n\t\
Error occurred at line {3} of file "{2}"\n\tat {4}

java.io.UnsupportedEncodingException: \
Error: Specified encoding not supported\n\t\
Error occurred at line {3} of file "{2}"\n\tat {4,time} on {4,date}

java.io.CharConversionException:\
Error: Character conversion failure.  Input data is not in specified format.

# A generic resource.  Display a message for any error or exception that
# is not handled by a more specific resource.
java.lang.Throwable:\
Error: {1}: {0}\n\t\
Error occurred at line {3} of file "{2}"\n\t{4,time,long} {4,date,long}
```

Exercises

14–1. Several internationalization-related classes, such as NumberFormat and Date-
    Format, have static methods named getAvailableLocales() that return an
    array of the Locale objects that they support. You can look up the name of
    the country of a given Locale object with the getDisplayCountry()
    method. Note that this method has two variants. One takes no arguments
    and displays the country name as appropriate in the default locale. The
    other version of getDisplayCountry() expects a Locale argument, and dis-
    plays the country name in the language of the specified locale.

    Write a program that displays the country names for all locales returned by
    NumberFormat.getAvailableLocales(). Using the static locale constants
    defined by the Locale class, display each country name in English, French,
    German, and Italian.

14–2. Write a multi-city digital clock applet that displays the current date and time
    in the cities Washington, London, Paris, Bonn, Beijing, and Tokyo. Display
    the dates and times using the customary formats for those cities. Consult a
    map, or search the Internet, to determine the timezones for each of these
    cities.

14–3. Example 14-5 shows how you can use a ResourceBundle to internationalize
    the text that appears within menus in your application. One feature of the
    AWT that discourages internationalization is that the Button, Menu, and
    MenuItem constructors, among others, are passed the labels that they are to
    display. This makes it very tempting for programmers to hardcode these
    labels into their programs.

Create internationalized subclasses of these classes named IButton, IMenu, and IMenuItem that instead take resource names as their constructor arguments. Each class should look up a resource bundle named "Labels" and use this bundle to look up the button or menu label that corresponds to the resource name passed to the constructor. If the bundle does not exist, or if a given resource is not defined in it, the IButton, IMenu, and IMenuItem classes should default to using the resource names as their labels. Write a simple test program (and some test property files) that demonstrate these new classes under two or three different locales.

CHAPTER 15

Remote Method Invocation

This chapter presents examples of using the remote method invocation (RMI) capabilities of the `java.rmi` and `java.rmi.server` packages that are part of Java 1.1. Remote method invocation is a powerful technology for developing networked applications without having to worry about the low-level networking details. RMI transcends the client/server model of computing with a more general "remote object" model. In this model, the "server" defines objects that "clients" can use remotely. Clients invoke methods of a remote object exactly as if it were a local object running in the same virtual machine as the client. RMI hides the underlying mechanism for transporting method arguments and return values across the network. An argument or return value can be a primitive value or any `Serializable` object.

An important limitation of RMI is that it only works when both the client and the server are Java applications. In this way, it is not as general as the CORBA architecture, which is independent of programming language.

To develop an RMI-based application, you need to follow these steps:

*   Create an interface that extends the `java.rmi.Remote` interface. This interface defines the exported methods that the remote object implements (i.e., the methods the "server" implements and that "clients" can invoke remotely). Each method in this interface must be declared to throw a `java.rmi.RemoteException`, which is the superclass of many more specific RMI exception classes. Every remote method must declare that it can throw a `RemoteException` because there are quite a few things that can go wrong during the remote method invocation process over a network.

*   Define a subclass of `java.rmi.server.UnicastRemoteObject` that implements your `Remote` interface. This class represents the remote object (or "server" object). Other than declaring its remote methods to throw `RemoteException` objects, the remote object does not need to do anything special to allow its

methods to be invoked remotely. The UnicastRemoteObject and the rest of the RMI infrastructure handle this automatically.

- Write a program (a "server") that creates an instance of your remote object. Export the object, making it available for use by clients, by registering the object by name with a registry service. This is usually done with the java.rmi.Naming class and the *rmiregistry* program. A server program may also act as its own registry server by using the LocateRegistry class and Registry interface of the java.rmi.registry package.

- After you compile the server program with *javac*, use *rmic* to generate a "stub" and a "skeleton" for the remote object. With RMI, the client and server do not communicate directly. On the client side, the client's reference to a remote object is implemented as an instance of a "stub" class. When the client invokes a remote method, it is a method of this stub object that is actually called. The stub does the necessary networking to pass that invocation to a "skeleton" class on the server. This skeleton translates the networked request into a method invocation on the server object, and passes the return value back to the stub, which passes it back to the client. This can be a complicated system, but fortunately, application programmers never have to think about stubs and skeletons; they are generated automatically by the *rmic* tool. Invoke *rmic* with the name of the remote object class (not the interface) on the command line. It creates and compiles two new classes with the suffixes _Stub and _Skel.

- If the server uses the default registry service provided by the Naming class, you must run the registry server, if it is not already running. You can run the registry server by invoking the *rmiregistry* program.

- Now you can write a client program to use the remote object exported by the server. The client must first obtain a reference to the remote object by using the Naming class to look up the object by name; the name is typically an *rmi:* URL. The remote reference that is returned is an instance of the Remote interface for the object (or more specifically, a "stub" object for the remote object). Once the client has this remote object, it can invoke methods on it exactly as it would invoke the methods of a local object. The only thing that it must be aware of is that all remote methods can throw RemoteException objects, and that in the presence of network errors, this can happen at unexpected times.

- RMI uses the serialization mechanism to transfer the stub object from the server to the client. Because a client may load an untrusted stub object, it should have a security manager installed to prevent a malicious (or just buggy) stub from deleting files or otherwise causing harm. The RMISecurityManager class is a suitable security manager that all RMI clients should install.

- Finally, start up the server program, and run the client!

The following sections of this chapter provides two complete RMI examples that follow the steps outlined above. The first example is a fairly simple remote banking program, while the second example is a complex and lengthy Multi-User Domain (MUD) system.

Remote Banking

Example 15-1 shows a class, Bank, that contains nested classes and interfaces for a remote bank client/server example. In this example, the RemoteBank interface defines remote methods to open and close accounts, deposit and withdraw money, check the account balance, and obtain the transaction history for an account. The Bank class contains all of the classes and interfaces required for the example except for the server class—the class that actually implements the RemoteBank interface. This server class is shown in Example 15-2; it would have been nested within the Bank class except that the Java 1.1 *rmic* compiler program does not understand nested classes and is not able to generate skeletons and stubs for them.

Example 15-1 defines the following nested classes and interfaces:

RemoteBank

> The Remote interface implemented by the bank server and used by the bank client.

FunnyMoney

> A trivial class that represents money in this banking example. It is nothing more than a wrapper around an int, but it serves to demonstrate that Serializable objects can be passed as arguments to remote methods and returned by remote methods.

BankingException

> A simple exception subclass that represents banking-related exceptions, such as "Insufficient funds." It demonstrates that remote method implementations on a server can throw exceptions that are transported across the network and thrown in the client program.

Client

> This class is a standalone program that serves as a simple client to the bank server. It uses Naming.lookup() to look up the desired RemoteBank object in the system registry, and then invokes various methods of that RemoteBank object, depending on its command-line arguments. It is really as simple as that; the use of RMI is almost transparent.

A session using the Bank.Client class might look as follows:

```
% java Bank\$Client open david javanut
Account opened.
% java Bank\$Client deposit david javanut 1000
Deposited 1000 wooden nickels.
% java Bank\$Client withdraw david javanut 300
Withdrew 300 wooden nickels.
% java Bank\$Client balance david javanut
You have 700 wooden nickels in the bank.
% java Bank\$Client history david javanut
Account opened at Thu Jul 10 12:44:32 EDT 1997
Deposited 1000 on Thu Jul 10 12:44:47 EDT 1997
Withdrew 300 on Thu Jul 10 12:44:59 EDT 1997
% java Bank\$Client close david javanut
700 wooden nickels returned to you.
Thanks for banking with us.
```

In the example session above, the bank client is running on the same host as the server. This need not be the case; the Client class looks for a system property named bank to specify what bank server to connect to. So you could invoke the client program like this:

```
% java -Dbank=rmi://bank.trustme.com/TrustyBank Bank\$Client open david javanut
```

Example 15-1: Bank.java

```java
import java.rmi.*;
import java.util.Vector;

/**
 * This class is a placeholder that simply contains other classes and
 * for interfaces remote banking.
 **/
public class Bank {
  /**
   * This is the interface that defines the exported methods of the
   * bank server.
   **/
  public interface RemoteBank extends Remote {
    /** Open a new account, with the specified name and password */
    public void openAccount(String name, String password)
        throws RemoteException, BankingException;

    /** Close the named account */
    public FunnyMoney closeAccount(String name, String password)
        throws RemoteException, BankingException;

    /** Deposit money into the named account */
    public void deposit(String name, String password, FunnyMoney money)
        throws RemoteException, BankingException;

    /** Withdraw the specified amount of money from the named account */
    public FunnyMoney withdraw(String name, String password, int amount)
        throws RemoteException, BankingException;

    /** Return the amount of money in the named account */
    public int getBalance(String name, String password)
        throws RemoteException, BankingException;

    /**
     * Return a Vector of Strings that list the transaction history
     * of the named account
     **/
    public Vector getTransactionHistory(String name, String password)
        throws RemoteException, BankingException;
  }

  /**
   * This simple class represents a monetary amount.  This implementation
   * is really nothing more than a wrapper around an integer.  It is a useful
   * to demonstrate that RMI can accept arbitrary non-String objects as
   * arguments and return them as values, as long as they are Serializable.
   * A more complete implementation of this FunnyMoney class might bear
   * a serial number, a digital signature, and other security features to
   * ensure that it is unique and non-forgable.
   **/
  public static class FunnyMoney implements java.io.Serializable {
```

Example 15–1: Bank.java (continued)

```
   public int amount;
   public FunnyMoney(int amount) { this.amount = amount; }
}

/**
 * This is a type of exception used to represent exceptional conditions
 * related to banking, such as "Insufficient Funds" and  "Invalid Password"
 **/
public static class BankingException extends Exception {
  public BankingException(String msg) { super(msg); }
}

/**
 * This class is a simple stand-alone client program that interacts
 * with a RemoteBank server.  It invokes different RemoteBank methods
 * depending on its command-line arguments, and demonstrates just how
 * simple it is to interact with a server using RMI.
 **/
public static class Client {
  public static void main(String[] args) {
    try {
      // Set the standard RMI security manager so that we can safely load
      // untrusted RemoteBank stub code over the network.
      System.setSecurityManager(new RMISecurityManager());

      // Figure out what RemoteBank to connect to by reading a system
      // property (specified on the command line with a -D option to java)
      // or, if it is not defined, use a default URL.  Note that by default
      // this client tries to connect to a server on the local machine
      String url = System.getProperty("bank", "rmi:///FirstRemote");

      // Now look up that RemoteBank server using the Naming object, which
      // contacts the rmiregistry server.  Given the url, this call returns
      // a RemoteBank object whose methods may be invoked remotely
      RemoteBank bank = (RemoteBank) Naming.lookup(url);

      // Convert the user's command to lower case
      String cmd = args[0].toLowerCase();

      // Now, go test the command against a bunch of possible options
      if (cmd.equals("open")) {             // Open an account
        bank.openAccount(args[1], args[2]);
        System.out.println("Account opened.");
      }
      else if (cmd.equals("close")) {       // Close an account
        FunnyMoney money = bank.closeAccount(args[1], args[2]);
        // Note that FunnyMoney currency is denominated in wooden nickels
        System.out.println(money.amount+" wooden nickels returned to you.");
        System.out.println("Thanks for banking with us.");
      }
      else if (cmd.equals("deposit")) {    // Deposit money
        FunnyMoney money = new FunnyMoney(Integer.parseInt(args[3]));
        bank.deposit(args[1], args[2], money);
        System.out.println("Deposited " + money.amount + " wooden nickels.");
      }
      else if (cmd.equals("withdraw")) {   // Withdraw money
        FunnyMoney money = bank.withdraw(args[1], args[2],
                                         Integer.parseInt(args[3]));
```

Example 15–1: Bank.java (continued)

```
            System.out.println("Withdrew " + money.amount + " wooden nickels.");
          }
          else if (cmd.equals("balance")) {    // Check account balance
            int amt = bank.getBalance(args[1], args[2]);
            System.out.println("You have "+amt+" wooden nickels in the bank.");
          }
          else if (cmd.equals("history")) {    // Get transaction history
            Vector transactions = bank.getTransactionHistory(args[1], args[2]);
            for(int i = 0; i < transactions.size(); i++)
              System.out.println(transactions.elementAt(i));
          }
          else System.out.println("Unknown command");
        }
        // Catch and display RMI exceptions
        catch (RemoteException e) { System.err.println(e); }
        // Catch and display Banking related exceptions
        catch (BankingException e) { System.err.println(e.getMessage()); }
        // Other exceptions are probably user syntax errors, so show usage.
        catch (Exception e) {
          System.err.println(e);
          System.err.println("Usage: java [-Dbank=<url>] Bank$Client " +
                             "<cmd> <name> <password> [<amount>]");
          System.err.println("where cmd is: open, close, deposit, " +
                             "withdraw, balance, history");
        }
      }
    }
  }
}
```

A Bank Server

Example 15-1 defined a RemoteBank interface and a bank client program. Example 15-2 is a RemoteBankServer class that implements the RemoteBank interface and acts as a server for the Bank.Client program. This class includes a main() method so it can be run as a standalone program. This method creates a Remote-BankServer object and registers it with Naming.rebind(), so that clients can look it up. It reads the system property bankname to determine what name to use to register the bank, but uses the name FirstRemote by default. (This is the same name that the Bank.Client uses by default as well.)

RemoteBankServer implements the RemoteBank interface, so it provides implementations for all the remote methods defined by that interface. It also defines some utility methods that are not remote methods, but that are used by the remote methods. Note that RemoteBankServer includes a nested Account class that stores all of the information about a single bank account. It maintains a hashtable that maps from account names to Account objects. The various remote methods look up the named account, verify the password, and operate on the account in some way. Any RMI remote object must be able to handle multiple, concurrent method invocations because multiple clients can be using the object at the same time. RemoteBankServer uses synchronized methods and synchronized statements to prevent two clients from opening, closing, or modifying the same account at the same time.

Before you can run this `RemoteBankServer` program, you must compile it, generate stub and skeleton classes, and start the *rmiregistry* service (if it is not already running). You might do all this with commands like the following (on a UNIX system):

```
% javac RemoteBankServer.java
% rmic RemoteBankServer
% rmiregistry &
% java RemoteBankServer
FirstRemote is open and ready for customers.
```

Note that Example 15-2 contains a fatal flaw: if the bank server crashes, all bank account data is lost, which is likely to result in angry customers! Chapter 16, *Database Access with SQL*, includes another implementation of the `RemoteBank` interface. This implementation uses a database to store account data in a more persistent way.

Example 15-2: RemoteBankServer.java

```java
import java.rmi.*;
import java.rmi.server.*;
import java.util.*;
import Bank.*;

/**
 * This class implements the remote methods defined by the RemoteBank
 * interface.  It has a serious shortcoming, though: all account data is
 * lost when the server goes down.
 **/
public class RemoteBankServer extends UnicastRemoteObject implements RemoteBank
{
  /**
   * This nested class stores data for a single account with the bank
   **/
  class Account {
    String password;             // account password
    int balance;                 // account balance
    Vector transactions = new Vector();   // account transaction history
    Account(String password) {
      this.password = password;
      transactions.addElement("Account opened at " + new Date());
    }
  }

  /**
   * This hashtable stores all open accounts and maps from account name
   * to Account object
   **/
  Hashtable accounts = new Hashtable();

  /**
   * This constructor doesn't do anything, but because it throws the
   * same exception that the superclass constructor throws, it must be
   * declared.
   **/
  public RemoteBankServer() throws RemoteException { super(); }

  /**
   * Open a bank account with the specified name and password
```

Example 15-2: RemoteBankServer.java (continued)

```
 * This method is synchronized to make it thread safe, since it
 * manipulates the accounts hashtable.
 **/
public synchronized void openAccount(String name, String password)
    throws RemoteException, BankingException {
  // Check if there is already an account under that name
  if (accounts.get(name) != null)
    throw new BankingException("Account already exists.");
  // Otherwise, it doesn't exist, so create it.
  Account acct = new Account(password);
  // And register it
  accounts.put(name, acct);
}

/**
 * This convenience method is not a remote method.  Given a name and password
 * it checks to see if an account with that name and password exists.  If
 * so, it returns the Account object.  Otherwise, it throws an exception.
 **/
public Account verify(String name, String password)
    throws BankingException {
  synchronized(accounts) {
    Account acct = (Account)accounts.get(name);
    if (acct == null) throw new BankingException("No such account");
    if (!password.equals(acct.password))
      throw new BankingException("Invalid password");
    return acct;
  }
}

/**
 * Close the named account.  This method is synchronized to make it
 * thread safe, since it manipulates the accounts hashtable.
 **/
public synchronized FunnyMoney closeAccount(String name, String password)
    throws RemoteException, BankingException {
  Account acct;
  acct = verify(name, password);
  accounts.remove(name);
  // Before changing the balance or transactions of any account, we first
  // have to obtain a lock on that account to be thread safe.
  synchronized (acct) {
    int balance = acct.balance;
    acct.balance = 0;
    return new FunnyMoney(balance);
  }
}

/** Deposit the specified FunnyMoney to the named account */
public void deposit(String name, String password, FunnyMoney money)
    throws RemoteException, BankingException {
  Account acct = verify(name, password);
  synchronized(acct) {
    acct.balance += money.amount;
    acct.transactions.addElement("Deposited " + money.amount +
                                 " on " + new Date());
  }
}
```

Example 15-2: RemoteBankServer.java (continued)

```
/** Withdraw the specified amount from the named account */
public FunnyMoney withdraw(String name, String password, int amount)
    throws RemoteException, BankingException {
  Account acct = verify(name, password);
  synchronized(acct) {
    if (acct.balance < amount)
      throw new BankingException("Insufficient Funds");
    acct.balance -= amount;
    acct.transactions.addElement("Withdrew " + amount + " on "+new Date());
    return new FunnyMoney(amount);
  }
}

/** Return the current balance in the named account */
public int getBalance(String name, String password)
    throws RemoteException, BankingException {
  Account acct = verify(name, password);
  synchronized(acct) { return acct.balance; }
}

/**
 * Return a Vector of strings containing the transaction history
 * for the named account
 **/
public Vector getTransactionHistory(String name, String password)
    throws RemoteException, BankingException {
  Account acct = verify(name, password);
  synchronized(acct) { return acct.transactions; }
}

/**
 * The main program that runs this RemoteBankServer.
 * Create a RemoteBankServer object and give it a name in the registry.
 * Read a system property to determine the name, but use "FirstRemote"
 * as the default name.  This is all that is necessary to set up the
 * service.  RMI takes care of the rest.
 **/
public static void main(String[] args) {
  try {
    // Create a bank server object
    RemoteBankServer bank = new RemoteBankServer();
    // Figure out what to name it
    String name = System.getProperty("bankname", "FirstRemote");
    // Name it that
    Naming.rebind(name, bank);
    // Tell the world we're up and running
    System.out.println(name + " is open and ready for customers.");
  }
  catch (Exception e) {
    System.err.println(e);
    System.err.println("Usage: java [-Dbankname=<name>] RemoteBankServer");
    System.exit(1); // Force an exit because there might be other threads
  }
}
}
```

Remote Method Invocation

A Multi-User Domain

A Multi-User Domain, or MUD, is a program (a server) that allows multiple people (clients) to interact with each other and with a shared virtual environment. The environment is typically a series of rooms or places linked to each other by various exits. Each room or place has a textual description that serves as the backdrop and sets the tone for the interactions between users. Many early MUDs were set in dungeons, with place descriptions reflecting the dark, underground nature of that imaginary environment. In fact, the MUD acronym originally stood for "Multi-User Dungeon." Some MUDs serve primarily as chat rooms for their clients, while others have more of the flavor of old-style adventure games, where the focus is on exploring the environment and problem solving. Others are exercises in creativity and group dynamics, allowing users to add new places and items to the MUD.

Example 15-3 through Example 15-7 show classes and interfaces used to define a simple user-extensible MUD system. A program like this MUD example clearly demonstrates how the RMI programming paradigm transcends the client/server model. As we'll see, MudServer and MudPlace are server objects that create the MUD environment within which users interact. But at the same time, each user within the MUD is represented by a MudPerson remote object that acts as a server when interacting with other users. Rather than having a single server and a set of clients, then, this system is really a distributed network of remote objects, all communicating with each other. Which objects are servers and which are clients really depends on your point of view.

In order to understand the MUD system, an overview of its architecture is useful. The MudServer class is a simple remote object (and standalone server program) that defines the entrance to a MUD and keeps track of the names of all the places within a MUD. Despite its name, the MudServer object does not provide the services that most users think of as "the MUD." That is the job of the MudPlace class.

Each MudPlace object represents a single place within the MUD. Each place has a name, a description, and lists of the items in the place, all of the people (users) currently in the place, all of the exits from the place, and the other places to which those exits lead. An exit may lead to an adjoining MudPlace on the same server, or it may lead to a MudPlace object in a different MUD on a different server altogether. Thus, the MUD environment that a user interacts with is really a network of MudPlace objects. It is the descriptions of places and items, and the complexity of the linkages between places, that give the MUD the richness that make it interesting to a user.

The users, or people, in a MUD are represented by MudPerson objects. MudPerson is a remote object that defines two methods. One method returns a description of the person (i.e., what other people see when they look at this person) and the other method delivers a message to the person (or to the user that the MudPerson represents). These methods allow users to look at each other and to talk to each other. When two users run into each other in a given MudPlace and begin to talk to each other, the MudPlace and the server on which the MUD is running are no longer relevant—the two MudPerson objects can communicate directly with each other through the power of RMI.

The examples that follow are long and somewhat complex, but are worth studying carefully. Given the complexity of the MUD system being developed, however, the classes and interfaces defined below are actually surprisingly simple. As you'll see, remote method invocation techniques are very powerful in systems like this one.

Remote MUD Interfaces

Example 15-3 is a Mud class that serves as a placeholder for nested classes and interfaces (and one constant) used by the rest of the MUD system. Most importantly, Mud defines three Remote interfaces: RemoteMudServer, RemoteMudPerson, and RemoteMudPlace. These define the remote methods that are implemented by the MudServer, MudPerson, and MudPlace objects, respectively.

Example 15–3: Mud.java

```
import java.rmi.*;
import java.util.Vector;
import java.io.IOException;

/**
 * This class defines three nested Remote interfaces for use by our MUD game.
 * It also defines a bunch of exception subclasses, and a constant string
 * prefix used to create unique names when registering MUD servers
 **/
public class Mud {
  /**
   * This interface defines the exported methods of the MUD server object
   **/
  public interface RemoteMudServer extends Remote {
    /** Return the name of this MUD */
    public String getMudName() throws RemoteException;

    /** Return the main entrance place for this MUD */
    public RemoteMudPlace getEntrance() throws RemoteException;

    /** Look up and return some other named place in this MUD */
    public RemoteMudPlace getNamedPlace(String name)
        throws RemoteException, NoSuchPlace;

    /**
     * Dump the state of the server to a file so that it can be restored later
     * All places, and their exits and things are dumped, but the "people"
     * in them are not.
     **/
    public void dump(String password, String filename)
        throws RemoteException, BadPassword, IOException;
  }

  /**
   * This interface defines the methods exported by a "person" object that
   * is in the MUD.
   **/
  public interface RemoteMudPerson extends Remote {
    /** Return a full description of the person */
    public String getDescription() throws RemoteException;

    /** Deliver a message to the person */
```

Example 15–3: Mud.java (continued)

```
    public void tell(String message) throws RemoteException;
}

/**
 * This is the most important remote interface for the MUD.  It defines the
 * methods exported by the "places" or "rooms" within a MUD.  Each place
 * has a name and a description, and also maintains a list of "people" in
 * the place, things in the place, and exits from the place.  There are
 * methods to get a list of names for these people, things, and exits.  There
 * are methods to get the RemoteMudPerson object for a named person, to get
 * a description of a named thing, and to go through a named exit.
 * There are methods for interacting with other people in the MUD.
 * There are methods for building the MUD by creating and destroying
 * things, adding new places (and new exits to those places), for linking
 * a place through a new exit to some other place (possibly on another
 * MUD server), and for closing down an existing exit.
 **/
public interface RemoteMudPlace extends Remote {
  /** Look up the name of this place */
  public String getPlaceName() throws RemoteException;

  /** Get a description of this place */
  public String getDescription() throws RemoteException;

  /** Find out the names of all people here */
  public Vector getNames() throws RemoteException;

  /** Get the names of all things here */
  public Vector getThings() throws RemoteException;

  /** Get the names of all ways out of here */
  public Vector getExits() throws RemoteException;

  /** Get the RemoteMudPerson object for the named person. */
  public RemoteMudPerson getPerson(String name)
      throws RemoteException, NoSuchPerson;

  /** Get more details about a named thing */
  public String examineThing(String name) throws RemoteException,NoSuchThing;

  /** Use the named exit */
  public RemoteMudPlace go(RemoteMudPerson who, String direction)
      throws RemoteException,NotThere,AlreadyThere,NoSuchExit,LinkFailed;

  /** Send a message of the form "David: hi everyone" */
  public void speak(RemoteMudPerson speaker, String msg)
      throws RemoteException, NotThere;

  /** Send a message of the form "David laughs loudly" */
  public void act(RemoteMudPerson speaker, String msg)
      throws RemoteException, NotThere;

  /** Add a new thing in this place */
  public void createThing(RemoteMudPerson who, String name,
                          String description)
      throws RemoteException, NotThere, AlreadyThere;

  /** Remove a thing from this place */
```

Example 15-3: Mud.java (continued)

```java
    public void destroyThing(RemoteMudPerson who, String thing)
        throws RemoteException, NotThere, NoSuchThing;

    /** Create a new place, bi-directionally linked to this one by an exit */
    public void createPlace(RemoteMudPerson creator,
                            String exit, String entrance,
                            String name, String description)
        throws RemoteException,NotThere,ExitAlreadyExists,PlaceAlreadyExists;

    /**
     * Link this place (unidirectionally) to some existing place.  The
     * destination place may even be on another server.
     **/
    public void linkTo(RemoteMudPerson who, String exit,
                       String hostname, String mudname, String placename)
        throws RemoteException, NotThere, ExitAlreadyExists, NoSuchPlace;

    /** Remove an existing exit */
    public void close(RemoteMudPerson who, String exit)
        throws RemoteException, NotThere, NoSuchExit;

    /**
     * Remove this person from this place, leaving them nowhere.
     * Send the specified message to everyone left in the place.
     **/
    public void exit(RemoteMudPerson who, String message)
        throws RemoteException, NotThere;

    /**
     * Put a person in a place, assigning their name, and sending the
     * specified message to everyone else in the place.  The client should
     * not make this method available to the user.  They should use go()
     * instead.
     **/
    public void enter(RemoteMudPerson who, String name, String message)
        throws RemoteException, AlreadyThere;

    /**
     * Return the server object of the MUD that "contains" this place
     * This method should not be directly visible to the player
     **/
    public RemoteMudServer getServer() throws RemoteException;
}

/**
 * This is a generic exception class that serves as the superclass
 * for a bunch of more specific exception types
 **/
public static class MudException extends Exception {}

/**
 * These specific exception classes are thrown in various contexts.
 * The exception class name contains all the information about the exception;
 * no detail messages are provided by these classes.
 **/
public static class NotThere extends MudException {}
public static class AlreadyThere extends MudException {}
public static class NoSuchThing extends MudException {}
```

Example 15-3: Mud.java (continued)

```
public static class NoSuchPerson extends MudException {}
public static class NoSuchExit extends MudException {}
public static class NoSuchPlace extends MudException {}
public static class ExitAlreadyExists extends MudException {}
public static class PlaceAlreadyExists extends MudException {}
public static class LinkFailed extends MudException {}
public static class BadPassword extends MudException {}

/**
 * This constant is used as a prefix to the MUD name when the server
 * registers the mud with the RMI Registry, and when the client looks
 * up the MUD in the registry.  Using this prefix helps prevent the
 * possibility of name collisions.
 **/
static final String mudPrefix = "com.davidflanagan.mud.";
}
```

The MUD Server

Example 15-4 shows the MudServer class. This class is a standalone program that starts a MUD running; it also provides the implementation of the RemoteMudServer interface. As noted above, a MudServer object merely serves as the entrance to a MUD: it is not the MUD itself. Therefore, this is a fairly simple class. One of its most interesting features is the use of the serialization classes of java.io and the compression classes of java.util.zip to save the state the MUD, so that it can be restored later.

Example 15-4: MudServer.java

```
import java.rmi.*;
import java.rmi.server.*;
import java.rmi.registry.*;
import java.io.*;
import java.util.Hashtable;
import java.util.zip.*;

/**
 * This class implements the RemoteMudServer interface.  It also defines a
 * main() method so you can run it as a standalone program that will
 * set up and initialize a MUD server.  Note that a MudServer maintains an
 * entrance point to a MUD, but it is not the MUD itself.  Most of the
 * interesting MUD functionality is defined by the RemoteMudPlace interface
 * and implemented by the RemotePlace class.  In addition to being a remote
 * object, this class is also Serializable, so that the state of the MUD
 * can be saved to a file and later restored.  Note that the main() method
 * defines two ways of starting a MUD: one is to start it from scratch with
 * a single initial place, and another is to restore an existing MUD from a
 * file.
 **/
public class MudServer extends UnicastRemoteObject
                       implements RemoteMudServer, Serializable {
    MudPlace entrance;     // The standard entrance to this MUD
    String password;       // The password required to dump() the state of the MUD
    String mudname;        // The name that this MUD is registered under
    Hashtable places;      // A mapping of place names to places in this MUD
```

Example 15-4: MudServer.java (continued)

```
/**
 * Start a MUD from scratch, with the given name and password.  Create
 * an initial MudPlace object as the entrance, giving it the specified
 * name and description.
 **/
public MudServer(String mudname, String password,
                 String placename, String description)
     throws RemoteException {
  this.mudname = mudname;
  this.password = password;
  this.places = new Hashtable();
  // Create the entrance place
  try { this.entrance = new MudPlace(this, placename, description); }
  catch (PlaceAlreadyExists e) {} // Should never happen
}

/** For serialization only.  Never call this constructor. */
public MudServer() throws RemoteException {}

/** This remote method returns the name of the MUD */
public String getMudName() throws RemoteException { return mudname; }

/** This remote method returns the entrance place of the MUD */
public RemoteMudPlace getEntrance() throws RemoteException {
  return entrance;
}

/**
 * This remote method returns a RemoteMudPlace object for the named place.
 * In this sense, a MudServer acts as like an RMI Registry object, returning
 * remote objects looked up by name.  It is simpler to do it this way than
 * to use an actual Registry object.  If the named place does not exist,
 * it throws a NoSuchPlace exception
 **/
public RemoteMudPlace getNamedPlace(String name)
     throws RemoteException, NoSuchPlace {
  RemoteMudPlace p = (RemoteMudPlace) places.get(name);
  if (p == null) throw new NoSuchPlace();
  return p;
}

/**
 * Define a new placename to place mapping in our hashtable.
 * This is not a remote method.  The MudPlace() constructor calls it
 * to register the new place it is creating.
 **/
public void setPlaceName(RemoteMudPlace place, String name)
     throws PlaceAlreadyExists {
  if (places.containsKey(name)) throw new PlaceAlreadyExists();
  places.put(name, place);
}

/**
 * This remote method serializes and compresses the state of the MUD
 * to a named file, if the specified password matches the one specified
 * when the MUD was initially created.  Note that the state of a MUD
```

Example 15–4: MudServer.java (continued)

```java
     * consists of all places in the MUD, with all things and exits in those
     * places.  The people in the MUD are not part of the state that is saved.
     **/
    public void dump(String password, String f)
          throws RemoteException, BadPassword, IOException {
      if ((this.password != null) && !this.password.equals(password))
        throw new BadPassword();
      ObjectOutputStream out =
        new ObjectOutputStream(new GZIPOutputStream(new FileOutputStream(f)));
      out.writeObject(this);
      out.close();
    }


    /**
     * This main() method defines the standalone program that starts up a MUD
     * server.  If invoked with a single argument, it treats that argument as
     * the name of a file containing the serialized and compressed state of an
     * existing MUD, and recreates it.  Otherwise, it expects four command-line
     * arguments: the name of the MUD, the password, the name of the entrance
     * place for the MUD, and a description of that entrance place.
     * Besides creating the MudServer object, this program sets an appropriate
     * security manager, and uses the default rmiregistry to register the
     * the MudServer under its given name.
     **/
    public static void main(String[] args) {
      try {
        MudServer server;
        if (args.length == 1) {
          // Read the MUD state in from a file
          FileInputStream f = new FileInputStream(args[0]);
          ObjectInputStream in = new ObjectInputStream(new GZIPInputStream(f));
          server = (MudServer) in.readObject();
        }
        // Otherwise, create an initial MUD from scratch
        else server = new MudServer(args[0], args[1], args[2], args[3]);

        System.setSecurityManager(new RMISecurityManager());
        Naming.rebind(Mud.mudPrefix + server.mudname, server);
      }
      // Display an error message if anything goes wrong.
      catch (Exception e) {
        System.out.println(e);
        System.out.println("Usage: java MudServer <savefile>\n" +
                           "   or: java MudServer <mudname> <password> " +
                           "<placename> <description>");
        System.exit(1);
      }
    }

    /** This constant is a version number for serialization */
    static final long serialVersionUID = 7453281245880199453L;
}
```

The MudPlace Class

Example 15-5 is the MudPlace class that implements the RemoteMudPlace interface and acts as a server for a single place or room within the MUD. It is this class that holds the description of a place and maintains the lists of the people and items in a place and the exits from a place. This is a long class, but many of the remote methods it defines have simple or even trivial implementations. The go(), createPlace(), and linkTo() methods are among the more complex and interesting methods; they manage the network of connections between MudPlace objects.

Note that the MudPlace class is Serializable, so that a MudPlace (and all places it is connected to) can be serialized along with the MudServer that refers to them. However, the names and people fields are declared transient, so they are not serialized along with the place.

Example 15-5: MudPlace.java

```java
import java.rmi.*;
import java.rmi.server.*;
import java.rmi.registry.*;
import java.io.*;
import java.util.*;

/**
 * This class implements the RemoteMudPlace interface and exports a
 * bunch of remote methods that are at the heart of the MUD.  The
 * MudClient interacts primarily with these methods.  See the comment
 * for RemoteMudPlace for an overview.
 * The MudPlace class is Serializable so that places can be saved to disk
 * along with the MudServer that contains them.  Note, however that the
 * names and people fields are marked transient, so they are not serialized
 * along with the place (because it wouldn't make sense to try to save
 * RemoteMudPerson objects, even if they could be serialized).
 **/
public class MudPlace extends UnicastRemoteObject
                      implements RemoteMudPlace, Serializable {
  String placename, description;        // information about the place itself
  Vector exits = new Vector();          // names of exits from this place
  Vector destinations = new Vector();   // where the exits go to
  Vector things = new Vector();         // names of things in this place
  Vector descriptions = new Vector();   // descriptions of those things
  transient Vector names = new Vector();   // names of people in this place
  transient Vector people = new Vector(); // the RemoteMudPerson objects
  MudServer server;                     // the server for this place

  /** A no-arg constructor for de-serialization only.  Do not call it */
  public MudPlace() throws RemoteException { super(); }

  /**
   * This constructor creates a place, and calls a server method
   * to register the object so that it will be accessible by name
   **/
  public MudPlace(MudServer server, String placename, String description)
       throws RemoteException, PlaceAlreadyExists {
    this.server = server;
    this.placename = placename;
    this.description = description;
```

Example 15–5: MudPlace.java (continued)

```
    server.setPlaceName(this, placename);  // Register the place
  }

  /** This remote method returns the name of this place */
  public String getPlaceName() throws RemoteException { return placename; }

  /** This remote method returns the description of this place */
  public String getDescription() throws RemoteException { return description; }

  /** This remote method returns a Vector of names of people in this place */
  public Vector getNames() throws RemoteException { return names; }

  /** This remote method returns a Vector of names of things in this place */
  public Vector getThings() throws RemoteException { return things; }

  /** This remote method returns a Vector of names of exits from this place */
  public Vector getExits() throws RemoteException { return exits; }

  /**
   * This remote method returns a RemoteMudPerson object corresponding to
   * the specified name, or throws an exception if no such person is here
   **/
  public RemoteMudPerson getPerson(String name)
      throws RemoteException, NoSuchPerson {
    synchronized(names) {
      // What about when there are 2 of the same name?
      int i = names.indexOf(name);
      if (i == -1) throw new NoSuchPerson();
      return (RemoteMudPerson) people.elementAt(i);
    }
  }

  /**
   * This remote method returns a description of the named thing, or
   * throws an exception if no such thing is in this place.
   **/
  public String examineThing(String name) throws RemoteException, NoSuchThing {
    synchronized(things) {
      int i = things.indexOf(name);
      if (i == -1) throw new NoSuchThing();
      return (String) descriptions.elementAt(i);
    }
  }

  /**
   * This remote method moves the specified RemoteMudPerson from this place
   * in the named direction (i.e. through the named exit) to whatever place
   * is there.  It throws exceptions if the specified person isn't in this
   * place to begin with, or if they are already in the place through the exit
   * or if the exit doesn't exist, or if the exit links to another MUD server
   * and the server is not functioning.
   **/
  public RemoteMudPlace go(RemoteMudPerson who, String direction)
      throws RemoteException, NotThere, AlreadyThere, NoSuchExit, LinkFailed {
    // Make sure the direction is valid, and get destination if it is
    Object destination;
    synchronized(exits) {
      int i = exits.indexOf(direction);
```

Example 15-5: MudPlace.java (continued)

```
    if (i == -1) throw new NoSuchExit();
    destination = destinations.elementAt(i);
  }

  // If destination is a string, it is a place on another server, so connect
  // to that server.  Otherwise, it is a place already on this server.
  // Throw an exception if we can't connect to the server.
  RemoteMudPlace newplace;
  if (destination instanceof String) {
    try {
      String t = (String) destination;
      int pos = t.indexOf('@');
      String url = t.substring(0, pos);
      String placename = t.substring(pos+1);
      RemoteMudServer s = (RemoteMudServer) Naming.lookup(url);
      newplace = s.getNamedPlace(placename);
    }
    catch (Exception e) { throw new LinkFailed(); }
  }
  // If the destination is not a string, then it is a Place
  else newplace = (RemoteMudPlace) destination;

  // Make sure the person is here and get their name.
  // Throw an exception if they are not here
  String name = verifyPresence(who);

  // Move the person out of here, and tell everyone who remains about it.
  this.exit(who, name + " has gone " + direction);

  // Put the person into the new place.
  // Send a message to everyone already in that new place
  String fromwhere;
  if (newplace instanceof MudPlace) // going to a local place
    fromwhere = placename;
  else
    fromwhere = server.getMudName() + "." + placename;
  newplace.enter(who, name, name + " has arrived from: " + fromwhere);

  // Return the new RemoteMudPlace object to the client so they
  // know where they are now at.
  return newplace;
}

/**
 * This remote method sends a message to everyone in the room.  Used to
 * say things to everyone.  Requires that the speaker be in this place.
 **/
public void speak(RemoteMudPerson speaker, String msg)
    throws RemoteException, NotThere {
  String name = verifyPresence(speaker);
  tellEveryone(name + ":" + msg);
}

/**
 * This remote method sends a message to everyone in the room.  Used to
 * do things that people can see.  Requires that the actor be in this place.
 **/
public void act(RemoteMudPerson actor, String msg)
```

Example 15–5: MudPlace.java (continued)

```
      throws RemoteException, NotThere {
  String name = verifyPresence(actor);
  tellEveryone(name + " " + msg);
}


/**
 * This remote method creates a new thing in this room.
 * It requires that the creator be in this room.
 **/
public void createThing(RemoteMudPerson creator,
                        String name, String description)
     throws RemoteException, NotThere, AlreadyThere {
  // Make sure the creator is here
  String creatorname = verifyPresence(creator);
  synchronized(things) {
    // Make sure there isn't already something with this name.
    if (things.indexOf(name) != -1) throw new AlreadyThere();
    // Add the thing name and descriptions to the appropriate lists
    things.addElement(name);
    descriptions.addElement(description);
  }
  // Tell everyone about the new thing and its creator
  tellEveryone(creatorname + " has created a " + name);
}


/**
 * Remove a thing from this room.  Throws exceptions if the person
 * who removes it isn't themselves in the room, or if there is no
 * such thing here.
 **/
public void destroyThing(RemoteMudPerson destroyer, String thing)
     throws RemoteException, NotThere, NoSuchThing {
  // Verify that the destroyer is here
  String name = verifyPresence(destroyer);
  synchronized(things) {
    // Verify that there is a thing by that name in this room
    int i = things.indexOf(thing);
    if (i == -1) throw new NoSuchThing();
    // And remove its name and description from the lists
    things.removeElementAt(i);
    descriptions.removeElementAt(i);
  }
  // Let everyone know of the demise of this thing.
  tellEveryone(name + " had destroyed the " + thing);
}


/**
 * Create a new place in this MUD, with the specified name an description.
 * The new place is accessible from this place through
 * the specified exit, and this place is accessible from the new place
 * through the specified entrance.  The creator must be in this place
 * in order to create a exit from this place.
 **/
public void createPlace(RemoteMudPerson creator,
                        String exit, String entrance, String name,
                        String description)
     throws RemoteException,NotThere,ExitAlreadyExists,PlaceAlreadyExists {
  // Verify that the creator is actually here in this place
```

Example 15-5: MudPlace.java (continued)

```
   String creatorname = verifyPresence(creator);
   synchronized(exits) {  // Only allow one client to change exits at a time
     // Check that the exit doesn't already exist.
     if (exits.indexOf(exit) != -1) throw new ExitAlreadyExists();
     // Create the new place, registering its name with the server
     MudPlace destination = new MudPlace(server, name, description);
     // Link from there back to here
     destination.exits.addElement(entrance);
     destination.destinations.addElement(this);
     // And link from here to there
     exits.addElement(exit);
     destinations.addElement(destination);
   }
   // Let everyone know about the new exit, and the new place beyond
   tellEveryone(creatorname + " has created a new place: " + exit);
 }

 /**
  * Create a new exit from this mud, linked to a named place in a named
  * MUD on a named host (this can also be used to link to a named place in
  * the current MUD, of course).  Because of the possibilities of deadlock,
  * this method only links from here to there; it does not create a return
  * exit from there to here.  That must be done with a separate call.
  **/
 public void linkTo(RemoteMudPerson linker, String exit,
                    String hostname, String mudname, String placename)
     throws RemoteException, NotThere, ExitAlreadyExists, NoSuchPlace {
   // Verify that the linker is actually here
   String name = verifyPresence(linker);

   // Check that the link target actually exists.  Throw NoSuchPlace if not.
   // Note that NoSuchPlace may also mean "NoSuchMud" or "MudNotResponding".
   String url = "rmi://" + hostname + '/' + Mud.mudPrefix + mudname;
   try {
     RemoteMudServer s = (RemoteMudServer) Naming.lookup(url);
     RemoteMudPlace destination = s.getNamedPlace(placename);
   }
   catch (Exception e) { throw new NoSuchPlace(); }

   synchronized(exits) {
     // Check that the exit doesn't already exist.
     if (exits.indexOf(exit) != -1) throw new ExitAlreadyExists();
     // Add the exit, to the list of exit names
     exits.addElement(exit);
     // And add the destination to the list of destinations.  Note that
     // the destination is stored as a string rather than as a RemoteMudPlace.
     // This is because if the remote server goes down then comes back up
     // again, a RemoteMudPlace is not valid, but the string still is.
     destinations.addElement(url + '@' + placename);
   }
   // Let everyone know about the new exit and where it leads
   tellEveryone(name + " has linked " + exit + " to " +
                "'" + placename + "' in MUD '" + mudname +
                "' on host " + hostname);
 }

 /**
  * Close an exit that leads out of this place.
```

Example 15-5: MudPlace.java (continued)

```
   * It does not close the return exit from there back to here.
   * Note that this method does not destroy the place that the exit leads to.
   * In the current implementation, there is no way to destroy a place.
   **/
  public void close(RemoteMudPerson who, String exit)
       throws RemoteException, NotThere, NoSuchExit {
    // check that the person closing the exit is actually here
    String name = verifyPresence(who);
    synchronized(exits) {
      // Check that the exit exists
      int i = exits.indexOf(exit);
      if (i == -1) throw new NoSuchExit();
      // Remove it and its destination from the lists
      exits.removeElementAt(i);
      destinations.removeElementAt(i);
    }
    // Let everyone know that the exit doesn't exist anymore
    tellEveryone(name + " has closed exit " + exit);
  }

  /**
   * Remove a person from this place.  If there is a message, send it to
   * everyone who is left in this place.  If the specified person is not here,
   * this method does nothing and does not throw an exception.  This method
   * is called by go(), and the client should call it when the user quits.
   * The client should not allow the user to invoke it directly, however.
   **/
  public void exit(RemoteMudPerson who, String message) throws RemoteException{
    String name;
    synchronized(names) {
      int i = people.indexOf(who);
      if (i == -1) return;
      names.removeElementAt(i);
      people.removeElementAt(i);
    }
    if (message != null) tellEveryone(message);
  }

  /**
   * This method puts a person into this place, assigning them the
   * specified name, and displaying a message to anyone else who is in
   * that place.  This method is called by go(), and the client should
   * call it to initially place a person into the MUD.  Once the person
   * is in the MUD, however, the client should restrict them to using go()
   * and should not allow them to call this method directly.
   * If there have been networking problems, a client might call this method
   * to restore a person to this place, in case they've been bumped out.
   * (A person will be bumped out of a place if the server tries to send
   * a message to them and gets a RemoteException.)
   **/
  public void enter(RemoteMudPerson who, String name, String message)
       throws RemoteException, AlreadyThere {
    // Send the message to everyone who is already here.
    if (message != null) tellEveryone(message);

    // Add the person to this place.
    synchronized (names) {
      if (people.indexOf(who) != -1) throw new AlreadyThere();
```

Example 15–5: MudPlace.java (continued)

```
      names.addElement(name);
      people.addElement(who);
  }
}

/**
 * This final remote method returns the server object for the MUD in which
 * this place exists.  The client should not allow the user to invoke this
 * method.
 **/
public RemoteMudServer getServer() throws RemoteException { return server; }

/**
 * Create and start a thread that sends out a message everyone in this place.
 * If it gets a RemoteException talking to a person, it silently removes
 * that person from this place.  This is not a remote method, but is used
 * internally by a number of remote methods.
 **/
protected void tellEveryone(final String message) {
  // If there is no-one here, don't bother sending the message!
  if (people.size() == 0) return;
  // Make a copy of the people here now.  The message is sent asynchronously
  // and the list of people in the room may change before the message is
  // sent to everyone.
  final Vector recipients = (Vector) people.clone();
  // Create and start a thread to send the message, using an anonymous
  // class.  We do this because sending the message to everyone in this
  // place might take some time, (particularly on a slow or flaky network)
  // and we don't want to wait.
  new Thread() {
    public void run() {
      // Loop through the recipients
      for(int i = 0; i < recipients.size(); i++) {
        RemoteMudPerson person = (RemoteMudPerson)recipients.elementAt(i);
        // Try to send the message to each one.
        try { person.tell(message); }
        // If it fails, assume that that person's client or network has
        // failed, and silently remove them from this place.
        catch (RemoteException e) {
          try { MudPlace.this.exit(person, null); }
          catch (Exception ex) {}
        }
      }
    }
  }.start();
}

/**
 * This convenience method checks whether the specified person is here.
 * If so, it returns their name.  If not it throws a NotThere exception
 **/
protected String verifyPresence(RemoteMudPerson who) throws NotThere {
  int i = people.indexOf(who);
  if (i == -1) throw new NotThere();
  else return (String) names.elementAt(i);
}
```

Example 15–5: MudPlace.java (continued)

```
/**
 * This method is used for custom de-serialization.  Since the vectors of
 * people and of their names are transient, they are not serialized with
 * the rest of this place.  Therefore, when the place is de-serialized, those
 * vectors have to be recreated (empty).
 **/
private void readObject(ObjectInputStream in)
        throws IOException, ClassNotFoundException {
    in.defaultReadObject();  // Read most of the object as normal
    names = new Vector();    // Then recreate the names vector
    people = new Vector();   // and recreate the people vector
}

/** This constant is a version number for serialization */
static final long serialVersionUID = 5090967989223703026L;
}
```

The MudPerson Class

Example 15-6 shows the MudPerson class. This is the simplest of the remote objects in the MUD system. It implements the two remote methods defined by the RemoteMudPerson interface and also defines a few non-remote methods used by the MudClient class of Example 15-7. The remote methods are quite simple: one simply returns a description string to the caller and the other writes a message to a stream where the user can see it.

Example 15–6: MudPerson.java

```
import java.rmi.*;
import java.rmi.server.*;
import java.io.*;

/**
 * This is the simplest of the remote objects that we implement for the MUD.
 * It maintains only a little bit of state, and has only two exported
 * methods
 **/
public class MudPerson extends UnicastRemoteObject implements RemoteMudPerson {
    String name;            // The name of the person
    String description;     // The person's description
    PrintWriter tellStream; // Where to send messages we receive to

    public MudPerson(String n, String d, PrintWriter out)
            throws RemoteException {
        name = n;
        description = d;
        tellStream = out;
    }

    /** Return the person's name.  Not a remote method */
    public String getName() { return name; }

    /** Set the person's name.  Not a remote method */
    public void setName(String n) { name = n; }
```

Example 15–6: MudPerson.java (continued)

```
/** Set the person's description.  Not a remote method */
public void setDescription(String d) { description = d; }

/** Set the stream that messages to us should be written to.  Not remote. */
public void setTellStream(PrintWriter out) { tellStream = out; }

/** A remote method that returns this person's description */
public String getDescription() throws RemoteException { return description; }

/**
 * A remote method that delivers a message to the person.
 * I.e. it delivers a message to the user controlling the "person"
 **/
public void tell(String message) throws RemoteException {
  tellStream.println(message);
  tellStream.flush();
}
}
```

A MUD Client

Example 15-7 is a client program for the MUD system we've developed in the previous examples. It uses the `Naming.lookup()` method to look up the `RemoteMud-Server` object that represents a named MUD on a specified host. The program then calls `getEntrance()` or `getNamedPlace()` method of this `RemoteMudServer` object to obtain an initial `MudPlace` object into which to insert the user. Next, the program asks the user for a name and description of the `MudPerson` that will represent her in the MUD, creates a `MudPerson` object with that name and description, and then places it in the initial `RemoteMudPlace`. Finally, the program enters a loop that prompts the user to enter a command and processes the command. Most of the commands that this client supports simply invoke one of the remote methods of the `RemoteMudPlace` that represents the user's current location in the MUD. The end of the command loop consists of a number of catch clauses that handle the large number of things that can go wrong.

Example 15-7: MudClient.java

```
import java.rmi.*;
import java.rmi.server.*;
import java.rmi.registry.*;
import java.io.*;
import java.util.*;

/**
 * This class is a client program for the MUD.  The main() method sets up
 * a connection to a RemoteMudServer, gets the initial RemoteMudPlace object,
 * and creates a MudPerson object to represent the user in the MUD.  Then it
 * calls runMud() to put the person in the place, begins processing
 * user commands.  The getLine() and getMultiLine() methods are convenience
 * methods used throughout to get input from the user.
 **/
public class MudClient {
```

Example 15-7: MudClient.java (continued)

```java
/**
 * The main program.  It expects two or three arguments:
 *    0) the name of the host on which the mud server is running
 *    1) the name of the MUD on that host
 *    2) the name of a place within that MUD to start at (optional).
 *
 * It uses the Naming.lookup() method to obtain a RemoteMudServer object
 * for the named MUD on the specified host.  Then it uses the getEntrance()
 * or getNamedPlace() method of RemoteMudServer to obtain the starting
 * RemoteMudPlace object.  It prompts the user for a their name and
 * description, and creates a MudPerson object.  Finally, it passes
 * the person and the place to runMud() to begin interaction with the MUD.
 **/
public static void main(String[] args) {
  try {
    String hostname = args[0];    // Each MUD is uniquely identified by a
    String mudname = args[1];     //   host and a MUD name.
    String placename = null;      // Each place within a MUD has a unique name
    if (args.length > 2) placename = args[2];

    // Set the RMI security manager so that untrusted stub objects loaded
    // over the network can't cause havoc.
    System.setSecurityManager(new RMISecurityManager());

    // Look up the RemoteMudServer object for the named MUD using
    // the default registry on the specified host.  Note the use of
    // the Mud.mudPrefix constant to help prevent naming conflicts
    // in the registry.
    RemoteMudServer server =
      (RemoteMudServer)Naming.lookup("rmi://" + hostname + "/" +
                                     Mud.mudPrefix + mudname);

    // If the user did not specify a place in the mud, use getEntrance()
    // to get the initial place.  Otherwise, call getNamedPlace() to find
    // the initial place.
    RemoteMudPlace location = null;
    if (placename == null) location = server.getEntrance();
    else location = (RemoteMudPlace) server.getNamedPlace(placename);

    // Greet the user and ask for their name and description.
    // This relies on getLine() and getMultiLine() defined below.
    System.out.println("Welcome to " + mudname);
    String name = getLine("Enter your name: ");
    String description = getMultiLine("Please describe what " +
                                      "people see when they look at you:");

    // Define an output stream that the MudPerson object will use to
    // display messages sent to it to the user.  We'll use the console.
    PrintWriter myout = new PrintWriter(new OutputStreamWriter(System.out));

    // Create a MudPerson object to represent the user in the MUD.
    // Use the specified name and description, and the output stream.
    MudPerson me = new MudPerson(name, description, myout);

    // Lower this thread's priority one notch so that broadcast messages
    // can appear even when we're blocking for I/O.  This is necessary
    // on the Linux platform, but may not be necessary on all platforms.
```

Example 15-7: MudClient.java (continued)

```
        int pri = Thread.currentThread().getPriority();
        Thread.currentThread().setPriority(pri-1);

        // Finally, put the MudPerson into the RemoteMudPlace, and start
        // prompting the user for commands.
        runMud(location, me);
    }
    // If anything goes wrong, print a message and exit.
    catch (Exception e) {
      System.out.println(e);
      System.out.println("Usage: java MudClient <host> <mud> [<place>]");
      System.exit(1);
    }
  }

  /**
   * This method is the main loop of the MudClient.  It places the person
   * into the place (using the enter() method of RemoteMudPlace).  Then it
   * calls the look() method to describe the place to the user, and enters a
   * command loop to prompt the user for a command and process the command
   **/
  public static void runMud(RemoteMudPlace entrance, MudPerson me)
        throws RemoteException {
    RemoteMudPlace location = entrance;    // The current place
    String myname = me.getName();          // The person's name
    String placename = null;               // The name of the current place
    String mudname = null;                 // The name of the mud of that place

    try {
      // Enter the MUD
      location.enter(me, myname, myname + " has entered the MUD.");
      // Figure out where we are (for the prompt)
      mudname = location.getServer().getMudName();
      placename = location.getPlaceName();
      // Describe the place to the user
      look(location);
    }
    catch (Exception e) {
      System.out.println(e);
      System.exit(1);
    }

    // Now that we've entered the MUD, begin a command loop to process
    // the user's commands.  Note that there is a huge block of catch
    // statements at the bottom of the loop to handle all the things that
    // could go wrong each time through the loop.
    for(;;) {  // Loop until the user types "quit"
      try {     // Catch any exceptions that occur in the loop
        // Pause just a bit before printing the prompt, to give output
        // generated indirectly by the last command a chance to appear.
        try { Thread.sleep(200); } catch (InterruptedException e) {}

        // Display a prompt, and get the user's input
        String line = getLine(mudname + '.' + placename + "> ");

        // Break the input into a command and an argument that consists
        // of the rest of the line.  Convert the command to lowercase.
        String cmd, arg;
```

Remote Method Invocation

Example 15-7: MudClient.java (continued)

```
      int i = line.indexOf(' ');
      if (i == -1) { cmd = line; arg = null; }
      else {
        cmd = line.substring(0, i).toLowerCase();
        arg = line.substring(i+1);
      }
      if (arg == null) arg = "";

      // Now go process the command.  What follows is a huge repeated
      // if/else statement covering each of the commands supported by
      // this client.  Many of these commands simply invoke one of the
      // remote methods of the current RemoteMudPlace object.  Some have
      // to do a bit of additional processing.

      // LOOK: Describe the place and its things, people, and exits
      if (cmd.equals("look")) look(location);
      // EXAMINE: Describe a named thing
      else if (cmd.equals("examine"))
        System.out.println(location.examineThing(arg));
      // DESCRIBE: Describe a named person
      else if (cmd.equals("describe")) {
        try {
          RemoteMudPerson p = location.getPerson(arg);
          System.out.println(p.getDescription());
        }
        catch(RemoteException e) {
          System.out.println(arg + " is having technical difficulties.  " +
                             "No description is available.");
        }
      }
      // GO: Go in a named direction
      else if (cmd.equals("go")) {
        location = location.go(me, arg);
        mudname = location.getServer().getMudName();
        placename = location.getPlaceName();
        look(location);
      }
      // SAY: Say something to everyone
      else if (cmd.equals("say")) location.speak(me, arg);
      // DO: Do something that will be described to everyone
      else if (cmd.equals("do")) location.act(me, arg);
      // TALK: Say something to one named person
      else if (cmd.equals("talk")) {
        try {
          RemoteMudPerson p = location.getPerson(arg);
          String msg = getLine("What do you want to say?: ");
          p.tell(myname + " says \"" + msg + "\"");
        }
        catch (RemoteException e) {
          System.out.println(arg + " is having technical difficulties.  " +
                             "Can't talk to them.");
        }
      }
      // CHANGE: Change my own description
      else if (cmd.equals("change"))
        me.setDescription(getMultiLine("Describe yourself for others: "));
      // CREATE: Create a new thing in this place
      else if (cmd.equals("create")) {
```

Example 15-7: MudClient.java (continued)

```
    if (arg.length() == 0)
      throw new IllegalArgumentException("name expected");
    String desc = getMultiLine("Please describe the " + arg + ": ");
    location.createThing(me, arg, desc);
  }
  // DESTROY: Destroy a named thing
  else if (cmd.equals("destroy")) location.destroyThing(me, arg);
  // OPEN: Create a new place and connect this place to it through
  // the exit specified in the argument.
  else if (cmd.equals("open")) {
    if (arg.length() == 0)
      throw new IllegalArgumentException("direction expected");
    String name = getLine("What is the name of place there?: ");
    String back = getLine("What is the direction from " +
                          "there back to here?: ");
    String desc = getMultiLine("Please describe " + name + ":");
    location.createPlace(me, arg, back, name, desc);
  }
  // CLOSE: Close a named exit.  Note: only closes an exit
  // uni-directionally, and does not destroy a place.
  else if (cmd.equals("close")) {
    if (arg.length() == 0)
      throw new IllegalArgumentException("direction expected");
    location.close(me, arg);
  }
  // LINK: Create a new exit that connects to an existing place
  // that may be in another MUD running on another host
  else if (cmd.equals("link")) {
    if (arg.length() == 0)
      throw new IllegalArgumentException("direction expected");
    String host = getLine("What host are you linking to?: ");
    String mud = getLine("What is the name of the MUD on that host?: ");
    String place = getLine("What is the place name in that MUD?: ");
    location.linkTo(me, arg, host, mud, place);
    System.out.println("Don't forget to make a link from there " +
                       "back to here!");
  }
  // DUMP: Save the state of this MUD into the named file,
  // if the password is correct
  else if (cmd.equals("dump")) {
    if (arg.length() == 0)
      throw new IllegalArgumentException("filename expected");
    String password = getLine("Password: ");
    location.getServer().dump(password, arg);
  }
  // QUIT: Quit the game
  else if (cmd.equals("quit")) {
    try { location.exit(me, myname + " has quit."); }
    catch (Exception e) {}
    System.out.println("Bye.");
    System.out.flush();
    System.exit(0);
  }
  // HELP: Print out a big help message
  else if (cmd.equals("help")) {
    String help =
      "Commands are:\n" +
      "look: Look around\n" +
```

Example 15-7: MudClient.java (continued)

```
                "examine <thing>: examine the named thing in more detail\n" +
                "describe <person>: describe the named person\n" +
                "go <direction>: go in the named direction (i.e. a named exit)\n" +
                "say <message>: say something to everyone\n" +
                "do <message>: tell everyone that you are doing something\n" +
                "talk <person>: talk to one person.  Will prompt for message\n" +
                "change: change how you are described.  Will prompt for input\n" +
                "create <thing>: create a new thing.  Prompts for description \n" +
                "destroy <thing>: destroy a thing.\n" +
                "open <direction>: create an adjoining place. Prompts for input\n"+
                "close <direction>: close an exit from this place.\n" +
                "link <direction>: create an exit to an existing place,\n" +
                "    perhaps on another server.  Will prompt for input.\n" +
                "dump <filename>: save server state.  Prompts for password\n" +
                "quit: leave the Mud\n" +
                "help: display this message";
            System.out.println(help);
        }
        // Otherwise, this is an unrecognized command.
        else System.out.println("Unknown command.  Try 'help'.");
    }
    // Handle the many possible types of MudException
    catch (MudException e) {
        if (e instanceof NoSuchThing)
            System.out.println("There isn't any such thing here.");
        else if (e instanceof NoSuchPerson)
            System.out.println("There isn't anyone by that name here.");
        else if (e instanceof NoSuchExit)
            System.out.println("There isn't an exit in that direction.");
        else if (e instanceof NoSuchPlace)
            System.out.println("There isn't any such place.");
        else if (e instanceof ExitAlreadyExists)
            System.out.println("There is already an exit in that direction.");
        else if (e instanceof PlaceAlreadyExists)
            System.out.println("There is already a place with that name.");
        else if (e instanceof LinkFailed)
            System.out.println("That exit is not functioning.");
        else if (e instanceof BadPassword)
            System.out.println("Invalid password.");
        else if (e instanceof NotThere)      // Shouldn't happen
            System.out.println("You can't do that when you're not there.");
        else if (e instanceof AlreadyThere)  // Shouldn't happen
            System.out.println("You can't go there; you're already there.");
    }
    // Handle RMI exceptions
    catch (RemoteException e) {
        System.out.println("The MUD is having technical difficulties.");
        System.out.println("Perhaps the server has crashed:");
        System.out.println(e);
    }
    // Handle everything else that could go wrong.
    catch (Exception e) {
        System.out.println("Syntax or other error:");
        System.out.println(e);
        System.out.println("Try using the 'help' command.");
    }
  }
}
```

Example 15-7: MudClient.java (continued)

```
/**
 * This convenience method is used in several places in the
 * runMud() method above.  It displays the name and description of
 * the current place (including the name of the mud the place is in),
 * and also displays the list of things, people, and exits in
 * the current place.
 **/
public static void look(RemoteMudPlace p)
      throws RemoteException, MudException {
  String mudname = p.getServer().getMudName();   // Mud name
  String placename = p.getPlaceName();           // Place name
  String description = p.getDescription();       // Place description
  Vector things = p.getThings();                 // List of things here
  Vector names = p.getNames();                   // List of people here
  Vector exits = p.getExits();                   // List of exits from here

  // Print it all out
  System.out.println("You are in: " + placename + " of the Mud: " + mudname);
  System.out.println(description);
  System.out.print("Things here: ");
  for(int i = 0; i < things.size(); i++) {       // Display list of things
    if (i > 0) System.out.print(", ");
    System.out.print(things.elementAt(i));
  }
  System.out.print("\nPeople here: ");
  for(int i = 0; i < names.size(); i++) {        // Display list of people
    if (i > 0) System.out.print(", ");
    System.out.print(names.elementAt(i));
  }
  System.out.print("\nExits are: ");
  for(int i = 0; i < exits.size(); i++) {        // Display list of exits
    if (i > 0) System.out.print(", ");
    System.out.print(exits.elementAt(i));
  }
  System.out.println();                          // Blank line
  System.out.flush();                            // Make it appear now!
}

/** This static input stream reads lines from the console */
static BufferedReader in =
      new BufferedReader(new InputStreamReader(System.in));

/**
 * A convenience method for prompting the user and getting a line of
 * input.  It guarantees that the line is not empty and strips off
 * whitespace at the beginning and end of the line.
 **/
public static String getLine(String prompt) {
  String line = null;
  do {                             // Loop until a non-empty line is entered
    try {
      System.out.print(prompt);                  // Display prompt
      System.out.flush();                        // Display it right away
      line = in.readLine();                       // Get a line of input
      if (line != null) line = line.trim();     // Strip off whitespace
    } catch (Exception e) {}                      // Ignore any errors
```

Example 15–7: MudClient.java (continued)

```
    } while((line == null) || (line.length() == 0));
    return line;
}

/**
 * A convenience method for getting multi-line input from the user.
 * It prompts for the input, displays instructions, and guarantees that
 * the input is not empty.  It also allows the user to enter the name of
 * a file from which text will be read.
 **/
public static String getMultiLine(String prompt) {
  String text = "";
  for(;;) {  // We'll break out of this loop when we get non-empty input
    try {
      BufferedReader br = in;        // The stream to read from
      System.out.println(prompt);    // Display the prompt
      // Display some instructions
      System.out.println("You can enter multiple lines.  " +
                         "End with a '.' on a line by itself.\n" +
                         "Or enter a '<<' followed by a filename");
      // Make the prompt and instructions appear now.
      System.out.flush();
      // Read lines
      String line;
      while((line = br.readLine()) != null) {    // Until EOF
        if (line.equals(".")) break;             // Or until a dot by itself
        // Or, if a file is specified, start reading from it instead of
        // from the console.
        if (line.trim().startsWith("<<")) {
          String filename = line.trim().substring(2).trim();
          br = new BufferedReader(new FileReader(filename));
          continue;  // Don't count the << line as part of the input
        }
        else text += line + "\n";  // Add the line to the collected input
      }
      // If we got at least one line, return it.  Otherwise, chastise the
      // user and go back to the prompt and the instructions.
      if (text.length() > 0) return text;
      else System.out.println("Please enter at least one line.");
    }
    // If there were errors, for example an IO error reading a file,
    // display the error and loop again, displaying prompt and instructions
    catch(Exception e) { System.out.println(e); }
  }
}
}
```

Exercises

15–1. Modify the remote banking example in this chapter so that bank customers are allowed to borrow money from the bank against some maximum line of credit and can also apply money from their account to pay off their debt. Add borrow() and repay() methods to the RemoteBank interface, implement these methods in the server, and modify the client so that it can call these methods when the user requests them.

15-2. The *rmiregistry* program provides a simple name service for RMI programs—it allows servers to register names for the remote objects they
serve, and it allows clients to look up those remote objects by name.
Because it is a global registry, shared by any number of remote services,
there is a possibility of name collisions. For this reason, if a service needs to
define names for a number of remote objects, it should usually provide its
own custom registry. That way, a client can use the global registry to look
up the service's custom naming registry, and then it can use this custom
registry to look up particular named objects for that service.

Use RMI to write a server that provides such a custom naming service. It
should export remote methods that correspond to the bind(), rebind(),
unbind(), and lookup() methods of the Naming class. You will probably
want to use the java.util.Hashtable class to associate names with remote
objects.

15-3. The MUD example of this chapter uses remote objects to represent the
rooms or places in the MUD and the people interacting in the MUD. Things
that appear in the MUD, however, are not remote objects—they are simply
part of the state of each room in the MUD.

Modify the example so that things are true remote objects. Define a
MudThing interface that extends Remote. It should have a getDescription()
method that returns the description of a thing. Modify the MudPlace interface and RemoteMudPlace class to have methods that allow MudThing objects
to be added to and removed from a place.

Define a trivial implementation of MudThing that simply returns a static
string from its getDescription() method. Then, define another implementation of MudThing, named Clock. This class should have more dynamic
behavior: whenver its getDescription() method is called, it should return
a string that displays the current time. Modify the MUD server so that it
places a Clock object in the entrance to the MUD.

15-4. Modify the MUD example again so that MudPerson objects can pick up
MudThing objects they find in a MudPlace, carry them around, drop them in
other places, and give them to other people. Implement at least three new
methods: pickup(), drop(), and give(). Modify the MUD client so that it
supports pickup, drop, and give commands.

Remote Method Invocation

CHAPTER 16

Database Access
with SQL

This chapter provides examples of using Java Database Connectivity (JDBC)—also known as the `java.sql` package—to query and update databases. JDBC is an API that allows a Java program to communicate with a database server using SQL (Structured Query Language) commands. Note that JDBC is a SQL API, not an embedded SQL mechanism for Java.

The `java.sql` package provides a fairly straightforward mechanism for sending SQL queries to a database and for receiving query results. Thus, assuming that you already have experience working with databases and SQL, this chapter should be relatively easy to understand. On the other hand, if you have not worked with databases before, you'll need to learn basic SQL syntax and some general database programming concepts before you can really take advantage of the examples in this chapter, and JDBC in general. I'll try to explain some of the basic concepts as I go along, so that you can get a sense of what is possible with JDBC, but full coverage of database programming is beyond the scope of this chapter.

Furthermore, in order to run the examples in this chapter, you need access to a database and you have to obtain and install a JDBC driver for it.* You need to know how to create a database and otherwise administer the database server. If you are new to databases, figuring out how to do this can actually be more difficult than learning how to program with JDBC. You also need to know at least the basics of the SQL language. Your database documentation should include reference material for the version of SQL that your database supports.

---

*In addition to the commercial database systems available from various vendors, there are several free (or inexpensive) database products available on the Net, including PostgreSQL, MySQL, and msql. Unfortunately, these products are not as full-featured as their commercial cousins, and, more importantly, as of this writing their JDBC drivers are not fully functional or fully debugged.

Accessing a Database

Example 16-1 shows a program that connects to a database and then loops, prompting the user for a SQL statement, sending that statement to the database, and displaying the results. It demonstrates the four most important (JDBC)" techniques for JDBC programming: registering a database driver, using the `DriverManager` class to obtain a `Connection` object that represents a database connection, sending a SQL statement to the database using the `Statement` object, and retrieving the results of a query with a `ResultSet` object. Before we look at the specifics of the `ExecuteSQL` program, let's examine these basic techniques.

One of the interesting things about the `java.sql` package is that its most important members, such as `Connection`, `Statement`, and `ResultSet`, are interfaces instead of classes. The whole point of JDBC is to hide the specifics of accessing particular kinds of database systems and these interfaces make that possible. A JDBC driver is a set of classes that implement the interfaces for a particular database system; different database systems require different drivers. As an application programmer, you don't have to worry about the implementation of these underlying classes. All you have to worry about is writing code that uses the methods defined by the various interfaces.

The `DriverManager` class is responsible for keeping track of all the JDBC drivers that are available on a system. So, the first task of a JDBC program is to load an appropriate driver for the type of database being used. The `Class.forName()` method provides one way of doing this. This method takes a `String` argument that specifies a class name, so it is easy to pass the driver name to the program on the command line. When a driver class is loaded with `Class.forName()`, a static initializer of the driver takes care of registering the driver with the `DriverManager`. Note that this step simply loads a driver and registers it with the `DriverManager`; it does not specify that the program actually uses that driver. The driver selection step comes next, when the program actually connects to a database.

After the required driver is loaded (and has registered itself), a JDBC program can connect to the database by calling `DriverManager.getConnection()`. You specify the database to connect to with a *jdbc:* URL. This URL has the following general syntax:

```
jdbc:subprotocol://host:port/databasename
```

The *subprotocol* of the URL identifies the particular database system that is being used. The `DriverManager` class uses that part of the URL to select an appropriate JDBC driver from the list of drivers that have been registered. If the `DriverManager` cannot find a JDBC driver for the database, it throws a `SQLException`.

I used the free Postgres database while developing the examples in this chapter, so I had to use a URL like the following to connect to my database:

```
jdbc:postgres95:///apidb
```

Note that the *host* and *port* are omitted from this URL. By default, *host* is set to the current host if it is not specified. If *port* is not specified, it defaults to the default port for the database server being used. In this case, *port* is set to port 5432, which is the default port for the Postgres database server.

DriverManager.getConnection() returns an object that implements the Connection interface. This object represents the connection to the database; you use it to interact with the database. The createStatement() method of the Connection object creates an object that implements the Statement interface, which is what you use to send SQL queries and updates to the database. The executeQuery() and executeUpdate() methods of the Statement object send queries and updates, respectively, while the general-purpose execute() method sends a statement that can be either a query or an update.

After you have sent a query to the database, you use the getResultSet() method of Statement to retrieve an object that implements the ResultSet interface. This object represents the values returned by the SQL query; it is organized into columns and rows like a table. A ResultSet offers its data one row at a time; you use next() to move from the current row to the next row. ResultSet provides numerous getX() methods that allow you to retrieve the data from each column of the current row as a number of different types.

Now that you understand the basic techniques used in a JDBC program, let's get back to Example 16-1. The ExecuteSQL program uses all of the techniques we've just discussed to connect to a database, execute SQL statements, and display the results. The program parses its command-line arguments to determine the class name of the JDBC driver, the URL of the database, and other parameters necessary to connect to the database. For example, you might invoke the ExecuteSQL program and enter a simple query like this:

```
% java ExecuteSQL -d postgres95.PGDriver -u java -p nut jdbc:postgres95:///api
sql> SELECT * FROM package WHERE name LIKE '%.rmi%'
+----+--------------------------------+
| id |              name              |
+----+--------------------------------+
| 14 | java.rmi                       |
| 15 | java.rmi.dgc                   |
| 16 | java.rmi.registry              |
| 17 | java.rmi.server                |
+----+--------------------------------+
sql> quit
```

Notice that ExecuteSQL uses the execute() method of its Statement object to execute SQL statements. Since the user is allowed to enter any kind of SQL statement, we have to use this general-purpose method. If execute() returns true, the SQL statement was a query, so the program retrieves the ResultSet and displays the results of the query. Otherwise, the statement was an update, so the program simply outputs information about how many rows in the database were affected by the update.

The printResultsTable() method handles displaying the results of a query. This method gets a ResultSetMetaData object to find out some information about the data returned by the query, so it can format the results appropriately.

There are two other important JDBC programming techniques to note in Example 16-1. The first is the handling of SQLException exceptions that are thrown. The SQLException object supports the standard exception message with getMessage(), but it may also contain an additional message sent by the database server. You obtain this message by calling the getSQLState() method of the exception object.

The second technique is the handling of warnings. The SQLWarning class is a sub-class of SQLException, but warnings, unlike exceptions, are not thrown. When a SQL command is executed, any warnings reported by the server are stored in a linked-list of SQLWarning objects. You obtain the first SQLWarning object in this list by calling the getWarnings() method of the Connection object. If there are any additional SQLWarning objects, you get the next one by calling the getNext-Warning() method of the current SQLWarning object. In Example 16-1, these warnings are displayed using a finally clause, so that they appear both when an exception is thrown and when execution completes normally.

Example 16-1: ExecuteSQL.java

```java
import java.sql.*;
import java.io.*;

/**
 * A general-purpose SQL interpreter program.
 **/
public class ExecuteSQL {
  public static void main(String[] args) {
    Connection conn = null;  // Our JDBC connection to the database server
    try {
      String driver = null, url = null, user = "", password = "";

      // Parse all the command-line arguments
      for(int n = 0; n < args.length; n++) {
        if (args[n].equals("-d")) driver = args[++n];
        else if (args[n].equals("-u")) user = args[++n];
        else if (args[n].equals("-p")) password = args[++n];
        else if (url == null) url = args[n];
        else throw new IllegalArgumentException("Unknown argument.");
      }

      // The only required argument is the database URL.
      if (url == null)
        throw new IllegalArgumentException("No database specified");

      // If the user specified the classname for the DB driver, load
      // that class dynamically.  This gives the driver the opportunity
      // to register itself with the DriverManager.
      if (driver != null) Class.forName(driver);

      // Now open a connection the specified database, using the user-specified
      // username and password, if any.  The driver manager will try all of
      // the DB drivers it knows about to try to parse the URL and connect to
      // the DB server.
      conn = DriverManager.getConnection(url, user, password);

      // Now create the statement object we'll use to talk to the DB
      Statement s = conn.createStatement();

      // Get a stream to read from the console
      BufferedReader in = new BufferedReader(new InputStreamReader(System.in));

      // Loop forever, reading the user's queries and executing them
      while(true) {
        System.out.print("sql> ");       // prompt the user
        System.out.flush();              // make the prompt appear immediately
        String sql = in.readLine();      // get a line of input from the user
```

Example 16-1: ExecuteSQL.java (continued)

```
                // Quit when the user types "quit".
                if ((sql == null) || sql.equals("quit")) break;

                // Ignore blank lines
                if (sql.length() == 0) continue;

                // Now, attempt to execute the user's line of SQL and display results.
                try {
                  // We don't know if this is a query or some kind of update, so we
                  // use execute() instead of executeQuery() or executeUpdate()
                  // If the return value is true, it was a query, else an update
                  boolean status = s.execute(sql);
                  // Loop until there are no more results to return
                  do {
                    if (status) { // statement was a query that returns a ResultSet
                      // Get the set of results and display them
                      ResultSet rs = s.getResultSet();
                      printResultsTable(rs, System.out);
                    }
                    else {
                      // If the SQL command that was executed was some kind of update
                      // rather than a query, then it doesn't return a ResultSet.
                      // Instead, we just print the number of rows that were affected.
                      int numUpdates = s.getUpdateCount();
                      System.out.println("Ok. " + numUpdates + " rows affected.");
                    }
                    // Now go see if there are even more results, and
                    // continue the results display loop if there are.
                    status = s.getMoreResults();
                  // With some buggy JDBC drivers, this condition causes an infinite
                  // loop with SQL updates.  If that happens, change to:  while(status);
                  } while(status || s.getUpdateCount() != -1);
                }
                // If a SQLException is thrown, display an error message.  Note that
                // SQLExceptions can have a general message and a DB-specific message
                // returned by getSQLState()
                catch (SQLException e) {
                  System.err.println("SQLException: " + e.getMessage() + ":" +
                                     e.getSQLState());
                }
                // Each time through this loop, check to see if any warnings were
                // issued.  Note that there can be a whole chain of warnings.
                finally { // print out any warnings that occurred
                  for(SQLWarning w=conn.getWarnings(); w != null; w=w.getNextWarning())
                    System.err.println("WARNING: " + w.getMessage() +
                                       ":" + w.getSQLState());
                }
            }
        }
    // Handle exceptions that occur during argument parsing, database
    // connection setup, etc.  For SQLExceptions, print the details.
    catch (Exception e) {
      System.err.println(e);
      if (e instanceof SQLException)
        System.err.println("SQL State: " + ((SQLException)e).getSQLState());
      System.err.println("Usage: java ExecuteSQL [-d <driver>] [-u <user>] " +
                         "[-p <password>] <database URL>");
    }
```

Example 16-1: ExecuteSQL.java (continued)

```
      // Be sure to always close the database connection when we exit, whether
      // we exit because the user types 'quit' or because of an exception thrown
      // while setting things up.  Closing this connection also implicitly
      // closes any open statements and result sets associated with it.
      finally {
        try { conn.close(); } catch (Exception e) {}
      }
    }


    /**
     * This method attempts to output the contents of a ResultSet in a
     * textual table.  It relies on the ResultSetMetaData class, but a fair
     * bit of the code is simple string manipulation.
     **/
    static void printResultsTable(ResultSet rs, OutputStream output)
        throws SQLException {
      // Set up the output stream
      PrintWriter out = new PrintWriter(new OutputStreamWriter(output));

      // Get some "meta data" (column names, etc.) about the results
      ResultSetMetaData metadata = rs.getMetaData();

      // Variables to hold important data about the table to be displayed
      int numcols = metadata.getColumnCount();// how many columns
      String[] labels = new String[numcols];  // the column labels
      int[] colwidths = new int[numcols];      // the width of each
      int[] colpos = new int[numcols];         // start position of each
      int linewidth;                           // total width of table

      // Figure out how wide the columns are, where each one begins,
      // how wide each row of the table will be, etc.
      linewidth = 1; // for the initial '|'.
      for(int i = 0; i < numcols; i++) {       // for each column
        colpos[i] = linewidth;                 // save its position
        labels[i] = metadata.getColumnLabel(i+1); // get its label
        // Get the column width.  If the db doesn't report one, guess
        // 30 characters.  Then check the length of the label, and use
        // it if it is larger than the column width
        int size =  metadata.getColumnDisplaySize(i+1);
        if (size == -1) size = 30;             // some drivers return -1...
        int labelsize = labels[i].length();
        if (labelsize > size) size = labelsize;
        colwidths[i] = size + 1;               // save the column the size
        linewidth += colwidths[i] + 2;         // increment total size
      }

      // Create a horizontal divider line we use in the table.
      // Also create a blank line that is the initial value of each
      // line of the table
      StringBuffer divider = new StringBuffer(linewidth);
      StringBuffer blankline = new StringBuffer(linewidth);
      for(int i = 0; i < linewidth; i++) {
        divider.insert(i, '-');
        blankline.insert(i, " ");
      }
      // Put special marks in the divider line at the column positions
      for(int i=0; i<numcols; i++) divider.setCharAt(colpos[i]-1,'+');
      divider.setCharAt(linewidth-1, '+');
```

Example 16-1: ExecuteSQL.java (continued)

```java
// Begin the table output with a divider line
out.println(divider);

// The next line of the table contains the column labels.
// Begin with a blank line, and put the column names and column
// divider characters "|" into it.  overwrite() is defined below.
StringBuffer line = new StringBuffer(blankline.toString());
line.setCharAt(0, '|');
for(int i = 0; i < numcols; i++) {
  int pos = colpos[i] + 1 + (colwidths[i]-labels[i].length())/2;
  overwrite(line, pos, labels[i]);
  overwrite(line, colpos[i] + colwidths[i], " |");
}

// Then output the line of column labels and another divider
out.println(line);
out.println(divider);

// Now, output the table data.  Loop through the ResultSet, using
// the next() method to get the rows one at a time. Obtain the
// value of each column with getObject(), and output it, much as
// we did for the column labels above.
while(rs.next()) {
  line = new StringBuffer(blankline.toString());
  line.setCharAt(0, '|');
  for(int i = 0; i < numcols; i++) {
    Object value = rs.getObject(i+1);
    if (value != null)
      overwrite(line, colpos[i] + 1, value.toString().trim());
    overwrite(line, colpos[i] + colwidths[i], " |");
  }
  out.println(line);
}
// Finally, end the table with one last divider line.
out.println(divider);
out.flush();
}

/** This utility method is used when printing the table of results */
static void overwrite(StringBuffer b, int pos, String s) {
  int len = s.length();
  for(int i = 0; i < len; i++) b.setCharAt(pos+i, s.charAt(i));
}
}
```

Using Database Metadata

Sometimes, in addition to querying and updating the data in a database, you also want to retrieve information about the database itself and its contents. This information is called "metadata." The DatabaseMetaData interface allows you to do retrieve this kind of information. You can obtain an object that implements this interface by calling the getMetaData() method of the Connection object, as shown in Example 16-2.

After GetDBInfo opens a database Connection and obtains a DatabaseMetaData object, it displays some general information about the database server and JDBC driver. Then, if the user just specified a database name on the command line, the program lists all of the tables in that database. If the user specified a database name and a table name, however, the program lists the name and data type of each column in that table.

An interesting feature of this GetDBInfo program is how it obtains the parameters needed to connect to the database. The example operates on the premise that at any given site, it is typically used to connect to the same database server, using the same database driver, and may also be used with the same database user name and password. So, instead of requiring the user to type all this cumbersome information on the command line each time the program is run, the program reads default values from a file named *DB.props* that is stored in the same directory as the *GetDBInfo.class* file. In order to run Example 16-2, you have to create an appropriate *DB.props* file for your system. On my system, this file contains:

```
# The name of the JDBC driver class
driver=postgres95.PGDriver
# The URL that specifies the database server.
# It should not include the name of the database to connect to
server=jdbc:postgres95:///
# The database account name
user=david
# The password for the specified account.  Not specified here
# Uncomment the line below to specify a password
#password=
```

Lines that begin with # are comments, obviously. The *name=value* format is the standard file format for the java.util.Properties object that is used to read the contents of this file.

After the program reads the default values from the *DB.props* file, it parses its command line arguments, which can override the driver, server, user, and password properties specified in the file. The name of the database to connect to must be specified on the command line; the database name is simply appended to the server URL. The name of a table in the database can optionally be specified on the command line. For example, you might run the program as follows:

```
% java GetDBInfo api class
DBMS: Postgres95 1.0
JDBC Driver: PGDriver 1.1
Database: jdbc:postgres95://:5432/api
User: david
Columns of class:
        id : int2
        packageid : int2
        name : varchar
```

Example 16-2: GetDBInfo.java

```
import java.sql.*;
import java.util.Properties;

/**
 * This class uses the DatabaseMetaData class to obtain information about
 * the database, the JDBC driver, and the tables in the database, or about
 * the columns of a named table.
 **/
```

Example 16-2: GetDBInfo.java (continued)

```
public class GetDBInfo {
    public static void main(String[] args) {
        Connection c = null;  // The JDBC connection to the database server
        try {
            // Look for the properties file DB.props in the same directory as
            // this program.  It will contain default values for the various
            // parameters needed to connect to a database
            Properties p = new Properties();
            try { p.load(GetDBInfo.class.getResourceAsStream("DB.props")); }
            catch (Exception e) {}

            // Get default values from the properties file
            String driver = p.getProperty("driver");        // Name of driver class
            String server = p.getProperty("server", "");     // JDBC URL for server
            String user = p.getProperty("user", "");         // db user name
            String password = p.getProperty("password", ""); // db account password

            // These variables don't have defaults
            String database = null;  // The db name (to be appended to server URL)
            String table = null;     // The optional name of a table in the db

            // Parse the command-line arguments to override the default values above
            for(int i = 0; i < args.length; i++) {
                if (args[i].equals("-d")) driver = args[++i];      // -d <driver>
                else if (args[i].equals("-s")) server = args[++i]; // -s <server>
                else if (args[i].equals("-u")) user = args[++i];   // -u <user>
                else if (args[i].equals("-p")) password = args[++i]; // -p <password>
                else if (database == null) database = args[i];     // <dbname>
                else if (table == null) table = args[i];           // <tablename>
                else throw new IllegalArgumentException("Unknown argument: "+args[i]);
            }

            // Make sure that at least a server or a database were specified.
            // If not, we have no idea what to connect to, and cannot continue.
            if ((server.length() == 0) && (database.length() == 0))
                throw new IllegalArgumentException("No database or server specified.");

            // Load the db driver, if any was specified.
            if (driver != null) Class.forName(driver);

            // Now attempt to open a connection to the specified database on
            // the specified server, using the specified name and password
            c = DriverManager.getConnection(server+database, user, password);

            // Get the DatabaseMetaData object for the connection.  This is the
            // object that will return us all the data we're interested in here.
            DatabaseMetaData md = c.getMetaData();

            // Display information about the server, the driver, etc.
            System.out.println("DBMS: " + md.getDatabaseProductName() +
                               " " + md.getDatabaseProductVersion());
            System.out.println("JDBC Driver: " + md.getDriverName() +
                               " " + md.getDriverVersion());
            System.out.println("Database: " + md.getURL());
            System.out.println("User: " + md.getUserName());

            // Now, if the user did not specify a table, then display a list of
            // all tables defined in the named database.  Note that tables are
```

Example 16-2: GetDBInfo.java (continued)

```
            // returned in a ResultSet, just like query results are.
            if (table == null) {
              System.out.println("Tables:");
              ResultSet r = md.getTables("", "", "%", null);
              while(r.next()) System.out.println("\t" + r.getString(3));
            }
            // Otherwise, list all columns of the specified table.
            // Again, information about the columns is returned in a ResultSet
            else {
              System.out.println("Columns of " + table + ": ");
              ResultSet r = md.getColumns("", "", table, "%");
              while(r.next())
                System.out.println("\t" + r.getString(4) + " : " + r.getString(6));
            }
          }
          // Print an error message if anything goes wrong.
          catch (Exception e) {
            System.err.println(e);
            if (e instanceof SQLException)
              System.err.println(((SQLException)e).getSQLState());
            System.err.println("Usage: java GetDBInfo [-d <driver] [-s <dbserver>]\n"
                             + "\t[-u <username>] [-p <password>] <dbname>");
          }
          // Always remember to close the Connection object when we're done!
          finally {
            try { c.close(); } catch (Exception e) {}
          }
        }
      }
    }
```

Building a Database

Example 16-3 shows a program, MakeAPIDB, that takes a list of class names and uses the Java Reflection API to build a database of those classes, the packages that they belong to, and all of the methods and fields defined by the classes. Example 16-4 shows a program that makes use of the database created by this example.

MakeAPIDB uses the SQL CREATE TABLE statement to add three tables, named package, class, and member, to the database. The program then inserts data into those tables using INSERT INTO statements. The program uses the same INSERT INTO statements repeatedly, as it iterates though the list of class names. In this type of situation, you can often increase the efficiency of your insertions if you use PreparedStatement objects to execute the statements.

A prepared statement is essentially a blueprint for the statements you need to execute. When you send a SQL statement to the database, the database interprets the SQL and creates a template for executing the statement. If you are sending the same SQL statement repeatedly, only with different input parameters, the database still has to interpret the SQL each time. On database platforms that support prepared statements, you can eliminate this inefficiency by sending a prepared statement to the database before you actually make any calls to the database. The database interprets the prepared statement and creates its template just once. Then, when you execute the prepared statement repeatedly with different input parameters, the database uses the template it has already created. JDBC provides the PreparedStatement class to support prepared statements, but it does not guarantee that the underlying database actually takes advantage of them.

You create a PreparedStatement with the prepareStatement() method of a Connection object, as shown in Example 16-3. MakeAPIDB passes a SQL statement to prepareStatement(), substituting ? placeholders for the variable parameters in the statement. Later, before the program executes the prepared statement, it binds values to these parameters using the various setX() methods (e.g., setInt() and setString()) of the PreparedStatement object. Each setX() method takes two arguments: a parameter index (starting with 1) and a value. Then the program calls the executeUpdate() method of the PreparedStatement to execute the statement. (PreparedStatement also provides execute() and executeQuery() methods, just like Statement.)

MakeAPIDB expects its first argument to be the name of a file that contains a list of classes to be placed into the database. The classes should be listed one to a line; each line must contain a fully-qualified class name (i.e., it must specify both package name and class name). Such a file might contain lines like the following:

```
java.applet.Applet
java.applet.AppletContext
java.applet.AppletStub
        ...
java.util.zip.ZipOutputStream
```

The program reads database parameters from a Properties file named *APIDB.props* in the current directory, or from an alternate Properties file specified as the second command-line argument. This Properties file is similar to, but not quite the same as, the one used in conjunction with Example 16-2; it should contain properties named driver, database, user, and password. On my system, the *APIDB.props* file looks as follows:

```
# The full classname of the JDBC driver to load
driver=postgres95.PGDriver
# The URL of the server and database to connect to
database=jdbc:postgres95:///APIDB
# The name of the database user account
user=david
# The password for the database user account.
# Uncomment the line below to specify a password
#password=
```

Note that before you run this program, you must create the database for it on your database server. To do this, you'll have to follow the instructions provided by your database vendor.

Example 16-3: MakeAPIDB.java

```
import java.sql.*;
import java.lang.reflect.*;
import java.io.*;
import java.util.*;

/**
 * This class is a standalone program that reads a list of classes and
```

Example 16–3: MakeAPIDB.java (continued)

```
 * builds a database of packages, classes, and class fields and methods.
 **/
public class MakeAPIDB {
  public static void main(String args[]) {
    Connection c = null;        // The connection to the database
    try {
      // Read the names of classes to index from a file specified by args[0]
      Vector classnames = new Vector();
      BufferedReader in = new BufferedReader(new FileReader(args[0]));
      String name;
      while((name = in.readLine()) != null) classnames.addElement(name);

      // Now determine the values needed to set up the database connection
      // The program attempts to read a property file named "APIDB.props",
      // or optionally specified by args[1]. This property file (if any)
      // may contain "driver", "database", "user", and "password" properties
      // that specify the necessary values for connecting to the db.
      // If the properties file does not exist, or does not contain the named
      // properties, defaults will be used.
      Properties p = new Properties();              // Empty properties
      try { p.load(new FileInputStream(args[1])); } // Try to load properties
      catch (Exception e1) {
        try { p.load(new FileInputStream("APIDB.props")); }
        catch (Exception e2) {}
      }

      // Read values from Properties file, using the specified defaults if
      // they are not found.  These defaults will probably not work for you!
      String driver = p.getProperty("driver", "postgres95.PGDriver");
      String database = p.getProperty("database","jdbc:postgres95:///APIDB");
      String user = p.getProperty("user", "");
      String password = p.getProperty("password", "");

      // Load the database driver
      Class.forName(driver);

      // And set up a connection to the specified database
      c = DriverManager.getConnection(database, user, password);

      // Create three new tables for our data
      // The package table contains a package id and a package name
      // The class table contains a class id, a package id, and a class name
      // The member table contains a class id, a member name, and an int
      // that indicates whether the class member is a field or a method.
      Statement s = c.createStatement();
      s.executeUpdate("CREATE TABLE package " +
                      "(id SMALLINT, name VARCHAR(80))");
      s.executeUpdate("CREATE TABLE class " +
                      "(id SMALLINT, packageId SMALLINT, name VARCHAR(48))");
      s.executeUpdate("CREATE TABLE member " +
                      "(classId SMALLINT,name VARCHAR(48),isField SMALLINT)");

      // Prepare some statements that will be used to insert records into
      // these three tables.
      insertpackage = c.prepareStatement("INSERT INTO package VALUES(?,?)");
      insertclass = c.prepareStatement("INSERT INTO class VALUES(?,?,?)");
      insertmember = c.prepareStatement("INSERT INTO member VALUES(?,?,?)");
```

Example 16-3: MakeAPIDB.java (continued)

```java
    // Now loop through the list of classes and store them all in the tables
    for(int i = 0; i < classnames.size(); i++)
      storeClass((String)classnames.elementAt(i));
  }
  catch (Exception e) {
    System.err.println(e);
    if (e instanceof SQLException)
      System.err.println("SQLState: " + ((SQLException)e).getSQLState());
    System.err.println("Usage: java MakeAPIDB <classlistfile> <propfile>");
  }
  // When we're done, close the connection to the database
  finally { try { c.close(); } catch (Exception e) {} }
}

/**
 * This hash table records the mapping between package names and package
 * id.  This is the only one we need to store temporarily.  The others are
 * stored in the db and don't have to be looked up by this program
 **/
static Hashtable package_to_id = new Hashtable();

// Counters for the package and class identifier columns
static int packageId = 0, classId = 0;

// Some prepared SQL statements for use in inserting
// new values into the tables.  Initialized in main() above.
static PreparedStatement insertpackage, insertclass, insertmember;

/**
 * Given a fully-qualified classname, this method stores the package name
 * in the package table (if it is not already there), stores the class name
 * in the class table, and then uses the Java Reflection API to look up all
 * methods and fields of the class, and stores those in the member table.
 **/
public static void storeClass(String name)
    throws SQLException, ClassNotFoundException {
  String packagename, classname;

  // Dynamically load the class.
  Class c = Class.forName(name);

  // Display output so the user knows that the program is progressing
  System.out.println("Storing data for: " + name);

  // Figure out the packagename and the classname
  int pos = name.lastIndexOf('.');
  if (pos == -1) {
    packagename = "";
    classname = name;
  }
  else {
    packagename = name.substring(0,pos);
    classname = name.substring(pos+1);
  }

  // Figure out what the package id is.  If there is one, then this package
  // has already been stored in the database.  Otherwise, assign an id,
  // and store it and the packagename in the db.
```

Example 16–3: MakeAPIDB.java (continued)

```
Integer pid;
pid = (Integer)package_to_id.get(packagename);  // Check hashtable
if (pid == null) {
  pid = new Integer(++packageId);               // Assign an id
  package_to_id.put(packagename, pid);          // Remember it in the hashtable
  insertpackage.setInt(1,packageId);            // Set args to PreparedStatement
  insertpackage.setString(2,packagename);
  insertpackage.executeUpdate();                // Insert the package into db
}

// Now, store the classname in the class table of the database.
// This record includes the package id, so that the class is linked to
// the package that contains it.  To store the class, we set arguments
// to the PreparedStatement, then execute that statement
insertclass.setInt(1, ++classId);           // Set class identifier
insertclass.setInt(2, pid.intValue());      // Set package identifier
insertclass.setString(3, classname);        // Set class name
insertclass.executeUpdate();                // Insert the class record

// Now, get a list of all non-private methods of the class, and
// insert those into the "members" table of the database.  Each
// record includes the class id of the containing class, and also
// a value that indicates that these are methods, not fields.
Method[] methods = c.getDeclaredMethods();           // Get a list of methods
for(int i = 0; i < methods.length; i++) {            // For all non-private
  if (Modifier.isPrivate(methods[i].getModifiers())) continue;
  insertmember.setInt(1, classId);                   // Set the class id
  insertmember.setString(2, methods[i].getName()); // Set the method name
  insertmember.setInt(3, 0);                         // It is not a field
  insertmember.executeUpdate();                      // Insert the record
}

// Do the same thing for the non-private fields of the class
Field[] fields = c.getDeclaredFields();            // Get a list of fields
for(int i = 0; i < fields.length; i++) {           // For each non-private
  if (Modifier.isPrivate(fields[i].getModifiers())) continue;
  insertmember.setInt(1, classId);                 // Set the class id
  insertmember.setString(2, fields[i].getName());  // Set the field name
  insertmember.setInt(3, 1);                       // It is a field
  insertmember.executeUpdate();                    // Insert the record
}
  }
}
```

Database Access with SQL

Using the API Database

Example 16-4 displays a program, LookupAPI, that makes use of the database built by the MakeAPIDB program of Example 16-3. LookupAPI behaves as follows:

- When invoked with the name of a class member, it lists the full name (including package and class) of each field and/or method that has that name.

- When run with the name of a class, it lists the full name of every class in any package that has that name.

- When called with a portion of a package name, it lists the names of all the packages that contain that string.

- When invoked with the -l option and a class name, it lists every member of every class that has that name.

- When run with the -l option and a portion of a package name, it lists all of the classes and interfaces in any package that matches that string.

LookupAPI reads the same *APIDB.props* property file that MakeAPIDB does. Or, alternatively, it reads a property file specified on the command line following a -p flag. Using the database connection parameters in the property file, the program connects to a database and executes the necessary SQL queries to return the desired information. Note that it calls the setReadOnly() method of the Connection object. Doing this provides a hint that the program only performs queries and does not modify the database in any way. For some database systems, this may improve efficiency. Other than the setReadOnly() method, this example does not introduce any new JDBC features. It simply serves as a real-world application of a database and demonstrates some of the powerful database queries that can be expressed using SQL.

Example 16-4: LookupAPI.java

```java
import java.sql.*;
import java.io.FileInputStream;
import java.util.Properties;

/**
 * This program uses the database created by MakeAPIDB.  It opens a connection
 * to a database using the same property file used by MakeAPIDB.  Then it
 * queries that database in several interesting ways to obtain useful
 * information about Java APIs.  It can be used to look up the fully-qualified
 * name of a member, class, or package, or it can be used to list the members
 * of a class or package.
 **/
public class LookupAPI {
  public static void main(String[] args) {
    Connection c = null;                // JDBC connection to the database
    try {
      // Some default values
      String target = null;             // The name to look up
      boolean list = false;             // List members or lookup name?
      String propfile = "APIDB.props";  // The properties file of db parameters

      // Parse the command-line arguments
      for(int i = 0; i < args.length; i++) {
        if (args[i].equals("-l")) list = true;
        else if (args[i].equals("-p")) propfile = args[++i];
        else if (target != null)
          throw new IllegalArgumentException("Unexpected argument: " +args[i]);
        else target = args[i];
      }
      if (target == null)
        throw new IllegalArgumentException("No target specified");

      // Now determine the values needed to set up the database connection
      // The program attempts to read a property file named "APIDB.props",
      // or optionally specified with the -p argument.  This property file
```

Example 16-4: LookupAPI.java (continued)

```
        // may contain "driver", "database", "user", and "password" properties
        // that specify the necessary values for connecting to the db.
        // If the properties file does not exist, or does not contain the named
        // properties, defaults will be used.
        Properties p = new Properties();              // Empty properties
        try { p.load(new FileInputStream(propfile)); } // Try to load props
        catch (Exception e) {}

        // Read values from Properties file, using defaults if not found.
        // These defaults will probably not work for you!
        String driver = p.getProperty("driver", "postgres95.PGDriver");
        String database = p.getProperty("database","jdbc:postgres95:///APIDB");
        String user = p.getProperty("user", "");
        String password = p.getProperty("password", "");

        // Load the database driver
        Class.forName(driver);

        // And set up a connection to the specified database
        c = DriverManager.getConnection(database, user, password);

        // Tell it we will not do any updates.  This hint may improve efficiency.
        c.setReadOnly(true);

        // If the "-l" option was given, then list the members of the named
        // package or class.  Otherwise, lookup all matches for the specified
        // member, class, or package.
        if (list) list(c, target);
        else lookup(c, target);
    }
    // If anything goes wrong, print the exception and a usage message.  If
    // a SQLException is thrown, display the extra state message it includes.
    catch (Exception e) {
      System.out.println(e);
      if (e instanceof SQLException)
        System.out.println(((SQLException) e).getSQLState());
      System.out.println("Usage: java LookupAPI [-l] [-p <propfile>] target");
    }
    // Always close the DB connection when we're done with it.
    finally {
      try { c.close(); } catch (Exception e) {}
    }
  }

  /**
   * This method looks up all matches for the specified target string in the
   * database.  First, it prints the full name of any members by that name.
   * Then it prints the full name of any classes by that name.  Then it prints
   * the name of any packages that contain the specified name
   **/
  public static void lookup(Connection c, String target) throws SQLException {
    // Create the Statement object we'll use to query the database
    Statement s = c.createStatement();

    // Go find all class members with the specified name
    s.executeQuery("SELECT DISTINCT " +
                "package.name, class.name, member.name, member.isField " +
                "FROM package, class, member " +
```

Example 16–4: LookupAPI.java (continued)

```
                    "WHERE member.name='" + target + "' " +
                    "   AND member.classId=class.id " +
                    "   AND class.packageId=package.id");

    // Loop through the results, and print them out (if there are any).
    ResultSet r = s.getResultSet();
    while(r.next()) {
      String pkg = r.getString(1);      // package name
      String cls = r.getString(2);      // class name
      String member = r.getString(3);   // member name
      int isField = r.getInt(4);                // is the member a field?
      // Display this match
      System.out.println(pkg + "." + cls + "." + member +
                         ((isField==1)?"":"()"));
    }

    // Now look for a class with the specified name
    s.executeQuery("SELECT package.name, class.name " +
                   "FROM package, class " +
                   "WHERE class.name='" + target + "' " +
                   "   AND class.packageId=package.id");
    // Loop through the results and print them out
    r = s.getResultSet();
    while(r.next()) System.out.println(r.getString(1) + "." +
                                       r.getString(2));

    // Finally, look for a package that matches a part of of the name.
    // Note the use of the SQL LIKE keyword and % wildcard characters
    s.executeQuery("SELECT name FROM package " +
                   "WHERE name LIKE '%." + target + ".%' " +
                   "   OR name LIKE '" + target + ".%' " +
                   "   OR name LIKE '%." + target + "'");
    // Loop through the results and print them out
    r = s.getResultSet();
    while(r.next()) System.out.println(r.getString(1));

    // Finally, close the Statement object
    s.close();
  }

  /**
   * This method looks for classes with the specified name, or packages
   * that contain the specified name.  For each class it finds, it displays
   * all methods and fields of the class.  For each package it finds, it
   * displays all classes in the package.
   **/
  public static void list(Connection conn, String target) throws SQLException {
    // Create two Statement objects to query the database with
    Statement s = conn.createStatement();
    Statement t = conn.createStatement();

    // Look for a class with the given name
    s.executeQuery("SELECT package.name, class.name " +
                   "FROM package, class " +
                   "WHERE class.name='" + target + "' " +
                   "   AND class.packageId=package.id");
```

Example 16-4: LookupAPI.java (continued)

```
    // Loop through all matches
    ResultSet r = s.getResultSet();
    while(r.next()) {
      String p = r.getString(1);  // package name
      String c = r.getString(2);  // class name
      // Print out the matching class name
      System.out.println("class " + p + "." + c + " {");

      // Now query all members of the class
      t.executeQuery("SELECT DISTINCT member.name, member.isField " +
                     "FROM package, class, member " +
                     "WHERE package.name = '" + p + "' " +
                     "  AND class.name = '" + c + "' " +
                     "  AND member.classId=class.id " +
                     "  AND class.packageId=package.id " +
                     "ORDER BY member.isField, member.name");

      // Loop through the ordered list of all members, and print them out
      ResultSet r2 = t.getResultSet();
      while(r2.next()) {
        String m = r2.getString(1);
        int isField = r2.getInt(2);
        System.out.println("  " + m + ((isField == 1)?"":"()"));
      }
      // End the class listing
      System.out.println("}");
    }

    // Now go look for a package that matches the specified name
    s.executeQuery("SELECT name FROM package " +
                   "WHERE name LIKE '%." + target + ".%' " +
                   "  OR name LIKE '" + target + ".%' " +
                   "  OR name LIKE '%." + target + "'");
    // Loop through any matching packages
    r = s.getResultSet();
    while(r.next()) {
      // Display the name of the package
      String p = r.getString(1);
      System.out.println("Package " + p + ": ");

      // Get a list of all classes and interfaces in the package
      t.executeQuery("SELECT class.name FROM package, class " +
                     "WHERE package.name='" + p + "' " +
                     "  AND class.packageId=package.id " +
                     "ORDER BY class.name");
      // Loop through the list and print them out.
      ResultSet r2 = t.getResultSet();
      while(r2.next()) System.out.println("  " + r2.getString(1));
    }

    // Finally, close both Statement objects
    s.close(); t.close();
  }
}
```

Atomic Transactions

By default, a newly-created database Connection object is in "auto commit" mode. That means that each update to the database is treated as a separate transaction and is automatically committed to the database. Sometimes, however, you want to be able to group several updates into a single "atomic" transaction, with the property that either all of the updates complete successfully or no updates occur at all. With a database system (and JDBC driver) that supports it, you can take the Connection out of "auto commit" mode and explicitly call commit() to commit a batch of transactions or call rollback() to abort a batch of transactions, undoing the ones that have already been done.

Example 16-5 displays a class that uses atomic transactions to ensure database consistency. The example is an implementation of the RemoteBank interface that was developed in Chapter 15, *Remote Method Invocation*. As you may recall, the RemoteBankServer class developed in Chapter 15 did not provide any form of persistent storage for its bank account data. Example 16-5 addresses this problem by implementing a RemoteBank that uses a database to store all user account information.

After the RemoteDBBankServer creates its Connection object, it calls setAutoCommit() with the argument false to turn off "auto commit" mode. Then, for example, the openAccount() method groups three transactions into a single, atomic transaction: adding the account to the database, creating a table for the account history, and adding an initial entry into the history. If all three of these transactions are successful (i.e., they don't throw any exceptions), openAccount() calls commit() to commit the transactions to the database. However, if any one of the transactions throws an exception, the catch clause takes care of calling rollback() to rollback any of the transactions that succeeded. All remote methods in RemoteDBBankServer use this technique to keep the account database consistent.

In addition to demonstrating the techniques of atomic transaction processing, the RemoteDBBankServer class provides further examples of using SQL queries to interact with a database.

Example 16–5: RemoteDBBankServer.java

```
import java.rmi.*;
import java.rmi.server.*;
import java.rmi.registry.*;
import java.sql.*;
import java.io.*;
import java.util.*;
import java.util.Date; // import explicitly to disambiguate from java.sql.Date
import Bank.*;

/**
 * This class is another implementation of the RemoteBank interface.
 * It uses a database connection as its back end, so that client data isn't
 * lost if the server goes down.  Note that it takes the database connection
 * out of "auto commit" mode and explicitly calls commit() and rollback() to
 * ensure that updates happen atomically.
 **/
public class RemoteDBBankServer extends UnicastRemoteObject
                                implements RemoteBank {
```

Example 16-5: RemoteDBBankServer.java (continued)

```
Connection db;   // The connection to the database that stores account info

/** The constructor.  Just save the database connection object away */
public RemoteDBBankServer(Connection db) throws RemoteException {
  this.db = db;
}

/** Open an account */
public synchronized void openAccount(String name, String password)
    throws RemoteException, BankingException {
  // First, check if there is already an account with that name
  Statement s = null;
  try {
    s = db.createStatement();
    s.executeQuery("SELECT * FROM accounts WHERE name='" + name + "'");
    ResultSet r = s.getResultSet();
    if (r.next()) throw new BankingException("Account already exists.");

    // If it doesn't exist, go ahead and create it
    // Also, create a table for the transaction history of this account and
    // insert an initial transaction into it.
    s = db.createStatement();
    s.executeUpdate("INSERT INTO accounts VALUES ('" + name + "', '" +
                    password + "', 0)");
    s.executeUpdate("CREATE TABLE " + name +
                    "_history (msg VARCHAR(80))");
    s.executeUpdate("INSERT INTO " + name + "_history " +
                    "VALUES ('Account opened at " + new Date() + "')");

    // And if we've been successful so far, commit these updates,
    // ending the atomic transaction.  All the methods below also use this
    // atomic transaction commit/rollback scheme
    db.commit();
  }
  catch(SQLException e) {
    // If an exception was thrown, "rollback" the prior updates,
    // removing them from the database.  This also ends the atomic
    // transaction.
    try { db.rollback(); } catch (Exception e2) {}
    // Pass the SQLException on in the body of a BankingException
    throw new BankingException("SQLException: " + e.getMessage() +
                               ": " + e.getSQLState());
  }
  // No matter what happens, don't forget to close the DB Statement
  finally { try { s.close(); } catch (Exception e) {} }
}

/**
 * This convenience method checks whether the name and password match
 * an existing account.  If so, it returns the balance in that account.
 * If not, it throws an exception.  Note that this method does not call
 * commit() or rollback(), so its query is part of a larger transaction.
 **/
public int verify(String name, String password)
    throws BankingException, SQLException {
  Statement s = null;
  try {
    s = db.createStatement();
```

Example 16–5: RemoteDBBankServer.java (continued)

```
      s.executeQuery("SELECT balance FROM accounts " +
                     "WHERE name='" + name + "' " +
                     " AND password = '" + password + "'");
    ResultSet r = s.getResultSet();
    if (!r.next())
      throw new BankingException("No such account or invalid password");
    return r.getInt(1);
  }
  finally { try { s.close(); } catch (Exception e) {} }
}

/** Close a named account */
public synchronized FunnyMoney closeAccount(String name, String password)
    throws RemoteException, BankingException {
  int balance = 0;
  Statement s = null;
  try {
    balance = verify(name, password);
    s = db.createStatement();
    // Delete the account from the accounts table
    s.executeUpdate("DELETE FROM accounts " +
                    "WHERE name = '" + name + "' " +
                    " AND password = '" + password + "'");
    // And drop the transaction history table for this account
    s.executeUpdate("DROP TABLE " + name + "_history");
    db.commit();
  }
  catch (SQLException e) {
    try { db.rollback(); } catch (Exception e2) {}
    throw new BankingException("SQLException: " + e.getMessage() +
                               ": " + e.getSQLState());
  }
  finally { try { s.close(); } catch (Exception e) {} }

  // Finally, return whatever balance remained in the account
  return new FunnyMoney(balance);
}

/** Deposit the specified money into the named account */
public synchronized void deposit(String name, String password,
                                 FunnyMoney money)
    throws RemoteException, BankingException {
  int balance = 0;
  Statement s = null;
  try {
    balance = verify(name, password);
    s = db.createStatement();
    // Update the balance
    s.executeUpdate("UPDATE accounts " +
                    "SET balance = " + balance + money.amount + " " +
                    "WHERE name='" + name + "' " +
                    " AND password = '" + password + "'");
    // Add a row to the transaction history
    s.executeUpdate("INSERT INTO " + name + "_history " +
                    "VALUES ('Deposited " + money.amount +
                    " at " + new Date() + "')");
    db.commit();
  }
```

Example 16-5: RemoteDBBankServer.java (continued)

```
      catch (SQLException e) {
        try { db.rollback(); } catch (Exception e2) {}
        throw new BankingException("SQLException: " + e.getMessage() +
                                   ": " + e.getSQLState());
      }
      finally { try { s.close(); } catch (Exception e) {} }
  }

  /** Withdraw the specified amount from the named account */
  public synchronized FunnyMoney withdraw(String name, String password,
                                          int amount)
       throws RemoteException, BankingException {
    int balance = 0;
    Statement s = null;
    try {
      balance = verify(name, password);
      if (balance < amount) throw new BankingException("Insufficient Funds");
      s = db.createStatement();
      // Update the account balance
      s.executeUpdate("UPDATE accounts " +
                      "SET balance = " + (balance - amount) + " " +
                      "WHERE name='" + name + "' " +
                      "  AND password = '" + password + "'");
      // Add a row to the transaction history
      s.executeUpdate("INSERT INTO " + name + "_history " +
                      "VALUES ('Withdrew " + amount +
                      " at " + new Date() + "')");
      db.commit();
    }
    catch (SQLException e) {
      try { db.rollback(); } catch (Exception e2) {}
      throw new BankingException("SQLException: " + e.getMessage() +
                                 ": " + e.getSQLState());
    }
    finally { try { s.close(); } catch (Exception e) {} }

    return new FunnyMoney(amount);
  }

  /** Return the balance of the specified account */
  public synchronized int getBalance(String name, String password)
       throws RemoteException, BankingException {
    int balance;
    try {
      // Get the balance
      balance = verify(name, password);
      // Commit the transaction
      db.commit();
    }
    catch (SQLException e) {
      try { db.rollback(); } catch (Exception e2) {}
      throw new BankingException("SQLException: " + e.getMessage() +
                                 ": " + e.getSQLState());
    }
    // Return the balance
    return balance;
  }
```

Example 16–5: RemoteDBBankServer.java (continued)

```
/** Get the transaction history of the named account */
public synchronized Vector getTransactionHistory(String name,
                                                 String password)
      throws RemoteException, BankingException {
  Statement s = null;
  Vector v = new Vector();
  try {
    // Call verify to check the password, even though we don't
    // care what the current balance is.
    verify(name, password);
    s = db.createStatement();
    // Request everything out of the history table
    s.executeQuery("SELECT * from " + name + "_history");
    // Get the results of the query and put them in a Vector
    ResultSet r = s.getResultSet();
    while(r.next()) v.addElement(r.getString(1));
    // Commit the transaction
    db.commit();
  }
  catch (SQLException e) {
    try { db.rollback(); } catch (Exception e2) {}
    throw new BankingException("SQLException: " + e.getMessage() +
                              ": " + e.getSQLState());
  }
  finally { try { s.close(); } catch (Exception e) {} }
  // Return the Vector of transaction history.
  return v;
}

/**
 * This main() method is the standalone program that figures out what
 * database to connect to with what driver, connects to the database,
 * creates a RemoteDBBankServer object, and registers it with the registry,
 * making it available for client use
 **/
public static void main(String[] args) {
  try {
    // Create a new Properties object.  Attempt to initialize it from
    // the BankDB.props file or the file optionally specified on the
    // command line, ignoring errors.
    Properties p = new Properties();
    try { p.load(new FileInputStream(args[0])); }
    catch (Exception e) {
      try { p.load(new FileInputStream("BankDB.props")); }
      catch (Exception e2) {}
    }

    // The BankDB.props file (or file specified on the command line)
    // must contain properties "driver" and "database", and may optionally
    // contain properties "user" and  "password".
    String driver = p.getProperty("driver");
    String database = p.getProperty("database");
    String user = p.getProperty("user", "");
    String password = p.getProperty("password", "");

    // Load the database driver class
    Class.forName(driver);
```

Example 16-5: RemoteDBBankServer.java (continued)

```
        // Connect to the database that stores our accounts
        Connection db = DriverManager.getConnection(database, user, password);

        // Configure the database to allow multiple queries and updates
        // to be grouped into atomic transactions
        db.setAutoCommit(false);
        db.setTransactionIsolation(Connection.TRANSACTION_READ_COMMITTED);

        // Create a server object that uses our database connection
        RemoteDBBankServer bank = new RemoteDBBankServer(db);

        // Read a system property to figure out how to name this server.
        // Use "SecondRemote" as the default.
        String name = System.getProperty("bankname", "SecondRemote");

        // Register the server with the name
        Naming.rebind(name, bank);

        // And tell everyone that we're up and running.
        System.out.println(name + " is open and ready for customers.");
      }
    catch (Exception e) {
      System.err.println(e);
      if (e instanceof SQLException)
        System.err.println("SQL State: " + ((SQLException)e).getSQLState());
      System.err.println("Usage: java [-Dbankname=<name>] RemoteDBBankServer "+
                         "[<dbpropsfile>]");
      System.exit(1);
    }
  }
}
```

Exercises

16-1. Before you can begin using JDBC, you must first have a database server and a JDBC driver for it and you must know how to administer the server in order to do things such as create new databases. If you are not already an experienced database programmer, learning to do all of this is more difficult than actually programming with JDBC. For this first exercise, therefore, obtain and install a database server if you do not already have one. Obtain and install a JDBC driver for it. Read the documentation for both the server and the driver. Learn the basics of the SQL language, if you do not already know it, and make a note of what SQL subset or SQL extensions are supported by your server and JDBC driver.

16-2. Example 16-1 is a general-purpose SQL interpreter program that displays database query results in a rudimentary text-based table format. Modify the program so that it outputs query results using HTML table syntax, resulting in output suitable for display in a Web browser. Test your program by issuing queries against some existing database.

16-3. If you are familiar with CGI programming, modify Example 16-1 again so that it can be used as a CGI script. Write an appropriate HTML front-end that communicates the user's SQL queries to the Java program on the back end and displays the HTML table output by your program.

16-4. Write a program to create a database table of all files and directories stored on your computer (or at least all files and directories beneath a specified directory). Each entry in the database table should include a filename, a size, a modification date, and a boolean value that indicates whether it is a file or a directory. Run this program to generate a database of files. Write a second program that allows a user to make useful queries against this database, such as "list all files larger than 1 megabyte that are older than 1 month," or "list all files with the extension *.java* that were modified today." Optionally, design and create a GUI that allows a user to issue this sort of complicated query without knowing SQL.

CHAPTER 17

Security and
Cryptography

Security is one of the key features that has made Java as successful as it has been. The Java SecurityManager mechanism allows untrusted programs, such as applets, to be executed safely, without fear that they will cause malicious damage, steal company secrets, or otherwise wreak havoc.

Java 1.1 introduces another layer to the Java security architecture, with the introduction of the java.security package and related packages. These packages support the generation of cryptographic message digests and digital signatures. Future releases of Java will also include encryption and decryption capabilities;[*] a beta-release of these features is available in the Java Cryptography Extension (JCE) add-on package to the JDK.

A Custom SecurityManager

Recall that in Chapter 9, *Networking*, we developed a general-purpose Server class that provides a network server infrastructure and can dynamically load named Service classes to perform any desired network service. These classes are loaded locally from the CLASSPATH and are therefore implicitly trusted—in other words, they can read and write files, perform arbitrary networking, and so on. In some situations, however, we might like to be able to safely run a server that loaded *untrusted* Service classes. Suppose, for example, that a system administrator wants to allow users to submit Service classes to be run, but doesn't really trust the users (or doesn't trust them to write bug-free code, at least).

Example 17-1 addresses this scenario. It defines a SafeServer class that uses the server infrastructure of the Server class, but loads the Service classes as untrusted code and imposes the restrictions of a custom SecurityManager on them. In order

---

[*] These capabilities may not be added directly to a java.security package, due to current U.S. export laws.

to impose SecurityManager restrictions on untrusted code but not on trusted code, the SecurityManager must be able to tell one from the other. This is accomplished by loading untrusted code with a custom ClassLoader, rather than with the normal Class.forName() method.

The SafeServer class defines nested classes for the custom SecurityManager and the custom ClassLoader. It also defines an example Service class, Prohibited-Service that attempts to perform operations prohibited by the security manager. The main() method of SafeServer creates and installs an instance of the custom ServiceSecurityManager class. Then it creates an instance of the nested Local-ClassLoader class that is used to load the untrusted code. The LocalClass-Loader() constructor is passed the name of a directory in which to look for the untrusted code. You must ensure that the untrusted code is *not* installed in the CLASSPATH; if it is it will be loaded as trusted code. Finally, the main() method creates a Server object to provide the server infrastructure, and then loads and instantiates any (untrusted) Service classes named on the command-line. Compare this main() method to the main() method of Server in Chapter 9, noting in particular how the classes are loaded.

The ServiceSecurityManager class is quite restrictive—it is even more restrictive than the one that applets are subjected to, for example. Given the limited nature of the tasks that Service classes must perform, however, this should not be a problem. After the ServiceSecurityManager is installed, its methods are invoked to determine whether any possibly sensitive operation is allowed to be performed. These methods simply return if permission is granted. Otherwise, they throw a SecurityException to prevent the code from being allowed to perform the operation. Like all security managers, our ServiceSecurityManager distinguishes trusted from untrusted code by calling the inClassLoader() method of its superclass. If any class that was loaded via a ClassLoader is on the call stack, this method returns true, which typically means that access to the operation should be denied.

Example 17–1: SafeServer.java

```
import java.net.*;
import java.io.*;
import Server.*;

/**
 * This class is a program that uses the Server class defined in Chapter 9.
 * Server would load arbitrary "Service" classes to provide services.
 * This class is an alternative program to start up a Server in a similar
 * way.  The difference is that this one uses a SecurityManager and a
 * ClassLoader to prevent the Service classes from doing anything damaging
 * or malicious on the local system.  This allows us to safely run Service
 * classes that come from untrusted sources.
 **/
public class SafeServer {
  public static void main(String[] args) {
    try {
      // Install the Security manager
      System.setSecurityManager(new ServiceSecurityManager());

      // Create the ClassLoader that we'll use to load Service classes.
      // The classes should be stored in (or beneath) the directory specified
```

Example 17-1: SafeServer.java (continued)

```
          // as the first command-line argument
          LocalClassLoader loader = new LocalClassLoader(args[0]);

          // Create a Server object that does no logging and
          // has a limit of five concurrent connections at once.
          Server server = new Server(null, 5);

          // Parse the argument list, which should contain Service name/port pairs.
          // For each pair, load the named Service using the class loader, then
          // instantiate it with newInstance(), then tell the server to start
          // running it.
          int i = 1;
          while(i < args.length) {
            Class serviceClass = loader.loadClass(args[i++]);       // dynamic load
            Service service = (Service)serviceClass.newInstance(); // instantiate
            int port = Integer.parseInt(args[i++]);                 // get port
            server.addService(service, port);                       // run service
          }
        }
        catch (Exception e) { // Display a message if anything goes wrong
          System.err.println(e);
          System.err.println("Usage: java SafeServer "  +
                          "<servicedir> <servicename> <port>\n" +
                          "\t\t[<servicename> <port> ... ]");
          System.exit(1);
        }
      }


/**
 * This is a fairly uptight security manager subclass.  Classes loaded by
 * a ClassLoader are highly restricted in what they are allowed to do.
 * This is okay, because our Service classes have a very narrowly defined
 * task: to read from one stream and send output to another.
 *
 * A SecurityManager consists of various methods that the system calls to
 * check whether certain sensitive operations should be allowed.  These
 * methods can throw a SecurityException to prevent the operation from
 * happening.  With this SecurityManager, we want to prevent untrusted
 * code that was loaded by a class loader from performing those sensitive
 * operations.  So we use the inherited SecurityManager methods to check
 * whether the call is being made by an untrusted class.  If it is, we
 * throw an exception.  Otherwise, we simply return, allowing the
 * operation to proceed normally.
 **/
public static class ServiceSecurityManager extends SecurityManager {
  /**
   * This is the basic method that tests whether there is a class loaded
   * by a ClassLoader anywhere on the stack.  If so, it means that that
   * untrusted code is trying to perform some kind of sensitive operation.
   * We prevent it from performing that operation by throwing an exception.
   * trusted() is called by most of the check...() methods below.
   **/
  protected void trusted() {
    if (inClassLoader()) throw new SecurityException();
  }

  /**
   * This is a variant on the trusted() method above.  There are a couple
```

Example 17-1: SafeServer.java (continued)

```
 * of methods that loaded code should not be able to call directly, but
 * which system methods invoked by the loaded code still need to be
 * able to call.  So for these, we only throw an exception if a
 * loaded class is the third thing on the call stack.  I.e. right above
 * this method and the check...() method that invoked it
 **/
protected void trustedOrIndirect() {
  if (classLoaderDepth() == 3) throw new SecurityException();
}

/**
 * Here's another variant.  It denies access if a loaded class attempts
 * the operation directly or through one level of indirection.  It is used
 * to prevent loaded code from calling Runtime.load(), or
 * System.loadLibrary() (which calls Runtime.load()).
 **/
protected void trustedOrIndirect2() {
  int depth = classLoaderDepth();
  if ((depth == 3) || (depth == 4)) throw new SecurityException();
}

/**
 * These are all the specific checks that a security manager can
 * perform.  They all just call one of the methods above and throw a
 * SecurityException if the operation is not allowed.  This
 * SecurityManager subclass is perhaps a little too restrictive.  For
 * example, it doesn't allow loaded code to read *any* system properties,
 * even though some of them are quite harmless.
 **/
public void checkCreateClassLoader() { trustedOrIndirect(); }
public void checkAccess(Thread g) { trusted(); }
public void checkAccess(ThreadGroup g) { trusted(); }
public void checkExit(int status) { trusted(); }
public void checkExec(String cmd) { trusted(); }
public void checkLink(String lib) { trustedOrIndirect2(); }
public void checkRead(FileDescriptor fd) { trusted(); }
public void checkRead(String file) { trusted(); }
public void checkRead(String file, Object context) { trusted(); }
public void checkWrite(FileDescriptor fd) { trusted(); }
public void checkWrite(String file) { trusted(); }
public void checkDelete(String file) { trusted(); }
public void checkConnect(String host, int port) { trusted(); }
public void checkConnect(String host,int port,Object context) {trusted();}
public void checkListen(int port) { trusted(); }
public void checkAccept(String host, int port) { trusted(); }
public void checkMulticast(InetAddress maddr) { trusted(); }
public void checkMulticast(InetAddress maddr, byte ttl) { trusted(); }
public void checkPropertiesAccess() { trustedOrIndirect(); }
public void checkPropertyAccess(String key) { trustedOrIndirect(); }
public void checkPrintJobAccess() { trusted(); }
public void checkSystemClipboardAccess() { trusted(); }
public void checkAwtEventQueueAccess() { trusted(); }
public void checkSetFactory() { trusted(); }
public void checkMemberAccess(Class clazz, int which) { trusted(); }
public void checkSecurityAccess(String provider) { trusted(); }

/** Loaded code can only load classes from java.* packages */
public void checkPackageAccess(String pkg) {
```

Example 17-1: SafeServer.java (continued)

```
        if (inClassLoader() && !pkg.startsWith("java."))
            throw new SecurityException();
    }

    /** Loaded code can't define classes in java.* or sun.* packages */
    public void checkPackageDefinition(String pkg) {
        if (inClassLoader() && (pkg.startsWith("java.")||pkg.startsWith("sun.")))
            throw new SecurityException();
    }

    /**
     * This is the one SecurityManager method that is different from the
     * others.  It indicates whether a top-level window should display an
     * "untrusted" warning.  The window is always allowed to be created, so
     * this method is not normally meant to throw an exception.  It should
     * return true if the window does not need to display the warning, and
     * false if it does.  In this example, however, our text-based Service
     * classes should never need to create windows, so we will actually
     * throw an exception to prevent any windows from being opened.
     **/
    public boolean checkTopLevelWindow(Object window) {
        trusted();
        return true;
    }
}


/**
 * In order to impose tight security restrictions on untrusted classes but
 * not on trusted system classes, we have to be able to distinguish between
 * those types of classes.  This is done by keeping track of how the classes
 * are loaded into the system.  By definition, any class that the interpreter
 * loads directly from the CLASSPATH is trusted.  This means that we can't
 * load untrusted code in that way--we can't load it with Class.forName().
 * Instead, we create a ClassLoader subclass to load the untrusted code.
 * This one loads classes from a specified directory (which should not
 * be part of the CLASSPATH).
 **/
public static class LocalClassLoader extends ClassLoader {
    /** This is the directory from which the classes will be loaded */
    String directory;

    /** The constructor.  Just initialize the directory */
    public LocalClassLoader(String dir) { directory = dir; }

    /** A convenience method that calls the 2-argument form of this method */
    public Class loadClass(String name) throws ClassNotFoundException {
        return loadClass(name, true);
    }

    /**
     * This is one abstract method of ClassLoader that all subclasses must
     * define.  Its job is to load an array of bytes from somewhere and to
     * pass them to defineClass().  If the resolve argument is true, it must
     * also call resolveClass(), which will do things like verify the presence
     * of the superclass.  Because of this second step, this method may be
     * called to load superclasses that are system classes, and it must take
     * this into account.
     **/
```

Example 17–1: SafeServer.java (continued)

```
public Class loadClass(String classname, boolean resolve)
  throws ClassNotFoundException {
  try {
    // Our ClassLoader superclass has a built-in cache of classes it has
    // already loaded.  So, first check the cache.
    Class c = findLoadedClass(classname);

    // After this method loads a class, it will be called again to
    // load the superclasses.  Since these may be system classes, we've
    // got to be able to load those too.  So try to load the class as
    // a system class (i.e. from the CLASSPATH) and ignore any errors
    if (c == null) {
      try { c = findSystemClass(classname); }
      catch (Exception e) {}
    }

    // If the class wasn't found by either of the above attempts, then
    // try to load it from a file in (or beneath) the directory
    // specified when this ClassLoader object was created.  Form the
    // filename by replacing all dots in the class name with
    // (platform-independent) file separators and by adding the
    // ".class" extension.
    if (c == null) {
      // Figure out the filename
      String filename = classname.replace('.',File.separatorChar)+".class";

      // Create a File object.  Interpret the filename relative to the
      // directory specified for this ClassLoader.
      File f = new File(directory, filename);

      // Get the length of the class file, allocate an array of bytes for
      // it, and read it in all at once.
      int length = (int) f.length();
      byte[] classbytes = new byte[length];
      DataInputStream in = new DataInputStream(new FileInputStream(f));
      in.readFully(classbytes);
      in.close();

      // Now call an inherited method to convert those bytes into a Class
      c = defineClass(classname, classbytes, 0, length);
    }

    // If the resolve argument is true, call the inherited resolveClass
    // method.
    if (resolve) resolveClass(c);

    // And we're done.  Return the Class object we've loaded.
    return c;
  }
  // If anything goes wrong, throw a ClassNotFoundException error
  catch (Exception e) { throw new ClassNotFoundException(e.toString()); }
}
}

/**
 * This is a demonstration service.  It attempts to do things that the
 * ServiceSecurityManager doesn't allow, and sends the results of
 * its attempts to the client.
```

Example 17-1: SafeServer.java (continued)

```
**/
public static class ProhibitedService implements Service {
  public void serve(InputStream i, OutputStream o) throws IOException {
    PrintWriter out = new PrintWriter(new OutputStreamWriter(o));
    out.print("Attempting to read a file...");
    try { new FileInputStream("testfile"); }
    catch (Exception e) { out.println("Failed: " + e); }
    out.print("Attempting to write a file...");
    try { new FileOutputStream("testfile"); }
    catch (Exception e) { out.println("Failed: " + e); }
    out.print("Attempting to read system property...");
    try { System.getProperty("java.version"); }
    catch (Exception e) { out.println("Failed: " + e); }
    out.print("Attempting to load a library...");
    try { Runtime.getRuntime().load("testlib"); }
    catch (Exception e) { out.println("Failed: " + e); }

    out.close();
    i.close();
  }
}
}
```

Message Digests and Digital Signatures

Java 1.1 introduced the java.security, java.security.acl, and java.security.interfaces packages, which provide a partial implementation of the Java Security API. This API includes classes for generating message digests and digital signatures, managing access control lists (ACLs), and performing simple key management. Future releases of Java will also include classes for encryption and decryption, although perhaps in a separate add-on package, due to current U.S. export laws.

Example 17-2 shows a program named Manifest that demonstrates the use of message digests and digital signatures. The Manifest program provides the following functionality:

- When you pass a list of filenames on the command line, the program reads each file, computes a message digest (or "cryptographic checksum") on the contents of the file, and then writes an entry in a manifest file (named *MANIFEST* by default) that specifies the filename and and its digest.

- If you use the optional -s flag to specify a signer, the program signs the contents of the manifest file and includes a digitial signature within the manifest.

- When you invoke the program with the -v option, it verifies an existing manifest file. First, it checks the digital signature, if any. If the signature is valid, it then reads each file named in the manifest and verifies that its digest matches the one specified in the manifest.

Using the Manifest program to create a signed manifest file and then later verify it accomplishes two goals. First, the message digests prove that the named files have not been maliciously or inadvertently modified or corrupted since the digests were computed. And second, the digital signature proves that the manifest file itself has not been modified since it was signed. (Attaching a digital signature to a file is like signing a legal document. By signing a manifest file, you are making the implicit assertion that the contents of the manifest are true and valid, and that you are willing to stake your trustworthiness on it.)

Digital signatures use public-key cryptography technology. A *private key* is used to create a digital signature and the corresponding *public key* is used to verify the signature. The classes of the java.security package rely on a "security database" where they can look up these keys. This database stores keys for various entities, which may be people, corporations, or other computers or programs. An entity with both a public and private key stored in the database is known as a *signer*, while an entity with only a public key is known as an *identity*.

In order to make this example work, you need to generate a public and private key pair for yourself (or for some test entity) and add those keys to the security database. By default, the security implementation shipped with the JDK uses a database that can be administered with the *javakey* program. Java implementations from other vendors may use other tools instead of *javakey*. Furthermore, some sites may customize their JDK installation to use a different security database.

If your system does use the *javakey* security database, you can add a new signer entry to it and generate public and private keys for that signer with commands like the following:

```
% javakey -cs david true
Created identity [Signer]david[identitydb.obj][trusted]
% javakey -gk david DSA 1024
Generated DSA keys for david (strength: 1024).
```

Alternatively, if you already have public and private keys that you want to use, you can use the -ic option to import your public key certificate into the database. You can also use the -ik option to import your public and private keys from X.509 formatted key files.

Example 17-2 uses the MessageDigest and DigestInputStream classes to compute message digests and the Signature class to compute digital signatures. To create a digital signature, the program also relies on a Signer and its associated PrivateKey object. To verify a digital signature, it uses an Identity and its associated PublicKey object. The Signer and Identity classes obtain the necessary key objects from the security database described above. The manifest file itself is created and read by a java.util.Properties object, which is ideal for this purpose. Message digests and digital signatures are stored in the manifest file using a simple hexadecimal encoding implemented by convenience methods that appear at the end of the example. (This is one shortcoming of the java.security package—it does not provide an easy way to convert an array of bytes to a portable textual representation.)

Example 17-2: Manifest.java

```
import java.security.*;
import java.io.*;
import java.util.*;
```

Example 17-2: Manifest.java (continued)

```java
public class Manifest {
  /**
   * This program creates a manifest file for the specified files, or verifies
   * an existing manifest file.  By default the manifest file is named
   * MANIFEST, but the -m option can be used to override this.  The -v
   * option specifies that the manifest should be verified.  Verification is
   * also the default option if no files are specified.
   **/
  public static void main(String[] args) {
    try {
      // Set the default values of the command-line arguments
      boolean verify = false;                  // Verify manifest or create one?
      String manifestfile = "MANIFEST";        // Manifest file name
      String digestAlgorithm = "MD5";          // Algorithm for message digests
      String signername = null;                // Signer.  No signature by default
      String signatureAlgorithm = "DSA";       // Algorithm for digital signatures
      Vector filelist = new Vector();          // The list of files to digest

      // Parse the command-line arguments, overriding the defaults above
      for(int i = 0; i < args.length; i++) {
        if (args[i].equals("-v")) verify = true;
        else if (args[i].equals("-m")) manifestfile = args[++i];
        else if (args[i].equals("-da") && !verify) digestAlgorithm = args[++i];
        else if (args[i].equals("-s") && !verify) signername = args[++i];
        else if (args[i].equals("-sa") && !verify)
          signatureAlgorithm = args[++i];
        else if (!verify) filelist.addElement(args[i]);
        else throw new IllegalArgumentException(args[i]);
      }

      // If -v was specified or no file were given, verify a manifest
      // Otherwise, create a new manifest for the specified files
      if (verify || (filelist.size() == 0)) verify(manifestfile);
      else create(manifestfile, digestAlgorithm,
                  signername, signatureAlgorithm, filelist);
    }
    // If anything goes wrong, display the exception, and print a usage message
    catch (Exception e) {
      System.err.println("\n" + e);
      System.err.println("Usage: java Manifest [-v] [-m <manifestfile>]\n" +
                         "   or: java Manifest " +
                         "[-m <manifestfile>] [-da <digest algorithm>]\n" +
                         "\t\t[-s <signer>] [-sa <signature algorithm>] " +
                         "files...");
    }
  }

  /**
   * This method creates a manifest file with the specified name, for
   * the specified vector of files, using the named message digest
   * algorithm.  If signername is non-null, it adds a digital signature
   * to the manifest, using the named signature algorithm.  This method can
   * throw a bunch of exceptions.
   **/
  public static void create(String manifestfile, String digestAlgorithm,
                            String signername, String signatureAlgorithm,
                            Vector filelist)
```

Example 17-2: Manifest.java (continued)

```
      throws NoSuchAlgorithmException, InvalidKeyException,
             SignatureException, IOException
{
    // For computing a signature, we have to process the files in a fixed,
    // repeatable order, so copy the filenames into an array and sort it.
    // Use the Sorter class from Chapter 2.
    String[] files = new String[filelist.size()];
    filelist.copyInto(files);
    Sorter.sortAscii(files);

    Properties manifest = new Properties(), metadata = new Properties();
    MessageDigest md = MessageDigest.getInstance(digestAlgorithm);
    Signature signature = null;
    byte[] digest;

    // If a signer name has been specified, then prepare to sign the manifest
    if (signername != null) {
      // Look up the signer object
      Signer signer =
        (Signer)IdentityScope.getSystemScope().getIdentity(signername);
      // Get a Signature object
      signature = Signature.getInstance(signatureAlgorithm);
      // And prepare to create a signature for the specified signer
      signature.initSign(signer.getPrivateKey());
    }

    // Now, loop through the files, in a well-known alphabetical order
    System.out.print("Computing message digests");
    for(int i = 0; i < files.length; i++) {
      // Compute the digest for each one, and skip files that don't exist.
      try { digest = getFileDigest(files[i], md); }
      catch (IOException e) {
        System.err.println("\nSkipping " + files[i] + ": " + e);
        continue;
      }
      // If we're computing a signature, use the bytes of the filename and
      // of the digest as part of the data to sign.
      if (signature != null) {
        signature.update(files[i].getBytes());
        signature.update(digest);
      }
      // Store the filename and the encoded digest bytes in the manifest
      manifest.put(files[i], hexEncode(digest));
      System.out.print('.');
      System.out.flush();
    }

    // If a signer was specified, compute digital signature for the manifest
    byte[] signaturebytes = null;
    if (signature != null) {
      System.out.print("done\nComputing digital signature...");
      System.out.flush();

      // Compute the digital signature by encrypting a message digest of all
      // the bytes passed to the update() method using the private key of the
      // signer.  This is a time consuming operation.
      signaturebytes = signature.sign();
    }
```

Example 17-2: Manifest.java (continued)

```
  // Tell the user what comes next
  System.out.print("done\nWriting manifest...");
  System.out.flush();

  // Store some metadata about this manifest, including the name of the
  // message digest algorithm it uses
  metadata.put("__META.DIGESTALGORITHM", digestAlgorithm);
  // If we're signing the manifest, store some more metadata
  if (signername != null) {
    // Store the name of the signer
    metadata.put("__META.SIGNER", signername);
    // Store the name of the algorithm
    metadata.put("__META.SIGNATUREALGORITHM", signatureAlgorithm);
    // And generate the signature, encode it, and store it
    metadata.put("__META.SIGNATURE", hexEncode(signaturebytes));
  }

  // Now, save the manifest data and the metadata to the manifest file
  FileOutputStream f = new FileOutputStream(manifestfile);
  manifest.save(f, "Manifest message digests");
  metadata.save(f, "Manifest metadata");
  System.out.println("done");
}


/**
 * This method verifies the digital signature of the named manifest
 * file, if it has one, and if that verification succeeds, it verifies
 * the message digest of each file in filelist that is also named in the
 * manifest.  This method can throw a bunch of exceptions
 **/
public static void verify(String manifestfile)
     throws NoSuchAlgorithmException, SignatureException,
            InvalidKeyException, IOException
{
  Properties manifest = new Properties();
  manifest.load(new FileInputStream(manifestfile));
  String digestAlgorithm = manifest.getProperty("__META.DIGESTALGORITHM");
  String signername = manifest.getProperty("__META.SIGNER");
  String signatureAlgorithm =
    manifest.getProperty("__META.SIGNATUREALGORITHM");
  String hexsignature = manifest.getProperty("__META.SIGNATURE");

  // Get a list of filenames in the manifest.  Use an Enumeration to
  // get them into a Vector, then allocate an array and copy them into that.
  Vector filelist = new Vector();
  Enumeration names = manifest.propertyNames();
  while(names.hasMoreElements()) {
    String s = (String)names.nextElement();
    if (!s.startsWith("__META")) filelist.addElement(s);
  }
  String[] files = new String[filelist.size()];
  filelist.copyInto(files);

  // If the manifest contained metadata about a digital signature, then
  // verify that signature first
  if (signername != null) {
    System.out.print("Verifying digital signature...");
    System.out.flush();
```

Example 17-2: Manifest.java (continued)

```
    // To verify the signature, we must process the files in exactly the
    // same order we did when we created the signature.  We guarantee
    // this order by sorting the filenames.
    Sorter.sortAscii(files);

    // Get the Signer identity, create a Signature object, and initialize
    // it for signature verification, using the signer's public key
    Identity signer =
        (Identity)IdentityScope.getSystemScope().getIdentity(signername);
    Signature signature = Signature.getInstance(signatureAlgorithm);
    signature.initVerify(signer.getPublicKey());

    // Now loop through these files in their known sorted order
    // For each one, send the bytes of the filename and of the digest
    // to the signature object for use in computing the signature.
    // It is important that this be done in exactly the same order when
    // verifying the signature as it was done when creating the signature.
    for(int i = 0; i < files.length; i++) {
      signature.update(files[i].getBytes());
      signature.update(hexDecode(manifest.getProperty(files[i])));
    }

    // Now decode the signature read from the manifest file and pass it
    // to the verify() method of the signature object.  If the signature
    // is not verified, print an error message and exit.
    if (!signature.verify(hexDecode(hexsignature))) {
      System.out.println("\nManifest has an invalid digital signature");
      System.exit(0);
    }

    // Tell the user we're done with this lengthy computation
    System.out.println("verified.");
  }

  // Tell the user we're starting the next phase of verification
  System.out.print("Verifying file message digests");
  System.out.flush();

  // Get a MessageDigest object to compute digests
  MessageDigest md = MessageDigest.getInstance(digestAlgorithm);
  // Loop through all files
  for(int i = 0; i < files.length; i++) {
    // Look up the encoded digest from the manifest file
    String hexdigest = manifest.getProperty(files[i]);
    // Compute the digest for the file.
    byte[] digest;
    try { digest = getFileDigest(files[i], md); }
    catch (IOException e) {
      System.out.println("\nSkipping " + files[i] + ": " + e);
      continue;
    }

    // Encode the computed digest and compare it to the encoded digest
    // from the manifest.  If they are not equal, print an error message.
    if (!hexdigest.equals(hexEncode(digest)))
      System.out.println("\nFile '" + files[i] + "' failed verification.");

    // Send one dot of output for each file we process.  Since computing
```

Example 17-2: Manifest.java (continued)

```
    // message digests takes some time, this lets the user know that the
    // program is functioning and making progress
    System.out.print(".");
    System.out.flush();
  }
  // And tell the user we're done with verification.
  System.out.println("done.");
}

/**
 * This convenience method is used by both create() and verify().  It
 * reads the contents of a named file and computes a message digest
 * for it, using the specified MessageDigest object.
 **/
public static byte[] getFileDigest(String filename, MessageDigest md)
      throws IOException {
  // Make sure there is nothing left behind in the MessageDigest
  md.reset();

  // Create a stream to read from the file and compute the digest
  DigestInputStream in =
    new DigestInputStream(new FileInputStream(filename),md);

  // Read to the end of the file, discarding everything we read.
  // The DigestInputStream automatically passes all the bytes read to
  // the update() method of the MessageDigest
  while(in.read(buffer) != -1) /* do nothing */ ;

  // Finally, compute and return the digest value.
  return md.digest();
}

/** This static buffer is used by getFileDigest() above */
public static byte[] buffer = new byte[4096];

/** This array is used to convert from bytes to hexadecimal numbers */
static final char[] digits = { '0', '1', '2', '3', '4', '5', '6', '7',
                               '8', '9', 'a', 'b', 'c', 'd', 'e', 'f'};

/**
 * A convenience method to convert an array of bytes to a String.  We do
 * this simply by converting each byte to two hexadecimal digits.  Something
 * like Base 64 encoding is more compact, but harder to encode.
 **/
public static String hexEncode(byte[] bytes) {
  StringBuffer s = new StringBuffer(bytes.length * 2);
  for(int i = 0; i < bytes.length; i++) {
    byte b = bytes[i];
    s.append(digits[(b & 0xf0) >> 4]);
    s.append(digits[b & 0x0f]);
  }
  return s.toString();
}

/**
 * A convenience method to convert in the other direction, from a string
 * of hexadecimal digits to an array of bytes.
 **/
```

Example 17-2: Manifest.java (continued)

```
public static byte[] hexDecode(String s) throws IllegalArgumentException {
  try {
    int len = s.length();
    byte[] r = new byte[len/2];
    for(int i = 0; i < r.length; i++) {
      int digit1 = s.charAt(i*2), digit2 = s.charAt(i*2 + 1);
      if ((digit1 >= '0') && (digit1 <= '9')) digit1 -= '0';
      else if ((digit1 >= 'a') && (digit1 <= 'f')) digit1 -= 'a' - 10;
      if ((digit2 >= '0') && (digit2 <= '9')) digit2 -= '0';
      else if ((digit2 >= 'a') && (digit2 <= 'f')) digit2 -= 'a' - 10;
      r[i] = (byte)((digit1 << 4) + digit2);
    }
    return r;
  }
  catch (Exception e) {
    throw new IllegalArgumentException("hexDecode(): invalid input");
  }
}
}
```

Digitally Signed Objects

Example 17-3 defines a SignedObject class, which, as its name suggests, is an object that bears a digital signature. If you are writing an object (typically for use in some sort of distributed system) that needs a digital signature for verification, you can simply extend the SignedObject class instead of extending Object. To compute a digital signature and attach it to the object, call sign(), passing the name of the signer and, optionally, the name of the digital signature algorithm to be used. (The default algorithm is DSA.)

Once an object has been signed, it carries the signature with it, when serialized or passed as an argument to a remote method, for example. When any fields of the object change, however, the signature is no longer valid and removeSignature() should be called. You can verify the signature by calling verify(), which returns true if the verification succeeds or false if it fails. Note that both sign() and verify() are time-consuming operations, and that these methods can throw a number of different exceptions.

Example 17-3 includes a simple SignedString subclass of SignedObject, as well as RMI server and client programs that demonstrate and test SignedObject. You can test out this system with commands like the following (on a UNIX system):

```
% javac SignedObject.java
% rmic SignedStringServer
% rmiregistry &
% java SignedStringServer "Testing, 1, 2, 3, testing." david &
Ready for clients
% java SignedStringClient
Verified SignedString: Testing, 1, 2, 3, testing.
```

See Chapter 15, *Remote Method Invocation*, for more details on RMI.

Example 17–3: SignedObject.java

```
import java.io.*;
import java.security.*;
import java.rmi.*;              // Used for the test programs only
import java.rmi.server.*;

/**
 * A SignedObject is exactly that--an object that bears a digital signature.
 * Subclass this class to add a digital signature to any class you want.
 * Note, however, that the signature is computed using serialization, so only
 * the serializable, non-transient fields of a subclass are included in
 * the signature computation.
 **/
public class SignedObject implements Serializable {
  protected String signername;           // Who is doing the signing
  protected String algorithm;            // What algorithm to use.
  private byte[] signature;              // The bytes of the signature
  transient private boolean signing = false; // A flag used below.

  /**
   * This method computes a digital signature for the current state of the
   * object, excluding the signature-related state of this class.
   * That is, the signature is based only on the state of the subclasses.
   * The arguments specify who is signing the object, and what digital
   * signature algorithm to use.
   *
   * Note that no other threads should be modifying the object while
   * this computation is being performed.  If a subclass will be used in a
   * multi-threaded environment, this means that methods of the subclass
   * that modify its state should be synchronized like this one is.
   **/
  public synchronized void sign(String signername, String algorithm)
       throws IOException, InvalidKeyException,
        SignatureException, NoSuchAlgorithmException
  {
    // Save the arguments for use by verify()
    this.signername = signername;
    this.algorithm = algorithm;

    // Get a Signature object to compute the signature with
    Signature s = Signature.getInstance(algorithm);

    // Get a Signer object representing the signer
    Signer signer =
      (Signer)IdentityScope.getSystemScope().getIdentity(signername);

    // Initialize the Signature object using the PrivateKey of the Signer
    s.initSign(signer.getPrivateKey());

    // Create an ObjectOutputStream that writes its output to a
    // ByteArrayStream.  This is how we capture the state of the object
    // so that it can be signed.
    ByteArrayOutputStream bout = new ByteArrayOutputStream();
    ObjectOutputStream out = new ObjectOutputStream(bout);

    // Now serialize the object, capturing its state.  We have to set a flag
    // before we do this, so that the signer name, algorithm, and signature
    // itself are not included in this serialized state.  See writeObject()
    // below to see how this works.
```

Example 17–3: SignedObject.java (continued)

```java
    signing = true;
    out.writeObject(this);
    signing = false;

    // Now tell the Signature object about the bytes of serialized state
    // that were stored by the ByteArrayOutputStream
    s.update(bout.toByteArray());

    // And finally, compute the signature
    this.signature = s.sign();
  }

  /** A simpler version of sign(), that defaults to using the DSA algorithm */
  public synchronized void sign(String signername)
      throws IOException, InvalidKeyException,
        SignatureException, NoSuchAlgorithmException {
    sign(signername, "DSA");
  }

  /**
   * This method verifies the signature of any SignedObject subclass.
   * It works much like the sign() method, and is also synchronized.
   **/
  public synchronized boolean verify()
      throws IOException, InvalidKeyException,
        SignatureException, NoSuchAlgorithmException
  {
    // Make sure the object is actually signed.
    if (signature == null)
      throw new SignatureException("Object is not signed");

    // Get the signature, signer and public key, and initialize, like above,
    // except that this time use a PublicKey instead of a PrivateKey
    Signature s = Signature.getInstance(algorithm);
    Identity signer =
      (Identity)IdentityScope.getSystemScope().getIdentity(signername);
    s.initVerify(signer.getPublicKey());

    // Create streams and capture the current state of the object
    // (excluding the signature bytes themselves) in a byte array
    ByteArrayOutputStream bout = new ByteArrayOutputStream();
    ObjectOutputStream out = new ObjectOutputStream(bout);
    signing = true;
    out.writeObject(this);
    signing = false;

    // Pass state of the object to the Signature, and verify the stored
    // signature bytes against that state.  Return the result of verification.
    s.update(bout.toByteArray());
    return s.verify(this.signature);
  }

  /**
   * When the contents of the object change, the signature becomes invalid.
   * When this happens, the signature should be erased, because validation
   * is guaranteed to fail.
   **/
```

Example 17-3: SignedObject.java (continued)

```java
  public void removeSignature() {
    signature = null; signername = null; algorithm = null;
  }

  /**
   * This method is invoked to allow custom serialization.
   * We only write out our signature-related state when we are not computing
   * or verifying a signature.  When we are computing or verifying, only our
   * subclass state gets written out.  If we don't do this, verification will
   * fail because the signature[] array will obviously be different on
   * verification than it is when the signature is generated.
   **/
  private void writeObject(ObjectOutputStream out) throws IOException {
    if (!signing) out.defaultWriteObject();
  }
}

/**
 * This class is a simple SignedObject subclass.
 * This and the following interface and classes are used to test SignedObject.
 **/
class SignedString extends SignedObject {
  public String s;
  public SignedString(String s) { this.s = s; }
}

/**
 * This interface extends Remote.  It is part of an RMI example using our
 * SignedString class above.
 **/
interface RemoteSignedString extends Remote {
  public SignedString getString() throws RemoteException;
}

/**
 * This is a simple RMI server class and a program to start and register the
 * server.  The server creates a SignedString object, signs it, and then
 * exports it to clients through the RemoteSignedString getString() method.
 **/
class SignedStringServer extends UnicastRemoteObject
                    implements RemoteSignedString
{
  SignedString s;  // The state of the server object

  /** The constructor.  Initialize the SignedString */
  public SignedStringServer(SignedString s) throws RemoteException {this.s=s;}

  /** This is the remote method exported by the server */
  public SignedString getString() throws RemoteException { return s; }

  /** The main program that creates and registers the server object */
  public static void main(String[] args)
      throws NoSuchAlgorithmException, InvalidKeyException,
        IOException, SignatureException
  {
    SignedString ss = new SignedString(args[0]);        // create object
    ss.sign(args[1]);                                   // sign it
    SignedStringServer sss = new SignedStringServer(ss); // start server
```

Example 17-3: SignedObject.java (continued)

```
    Naming.rebind("SignedStringServer", sss);          // register server
    System.out.println("Ready for clients");           // up and running!
  }
}


/**
 * This class is a client that connects to a RemoteSignedString server and
 * calls the getString() method to obtain a SignedString.  It then verifies
 * the signature of the object that it has just downloaded over a network
 * from an entirely different Java VM.  The client takes an optional hostname
 * argument on the command line.
 **/
class SignedStringClient {
  public static void main(String[] args)
        throws NoSuchAlgorithmException, InvalidKeyException,
          IOException, SignatureException, NotBoundException
  {
    // Look up the server
    RemoteSignedString rss =
      (RemoteSignedString) Naming.lookup("rmi://" +
                                    ((args.length>0)?args[0]:"") +
                                    "/SignedStringServer");

    // Invoke a remote method of the server to get a SignedString
    SignedString ss = rss.getString();

    // Now verify the signature on that SignedString.
    if (ss.verify()) System.out.println("Verified SignedString: " + ss.s);
    else System.out.println("SignedString failed verification");
  }
}
```

Exercises

17-1. Modify the SecurityManager in Example 17-1 so that untrusted Service classes are not quite so severely restricted. Allow them to read certain system properties, such as java.version, and allow them to read and write files stored within some predetermined scratch directory, such as */tmp/scratch* (on a UNIX system).

17-2. Modify the ClassLoader in Example 17-1 so that Service classes specified by URL can be loaded over the network. Note that in order to prevent name conflicts, you'll want to use a unique ClassLoader object for every combination of host and port from which a class is to be loaded.

17-3. Consider the remote banking example of Chapters 15 and 16. A flaw in the security of this remote banking scheme is that customer passwords are stored in "plain text" by the bank server. If the security of the server is compromised, all customer passwords might be stolen. To guard against this scenario, it is common to use a "one-way function" to encrypt the passwords. Message digests, such as those used in Example 17-2, provide exactly this kind of a one-way function. Computing a message digest for a password is relatively easy, but going in the opposite direction from digest to password is very difficult or impossible.

Modify the bank example so that it does not store passwords directly, but instead stores the message digests of the passwords. To verify a user's password, your modified program has to compute a digest for the supplied password and compare it to the stored digest. If they match, you can assume that the passwords match. (There is actually an infinitesimally small chance that two different passwords will produce the same message digest, but you can disregard this possibility.)

17-4. The remote banking example uses a trivial class named FunnyMoney to represent currency that is transferred between the bank and its customers. Modify the example so that every FunnyMoney object bears the digital signature of the bank that issues it. The signature should be computed based on the amount of money that the FunnyMoney object represents, so that this value cannot be modified without invalidating the signature. You may also want to include a unique serial number in each FunnyMoney object so that it cannot be copied and spent multiple times!

Modify the bank server so that it verifies the signature on any FunnyMoney objects passed to it by a client, and modify the client so that it verifies the signature on any FunnyMoney objects passed by the server. In order to do this, you have to use the *javakey* tool to create a public/private key pair for the bank server.

17-5. There are many services like the remote banking example that rely on password authentication. Design and implement a generic password-based authentication service that the remote bank and other services can rely on. It should export methods to register a new user and password, to authenticate a user by verifying the password they supply, and to change the password of a user. The service should have some form of persistant storage of names and passwords. You can use JDBC to store this data in a database or you can simply store it in a file. As in Exercise 17-3, the service should store message digests of the passwords, not the passwords themselves.

If, by the time you read this, the Java Cryptography Extension (JCE) has been released, take advantage of its encryption and decryption features to add extra security to your authentication service. Instead of transmitting passwords over the network in "plain text," first have the client encrypt them using a public key that belongs to the authentication server. Then only your server can decrypt the password and check its validity. To prevent a Net snooper from capturing the encrypted password and replaying it at a later time, encrypt the current time along with the password, and have the server check that the encrypted password is not long out of date.

Index

events (cont'd)
  event source, 87, 89
  EventObject class, 87
  EventTester1 class, 85
  EventTester2 class, 99
  for GUIs, 105
  Java 1.0 model, 78–83
  Java 1.1 model, 78
  low-level handling, 96
  methods, 88–89
  types, 80
  user inputs, 85
event listeners, 47, 87–89, 247
  EventListener interfaces, 88
  naming convention, 89
  registering, 89, 96
exceptions
  BankingException, 293
  defined, 11
  Exception class, 14
  handling, 13–14
  NullPointerException, 177
  PrintCanceledException, 176
  RemoteException, 291
  SecurityException, 350
  SQLException, 325–326
  throwing, 11, 14
execute(), 326
executeQuery(), 326
ExecuteSQL class, 326
executeUpdate(), 326, 334
extends keyword, 23
external classes, for Scribble class,
    91–92
Externalizable interface, 267, 270

F

FactComputer class, 13
factorial(), 9, 13
Factorial class, 9
factorials
  computing big, 12–13
  caching, 10–12
  computing, 9–10
  exception handling, 13–14
  factorial classes, 9–12
  recursive, 10
FactQuoter class, 14

FeatureDescriptor class, 235, 244
Fibonacci series, 6
fields
  declaring transient, 268
  defined, 20
  Field class, 257
  field key, 82
  modifier constants, 82
  nonstatic, 11
  static (class), 10, 20
  visibility levels, 20
files
  copying contents of, 157–159
  deleting, 155
  File class, 152, 157, 159
    methods of, 155–156
  FileCopy class, 157
  FileDescriptor class, 267
  FileDialog component, 107
  FileInputStream class, 153
  FileListener class, 162
  FilenameFilter class, 162
  FileOutputStream class, 154, 157
  FileReader class, 154, 159
  FileViewer class, 159
  FileWriter class, 155
  InputStream class, 157
  List component, 162
fill field (GridBagConstraints), 115
filtering
  FilterInputStream class, 153
  FilterOutputStream class, 154
  FilterReader class, 154, 169
  FilterWriter class, 155
  images, 70–73
  pipes and, 226
  position dependence, 72
filterRGB(), 71
finally statement, 157
finger, 196–197
first(), 114
FizzBuzz games, 3–7
  FizzBuzz classes, 4, 8
flipping images, 70
FlowLayout layout manager, 111
flush(), 173, 175
fonts
  applet, 57
  Font class, 42, 57

About the Author

David Flanagan is the author of the bestselling *Java in a Nutshell*. When David isn't busy writing about Java, he is a consulting computer programmer, user interface designer, and trainer. His other books with O'Reilly & Associates include *JavaScript: The Definitive Guide, Netscape IFC in a Nutshell, X Toolkit Intrinsics Reference Manual,* and *Motif Tools: Streamlined GUI Design and Programming with the Xmt Library.* David has a degree in computer science and engineering from the Massachusetts Institute of Technology.

Colophon

The animal featured on the cover of *Java Examples in a Nutshell* is an alligator. There are only two species of alligator: the American alligator (*Alligator mississippiensis*), found in the southeastern coastal plain of the United States, and the smaller Chinese alligator (*Alligator sinensis*), found in the lower valley of the Yangtze River. Both alligators are related to the more widely distributed crocodile.

The alligator is a much-studied animal, and so a great deal is known about its life cycle. Female alligators lay 30 to 80 eggs at a time. The mother allows the sun to incubate the eggs, but stays nearby. After about 60 days the eggs hatch, and the young call out for their mother. The mother then carries or leads them to the water, where they live with her for a year.

Alligators eat a varied diet of insects, fish, shellfish, frogs, water birds, and small mammals. Alligator attacks on humans are rare. Although normally slow-moving animals, alligators can charge quickly for short distances when they or their young are in danger.

Alligators have been hunted extensively for their skin. The American alligator was placed on the endangered species list in 1969, then declared to be out of danger in 1987. The Chinese alligator remains on the endangered list.

Edie Freedman designed the cover of this book, using a 19th-century engraving from the Dover Pictorial Archive. The cover layout was produced with Quark XPress 3.3 using the ITC Garamond font.

The inside layout was designed by Edie Freedman and Nancy Priest and implemented in gtroff by Lenny Muellner. The text and heading fonts are ITC Garamond Light and Garamond Book. Figures were created by Robert

Romano in Macromedia Freehand 5.0 and Adobe Photoshop. This colophon was written by Clairemarie Fisher O'Leary.

Whenever possible, our books use RepKover™, a durable and flexible lay-flat binding. If the page count exceeds RepKover's limit, perfect binding is used.

Java

Java Cryptography

By Jonathan B. Knudsen
1st Edition May 1998
362 pages, ISBN 1-56592-402-9

Java Cryptography teaches you how to write secure programs using Java's cryptographic tools. It includes thorough discussions of the java.security package and the Java Cryptography Extensions (JCE), showing you how to use security providers and even implement your own provider. It discusses authentication, key management, public and private key encryption, and includes a secure talk application that encrypts all data sent over the network. If you work with sensitive data, you'll find this book indispensable.

Java Distributed Computing

By Jim Farley
1st Edition January 1998
384 pages, ISBN 1-56592-206-9

Java Distributed Computing offers a general introduction to distributed computing, meaning programs that run on two or more systems. It focuses primarily on how to structure and write distributed applications and discusses issues like designing protocols, security, working with databases, and dealing with low bandwidth situations.

Java Network Programming

By Elliotte Rusty Harold
1st Edition February 1997
442 pages, ISBN 1-56592-227-1

The network is the soul of Java. Most of what is new and exciting about Java centers around the potential for new kinds of dynamic networked applications. *Java Network Programming* teaches you to work with Sockets, write network clients and servers, and gives you an advanced look at the new areas like multicasting, using the server API, and RMI. Covers Java 1.1.

Java Security

By Scott Oaks
1st Edition May 1998
474 pages, ISBN 1-56592-403-7

This essential Java 2 book covers Java's security mechanisms and teaches you how to work with them. It discusses class loaders, security managers, access lists, digital signatures, and authentication and shows how to use these to create and enforce your own security policy.

Java Threads, 2nd Edition

By Scott Oaks & Henry Wong
2nd Edition January 1999
336 pages, ISBN 1-56592-418-5

Revised and expanded to cover Java 2, *Java Threads, 2nd Edition* shows you how to take full advantage of Java's thread facilities: where to use threads to increase efficiency, how to use them effectively, and how to avoid common mistakes. It thoroughly covers the Thread and ThreadGroup classes, the Runnable interface, and the language's synchronized operator. The book pays special attention to threading issues with Swing, as well as problems like deadlock, race condition, and starvation to help you write code without hidden bugs.

Java I/O

By Elliotte Rusty Harold
1st Edition March 1999
596 pages, ISBN 1-56592-485-1

All of Java's Input/Output (I/O) facilities are based on streams, which provide simple ways to read and write data of different types. Java I/O tells you all you need to know about the four main categories of streams and uncovers less-known features to help make your I/O operations more efficient. Plus, it shows you how to control number formatting, use characters aside from the standard ASCII character set, and get a head start on writing truly multilingual software.

O'REILLY®

TO ORDER: **800-998-9938** • *order@oreilly.com* • *http://www.oreilly.com/*
OUR PRODUCTS ARE AVAILABLE AT A BOOKSTORE OR SOFTWARE STORE NEAR YOU.
FOR INFORMATION: **800-998-9938** • **707-829-0515** • *info@oreilly.com*

Java

Java Fundamental Classes Reference

By Mark Grand & Jonathan Knudsen
1st Edition May 1997
1114 pages, ISBN 1-56592-241-7

The *Java Fundamental Classes Reference* provides complete reference documentation on the core Java 1.1 classes that comprise the java.lang, java.io, java.net, java.util, java.text, java.math, java.lang.reflect, and java.util.zip packages. Part of O'Reilly's Java documentation series, this edition describes Version 1.1 of the Java Development Kit. It includes easy-to-use reference material and provides lots of sample code to help you learn by example.

Java Language Reference, 2nd Edition

By Mark Grand
2nd Edition July 1997
492 pages, ISBN 1-56592-326-X

This book helps you understand the subtle nuances of Java – from the definition of data types to the syntax of expressions and control structures – so you can ensure your programs run exactly as expected. The second edition covers the language features that have been added in Java 1.1, such as inner classes, class literals, and instance initializers.

Java Virtual Machine

By Jon Meyer & Troy Downing
1st Edition March 1997
452 pages, Includes diskette
ISBN 1-56592-194-1

This book is a comprehensive programming guide for the Java Virtual Machine (JVM). It gives readers a strong overview and reference of the JVM so that they may create their own implementations or write their own compilers that create Java object code.

Java AWT Reference

By John Zukowski
1st Edition April 1997
1074 pages, ISBN 1-56592-240-9

The *Java AWT Reference* provides complete reference documentation on the Abstract Window Toolkit (AWT), a large collection of classes for building graphical user interfaces in Java. Part of O'Reilly's Java documentation series, this edition describes both Version 1.0.2 and Version 1.1 of the Java Development Kit, includes easy-to-use reference material on every AWT class, and provides lots of sample code.

Exploring Java, 2nd Edition

By Pat Niemeyer & Josh Peck
2nd Edition September 1997
614 pages, ISBN 1-56592-271-9

Whether you're just migrating to Java or working steadily in the forefront of Java development, this book gives a clear, systematic overview of the language. It covers the essentials of hot topics like Beans and RMI, as well as writing applets and other applications, such as networking programs, content and protocol handlers, and security managers.

Developing Java Beans

By Robert Englander
1st Edition June 1997
316 pages, ISBN 1-56592-289-1

Developing Java Beans is a complete introduction to Java's component architecture. It describes how to write Beans, which are software components that can be used in visual programming environments. This book discusses event adapters, serialization, introspection, property editors, and customizers, and shows how to use Beans within ActiveX controls.

Java

Java Servlet Programming

By Jason Hunter with William Crawford
1st Edition November 1998
528 pages, ISBN 1-56592-391-X

Java servlets offer a fast, powerful, portable replacement for CGI scripts. *Java Servlet Programming* covers everything you need to know to write effective servlets. Topics include: serving dynamic Web content, maintaining state information, session tracking, database connectivity using JDBC, and applet-servlet communication.

Java Swing

By Robert Eckstein, Marc Loy & Dave Wood
1st Edition September 1998
1252 pages, ISBN 1-56592-455-X

The Swing classes eliminate Java's biggest weakness: its relatively primitive user interface toolkit. *Java Swing* helps you to take full advantage of the Swing classes, providing detailed descriptions of every class and interface in the key Swing packages. It shows you how to use all of the new components, allowing you to build state-of-the-art user interfaces and giving you the context you need to understand what you're doing. It's more than documentation; *Java Swing* helps you develop code quickly and effectively.

Java Power Reference

By David Flanagan
1st Edition March 1999
64 pages, Features CD-ROM
ISBN 1-56592-589-0

Java Power Reference is a searchable, browser-based resource that documents all the packages and classes of the Java 2™ platform on a single CD-ROM. Based on the clear, concise quick-reference style of the bestselling *Java in a Nutshell*, the *Java Power Reference* provides a unique view of the functionality of the Java APIs. In addition to the CD-ROM, the package contains a concise printed overview of the newly released Java 2 platform.

Enterprise JavaBeans

By Richard Monson-Haefel
1st Edition June 1999
336 pages, ISBN 1-56592-605-6

Enterprise JavaBeans is a thorough introduction to EJB for the enterprise software developer. It shows how to get started developing enterprise Beans, how to deploy those Beans in a server, and how to use those Beans to create applications that do useful tasks. The end result is a highly flexible system built from components that can easily be reused and that can be changed to suit your needs without upsetting other parts of the system.

Java 2D Graphics

By Jonathan Knudsen
1st Edition May 1999
366 pages, ISBN 1-56592-484-3

Java 2D Graphics describes the 2D API from top to bottom, demonstrating how to set line styles and pattern fills as well as more advanced techniques of image processing and font handling. You'll see how to create and manipulate the three types of graphics objects: shapes, text, and images. Other topics include image data storage, color management, font glyphs, and printing.

Web Programming

Practical Internet Groupware

By Jon Udell
1st Edition October 1999
524 pages, ISBN 1-56592-537-8

This revolutionary book tells users, programmers, IS managers, and system administrators how to build Internet groupware applications that organize the casual and chaotic transmission of online information into useful, disciplined, and documented data.

Web Programming

CGI Programming with Perl, 2nd Edition

By Shishir Gundavaram
2nd Edition June 2000 (est.)
450 pages (est.), ISBN 1-56592-419-3

Completely rewritten, this comprehensive explanation of CGI for those who want to provide their own Web servers features Perl 5 techniques and shows how to use two popular Perl modules, CGI.pm and CGI_lite. It also covers speed-up techniques, such as FastCGI and mod_perl, and new material on searching and indexing, security, generating graphics through ImageMagick, database access through DBI, Apache configuration, and combining CGI with JavaScript.

Dynamic HTML: The Definitive Reference

By Danny Goodman
1st Edition July 1998
1088 pages, ISBN 1-56592-494-0

Dynamic HTML: The Definitive Reference is an indispensable compendium for Web content developers. It contains complete reference material for all of the HTML tags, CSS style attributes, browser document objects, and JavaScript objects supported by the various standards and the latest versions of Netscape Navigator and Microsoft Internet Explorer.

PHP Pocket Reference

By Rasmus Lerdorf
1st Edition January 2000
120 pages, ISBN 1-56592-769-9

The *PHP Pocket Reference* is a handy quick reference for PHP, an open-source, HTML-embedded scripting language that can be used to develop web applications. This small book acts both as a perfect tutorial for learning the basics of PHP syntax and as a reference to the vast array of functions provided by PHP.

JavaScript: The Definitive Guide, 3rd Edition

By David Flanagan
3rd Edition June 1998
800 pages, ISBN 1-56592-392-8

This third edition of the definitive reference to JavaScript covers the latest version of the language, JavaScript 1.2, as supported by Netscape Navigator 4 and Internet Explorer 4. JavaScript, which is being standardized under the name ECMAScript, is a scripting language that can be embedded directly in HTML to give Web pages programming-language capabilities.

Learning VBScript

By Paul Lomax
1st Edition July 1997
616 pages, Includes CD-ROM
ISBN 1-56592-247-6

This definitive guide shows Web developers how to take full advantage of client-side scripting with the VBScript language. In addition to basic language features, it covers the Internet Explorer object model and discusses techniques for client-side scripting, like adding ActiveX controls to a Web page or validating data before sending it to the server. Includes CD-ROM with over 170 code samples.

ASP in a Nutshell

By A. Keyton Weissinger
1st Edition February 1999
426 pages, ISBN 1-56592-490-8

This detailed reference contains all the information Web developers need to create effective Active Server Pages (ASP) applications. It focuses on how features are used in a real application and highlights little-known or undocumented aspects, enabling even experienced developers to advance their ASP applications to new levels.

O'REILLY®

TO ORDER: **800-998-9938** • **order@oreilly.com** • **http://www.oreilly.com/**
OUR PRODUCTS ARE AVAILABLE AT A BOOKSTORE OR SOFTWARE STORE NEAR YOU.
FOR INFORMATION: **800-998-9938** • **707-829-0515** • **info@oreilly.com**

Web Programming

Writing Apache Modules with Perl and C

By Lincoln Stein & Doug MacEachern
1st Edition March 1999
746 pages, ISBN 1-56592-567-X

This guide to Web programming teaches you how to extend the capabilities of the Apache Web server. It explains the design of Apache, mod_perl, and the Apache API, then demonstrates how to use them to rewrite CGI scripts, filter HTML documents on the server-side, enhance server log functionality, convert file formats on the fly, and more.

Webmaster in a Nutshell, 2nd Edition

By Stephen Spainhour & Robert Eckstein
2nd Edition June 1999
540 pages, ISBN 1-56592-325-1

This indispensable book takes all the essential reference information for the Web and pulls it together into one volume. It covers HTML 4.0, CSS, XML, CGI, SSI, JavaScript 1.2, PHP, HTTP 1.1, and administration for the Apache server.

DocBook: The Definitive Guide

By Norman Walsh & Leonard Muellner
1st Edition October 1999
652 pages, Includes CD-ROM
ISBN 1-56592-580-7

DocBook is a Document Type Definition (DTD) for use with XML (the Extensible Markup Language) and SGML (the Standard Generalized Markup Language). DocBook lets authors in technical groups exchange and reuse technical information. This book contains an introduction to SGML, XML, and the DocBook DTD, plus the complete reference information for DocBook.

JavaScript Application Cookbook

By Jerry Bradenbaugh
1st Edition September 1999
478 pages, ISBN 1-56592-577-7

JavaScript Application Cookbook literally hands the Webmaster a set of ready-to-go, client-side JavaScript applications with thorough documentation to help them understand and extend the applications. By providing such a set of applications, *JavaScript Application Cookbook* allows Webmasters to immediately add extra functionality to their Web sites.

Web Authoring and Design

PNG: The Definitive Guide

By Greg Roelofs
1st Edition June 1999
344 pages, ISBN 1-56592-542-4

Targeted at graphic designers and programmers, *PNG: The Definitive Guide* is the first book devoted exclusively to teaching and documenting this important new and free image format. It is an indispensable compendium for Web content developers and programmers and is chock full of examples, sample code, and practical hands-on advice.

Web Design in a Nutshell

By Jennifer Niederst
1st Edition November 1998
580 pages, ISBN 1-56592-515-7

Web Design in a Nutshell contains the nitty-gritty on everything you need to know to design Web pages. Written by veteran Web designer Jennifer Niederst, this book provides quick access to the wide range of technologies and techniques from which Web designers and authors must draw. Topics include understanding the Web environment, HTML, graphics, multimedia and interactivity, and emerging technologies.

Web Authoring and Design

HTML: The Definitive Guide, 3rd Edition

By Chuck Musciano & Bill Kennedy
3rd Edition August 1998
576 pages, ISBN 1-56592-492-4

This complete guide is chock full of examples, sample code, and practical hands-on advice to help you create truly effective Web pages and master advanced features. Learn how to insert images, create useful links and searchable documents, use Netscape extensions, design great forms, and lots more. The third edition covers HTML 4.0, Netscape 4.5, and Internet Explorer 4.0, plus all the common extensions.

Designing Web Audio

By Josh Beggs & Dylan Thede
1st Edition October 2000 (est.)
250 pages (est.), Includes CD-ROM
ISBN 1-56592-353-7

Designing Web Audio is the most complete Internet audio guide on the market, loaded with informative real-world case studies, interviews with some of the world's leading audio and Web producers, and step-by-step instructions on how to use the most popular Web audio formats.

Designing with JavaScript, 2nd Edition

By Nick Heinle
2nd Edition October 2000 (est.)
300 pages (est.), ISBN 1-56592-360-X

By teaching JavaScript in the context of its most powerful capability – document manipulation through the DOM – *Designing with JavaScript, 2nd Edition*, not only teaches the language, not only teaches object, library, and DOM concepts, but also provides Web developers with useful strategies and techniques from the first page to the last. Heinle has written sophisticated JavaScript libraries for improved and easier use of form validation, browser detection, cookies, and more.

Photoshop for the Web, 2nd Edition

By Mikkel Aaland
2nd Edition November 1999
246 pages
Including multipage color insert
ISBN 1-56592-641-2

In this second edition, author Mikkel Aaland updates Photoshop for the Web to include important new techniques and workarounds for the latest Photoshop release – version 5.5. In addition, the new edition covers the latest version of Adobe's ImageReady 2.0 Web graphics production software.

Web Navigation: Designing the User Experience

By Jennifer Fleming
1st Edition September 1998
288 pages, Includes CD-ROM
ISBN 1-56592-351-0

This book takes the first in-depth look at designing Web site navigation through design strategies to help you uncover solutions that work for your site and audience. It focuses on designing by purpose, with chapters on entertainment, shopping, identity, learning, information, and community sites. Comes with a CD-ROM containing software demos and a "netography" of related Web resources.

Information Architecture for the World Wide Web

By Louis Rosenfeld & Peter Morville
1st Edition February 1998
224 pages, ISBN 1-56592-282-4

Learn how to merge aesthetics and mechanics to design Web sites that "work." This book shows how to apply principles of architecture and library science to design cohesive Web sites and intranets that are easy to use, manage, and expand. Covers building complex sites, hierarchy design and organization, and techniques to make your site easier to search. For Webmasters, designers, and administrators.

How to stay in touch with O'Reilly

1. Visit Our Award-Winning Site

http://www.oreilly.com/

★ "Top 100 Sites on the Web" —*PC Magazine*
★ "Top 5% Web sites" —*Point Communications*
★ "3-Star site" —*The McKinley Group*

Our web site contains a library of comprehensive product information (including book excerpts and tables of contents), downloadable software, background articles, interviews with technology leaders, links to relevant sites, book cover art, and more. File us in your Bookmarks or Hotlist!

2. Join Our Email Mailing Lists

New Product Releases

To receive automatic email with brief descriptions of all new O'Reilly products as they are released, send email to:
listproc@online.oreilly.com
Put the following information in the first line of your message (*not* in the Subject field):
subscribe oreilly-news

O'Reilly Events

If you'd also like us to send information about trade show events, special promotions, and other O'Reilly events, send email to:
listproc@online.oreilly.com
Put the following information in the first line of your message (*not* in the Subject field):
subscribe oreilly-events

3. Get Examples from Our Books via FTP

There are two ways to access an archive of example files from our books:

Regular FTP
- ftp to:
  ftp.oreilly.com
  (login: anonymous
  password: your email address)
- Point your web browser to:
  ftp://ftp.oreilly.com/

FTPMAIL
- Send an email message to:
  ftpmail@online.oreilly.com
  (Write "help" in the message body)

4. Contact Us via Email

order@oreilly.com
To place a book or software order online. Good for North American and international customers.

subscriptions@oreilly.com
To place an order for any of our newsletters or periodicals.

books@oreilly.com
General questions about any of our books.

software@oreilly.com
For general questions and product information about our software. Check out O'Reilly Software Online at **http://software.oreilly.com/** for software and technical support information. Registered O'Reilly software users send your questions to:
website-support@oreilly.com

cs@oreilly.com
For answers to problems regarding your order or our products.

booktech@oreilly.com
For book content technical questions or corrections.

proposals@oreilly.com
To submit new book or software proposals to our editors and product managers.

international@oreilly.com
For information about our international distributors or translation queries. For a list of our distributors outside of North America check out:
http://www.oreilly.com/www/order/country.html

5. Work with Us

Check out our website for current employment opportunites:
www.jobs@oreilly.com
Click on "Work with Us"

O'Reilly & Associates, Inc.
101 Morris Street, Sebastopol, CA 95472 USA
TEL   707-829-0515 or 800-998-9938
            (6am to 5pm PST)
FAX   707-829-0104

International Distributors

UK, EUROPE, MIDDLE EAST AND AFRICA (EXCEPT FRANCE, GERMANY, AUSTRIA, SWITZERLAND, LUXEMBOURG, LIECHTENSTEIN, AND EASTERN EUROPE)

INQUIRIES
O'Reilly UK Limited
4 Castle Street
Farnham
Surrey, GU9 7HS
United Kingdom
Telephone: 44-1252-711776
Fax: 44-1252-734211
Email: josette@oreilly.com

ORDERS
Wiley Distribution Services Ltd.
1 Oldlands Way
Bognor Regis
West Sussex PO22 9SA
United Kingdom
Telephone: 44-1243-779777
Fax: 44-1243-820250
Email: cs-books@wiley.co.uk

FRANCE

INQUIRIES
Éditions O'Reilly
18 rue Séguier
75006 Paris, France
Tel: 33-1-40-51-52-30
Fax: 33-1-40-51-52-31
Email: france@editions-oreilly.fr

ORDERS
GEODIF
61, Bd Saint-Germain
75240 Paris Cedex 05, France
Tel: 33-1-44-41-46-16 (French books)
Tel: 33-1-44-41-11-87 (English books)
Fax: 33-1-44-41-11-44
Email: distribution@eyrolles.com

GERMANY, SWITZERLAND, AUSTRIA, EASTERN EUROPE, LUXEMBOURG, AND LIECHTENSTEIN

INQUIRIES & ORDERS
O'Reilly Verlag
Balthasarstr. 81
D-50670 Köln
Germany
Telephone: 49-221-973160-91
Fax: 49-221-973160-8
Email: anfragen@oreilly.de (inquiries)
Email: order@oreilly.de (orders)

CANADA (FRENCH LANGUAGE BOOKS)
Les Éditions Flammarion ltée
375, Avenue Laurier Ouest
Montréal (Québec) H2V 2K3
Tel: 00-1-514-277-8807
Fax: 00-1-514-278-2085
Email: info@flammarion.qc.ca

HONG KONG
City Discount Subscription Service, Ltd.
Unit D, 3rd Floor, Yan's Tower
27 Wong Chuk Hang Road
Aberdeen, Hong Kong
Tel: 852-2580-3539
Fax: 852-2580-6463
Email: citydis@ppn.com.hk

KOREA
Hanbit Media, Inc.
Chungmu Bldg. 201
Yonnam-dong 568-33
Mapo-gu
Seoul, Korea
Tel: 822-325-0397
Fax: 822-325-9697
Email: hant93@chollian.dacom.co.kr

PHILIPPINES
Global Publishing
G/F Benavides Garden
1186 Benavides St.
Manila, Philippines
Tel: 632-254-8949/637-252-2582
Fax: 632-734-5060/632-252-2733
Email: globalp@pacific.net.ph

TAIWAN
O'Reilly Taiwan
No. 3, Lane 131
Hang-Chow South Road
Section 1, Taipei, Taiwan
Tel: 886-2-23968990
Fax: 886-2-23968916
Email: taiwan@oreilly.com

CHINA
O'Reilly Beijing
Room 2410
160, FuXingMenNeiDaJie
XiCheng District
Beijing
China PR 100031
Tel: 86-10-66412305
Fax: 86-10-86631007
Email: beijing@oreilly.com

INDIA
Computer Bookshop (India) Pvt. Ltd.
190 Dr. D.N. Road, Fort
Bombay 400 001 India
Tel: 91-22-207-0989
Fax: 91-22-262-3551
Email: cbsbom@giasbm01.vsnl.net.in

JAPAN
O'Reilly Japan, Inc.
Yotsuya's Building
7Banchi 6, Honshio-cho
Shinjuku-ku
Tokyo 160-0003 Japan
Tel: 81-3-3356-5227
Fax: 81-3-3356-5261
Email: japan@oreilly.com

ALL OTHER ASIAN COUNTRIES
O'Reilly & Associates, Inc.
101 Morris Street
Sebastopol, CA 95472 USA
Tel: 707-829-0515
Fax: 707-829-0104
Email: order@oreilly.com

AUSTRALIA
Woodslane Pty., Ltd.
7/5 Vuko Place
Warriewood NSW 2102
Australia
Tel: 61-2-9970-5111
Fax: 61-2-9970-5002
Email: info@woodslane.com.au

NEW ZEALAND
Woodslane New Zealand, Ltd.
21 Cooks Street (P.O. Box 575)
Waganui, New Zealand
Tel: 64-6-347-6543
Fax: 64-6-345-4840
Email: info@woodslane.com.au

LATIN AMERICA
McGraw-Hill Interamericana
Editores, S.A. de C.V.
Cedro No. 512
Col. Atlampa
06450, Mexico, D.F.
Tel: 52-5-547-6777
Fax: 52-5-547-3336
Email: mcgraw-hill@infosel.net.mx

O'REILLY™

O'Reilly & Associates, Inc.
101 Morris Street
Sebastopol, CA 95472-9902
1-800-998-9938

Visit us online at:
http://www.ora.com/
orders@ora.com

O'REILLY WOULD LIKE TO HEAR FROM YOU

Which book did this card come from?

_____

Where did you buy this book?
- ❏ Bookstore
- ❏ Direct from O'Reilly
- ❏ Bundled with hardware/software
- ❏ Other _____
- ❏ Computer Store
- ❏ Class/seminar

What operating system do you use?
- ❏ UNIX
- ❏ Windows NT
- ❏ Other _____
- ❏ Macintosh
- ❏ PC(Windows/DOS)

What is your job description?
- ❏ System Administrator
- ❏ Network Administrator
- ❏ Web Developer
- ❏ Other _____
- ❏ Programmer
- ❏ Educator/Teacher

❏ Please send me O'Reilly's catalog, containing
a complete listing of O'Reilly books and
software.

Name _____   Company/Organization _____

Address _____

City _____   State _____   Zip/Postal Code _____   Country _____

Telephone _____   Internet or other email address (specify network) _____

Nineteenth century wood engraving
of a bear from the O'Reilly &
Associates Nutshell Handbook®
Using & Managing UUCP.

BUSINESS REPLY MAIL
FIRST CLASS MAIL   PERMIT NO. 80   SEBASTOPOL, CA

Postage will be paid by addressee

O'Reilly & Associates, Inc.
101 Morris Street
Sebastopol, CA 95472-9902